The New York Times

DISUNION

The New York Times

DISUNION

A HISTORY OF THE CIVIL WAR

EDITED BY TED WIDMER

WITH CLAY RISEN AND GEORGE KALOGERAKIS

OXFORD

UNIVERSITY PRESS

OXFORD
UNIVERSITY PRESS

Oxford University Press is a department of the University of Oxford. It furthers
the University's objective of excellence in research, scholarship, and education
by publishing worldwide. Oxford is a registered trade mark of Oxford University
Press in the UK and certain other countries.

Published in the United States of America by Oxford University Press
198 Madison Avenue, New York, NY 10016, United States of America.

Library of Congress Cataloging-in-Publication Data
Names: Widmer, Edward L., editor. | Risen, Clay, editor. | Kalogerakis,
George, editor.
Title: The New York Times disunion : a history of the Civil War / edited by
Ted Widmer, with Clay Risen and George Kalogerakis.
Other titles: New York times
Description: New York : Oxford University Press, 2016. | Includes
bibliographical references and index.
Identifiers: LCCN 2016015114 | ISBN 9780190621834
Subjects: LCSH: United States—History—Civil War, 1861-1865.
Classification: LCC E468 .N493 2016 | DDC 973.7—dc23
LC record available at https://lccn.loc.gov/2016015114

1 3 5 7 9 8 6 4 2
Printed by Edwards Brothers Malloy, United States of America

CONTENTS

Foreword   xiii
    Ken Burns

Introduction   1
    Ted Widmer

1. **Secession**   5

Introduction   5
    Adam Goodheart

How Lincoln Undid the Union   7
    Richard Striner

Cup of Wrath and Fire   10
    David Blight

The Strange Victory of the Palmetto State   13
    Manisha Sinha

Learning from Buchanan   16
    Jean H. Baker

Confederates at the Gate   19
    Charles Lockwood and John Lockwood

How a Map Divided Virginia   23
    Susan Schulten

Texas Catches Fire   25
    Richard Parker

The Death Knell of Slavery   28
    Gregory P. Downs

2. **Slavery and Emancipation** 33

Introduction 33
  Manisha Sinha

Visualizing Slavery 35
  Susan Schulten

The Transatlantic Slave Trade and the Civil War 38
  David Eltis and David Richardson

What Lincoln Meant to the Slaves 41
  Steven Hahn

William Webb's World 43
  Susan Eva O'Donovan

A Capital under Slavery's Shadow 46
  Adam Goodheart

Black or White? 49
  Daniel J. Sharfstein

Was Freedom Enough? 52
  Gregory P. Downs and James Downs

Our Servants Do Pretty Much as They Please 55
  Adam Rothman

The Grove of Gladness 58
  Blain Roberts and Ethan J. Kytle

When Freedom Came to Charleston 62
  Blain Roberts and Ethan J. Kytle

3. **Women and the Home Front** 66

Introduction 66
  Nicole Etcheson

Women at War 69
  Elizabeth R. Varon

Laugh During Wartime 72
  Jon Grinspan

The Civil War's Rip Van Winkle 75
  Albin J. Kowalewski

General Butler and the Women 78
  Alecia P. Long

Scrapbooking the Civil War 80
  Ellen Gruber Garvey

The Civil War and the Fourth Estate 83
  Ford Risley

Making War on the Draft 86
  Nicole Etcheson

Going to the Fair 90
Jennifer R. Bridge

Albert Cashier's Secret 92
Jean R. Freedman

Blacks, Baseball, and the Civil War 95
George Kirsch

4. **The Battlefield** **99**
Introduction 99
Gary Gallagher

Blue, Gray, and Everything in Between 102
Michael O. Varhola

The War Comes Home for Lee 105
Jamie Stiehm

The Boys of War 107
Cate Lineberry

The Purchase by Blood 110
Carol Bundy

The Fighting Second 113
Lawrence A. Kreiser Jr.

Winning the Field but Not the War 116
James Q. Whitman

Striking the Blow at Fort Wagner 118
Glenn David Brasher

Life on the Battlefield 123
Carole Emberton

Left Behind at Chickamauga 126
Pat Leonard

Humanity and Hope in a Southern Prison 128
Peter Cozzens

How Coffee Fueled the Civil War 133
Jon Grinspan

Was the Burning of Columbia a War Crime? 135
Thom Bassett

5. **The West and Native Americans** **140**
Introduction 140
Boyd Cothran

The Bear Wars 142
Adam Goodheart

Sam Houston, We Have a Problem 144
Richard Parker

The Choctaw Confederates   148
    Adam Goodheart
How the West Was Won   151
    Susan Schulten
The Lone Star State Turns South   155
    Richard Parker
The Rise of the West   157
    Adam Arenson
Jennison's Jayhawkers   159
    Nicole Etcheson
The Cherokee Free Their Slaves   162
    Melinda Miller and Rachel Smith Purvis
Becoming Mark Twain   165
    Jim McWilliams

6. **Law and Rights**   **168**
Introduction   168
    John Fabian Witt
States' Rights, but to What?   170
    Paul Finkelman
Freedom and Restraint   174
    John Fabian Witt
The Lieber Code   177
    Rick Beard
Rape and Justice in the Civil War   180
    Crystal N. Feimster
Lincoln Answers His Critics   183
    Douglas L. Wilson
The Father of the Fourteenth Amendment   186
    Gerard Magliocca
The Great Writ, North and South   190
    Frank J. Williams
The Nashville Experiment   193
    William Moss Wilson
Lincoln, God, and the Constitution   196
    Joseph S. Moore
How the Civil War Changed the Constitution   199
    Paul Finkelman

7. **The Confederacy**   **204**
Introduction   204
    Stephanie McCurry

A Bad Document's Good Idea   206
   John J. Miller

Hastily Composed   208
   Adam Goodheart

The President and His General   212
   Phil Leigh

The Birth of "Dixie"   215
   Christian McWhirter

The Drought That Changed the War   218
   Kenneth W. Noe

The Free Men of Color Go to War   220
   Terry L. Jones

Passover in the Confederacy   225
   Sue Eisenfeld

Papers, Please!   228
   Yael A. Sternhell

Lee Surrendered, but His Lieutenants Kept Fighting   231
   Elizabeth R. Varon

Confederates in the Jungle   235
   Ron Soodalter

8. The Civil War and the World   **240**
Introduction   240
   Don H. Doyle

Lincoln's Mexican Visitor   242
   William Moss Wilson

The Other Emancipation Proclamation   246
   Adam Goodheart

Bully for Garibaldi   249
   Don H. Doyle

Why Bismarck Loved Lincoln   253
   Kenneth Weisbrode

Lincoln's PR Coup   256
   Aaron W. Marrs

Holland's Plan for America's Slaves   260
   Michael J. Douma

The Civil War and Hawaii   263
   Jeffrey Allen Smith

The Russians Are Coming!   266
   Rick Beard

Fighting off the Coast of France   270
   Jamie Malanowski

9. Abraham Lincoln and the Federal Government   **274**

Introduction   274
Louis P. Masur

The Sound of Lincoln's Silence   276
Harold Holzer

Seward's Folly   280
Russell McClintock

A Capitol Dilemma   283
Guy Gugliotta

Andrew Johnson's Difficult Task   287
Aaron Astor

The Do-Everything Congress   290
Mark Greenbaum

Lincoln's Letter to the Editor   293
Paul Finkelman

The Civil War's War on Fraud   296
Mark Greenbaum

Counting the Costs of the Civil War   299
Jeffrey Allen Smith and B. Christopher Frueh

Rewriting the Gettysburg Address   302
Martin P. Johnson

The Rise and Fall (and Rise) of Salmon P. Chase   305
Rick Beard

10. The Consequences of the Civil War   **310**

Introduction   310
Heather Cox Richardson

Remembering the Gettysburg Address   312
Joshua Zeitz

The Birth of Thanksgiving   316
Paul Quigley

My Civil War   318
Terry L. Jones

Teddy Roosevelt's Confederate Uncles   322
Edward P. Kohn

The Civil War's Environmental Impact   326
Ted Widmer

How the Civil War Created College Football   331
Amanda Brickell Bellows

How Lincoln Became Our Favorite President   334
Joshua Zeitz

How Kentucky Became a Confederate State   338
   Christopher Phillips
Was Abolitionism a Failure?   341
   Jon Grinspan
How the Civil War Changed the World   344
   Don Doyle

Afterword   349
   Ted Widmer
Acknowledgments   355
Contributors   357
Index   365

FOREWORD

The Old Guilts

Our decadent experimentation with disunion began in so many places that it is difficult to fix precisely its origin. Was it in the monumental hypocrisy of our founding, our ignominious acceptance of chattel slavery, even after a century of Enlightenment thinking had been artfully distilled, poetically articulated, and then proudly proclaimed to mankind that *we* the people believed in certain universal truths? Was it the corrupt bargains of the constitutional conventions and slavery's subsequent enshrinement into our manual of operation, with its sickening tolerance of "three-fifths of a person"?

Maybe it was the impertinence of a growing number of Americans, dedicated to abolition and emancipation, who threatened the immoral profits of the Southern states' "property." Maybe it was all the imperfect geographical compromises that dripped out over the ensuing decades, compromises that seemed to propel us inevitably toward carnage. Or was it the legislative and judicial embarrassments of the Fugitive Slave Act and the *Dred Scott* decision? Perhaps it was John Brown's murderous raid in Pottawatomie, "Bleeding" Kansas, followed by his blatant insurrection at Harpers Ferry. Or Nat Turner's own brave, futile attempt at liberation for his people and himself. Maybe it was, as Lincoln joked, "little" Stowe's "big" book. Perhaps, as the writer and historian Shelby Foote believed, it was our failure to compromise (our great "genius," he thought) that brought our civil war. Historians will forever debate and assign significance to each of these examples and dozens more.

Today, even with a century and a half between us and our greatest cataclysm, we have an eerie sense that so much of what seemed safely finished and distant about the Civil War now seems present, palpable, the underlying racial causes of the old conflict on nearly daily display. We begin to think with increasing alarm that it has always been with us; our interim historical glare has been distracted by other more "important" events. Black lives still don't matter, it seems, and we are faced with the crushing reality of a truth we thought had slipped into discarded cliché: that slavery and its consequences, including the Civil War, *are* our original sin. The jazz trumpeter and composer Wynton Marsalis says that in our country the question of race "is like the thing in the story, in the mythology that you have to do for the kingdom to be well." We are *not* well, and it becomes increasingly clear that the ghosts and echoes of our near-death experience have much to teach us today.

The Civil War has always been about voices. These voices are belligerent, angry, defiant, beseeching, scolding, coarse, arrogant, lawyerly, terrifying, bittersweet, posturing, forgiving, humane, and racist. Our remarkably literate population then ensured that these voices would issue from every region, race, station, and sex, expressing, it seems, almost every possible perspective. But the war itself was in some ways framed and bracketed by the voice and words of Abraham Lincoln in his two inaugural addresses, speeches that have had a hard time escaping the kudzu of sentimentality and nostalgia that has threatened to smother any serious consideration of those hard times. But once pruned of distracting hagiography, they are still hugely instructive to any understanding of "the irresistible conflict" he was charged with overseeing—and indeed to our perplexing present. (As a young man, years before the Civil War, Lincoln had presciently predicted, "As a nation of free men, we must live through all time or die by suicide.")

The first address is remembered for its beautiful and generous peroration, Lincoln's emotional plea that "we must not be enemies, but friends," that we were all, Southerner as well as Northerner, still connected by "mystic chords of memory"—music that, if listened to, would help us summon "the better angels of our nature." Most of this address, though, was a wily lawyer's insistent argument that secession was a kind of schizophrenia that, if not treated quickly, would blast us apart—if states could secede from countries, then counties could secede from states, towns from counties, neighborhoods and clans from those towns, a kind of tribal, hardly civilized madness.

His second inaugural, delivered with the sublime awareness that his victory was close at hand, that his Union *would* be preserved, is almost all peroration, an artful combination of Old Testament righteousness—"Yet, if God wills that it [the war] continue, until all the wealth piled up by the bond-man's two hundred and fifty years of unrequited toil shall be sunk, and until every drop of blood drawn with the lash, shall be paid by another drawn with the sword, as was said three thousand years ago, so still must be said, 'the judgments of the Lord are true and righteous altogether'"—and New Testament forgiveness and reconciliation: "With malice toward none; with charity for all." With these addresses and his Gettysburg speech, Lincoln gave us a new operating system, our 2.0, still fundamentally unamended in 150 years.

The poet and novelist Robert Penn Warren wrote an essay that expressed better than most the tensions of that long-ago moment and the way those tensions extend inexorably to our current predicament: "A civil war is, we may say, the prototype of all war, for in the person of fellow citizens who happen to be the enemy we meet again with the old ambivalence of love and hate and with all the old guilts, the blood brothers of our childhood."

It's very American to presume that all those guilts can be transformed into reparation and atonement, as in the story of the slaver who abandoned his errant path and wrote "Amazing Grace." But as the Civil War and our present day attest, the opposite is also true. Our ancient guilts and animosities more often metastasize into anger, violence, and brutality. That's very American too.

Ken Burns
Walpole, New Hampshire

The New York Times
DISUNION

Introduction

Ted Widmer

In the summer of 2010 two editors from the *New York Times*, Clay Risen and George Kalogerakis, invited me into their office to discuss an online history project. The 150th anniversary of the Civil War was approaching, and they wanted to celebrate it in a thoughtful way, taking advantage of the platform of the *Times*, the reach of the Internet, and the rise of a new cohort of historians, technologically literate and hungry for new ways to reach new audiences. The result was *Disunion*, an online series that launched on November 1, 2010, just before the anniversary of Lincoln's election as president.

The essays appeared in *Opinionator*, a suburb of the Opinion page, where writers were given more space to reflect than in the crowded confines of news reporting. On special occasions they made it onto the printed pages of the *Times*, but for the most part this experiment unfolded in cyberspace. We sometimes used the word *blog* to describe what was happening, but that casual term failed to convey the discipline and detail of *Disunion*. From the beginning, it maintained the highest standards of historical writing. Sources were listed, facts checked, and infelicities gently eliminated by the editors.

Soon a style emerged of a piece that was about a thousand words long, explaining a single, provocative point relating to the Civil War. It sometimes felt as if the *Times* had dispatched a new corps of reporters, trained in historical research, to cover something that happened a century and a half ago. The series was visually striking as well; the *Times* team carefully curated each piece and gave it appropriate illustrations. They read beautifully, especially on a large screen, where a well-crafted essay could become almost cinematic.

Some days it was hard to remember which century we were in. That was a tribute to the quality of those early pieces, which came in daily and quickly established their authority, even in a crowded news landscape. They were personal; they were vivid; they marched with military dispatch.

Readers responded immediately, not just to comment on pieces but to propose their own. Early articles by Adam Goodheart and Jamie Malanowski were helpful in establishing a tone that invited readers to the digital hearth. Soon other historians were joining them. The fresher the writing, the more other writers were attracted to it. *Disunion* had a rhythm of its own, true to the mildly subversive feel of the experiment. ("Can the

Times possibly be giving this much room to the Civil War?" some asked.) The pieces were published late in the evening, ahead of the next day's news cycle, when most of the country had gone to bed. It was especially attractive to young academics, naturally awake and caffeinated in the evening hours, but senior scholars also contributed, and some of the best articles came from amateur historians and high school teachers and park rangers. It was as if a clearing had been established during a pitched battle, and we were all free to run into this leafy glen, safe from harm.

Disunion easily accomplished its primary task of evoking the diurnal progress of the Civil War. But it did more than that. With its range of voices and its personal approach, it conveyed how present the Civil War remains. It's not just the unexploded ordnance that is still being dug up, even in 2016; some of our internal conflicts are not so far removed from those of 1861: anger at the federal government, unresolved racial tensions, simple helplessness before the constant onslaught of a 24-7 communications grid that matured during the war—including the distant, telegraphic ancestors of the wireless networks that made *Disunion* possible.

During the same years that the experiment ran, between 2010 and 2015, the United States saw many other reenactments of the Civil War, ranging from planned, ceremonial observances to the sudden eruptions of emotion that accompany the memory of this conflict and its unfinished business. Racial strife was a permanent feature of life in those years, even during a presidency that was supposed to inaugurate a postracial era. In 2015, as *Disunion* was ending its run and in the aftermath of a tragic act of racial violence in Charleston, a particularly bitter argument raged in South Carolina over whether the Confederate battle flag should fly next to the state house. (The flag was ultimately taken down.) Similar reassessments were taking place around the country, in New Orleans, in Birmingham, Alabama, and on college campuses everywhere. To be able to read about the Civil War in a forum as grounded as *Disunion* while these passions were roiling was reassuring.

Another reason for the salience of *Disunion* is that new information continues to come in. Given the abundance of books on the Civil War (more than fifteen thousand have been written about Lincoln alone), it's hard to believe that any information remains to be found. But it does, and always will, as records are unearthed or read in new ways. To cite one striking example: in 2012 a new historical consensus emerged that the accepted casualty figures for the war were too low by 20 percent; instead of 618,222 fatalities, 750,000 perished as a direct result of the conflict. *Disunion* proved to be a versatile channel for the rapid flow of these findings.

For those of us who had been trained to write in the conventional academic formats (fifty-minute lecture, journal article, book-length monograph), *Disunion* was liberating in every sense. It offered a chance to write something compact and clear for a wider audience. It discouraged the insider language that can separate the academy from the public and naturally encouraged a digital commons to emerge, in which we were all talking with one another. The essays linked to one another, readers wrote to writers, writers answered, and

Clay and George kept watch to ensure that standards of civility and grammar prevailed. To receive a response within minutes for a piece of historical research (often prepared quickly, in days rather than years) was exhilarating for most professional historians. This was something new under the sun. Normally historians do better with deep time than real time, but they stood up well under the scrutiny, and perhaps other experiments will follow, encouraging the lively study of other seminal historical episodes.

Originally our experiment was to last only six months, but, not unlike the experience of the war's early planners, we saw it outlast our naïve predictions of an early demise. Day after day the project rolled forward until we realized that we had to let it run its course and follow the entire war.

Determining when the conflict actually ended is not as simple as it sounds; perhaps we were reluctant to let go, or perhaps we were hesitant to pass a final verdict on this conflict that still feels so intensely alive, even as it recedes further into the past. Unlike most news stories, there was never a simple headline to *Disunion*. Instead a complex picture emerged of a war that reshaped everything that America had been to that point, and that still shapes and reshapes the country on a daily basis.

Certainly the memory of the war affected the United States during the centennial years, 1961 to 1965, when so many battles were fought to remember the war's intent, particularly the civil rights that had been promised a century earlier to African Americans. In other ways too the war lives on. For example, the ongoing battle to recognize the equal rights of women owes a great deal to the civil rights legislation of the 1960s, which specifically eliminated this form of discrimination. Each emancipation in our history has opened the door slightly for the one that followed, as Lincoln understood well—he argued that the war was being fought not only for the issues of its time, but "for a vast future" also. It was a particular pleasure to welcome so many women historians into what had traditionally been something of a fraternity. When the battles of the future come, the battles of the past will continue to bear upon the case.

Now that *Disunion* has ended, I have a deeper sense than ever of the Civil War's centrality to the national narrative. It defined how we *live* history and forever shaped the nation that we became afterward; Lincoln made that clear at Gettysburg. But it also changed the way we *write* history. From the beginning the war was a struggle among historians as well as a struggle among soldiers and politicians. Lincoln understood that intuitively even before he was elected; in his debates with Stephen Douglas, and then in his speech at Cooper Union, he went deeply into the story of the nation's founding. Throughout the war he was the historian in chief, in addition to everything else, and his major speeches offered a running commentary on the "astounding" time he inhabited.

Other historians went into the field, some literally, like the indefatigable Benson J. Lossing, trailing after the armies with his notebook in hand. Veterans of the fighting wrote prolifically about the conflict, their memoirs clogging the arteries of publishing until well into the twentieth century. Official government histories were commissioned soon after the cessation of hostilities; on June 23, 1874, Congress made an appropriation "to enable the Secretary of War to begin the publication of the Official Records of the War of the Rebellion both of the Union and Confederate Armies." The twentieth century showed no abatement in interest, nor it is likely that the twenty-first will lose the thread. There is something about the scale of the conflict, and the grandeur of those who waged it, that still commands respect—the same awe that Lincoln confessed in his second inaugural. Not all *Disunion* contributors agreed with one another; that would have been impossible, and undesirable. But we all felt respect for the war's magnitude, and the sacrifice it demanded.

Even as the war continues to recede far beyond the memory of anyone alive today, it speaks to all Americans who feel a connection to the founding ideals of the republic and the ongoing struggle to define them for new circumstances. As long as we remain less than perfect, we will want to learn from this epic struggle to resolve our contradictions. In other words, we will be studying the Civil War forever.

1. Secession

Introduction

ADAM GOODHEART

On November 1, 1860, a small Pennsylvania town drowsed in the waning light of an Indian summer. Almost nothing had happened lately that the two local newspapers found worthy of more than a cursory mention. The fall harvest was in; grain prices held steady. A new ice-cream parlor had opened in the Eagle Hotel on Chambersburg Street. Eight citizens had recently been married; eight others had died. It was an ordinary day in Gettysburg, Pennsylvania.

It was an ordinary day in America, one of the last such days for a very long time to come.

In dusty San Antonio, Texas, Colonel Robert E. Lee of the U.S. Army had just submitted a long report to Washington about recent skirmishes against marauding Comanche and Mexican banditti. In Louisiana, William Tecumseh Sherman was in the midst of a tedious week interviewing teenage applicants to the military academy where he served as superintendent. In Galena, Illinois, passersby might have seen a man in a shabby military greatcoat and slouch hat trudging to work that Thursday morning, as he did every weekday. He was Ulysses S. Grant, a middle-aged shop clerk in his family's leather-goods store. Even the most talked-about man in America was, in a certain sense, almost invisible—or at least inaudible.

On November 1, less than a week before Election Day, citizens of Springfield, Illinois, were invited to view a new portrait of Abraham Lincoln, just completed by a visiting artist and hung in the senate chamber of the state house. The likeness was said to be uncanny, but it was easy enough for viewers to reach their own conclusions, since the sitter could also be inspected in person in his office just across the hall. Politically, however, Lincoln was inscrutable. In keeping with long-standing tradition, he did not campaign at all that autumn, did not so much as deliver a single speech or grant a single interview to the press.

Lincoln and Hamlin campaign poster, 1860. Library of Congress Prints and Photographs Division, LC-DIG-pga-04545.

Instead Lincoln held court each day in his borrowed state house office, behind a desk piled high with gifts and souvenirs that supporters had sent him, including countless wooden knickknacks carved from bits and pieces of fence rails he had supposedly split in his youth. He shook hands with visitors, told funny stories, and answered mail. Only one modest public statement from him appeared in the *Illinois State Journal* that morning: a small front-page ad, sandwiched between those for a dentist and a saddle maker, offering the services of Lincoln & Herndon, attorneys at law.

The future is always a tough thing to predict, and perhaps it was especially so on the first day of that eventful month. Take the oil painting of Lincoln: it would be obsolete within weeks, when its subject unexpectedly grew a beard. (The distraught portraitist tried to daub in whiskers after the fact, succeeding only in wrecking his masterpiece.) Or, on a grander scale, consider an article in that morning's *New York Herald* using recent census data to project the country's growth over the next hundred years. By the late twentieth century, it stated confidently, America's population would grow to 300 million (pretty close to accurate), including 50 million slaves (a bit off). But, asked the author, could a nation containing so many different people and their opinions remain intact for that long? Impossible.

Between that November day and the first gunshots from Fort Sumter six months later, before the onset of the war, came disunion: seven states left before the fighting began, and four more just after. That they seceded over slavery is indisputable: as Mississippi's declaration of secession stated, "Our position is thoroughly identified with the institution of slavery—the greatest material interest of the world." And yet four slave states—Missouri, Kentucky, Maryland, and Delaware—stayed with the Union.

Was secession inevitable? Was war inevitable? Was the Confederacy—and with it, slavery—doomed? Writing about the past can be tricky, particularly when the subject is the Civil War, that famously unfinished conflict, when each week brought fresh reports of skirmishes between the ideological rearguards of the Union and Confederate armies, still going at it with gusto.

In many senses, though, the Civil War is a writer's—and reader's—dream. The 1860s were an unprecedented moment for documentation, for gathering and preserving the details of passing events and the texture of ordinary life. Starting just a few years before the war, America was photographed, lithographed, bound between the covers of mass-circulation magazines, and described by the very first generation of professional journalists.

Half a century ago, as the nation commemorated the war's centennial, a scruffy young man from Minnesota walked into the New York Public Library and began scrolling through reels of old microfilm, reading newspapers published all over the country between 1855 and 1865. As Bob Dylan would recount in the first volume of his memoir, *Chronicles*, he didn't know what he was looking for, much less what he would find. He just immersed himself in that time: the fiery oratory, the political cartoons, the "weird mind philosophies turned on their heads," the "epic, bearded characters." Much later he swore that this journey deep into the Civil War became "the all-encompassing template behind everything I would write."

How Lincoln Undid the Union

RICHARD STRINER

On December 11, 1860, with South Carolina's secession looming, President-elect Abraham Lincoln wrote a letter to Representative William Kellogg, a fellow Republican from Illinois. Publicly Lincoln was keeping silent on the emerging crisis. His letter was designed to achieve one objective: to sabotage a sectional compromise to save the Union.

Marked "Private & confidential," the letter instructed Kellogg to "entertain no proposition for a compromise in regard to the extension of slavery. The instant you do, they have us under again; all our labor is lost, and sooner or later must be done over.... Have none of it. The tug has to come & better now than later."

Lincoln was not speaking abstractly. The U.S. Capitol was buzzing with talk of a Union-saving deal. Indeed on December 18 Senator John J. Crittenden of Kentucky proposed a plan to preserve the Union through a series of actions to protect the institution of slavery. In other words, at the precise moment that a compromise to rescue the country seemed at hand, the incoming president worked aggressively to block it. Lincoln, whom historians often portray as being more interested in saving the Union than opposing slavery, chose to do the opposite.

Crittenden's plan consisted of a package of constitutional amendments and congressional resolutions, all of which would be "unamendable." Among their provisions, these amendments would have protected slavery in all of the slave states from future actions by Congress; permitted slavery to spread in all federal territories and future territories below the line of 36 degrees 30 minutes north latitude (which runs roughly along the northern border of North Carolina, Tennessee, Arkansas, Oklahoma, New Mexico, and Arizona); forbidden Congress to abolish slavery on federal property within a slave state; prevented Congress from interfering with the interstate slave trade; and indemnified owners whose runaway slaves could not be recovered under the Fugitive Slave Law.

The compromise won immediate praise; many politicians hailed it as a gesture of supreme wisdom that could forestall secession. Even William Seward, the New York senator whom Lincoln would soon tap to be secretary of state, seemed to support it.

But Lincoln—a protégé of Henry Clay, the Kentuckian who had orchestrated the great Missouri Compromise of 1820–21 and the Compromise of 1850—was not among those admirers. In fact he had taken preemptive action to undermine it. In the days leading up to its release he sent out a flurry of letters to congressional Republicans, giving orders to oppose any compromise. A few days after his letter to Kellogg he used even stronger language in a letter to Representative Elihu B. Washburne of Illinois: "Hold firm as with a chain of steel." He told Senator Lyman Trumbull of Illinois, "If any of our friends do prove false, and fix up a compromise on the territorial question, I am for fighting again."

Lincoln's letters proved decisive in the compromise's eventual defeat. To examine the plan the Senate had established the Committee of Thirteen; thanks in large part to Lincoln's goading, all five Republicans on the committee opposed it. Two Southern members of the committee, Robert Toombs and Jefferson Davis, voted against it on the grounds that such unified Republican opposition made the compromise worthless. When Crittenden took his plan to the Senate floor on January 16, 1861, it was voted down 25–23. Every one of the twenty-five no votes was cast by a Republican.

Cartoon depicting the difficulties of congressional compromises over slavery. Library of Congress Prints and Photographs Division, LC-USZ62-15644.

If Lincoln's efforts were so clear, why is there such a strong belief among historians and the public that he wanted to save the Union above all else? In part it's because Lincoln himself helped create that impression, saying in public the opposite of what he urged in private.

In a famous public letter that he sent in 1862 to the editor Horace Greeley, who then published it in his newspaper, the *New-York Tribune*, Lincoln wrote, "My paramount object in this struggle is to save the Union, and is not either to save or to destroy slavery. If I could save the Union without freeing any slave I would do it, and if I could save it by freeing all the slaves I would do it; and if I could save it by freeing some and leaving others alone I would also do that."

But Lincoln was being disingenuous. His object had always been to save the Union his way: with the institution of slavery on course for "ultimate extinction," as he put it in his 1858 "House Divided" speech. "I believe," he proclaimed in that fiery address,

this government cannot endure, permanently half slave and half free. I do not expect the Union to be dissolved—I do not expect the house to fall—but I do expect it will cease to be divided. It will become all one thing, or all the other. Either the opponents of slavery will arrest the further spread of it, and place it where the public mind shall rest in the belief that it is in course of ultimate extinction; or its advocates will push it forward, till it shall become alike lawful in all the States, old as well as new—North as well as South.

Lincoln meant to guarantee that his American "house" would be united in the right way, with slavery headed for extinction, not the wrong way, with slavery spreading.

Why did Lincoln write those misleading lines to Greeley? Because he was playing smart politics. He was preparing to unveil the Emancipation Proclamation, and he wanted to prevent a white-supremacist backlash by claiming that his policies on slavery were solely intended for the purpose of saving the Union—a Union that might never have been broken in the first place if Lincoln had not forged the "chain of steel" in the final months of 1860.

Cup of Wrath and Fire

DAVID BLIGHT

Few people in the North welcomed South Carolina's secession in December 1860, but Frederick Douglass, America's most prominent former slave and African American abolitionist, was one of them. From his editorial desk in Rochester, New York, Douglass heaped scorn on the Palmetto State's rash act, but he also relished it as an opportunity. He all but thanked the secessionists for "preferring to be a large piece of nothing, to being any longer a small piece of something."

Frederick Douglass. Library of Congress Prints and Photographs Division, LC-USZ62-15887.

To Douglass secessionists provided what he initially hoped would be the long-awaited opening for the antislavery cause: disunion, political crisis, and some form of sanctioned military action against slavery and the South. He would get his wish, but only after the tremendous confusion and fear of the secession winter of 1860–61.

Douglass's reactions to secession represented nearly twenty years of pent-up personal travail and abolitionist struggle as slavery grew across the cotton kingdom and into the American West and as the antislavery cause seemed to fail in electoral politics, the Supreme Court, and public opinion. Douglass and many of his fellow abolitionists had long yearned for a politics of disorder that might force the nation to confront, willingly or not, its future over slavery versus freedom in a rapidly expanding republic. Was that prospect now at hand?

"Her people [South Carolina's]," Douglass declared with anxious glee in his *Douglass Monthly*, "(except those of them held in slavery, which are more than half her population) have hailed the event as another and far more glorious Fourth of July, and are celebrating it with plenty of gunpowder and bad brandy, but as yet no balls, except those where perfumed ladies and gentlemen move their feet to the inspiring notes of the fiddle." With no veiled intent Douglass wished for a fight. "Other balls may yet come," he wrote, "and unless South Carolina shall retreat, or the Federal Government shall abdicate its functions, they must come." And he lampooned what South Carolinians imagined as "peaceful secession" celebrated by "bonfires, pyrotechnics . . . music and dancing." He cautioned Carolinians over their confidence about "a thing as easily done as the leaving of a society of Odd Fellows, or bidding good night to a spiritual circle."

Not that Douglass believed that South Carolina had a right to secede. The state, he wrote within a week of its act, was "out of the Union" only "on paper" and in "resolutions and telegrams." Governments "rest not upon paper, but upon power. They do not solicit obedience as a favor, but compel it as a duty." He acknowledged the "right of revolution" for a state or a political group but no constitutional "right of secession."

As a result, he believed, conflict was inevitable: "But revolution in this country is rebellion, and rebellion is treason, and treason is levying war against the United States, with something more than paper resolutions. . . . There must be swords, guns, powder, balls, and men behind them to use them." Secession therefore was no abstract debate over federalism or states' rights but a matter of power and guns. "The right of South Carolina to secede depends upon her ability to do so, and to stay so."

Douglass's sentiments were those of an antislavery activist who insisted that secession was intimately about slavery. He believed, as many reasonable Americans have ever since, that the significance of any exercise of a states' rights doctrine is in the issue for which it is employed. The prospect of civil war frightened him, but in January and February 1861 he cast the dreaded prospect in positive and apocalyptic language: "God in history everywhere pronouncing the doom of those nations which frame mischief by law" had caused a "concussion . . . against slavery which would now rock the land." National will and institutions had not solved the problem. "If there is not wisdom and virtue enough in the land to rid the country of slavery, then the next best thing is to let the South go . . . and be made to drink the wine cup of wrath and fire, which her long career of cruelty, barbarism and blood shall call down upon her guilty head."

From the snowy isolation of upstate New York Douglass could not easily define the course of disorder he sought as he watched several more Deep South states follow South Carolina out of the Union by February 1. His own confusion was not unlike the indecision, even incredulity of many Northern Republicans that winter. He had himself encountered the rage of a white mob on December 3 at Tremont Temple in Boston. At a gathering to commemorate the first anniversary of John Brown's execution, Douglass fought, according to one reporter, "like a trained pugilist" against those who shouted down and forcefully disrupted the antislavery gathering. For many, even in Boston, abolitionists had become easy scapegoats for the fear of disunion, disruption of the intersectional American economy, and the potential of war.

Above all, Douglass feared that the crisis would be resolved in yet further concessions to the South and slaveholders' interests. For a former slave and now a famous orator and editor—whose political consciousness had awakened with the Mexican War and the Compromise of 1850, who had seen the fate of slaves bandied about in one political crisis after another, who had struggled to preserve hope of freedom and citizenship in the face of the *Dred Scott* decision's egregious denials—a resolute stand by the North against secession and the "Slave Power" was hardly a sure thing. The best hopes for blacks, Douglass wrote in an editorial that winter, had always been dashed by the "old medicine of compromise."

He feared the same would be true in the latest crisis. As he watched Congress offer resolutions and conventions intended to settle the crisis, Douglass complained that South Carolina and her Northern enablers had "filled the air with whines of compromise." As March and the inauguration of Abraham Lincoln approached, Douglass, like so many Americans, felt powerless before events. Would Lincoln and the Republicans cave in to Southern demands and rebellion, or would they take a stand to defend federal authority and property?

Although it seemed unrealistic, what Douglass most desired was federal power marshaled for an organized war against the South and slavery. The necessity of a response to disunion might force Republicans into radical directions they would never take solely on their own accord. He wanted what Southerners most adamantly rejected: coercion against secession, even by force of arms.

But he warned about the tradition of compromise, feared Northerners had lost their "moral sense," lacked confidence in Lincoln's resolve, and worried that the abolition movement was about to be eclipsed by desire for a "peaceful disunion." In near despair in late February 1861, and employing his only weapon (a newspaperman's angry pen), Douglass envisioned a future when abolitionists would attack slavery in a foreign country by increasingly revolutionary means. "So much for the moral movement against slavery," he declared. "Hereafter, opposition to slavery will take a new form. . . . Slaves will run away, and humane men and women will help them; slaves will plot and conspire, and wise and brave men will help them. Abolition may be postponed, but it cannot be prevented. If it comes not from enlightenment . . . it will come from the fears of tyrants no longer able to hold down their rising slaves."

These sentiments and images of near race war are all the more interesting given the startling turn of events caused by the bombardment of one island fort in Charleston Harbor. Nothing explodes painful uncertainty like the awful clarity of war.

The Strange Victory of the Palmetto State

MANISHA SINHA

Less than two months separated South Carolina's decision to secede from the United States and the creation of a new country, the Confederate States of America. In that time six other states, constituting the entire Deep South—Mississippi, Florida, Alabama, Georgia, Louisiana, and Texas—had followed.

While each state had its share of secessionist fire-eaters, observers on all sides laid the blame firmly at the feet of the Palmetto State. Reverend R. J. Breckinridge of Kentucky, the pro-Union uncle of the Southern rights Democratic candidate in the 1860 presidential

John C. Calhoun. Library of Congress Prints and Photographs Division, LC-USZ62-76296.

election, blamed secession fever on "the chronic hatred of South Carolina to the national Union." Edmund Ruffin, an ardent Virginia secessionist, argued that it was natural for South Carolina to lead the secession movement because "the people of S.Ca. have been schooled and in training for 30 years in their political doctrines." Republican Party newspapers like the *New York Times* went so far as to call the seceded Lower South states the "Calhoun states" of America.

Though actual secession occurred quickly, South Carolina's leaders had been pushing the idea for decades without success. Criticized widely for its political distemper throughout the antebellum period, South Carolina remained immune to the charms of Jacksonian democracy and guided by the stern proslavery constitutional logic of John C. Calhoun. The state had gone to the brink in the 1830s, but the rest of the South held back; regional solidarity proved too thin to justify swift action. That changed over the next three decades, though, and in 1861, after nearly thirty years of resisting the siren call of secession from South Carolina, the cotton states followed its lead. What had changed?

Above all was a new sense of regional unity. When South Carolina seceded, emissaries from Alabama and Mississippi were on hand to commend the decision. There was also an element of strategy: immediately after it seceded South Carolina sent secession commissioners to the other Lower South states, urging disunion. It cleverly assigned to the more radicalized states of Florida, Alabama, and Mississippi fire-eating secessionists like Leonidas W. Spratt, father of the Southern movement to reopen the African slave trade; A. P. Calhoun, the son of John C. Calhoun; and Milledge Luke Bonham, later replaced by fellow congressman Armistead Burt. But it sent the more moderate, Democratic politicians James L. Orr and John L. Manning to Georgia and Louisiana, respectively, where Unionist sentiment still ran high. Many of these men had either lived in the states they were sent to or, like Manning and Calhoun, owned plantations there.

The Carolinian commissioners urged the speedy creation of a Southern nation and conveyed a united message in their speeches to the secession conventions of the cotton states. The North and the Republicans stood for "the social principle that equality is the right of man," according to Spratt, but the slave South embodied the "social principle that equality is not the right of man, but the right of equals only." Similarly John McQueen, the state's commissioner to Texas, argued that the "policy" of the "Black Republicans" was "the elevation of our own slaves to an equality with ourselves and our children."

As in South Carolina, most of these conventions were elected with large secessionist majorities. Only in Texas was the decision to secede ratified post facto in a statewide referendum. Following South Carolina's prompting, representatives of the seceded states met in Montgomery, Alabama, on February 4, and on February 8 they adopted a provisional constitution that explicitly recognized racial slavery.

Another factor contributing to regional unity under South Carolina's leadership was the changing nature of North-South politics. A faction of South Carolina's planter-politicians had been crying secession at least since the Nullification Crisis of 1828–32.

Under Calhoun's political tutelage, they argued that tariff laws formed a precedent for the federal government to interfere with the South's "domestick institution" of slavery, and threatened to leave the Union unless they were allowed to "nullify" federal laws within the state.

But the rest of the South wasn't convinced the Union was a bad deal for the region. After all, the long national ascendance of Virginia's revolutionary dynasty of Washington, Jefferson, Madison, and Monroe, as well as the resounding victory of Tennessee's Andrew Jackson in the 1828 presidential election, showed the South could exert significant power over national affairs. Moreover Jackson's presence in the White House during the Nullification Crisis pulled many Southern states into the Unionist orbit and away from South Carolina.

Change was already afoot, however. With the rise of the abolition movement in the 1830s and the sectional controversy over the expansion of slavery in the aftermath of the Mexican War, South Carolinians began to appear more in the garb of far-seeing prophets than fringe radicals to proslavery advocates in the rest of the region.

During the debates over the Compromise of 1850, a fairly strong secession movement arose not just in South Carolina but also in Alabama, Mississippi, and Georgia. Invoking and simultaneously subverting Patrick Henry's famous revolutionary slogan, the South Carolinian Edward Bryan proclaimed, "Give us slavery or give us death!" But a new split emerged, one between single-state secessionists, who believed in Calhoun's notion of absolute sovereignty that would allow any individual state to secede from the Union, and cooperationists, who argued that the South as a whole should secede. The latter won in 1850, and secession talk abated; ten years later the former won the day.

Why the flip? The Lower South states, with their large slave and slaveholding populations, started resembling South Carolina in more ways than one during the 1850s; with the demise of the Whig Party, they became one-party states and breeding grounds for Southern extremism. Slaveholders in those states became more receptive to radical ideas, like the Carolina-led movement to reopen the African slave trade. And they agreed with the contention of South Carolina's leaders that the opposition by the newly formed Republican Party to the extension of slavery was the first step toward general emancipation.

South Carolina not only inspired its fellow Lower South states to follow suit, but those states in turn worked on getting the Upper South to fall in line. Mississippi and Alabama dispatched emissaries to North Carolina, Maryland, Kentucky, and Missouri urging secession, though they took particular aim at Virginia. On February 13 three commissioners from South Carolina, Georgia, and Mississippi arrived simultaneously in that state. South Carolina's John S. Preston, who had earlier argued, "Slavery is our King—Slavery is our Truth—Slavery is our Divine Right," now told Virginians that the election of Lincoln meant the "annihilation" of Southern whites. But what had worked elsewhere failed here, and Virginians voted to stay within the Union.

But only for the moment. Indeed it was hardly a coincidence that a military showdown on Carolinian soil precipitated the secession of four Upper South states. South Carolina had already fired the first shot of the Civil War in January 1861, when artillery gunners opened fire on the ship *Star of the West*, sent to reinforce federal forces marooned at Fort Sumter, forcing it to turn back. When Confederate forces commenced bombardment of the fort on April 12, 1861, the Upper South had to choose sides. Virginia, Tennessee, Arkansas, and North Carolina rapidly seceded.

Despite their central role in fomenting secession, South Carolina's politicians did not dominate the Confederate government; in fact Virginia, though it entered the Confederacy late, soon became home to its capital. Nevertheless the Palmetto State had fulfilled the historical mission it had been rehearsing for years. As the unionist Reverend James W. Hunnicutt said of his native state, "The honor, the imperishable glory, of secession and inaugurating Civil War was reserved for South Carolina!"

Learning from Buchanan

JEAN H. BAKER

By mid-January 1861 a sleepless James Buchanan contemplated the remaining seven weeks of his presidency. Above all, he hoped to avoid the outbreak of civil war. He had come to Washington as a Northern Democrat who, through training, background, and conviction, believed himself well positioned to solve the sectional crisis.

Four years later, nearing his seventieth birthday, Buchanan wanted nothing more than to return to Wheatland, his home in Lancaster, Pennsylvania. He envisioned sitting at the mahogany desk in his study, explaining in his memoirs that the fault rested with the extremists in the North, who refused to allow Southern slaveholders their constitutional right to take slaves into the territories. He had always despised Republicans like William Seward and even President-elect Abraham Lincoln who threatened "the domestic institution" of slavery. One had only to consider John Brown's recent raid to understand the need to protect Southern rights.

In the second week of January 1861 Buchanan had received the attorney general of South Carolina, who brought an ominous letter from that state's governor, Francis Pickens, demanding that Fort Sumter, in Charleston Harbor, be handed over to South Carolina. It was a federal installation, and to do so would be treason. As commander in chief he had refused to send troops or naval forces when states had taken over installations in Texas or off the coast of Florida. But his new cabinet, formed after several Southern members resigned to join their states in secession, threatened to resign as well if he ordered Major Robert Anderson back to the less-fortified, landlocked Fort Moultrie. "No man can stand with you," his new attorney general, Jeremiah Black, had warned.

In this crisis Buchanan missed the congeniality of his former cabinet. Four of the original seven had been large slaveholders, and his special pet, Secretary of Treasury Howell Cobb of Georgia, had once owned over a thousand slaves. Gone in these frantic, chaotic days when "calamities never came alone" were the daily meetings that served as

James Buchanan. Library of Congress Prints and Photographs Division, LC-USZ62-96357.

family occasions for a lonely bachelor. As the president looked to the past with the future spinning out of control, they might have discussed what had gone wrong, though he had never considered such meetings as give-and-take sessions because he knew the answer: the fault lay with the aggressive Northern Republicans who refused to protect the rights of Southerners.

Buchanan had come to office with the best credentials of any president in American history. He had served in his state legislature, been elected to a congressional and then a Senate seat from Pennsylvania, and been considered for the Supreme Court. He even had foreign policy experience as James Polk's secretary of state and Franklin Pierce's minister to the Court of St. James's.

But there were troubling signs: Buchanan had won the 1856 three-way presidential race against a Republican and a Know Nothing with 45 percent of the popular vote and the electoral votes of only five Northern states. He paid little attention and gave jubilant supporters the watchwords of his forthcoming administration: the Republicans were a "dangerous geographical party. It was the southern people who still cherish a love for the Union." And as president he would protect them.

Buchanan found the solution to the nation's divisions in the *Dred Scott* case, then before the Supreme Court after a long history before lower courts. As president-elect, in a high-handed violation of the separation of powers, he had even urged Justice Robert C. Grier of Tennessee to find a comprehensive judgment that moved beyond the particulars of Dred Scott's individual status to that of all black Americans—slave and free, North and South. When such a decision was reached, slave owners could take slaves everywhere. Buchanan's goal of national harmony and constitutional government was enacted.

But like his predecessors, Buchanan was soon entangled in the controversial issue of slavery in Kansas. He intended to create a coalition of free-soil and proslavery Democrats, with partisan politics trumping any division over slavery, now protected by the *Dred Scott* decision as private property. But amid electoral fraud and violence there were two competing territorial governments in Kansas, one with a proslavery legislature and judiciary near Lecompton, the other a free-state government located in Topeka. Of course Buchanan supported the former, and when the Lecompton territorial government produced a constitution favoring slavery (boycotted by free-soil Kansans who represented the state's majority), he made the issue into an administrative measure, a litmus test for party loyalty.

Delighted Southerners now watched an unlikely slave state transformed into a probable one. But aggrieved Northern Democrats, including Stephen Douglas, saw the destruction of their party in the president's inability to treat both sides fairly. Even the lavish use of patronage did not win a majority in the House of Representatives. Buchanan had split the last remaining national organization in the United States.

The last year of Buchanan's presidency was the worst year of his life. His cabinet officers were among the most corrupt in American history. Secretary of War John Floyd even sent federal arms to the future states of the Confederacy. Then, on Christmas night 1860, Major Anderson moved to Fort Sumter, irritating South Carolinians whom Buchanan had spent four years appeasing. And while the president had approved an expedition to supply Anderson, he refused a more realistic one, proposed by Captain Gustavus Fox, to reinforce Fort Sumter using warships.

On March 4, 1861, Buchanan's tenure ended. As he and Lincoln rode back from the Capitol, he turned to the new president and said, "If you are as happy in entering the White House as I am in returning to Wheatland, you are a happy man."

The question remains why such an experienced and intelligent president failed so miserably. Americans lavish attention on their successful presidents, yet there is much to be learned from the failures. Buchanan did not suffer from feebleness or age or the insufficient powers of nineteenth-century executives. Rather he failed because he used that power with such partiality as an activist, ideologically driven executive. He chose sides in the great crisis and did not listen.

Indifferent toward slavery but greatly attached to the values of white Southerners, he went beyond political custom by castigating Republicans as disloyal. Yet his vision for the future of the United States was at odds with that of most Americans, whose definition of freedom did not include a slave republic dominated by a minority of slave owners. In one of the essential ingredients of successful leadership, Buchanan had failed to interpret his nation. Tragically his administration served to encourage the future enemies of the republic as he gave the Confederate States of America precious time and support to organize for war.

Confederates at the Gate

CHARLES LOCKWOOD AND JOHN LOCKWOOD

On April 8, 1861, the same day that President Lincoln notified South Carolina's governor that he intended to resupply Fort Sumter, ratcheting up the possibility of an armed Southern response, he also met with the governor of Pennsylvania, Andrew G. Curtin, at the White House. The president had more than Sumter on his mind; according to Curtin's

A view of Washington from Georgetown, 1860. Library of Congress Prints and Photographs Division, HABS DC, GEO, 1–13.

account, reported in the *New York Times*, Lincoln said he had "information of a design to attack the city of Washington," and he urged the governor, a close Republican Party ally, to ready his state's militia for a quick deployment to the Union capital.

The information had come via the inspector general of the District of Columbia Militia, Charles P. Stone, who had written to Secretary of State William H. Seward on April 5 describing recent reports of Confederate threats within the capital. An informant had warned Stone that "thousands of men in Washington, Virginia and Baltimore" were "ready to rise up armed" at Jefferson Davis's order and that the "attack on Fort Sumpter [*sic*] would be the Signal for action here, and plenty of men would rise to seize and hold the Capital until the Southern Army could reach here."

According to the information, Davis himself "would lead a company to take the Presidents House, and that the President, Cabinet Officers and General [Winfield] Scott would be made prisoners at the outset." Stone gave the story credence since he deemed it not improbable that "those who now rule the southern states intend to secure to themselves the prestige of possessing this capital."

Rumors of a secessionist conspiracy to capture Washington had circulated in both North and South since Lincoln's election. On Christmas Day 1860 the firebrand *Richmond Enquirer* had cried out, "Can there not be found men bold and brave enough in Maryland to unite with Virginians in seizing the Capital?" A week later the *New York Herald* warned of a plot to disrupt Lincoln's March 4 inauguration: "Already the border slave States of Maryland and Virginia are preparing to march a body of armed men to the federal capital to prevent the inauguration of the new President and to break up the government." The indecisiveness of the Buchanan administration, the newspaper cautioned, meant that there was "great danger that we may see the Capitol of the country seized, Mr. Lincoln driven out, and the government entirely broken up."

Dire warnings about Washington's safety were not limited to the sensationalist newspaper coverage. In early January Thomas H. Hicks, the governor of Maryland, cautioned that he had "been repeatedly warned by persons having the opportunity to know, and who are entitled to the highest confidence" that "secession leaders in Washington" had "resolved to seize the federal Capitol and the public archives, so that they may be in a position to be acknowledged by foreign governments."

Washington was undoubtedly easy prey. Located sixty miles south of the Mason-Dixon line, the city sat between two slave states that might easily follow the Deep South in seceding from the Union. What's more, its main transportation link to the North was the Baltimore & Ohio railroad line, a single track that served both north- and southbound traffic, with telegraph lines running alongside. Both the telegraph and the train lines could be torn up by a handful of men, severing Washington's physical and communication ties to the North. The city's natural defenses were nonexistent; in early 1861 its chief manmade fortification was Fort Washington, a decrepit structure built in 1809, located seven miles down the Potomac River and defended by exactly one soldier.

All was not hopeless, however; commanding the capital's defense was the storied general in chief of the Union Army, Winfield Scott. His 1846 conquest of Mexico City was one of the great triumphs of his long military career; now, fifteen years later, he was overseeing the rapid buildup of defenses around the capital.

The preparations began long before Lincoln took office. On December 2, 1860, President Buchanan requested that Scott move his New York–based military offices—and himself—back to Washington. This was no small request; the general lived in a fine brownstone at 24 West 12th Street off fashionable lower Fifth Avenue, ate at the best restaurants, and attended lavish parties and performances at the city's leading theaters. But recognizing the call to another historic duty, Scott arrived in Washington ten days later.

The general treated Washington as an unknown and potentially hostile territory, and his first step was to assess the local population. On the last day of the year he met with Charles Stone, a trustworthy former army colonel who had been living in Washington for several months. Stone told him, "It is my belief, General, that two-thirds of the fighting stock of this population would sustain the government in defending itself if called upon." That left another third loyal to the South—and that was counting only Washington residents, not secessionists in Virginia and Maryland. The next day Scott made Stone the inspector general of the District of Columbia Militia, where he could keep an eye on the armed unit's political sympathies and report back to Scott.

Colonel Stone stationed armed guards at the bridges over the Potomac and Anacostia rivers and at major roads leading into and out of the city. Still the number of troops available for Washington's defense was pitifully small because the majority of the army's sixteen thousand soldiers were deployed west of the Mississippi to guard the frontier. In early February President-elect Lincoln was forwarded a sobering note from Stone and Scott tallying the number of army troops available for the defense of the capital:

> Quartered at U.S. Arsenal 2 companies of Artillery say 12 guns—& . . . 130 men
> One company of Ordnance men . . . 50
> Quartered at Marine Barracks . . . 200
> At Fort McHenry 3 hours distant, two companies Artillery 6 guns . . . 120
> At West Point, under orders, 16 hours. One comp. Sappers . . . 100
> There are at Old Point Comfort which might in emergency be spared for this place,
>   24 hours distant . . . 200
> [Total] 800.

Without more troops the defense of Washington was impossible. In early January the *New York Herald* urged Congress to immediately call for sixty thousand troops to defend the capital, since the "pressing, immediate responsibility relates to the District of Columbia, and its defence against the attacks with which it is threatened." Without waiting for Congress to act, several Republican governors prepared their state militias for deployment to the capital in the event of an attack. John A. Andrew, sworn in as governor of Massachusetts on January 3, sent his military chief of staff to Washington to arrange the rapid dispatch of his state militia to the city in case secessionists moved against it.

Meanwhile rumors of a secessionist conspiracy being plotted within Washington were so rife that on January 26 a select committee of the House of Representatives opened an investigation into whether "any secret organization hostile to the government of the United States existed" in the city. After interviewing numerous witnesses, the committee concluded on February 14 that there was no secret plot to capture Washington—little comfort, because it also reported that Southern sympathies ran high and that many armed pro-Southern political clubs drilled there openly.

Lincoln's March 4 inauguration, conducted under heavy guard, passed without incident, and many believed that the threat to Washington had subsided. Still, parts of the city had taken on an eerie look. Houses sat empty because their former Southern inhabitants, including senators and congressmen, had returned home to their seceded states. Their window shutters were closed, and litter collected on their unswept sidewalks and front stoops. At night house after house sat silent and dark.

Jefferson Davis had departed Washington in January soon after Mississippi's vote to secede from the Union. His wife, Varina, apparently did not expect to remain gone for long. Colonel Stone reported that one of his informants, who had arrived in Washington from Montgomery, Alabama, in early April, had asked "Mrs. D. what she should say to her friends at Washington," to which Davis replied, "Tell them I shall be happy to see them in the White House at Washington in June."

On April 1, with war looming, Lincoln ordered Scott to "make short, comprehensive daily reports to me of what occurs in [your] Department, including movements" as well as "orders, and the receipt of intelligence." In his daily dispatch on April 8 Scott warned that army companies from Texas and Minnesota moving east might not arrive in the capital before it was attacked. Meanwhile he proposed mustering reliable volunteers from the District of Columbia Militia to supplement the regular army troops. On April 10 eight companies of District of Columbia volunteers were formally mustered to service of the federal government under the command of Colonel Stone.

In his April 10 diary entry a Patent Office examiner, Horatio Nelson Taft, whose daughter Julia and two sons were friends with Tad and Willie Lincoln, noted the presence of the new defenders throughout the city: "Guards are doubled at all the Public Buildings, and Military companies were on duty all last night." The night before, Taft had recorded in his diary, "Many are fearing an attack upon the City now, as it is thought that a War is about commencing."

That same day, with riflemen concealed in the shrubbery of the White House grounds for protection against a sudden attack, the *New York Herald* reported Lincoln's belief that once the first shots of the war had been fired, "this city will be the first that will be attacked."

Lincoln wasn't alone. With the fall of Fort Sumter, Varina Davis moved up the date she expected to take up residence at the White House. One prominent New York businessman reported to Seward, "[The] wife of the Rebel President Davis has had the impudence to send cards to her lady acquaintances at the Saint Nicholas"—a New York hotel popular among visiting Southerners—"inviting them to attend her reception in the White House at Washington on the first of May!"

How a Map Divided Virginia

SUSAN SCHULTEN

The secession crisis created tremendous turmoil in Virginia. The state initially considered leaving the Union in February 1861, and then again in early April, but on both occasions the proposal was defeated. This was partly a matter of geography: slavery was relatively rare in the western counties, and as the crisis intensified residents there began to see secession as primarily driven by the interests of slaveholders. As easterners became more strident about their rights, those in the west began to see themselves as a separate group with fundamentally different interests.

Just a few days after the Virginia delegates rejected secession, the crisis at Fort Sumter prompted Lincoln to call up seventy-five thousand volunteers. This was enough to force Virginians to reconsider, and this time the anger over military intervention convinced enough delegates to switch their vote, even as those in the western counties began to plan for their own secession from Richmond. Virginia's decision to secede was ratified by state voters on May 23, and just three days later General George McClellan, then commander of the army's Department of Ohio, invaded the western regions of the state to secure them for the Union.

But McClellan's soldiers weren't the only federal tool deployed to ensure Northern control over the breakaway counties. Just as Union forces were crossing the Ohio River, the U.S. Coast Survey issued a groundbreaking map of Virginia, the first ever to display census statistics cartographically.

The Coast Survey had experimented with cartographic techniques throughout the 1850s and introduced here a method of shading to represent "human" topography. The map has no legend, yet it is immediately clear that the darker areas represent a heavier density of slavery within the population. This technique visualized the stark inequality within Virginia, and it reinforced that message by ranking each county according to its dependence upon slavery in the chart on the left.

Anticipating the needs of a possible war, the Coast Survey established a separate lithographic division in May 1861 just to keep up with the demand for its maps. But this map of slavery was also made possible by the Census Office superintendent, who funneled the data collected from the 1860 enumeration directly to the Survey several months before releasing it to the public. Indeed Superintendent Joseph Kennedy had already turned the Census Office into a clearinghouse for Union propaganda: in an attempt to capitalize on divisions within Tennessee, North Carolina, and Virginia, Kennedy asked census workers

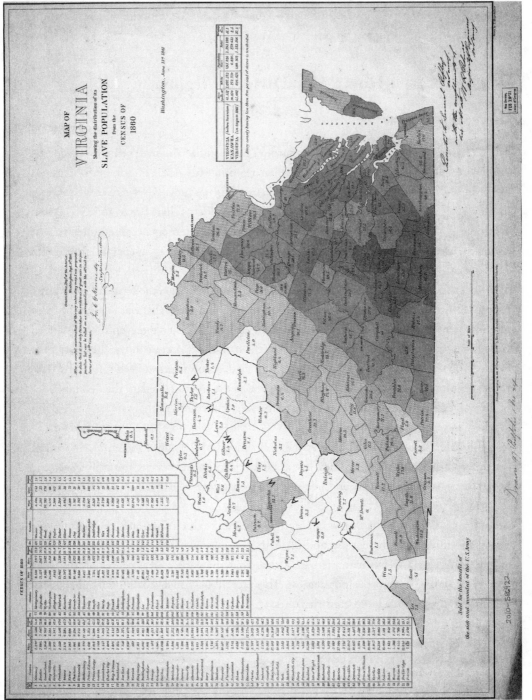

The distribution of slaves by county in Virginia. Courtesy of the Library of Congress.

to gauge Unionist sentiment within those states, and—with the help of Senator William Seward and Representative Charles Francis Adams—organized a massive mailing to undercut secessionist sentiment there. Thus he was only too happy to supply the Survey with the necessary data for its map of slavery.

In June McClellan's maneuvering enabled Unionists to meet in Wheeling, where they declared the government in Richmond to be illegal representatives of the state. In July Lincoln recognized the Unionists as the state's legitimate leaders, even as McClellan continued to battle against Robert E. Lee and his forces for control over these western counties. Captain William Palmer, who worked with the Coast Survey in 1861, sent one copy of the map directly to Secretary of the Navy Gideon Welles and several others to fellow army officers, which indicates that the map also had relevance for the military campaigns in Virginia.

The story of western Virginia is complex, and the map itself disguises this somewhat. Areas with a relatively small slave population generally sided against secession when the vote was taken on April 4, when it failed, then again on April 17, when it succeeded. However, this opposition to secession did not necessarily translate into abolition, or even resistance to slavery. When West Virginia finally became a state in June 1863, it passed rigid manumission laws that would have protected slavery for decades were it not for the Thirteenth Amendment. And in several counties the opposition to secession constituted a slim rather than a decisive majority; in other words, the map is not a transparent reflection of political sentiment. Yet it captured the imagination of the nation's leaders and the public, and it circulated widely throughout Washington.

By August the army had secured the western counties to the point that the residents could begin to organize themselves into a new state. At this moment of victory the Coast Survey issued a second edition of the map that boldly colored the proposed state of "Kanawha" in western Virginia. This edition also reinforced the initial message of the map with statistics showing that the vast majority of slaves had remained in Virginia.

Just a few weeks later the Coast Survey issued a final edition of the map to meet the overwhelming demand for copies, which suggests that the map itself was a successful experiment. In this final edition Superintendent Kennedy vouched for the accuracy of the map. More important, this final edition was accompanied by a second, even more ambitious map, one that pictured the distribution of slavery throughout the Southern states; it would become a favorite of Lincoln's as he navigated the complexities of total war.

Texas Catches Fire

RICHARD PARKER

Even as Texas prepared for war, its fate within the Confederacy sealed, parts of the state still seethed with Union sentiment. And no place was more fervently pro-Union that spring than Bexar County and its largest city, San Antonio, the home of the Alamo, the very cradle of Texas independence.

Indeed even as Union troops marched off to the coast to evacuate after surrendering their armory, Colonel C. A. Waite, who had arrived too late to stop the debacle, reported home on April 1, 1861, that Unionism in the city remained strong. Waite predicted that just "a few thousand dollars expended on the press would revolutionize sentiment in Texas."

Waite was wrong; two-thirds of Texas had voted to secede. Yet some Union sentiment would linger throughout the war. As many as a third of all Texans would continue to support the Union, historians later estimated. Some, out of love for Texas, would resign themselves to fight for the Confederacy. Some would be effectively silenced or would flee. And still others would pay for their loyalty with their lives, strung up or shot down.

James P. Newcomb was a young newspaperman in San Antonio who inadvertently tested Waite's thesis. Having started the *Weekly Alamo Express* the previous year, Newcomb made his pro-Union views widely known. He published notice of a public meeting in the plaza, to be held on April 9, for the purpose of "restoring harmony and prosperity to our distracted country." Two speakers addressed the crowd, and Newcomb later called it "a glorious night": "We have given the Reconstruction ball a roll. Let it be kept rolling over the state until all the opposition is crushed out." For good measure he added that the Confederacy was "conceived in sin" and called Jefferson Davis a weak, vile traitor.

Retribution came quick: Newcomb returned to find his office destroyed and his printing press at the bottom of the San Antonio River, courtesy of the pro-secession Knights of the Golden Circle and Confederate Rangers. Newcomb fled and, eventually, joined the Union Army.

Unionist sentiment took varying forms. Where Newcomb was outspoken, others simply and quietly refused to support the Confederacy—or the Union, for that matter. President Lincoln, who thought he saw a chance to break Texas off from the Confederacy, offered Sam Houston, ousted from the governorship in Austin, the chance to lead Union forces in retaking Texas. Yet Houston refused, not wanting Texans to spill the blood of other Texans. Learning that Waite was attempting to raise a force near Indianola to restore him to office as governor, he wrote to the army officer, "Allow me most respectfully to decline any such assistance of the United States government."

Others, like the politicians Eber Worthington Cave, B. H. Epperson, and James W. Throckmorton, embraced the cause of the Confederacy despite their misgivings. Throckmorton was the most outspoken Unionist at the Secession Convention, having opposed secession for two solid years, alongside Houston. He donned a gray uniform, however, and became a skilled soldier, organizing a hundred-man mounted rifle company, securing forts on the frontier, and joining the Sixth Texas Cavalry. He fought at the battles of Chustenahlah and Elkhorn Tavern and rose to the rank of brigadier general.

Andrew Jackson Hamilton would also become a brigadier general, but in the Union Army. A man who would not be silenced and would not sit idly by, he fled Austin upstream into the rough country of the Colorado River's bends, forests, and caves, crossing into Mexico and eventually making his way to Washington, where he would receive his commission. When the war was finally over, he was made provisional governor of Texas.

Altogether some two thousand Texans would fight for the Union. Edmund Jackson Davis, a south Texas judge, led the Union's First Texas Cavalry, which fought in south Texas early in the war. A second Texas Union cavalry regiment was led by John L. Haynes, a former state legislator from Rio Grande City, composed primarily of Mexicans. Both units would later fight in Louisiana.

Texas historians believe that about one-third of Texans actively or passively supported the Union as war unfurled. The common man, however, did not get a Union commission as general. Instead he usually got a threat. On May 25, 1861, a self-appointed Committee of Safety left an otherwise anonymous letter for a Mr. A. Newman, suspected of harboring abolitionist views: "Leave the country at once else you will be dealt with according to mob law."

In Cooke County, north of Dallas, a Unionist organization known as the Peace Party began to form in secret. But a drunken party leader revealed the group's plans, and Confederate officers penetrated the organization. The news spread like wildfire and ignited rumors of Unionists planning arson and murder. The population took matters into its own hands and hanged twenty-five Unionists without a trial. A little later another trial was held and more than forty were hanged.

But it would be Confederate conscription that would chafe the most at Texas Unionists. The German Americans of the Hill Country, in particular, would actively resist both conscription and the Confederacy. One plot called upon "all German Brothers" to "hang [Texans] by their feet and burn them from below." As the historian Mary Jo O'Rear

A funeral for German Americans in Texas. Library of Congress Prints and Photographs Division, LC-USZ61-2011.

writes, "Vague distrust exploded into blind rage." And that went for both sides: as dissent grew over the hot summer of 1862, Confederate cavalry and Partisan Rangers moved into the Hill Country, catching one hundred German Americans on the move to Mexico to join the federal army. On the banks of the clear Nueces River the Confederates killed thirty-two men in a surprise attack. Not a single prisoner was taken, according to the historian Claude Elliott. Nine more men were murdered after the fighting; the wounded were killed on the spot and the rest taken to White Oak Creek, where they were hanged or shot. The Confederates then made their way to Gillespie, where they captured and hanged another fifty men. The war, already raging in the East, had come home to Texas.

The Death Knell of Slavery

GREGORY P. DOWNS

When North Carolina finally voted to secede on May 20, 1861, the editor William Holden later wrote, the state's convention "looked like a sea partly in storm, partly calm, the secessionists shouting and throwing up their hats and rejoicing, the Conservatives sitting quietly, calm, and depressed." Even as they voted unanimously to leave the Union, North Carolina's leading politicians could not conceal the conflicts that would divide the state throughout the war.

Only three months earlier North Carolina voters had beaten back secessionists, refusing even to call a convention. And yet on that day in May the convention became the last official body to leave the Union, although Virginia's and Tennessee's secessions still awaited popular ratification. Indeed the state's change of heart and the evident fault lines at the fraught May convention remind us of three easy-to-overlook aspects of the Upper South's turn to the Confederacy.

Whites in the Upper South had argued about secession for decades, and objections to the right to secede did not disappear with the firing on Fort Sumter. Even as the state's politicians bowed to disunion, they disagreed about method.

In one of the stranger secession stories, North Carolina's conservatives paused on the precipice of disunion to beg the convention to consider not secession but revolution, a right that belonged to any people who could defend themselves. Put forward by George E. Badger, a former senator and secretary of the navy, a resolution of revolution garnered significant support, but not enough to derail the secessionists. Seeing failure, conservatives moved to make the secession vote unanimous, but their glum visages betrayed their misgivings.

Arguments about secession in the Upper South were not, however, arguments about slavery. Conservatives and secessionists defended slavery through different methods. In North Carolina, as in much of the Upper South, Unionists believed the nation the best, perhaps only safeguard for slavery. On the evening after the vote, hearing secessionists fire a hundred-gun salute at the state capitol, Badger called the sound "the death knell of slavery."

Senator George E. Badger. Library of Congress Prints and Photographs Division, LC-USZ62-110072.

Third, the Upper South's late decisions shaped the war to a degree largely forgotten today. Its secessions wounded the Union gravely and gave the Confederacy a much needed boost of soldiers and territory. North Carolina residents stocked the Confederate Army with 125,000 men and lost perhaps 35,000, arguably the most of any Southern state. Then, as white unanimity—and Confederate hopes—faded, Carolinians deserted at astonishing rates, and a peace movement spread across the state, seriously hindering the Southern war effort. Moreover slaves in the state gave the lie to any semblance of unanimity as they took their future in their own hands, running to Union lines and eventually serving in large numbers in the Northern army.

North Carolina illustrated these commitments and divisions because it was simultaneously deeply Southern and, in other ways, not quite Southern at all. Slavery stood at the center of North Carolina life, but plantations did not. Slaves made up about one-third of the state's 1 million people, a proportion notably smaller than South Carolina's or Mississippi's but slightly larger than Tennessee's or Virginia's. Of the roughly 25 percent of North Carolina families who owned slaves, 70 percent owned fewer than ten. Much of the state was full of small to middling farmers; 70 percent of farms were smaller than 100 acres. There were only two towns of five thousand people, and none had more than ten thousand.

The state's political divisions arose in part from geography. North Carolina had long been divided into three sections. Most slaves lived in a coastal plain of large-scale cotton and rice plantations. The state's two other regions had smaller but still substantial slave populations: a large central piedmont of middling staple and livestock farms, and the high western Appalachians. Westerners tended to fight against eastern planters on key issues like state spending on railroads and increased taxation on slaves. Eastern planters formed the backbone of early secessionist movements, while most Appalachian and particularly piedmont politicians argued for the Union.

But if the power of plantations divided the public, the importance of slavery did not. Across the state most leading men owned slaves. In 1860 more than 85 percent of the state legislators were slaveholders, the highest percentage in the South. Even Appalachian politicians vigorously supported slave orthodoxy. Defending slave owning was a way of protecting not plantations but property. "If they can take our niggers away from us they can take our cows and hosses, and everything else we've got!" one western slave owner warned his neighbors. Senator Thomas Clingman, a westerner who owned no slaves, was one of the country's most virulent defenders of slavery and secession.

Abraham Lincoln's election in November 1860 inspired secessionists in North Carolina, like their comrades in the Deep South, to push for a quick break. As rumors spread of slave uprisings and Northern plots, Clingman took to the Senate floor to warn that North Carolina should "expect to have slavery abolished by force of arms, and to see the South reduced to the condition of Jamaica or St. Domingo." Those attending a county meeting called Northern actions "intolerable" and promised to defend any of the "slave holding States" that "shall Secede."

The fervent talk worried Sallie Lenoir, a westerner. "I dread the dark future," she wrote. "If the South would only keep cool and try him [Lincoln] first I think we need not fear much but I cannot hope that."

During these winter months North Carolina Unionists worked diligently to block the state from joining its Deep South neighbors. The Constitution did not permit secession, argued William Graham, a former governor, and "the necessity for revolution does not yet exist."

Along with skepticism over the right of secession, Unionists disagreed with the strategy. Instead of protecting slavery, they argued, secession would destroy the institution. Holden, the state's leading Democrat and newspaperman, urged people to "watch and wait." Secession "would end in civil war, in military despotism, and in the destruction of slave property." A legislator warned that secession would "be bringing Canada down to the borders of the South. Our slaves would only have to step across the line, and they would be free."

As a compromise the state legislature called a February referendum on whether to hold a secession convention. The campaign was rough and ribald. In popular meetings in Raleigh, Unionist workingmen disrupted a secession meeting by burning tar barrels, ringing bells, and shouting down speakers. Another crowd shot a Confederate flag and chopped the flagpole to pieces. Unionists elsewhere promised, to the tune of "Dixie," "to live and die for Union."

On February 28 the state voted narrowly—by about 650 votes out of about 94,000—against a secession convention. And Unionist strength was greater than those numbers indicate: because some people voted both for the convention and for Unionist delegates, Unionists would have held about 80 of the 120 seats. Many Unionists in fact regretted the convention's defeat; had the convention met, it would have been controlled by conservatives. A future crisis, they feared, might prompt the election of more radical delegates.

At the same time, the Unionist victory was not as profound as it seemed. Many North Carolinians still hoped for an orderly resolution, perhaps from Virginia's Peace Conference. When the peace conference collapsed, one Unionist glumly warned, "There seems to be very little hope now."

Additionally many Unionists calculated their choices pragmatically. In times of peace, sticking with the Union might be the best way to protect slave property. If war broke out, however, most of them had no heart to fight the South and no faith in Northern support for protecting slavery in wartime. Many foresaw that an attack on Sumter would lead to a conflict the state could not avoid. Days before Sumter, with his state still in the Union, a North Carolina West Point cadet prepared to leave the school, believing, "There will be no compromise, and . . . the border states will be compelled to secede however unwilling they may be to do so." Once Lincoln called for troops, the secessionist governor John Ellis dismissed the government's "gross usurpation of power." The legislature called a May 20 convention and began to prepare for war.

Meanwhile Unionism in the state crumbled. Representative Zebulon Vance, a western Unionist, was gesturing to the heavens "for peace and the Union of our Fathers" when someone handed him news of Lincoln's call for troops. "When my hand came down," Vance recalled later, "it fell slowly and sadly by the side of a secessionist. I immediately, with altered voice and manner, called upon the assembled multitude to volunteer, not to fight against but for South Carolina."

As the state prepared for its May 20 convention, there was much anxiety but little public debate. "I tremble for you and for myself," Jonathan Worth, a state senator, wrote to his son. A conservative raised a Quaker, Worth refused to attend the convention but acceded to its results. "Peaceable secession would soon annihilate slavery. War, long continued, will ruin every peaceful citizen and end in the total overthrow of civil liberty and the abolition of slavery. I think the South is committing suicide, but my lot is cast with the South."

The immediate acquiescence to the strategy, if not the principle, of secession shows the deep limitations of Southern Unionism. While some scholars criticize Lincoln for not appealing to Southern Unionists, their loyalty was situational: Lincoln could keep the Upper South in the Union, or he could defend federal forts from Confederate seizure, but he could not do both.

White and black Carolinians watched and waited, some hopeful, some fearful, all unsure of what was to come. Hannah Crasson, a young slave near Raleigh, remembered that her master told her father and uncles that a Northern victory would mean freedom. The master's son, however, bragged "dey could eat breakfast at home, go and whup the North, and be back far dinner." Would the war bring freedom or Confederate triumph? Her master's son "went away, and it wuz four long years before he cum back to dinner," Crasson remembered. When he returned, she and her family were free.

2. Slavery and Emancipation

Introduction

Manisha Sinha

Abraham Lincoln called emancipation "the central act of my administration and the great event of the nineteenth century." Like all important historical milestones, emancipation was a complex process that involved many actors, including the slaves themselves, the Union Army, black and white abolitionists, Congress, and the president. Nor was emancipation simply a military act born of a wartime emergency but one that had a long prehistory in slave resistance, abolitionist activism, and the politics of antislavery.

Some recent historians have further complicated our understanding of the emancipatory legacy of the Civil War by pointing to the hurdles, shortcomings, and suffering of the newly freed. Notwithstanding this turn in the history of slavery and emancipation, Lincoln's assessment of the destruction of American slavery as a revolutionary act, with world-historical consequences, still holds.

Emancipation was not a singular event made possible by the stroke of a pen. The enslaved had resisted slavery from the moment of enslavement, and abolitionists had long agitated for an end to slavery. In the years prior to the Civil War fugitive slaves had exacerbated sectional tensions between free and slave states and called into question the national legitimacy of slavery. They anticipated the movement of thousands of slaves who defected to the Union Army lines and pressured the Lincoln administration to act on emancipation. Slaves saw Lincoln and the Union Army as their liberators before Lincoln and the Union Army saw themselves in that role. Their stories have added nuance and fullness to the traditional top-down histories of emancipation.

The historical drama of emancipation unfolded on the ground in countless stories of the slaves' jubilation, daily confrontations with whites who proclaimed that they had a divine right to own them, and at times tragic tales of their jagged road to freedom. If slaves fleeing for freedom had not seized the initiative, the process of emancipation would not have unfolded in precisely the manner it did. The contraband policy of the Union, which proclaimed slaves enemy property legitimately confiscated, recognized the principle of property in human beings but led to the liberation of millions of slaves from the Confederacy. For many Northern soldiers, encounters with contraband slaves were their first introduction to the horrors of slavery. Slaves who braved enemy fire, their master's wrath, and the Confederacy's punitive response and who, at times, brought valuable military information, converted many a midwestern farm boy to abolition. Their backs scarred from whippings bore silent witness to the harrowing stories told by fugitive slaves and abolitionists before the war.

Nor did emancipation, as federal policy, follow a straight line. The Lincoln administration's commitment to returning the fugitive slaves of Unionist slaveholders and those from the border slave states in the Union provoked an outcry among abolitionists and Radical Republicans. But in enacting the Confiscation Acts of 1861 and 1862 and the Militia Act of 1862, the Republican-dominated Congress stole a march on the president. These laws confiscated the slaves used in the rebellion and those of rebel slaveholders and pointed the way to black recruitment in the army. For enslaved men in the border states, enlistment in the Union Army was the only way to obtain freedom for themselves and their families, and they were quick to seize the opportunity even as their masters howled in protest. The capital of the nation was itself emancipated from the chokehold of slavery a year prior to Lincoln's historic Emancipation Proclamation.

Lincoln's proclamation, issued on January 1, 1863, the same day the black republic of Haiti declared its independence in 1804 and the United States and Britain abolished the African slave trade four years later, became sanctified in black and abolitionist memory. The Day of Jubilo, or Emancipation Day, would long be celebrated among African Americans after the war. Scholars who criticize the proclamation for its lack of moral grandeur or as an act born of military necessity overlook the fact that Lincoln and his contemporaries viewed the constitutional, military, moral, and political causes of emancipation as interconnected. Its purview was broader than the confiscation acts, as it freed all slaves in rebel areas even though it left out slaves in Union-controlled territory. And in calling for black recruitment into the Union Army and demanding freed people refrain from violence except in self-defense, it revealed the radical transformation the war had wrought. It linked black freedom with the powers of the federal government and the Union cause.

Perhaps the most important symbol of the emancipatory nature of the war was the presence of black soldiers in the Union Army. Former abolitionists recruited them and even served as officers in some black regiments. The Civil War alliance between them extended the antebellum logic that made the enslaved and abolitionists "allies for freedom." Black military service also became a powerful argument for African American citizenship, and black heroism in the fighting at places like Fort Wagner, Port Hudson, and Milliken's Bend convinced skeptical Northerners of the wisdom of emancipation. Lincoln himself traveled the road from colonization, the plan to colonize free blacks outside the country, to black rights within the country. When racist opposition to emancipation, illustrated most horrifically in the New York City Draft Riots of 1863, threatened his reelection, the votes of Union Army soldiers provided him with the margin of victory.

Emancipation made the slave's cause in the United States an international movement. It portended the destruction of slavery and its vestiges in Brazil and Cuba and finally put a halt to the infamous traffic in human beings from Africa. Republican revolutionaries and democrats all over Europe linked the fate of their nations and movements to the survival of the American republic and the emancipation of its slaves. Radical Republicans, abolitionists, and Lincoln fought hard for passage of the Thirteenth Amendment abolishing servitude at the end of the war. As the historian Armstead I. Robinson first argued, "A war fought to protect slavery ended in its destruction, and slaves whose permanent servitude was to be the Confederacy's triumphant reward helped deny slaveholders the fulfillment of their most cherished dream."

Visualizing Slavery

SUSAN SCHULTEN

The 1860 census was the last time the federal government took a count of the South's vast slave population. Several months later the U.S. Coast Survey—arguably the most important scientific agency in the nation at the time—issued two maps of slavery that drew on the census data, the first of Virginia and the second of Southern states as a whole. Though many Americans knew that dependence on slave labor varied throughout the South, these maps captured the complexity of the institution and struck a chord with a public hungry for information about the rebellion.

The map uses what was then a new technique in statistical cartography: each county not only displays its slave population numerically but is shaded (the darker the shading, the higher the number of slaves) to visualize the concentration of slavery across the region. The counties along the Mississippi River and in coastal South Carolina are almost black, while Kentucky and the Appalachians are nearly white.

The map reaffirmed the belief of many in the Union that secession was driven not by a notion of "state rights" but by the defense of a labor system. A table at the lower edge of the map measured each state's slave population, and contemporaries would have immediately noticed that this corresponded closely to the order of secession. South Carolina, which led the rebellion, was one of two states that enslaved a majority of its population, a fact starkly represented on the map.

Conversely the map illustrated the degree to which entire regions—like eastern Tennessee and western Virginia—were virtually devoid of slavery and thus potential sources of resistance to secession. Such a map might have reinforced President Abraham Lincoln's belief that secession was animated by a minority and could be reversed if Southern Unionists were given sufficient time and support.

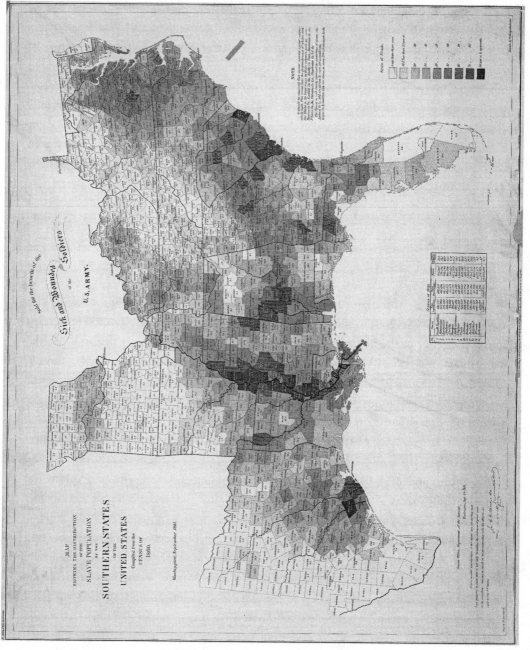

The U.S. Coast Survey's map of the slaveholding states. Courtesy of the Library of Congress.

The map quickly caught the public's attention and was reproduced throughout the war. Its banner headline, "For the benefit of the sick and wounded soldiers," also became the slogan of the Union's most important home front organization, the U.S. Sanitary Commission. The map gave a clear picture of what the Union was up against and allowed Northerners to follow the progress of the war and the liberation of slave populations.

We don't know when Lincoln first encountered the Coast Survey's map of slavery. But he became so taken with it that Francis Bicknell Carpenter included it in the lower right corner of his painting *President Lincoln Reading the Emancipation Proclamation to His Cabinet*. Carpenter spent the first six months of 1864 in the White House preparing the portrait and on more than one occasion found Lincoln poring over the map. Though the president had abundant maps at his disposal, only this one allowed him to focus on the Confederacy's greatest asset: its labor system. After January 1, 1863, when emancipation became law, the president could use the map to follow Union troops as they liberated slaves and destabilized the rebellion. Lincoln was enthusiastic about Carpenter's finished portrait and singled out the map as one of its most notable details.

Slavery also informed the painting in another way. Carpenter arranged the cabinet members according to his perception of their sentiment regarding emancipation: its two leading proponents, Secretary of the Treasury Salmon P. Chase (standing) and Secretary of War Edwin Stanton are to Lincoln's right, while Secretary of State William Seward sits in the foreground. To Lincoln's immediate left are the secretary of the navy, the secretary of the interior, and the postmaster general standing in the rear, while Attorney General Edward Bates sits at the far right of the portrait. Lincoln sits at the center, as Carpenter wrote, "nearest that representing the radical, but the uniting point of both." A copy of the antislavery *New-York Tribune* lies at Stanton's feet, while a portrait of Simon Cameron—the prior secretary of war, who urged emancipation early in the conflict—is visible beyond Stanton's head. The map lying across the table behind Seward is the Coast Survey's 1863 Map of the State of Virginia, which included both population statistics and concentric rings around Richmond to guide Union strategy.

It may seem odd that the Coast Survey, originally responsible for detailing the nation's coastlines and rivers, produced a map of slavery in the South. Yet over the preceding two decades its superintendent, Alexander Dallas Bache, had skillfully widened the Survey's work and made it a hub of mapmaking innovation. The Survey experimented with several new methods of cartographic representation, including the use of shading to represent the human population. As early as 1858 Bache had directed the Survey to produce maps of the rivers and coasts of the South in anticipation of a conflict. But the 1861 map was in a class by itself: a landmark cartographic achievement, a popular propaganda tool, and an eminently practical instrument of military policy. No wonder Lincoln liked it.

The Transatlantic Slave Trade and the Civil War

DAVID ELTIS AND DAVID RICHARDSON

The conclusion of the historian David Brion Davis's book *Inhuman Bondage* traces the significance of the Civil War in the ending of slavery elsewhere. It implicitly poses the question: What if the Confederacy had won recognition from Britain in 1862 and had survived the war? Our rather frightening answer is that the three great centers of slavery in the Americas—the United States South, Cuba, and Brazil—and the smaller plantation economy of Dutch Suriname would not have abolished slavery when they did.

The slave deck of the barque *Wildfire*, brought into Key West on April 30, 1860. Library of Congress Prints and Photographs Division, LC-USZ62-41678.

That the Civil War and the subsequent Thirteenth Amendment ended slavery in the United States is self-evident. What's less well known is that the Civil War also had immense significance for the ending of slavery elsewhere, especially in the Americas. Indeed few people recognize that it took a war to finally bring the brutal transatlantic slave trade to a close. In all likelihood, without a Union victory slavery would have remained a central institution underpinning global economic growth possibly until the present day.

It's true that only a small share—about 4 percent—of the total slaves carried off from Africa landed on the North American mainland. And an even smaller share of those destined for slavery in the rest of the Americas completed their voyage in vessels flying the U.S. flag or set sail from mainland ports. Yet small as the U.S. role was, there is no doubt that the federal government effectively protected transatlantic slave traders in the half-century before 1861 and that the outbreak of the Civil War just as effectively removed that protection. Indeed thanks to America's role, almost one-quarter of the total transatlantic slave trade occurred after the government banned American participation in the slave trade in 1807.

How was it possible for such a minor player to have such a large impact? The answer turns on the nature of the nascent system of international law that had emerged by the early nineteenth century and the fact that the transatlantic slave trade was perhaps the most thoroughly multinational business of the early modern era.

For one thing, Denmark, the United States, and Britain, the first nations to take action against the trade, might have banned their own citizens from participating and forbade the entry of slaves into their own territories, but without negotiating international treaties they could do nothing to stop foreign nationals carrying on the slave trade elsewhere— including the high seas.

After 1807 the British constructed an elaborate, costly, but ultimately ineffective network of treaties that allowed their cruisers to stop suspected slave vessels flying the flags of other nations. But it didn't cover all countries, and in these years slave ships sailed under the colors of Mexico, Russia, Sardinia, and Argentina, among many others, solely because these flags prevented British intervention. And as long as a single nation allowed its flag to be used in this way, and as long as Brazil and Cuba remained open to new arrivals from Africa, the transatlantic slave trade would continue.

Moreover France and the United States never allowed the British to stop and search their own merchant vessels. Instead they undertook to patrol the Atlantic themselves. The French at one stage assigned more than forty warships to slave trade duties. The American fleet, on the other hand, never exceeded six warships, and for years at a time the country deployed none at all. And neither nation sought permission to stop and search suspected slave ships operating under another flag. As a consequence the British Navy detained almost 1,600 of the nearly two thousand slave vessels detained in Atlantic waters in the era of suppression; the United States detained just sixty-eight.

Why such a half-hearted effort? The answer is simple. First, American administrations were often stocked with Southerners in key positions, such as secretary of state, secretary of the navy, and president, and they refused to take serious action against the foreign slave trade. Thus they tacitly allowed the Stars and Stripes to be used as a cover. In the absence of a treaty the British were reluctant to interfere with American shipping; only American naval ships could stop this practice, and even when they acted officers would usually detain a ship only if slaves were on board. (Thus ships heading to Africa, even if they were obviously slavers, were let go.)

But an unwillingness to enforce the law was just part of the story. American shipbuilders also sent a steady stream of fast-sailing vessels into the slave trade after 1830. The premium on speed partly had to do with voyage mortality risks and the high-value nature of the cargo; by the 1860s five hundred slaves could fetch close to half a million dollars in Cuba. The design of the slave vessel changed radically between 1800 and the mid-1830s, and the duration of the middle passage to Cuba declined by one-third between the 1790s and 1850s. Many of these fast slavers were yachts or clippers made in the United States; Baltimore in particular developed a reputation for constructing fast sailing vessels. In all, about one-third of the slave ships sailing after 1810 were built in American ports.

Second, the use of the U.S. flag by slave traders escalated after 1835. In the early years of suppression the Cuban trade was conducted under the Spanish flag, the traffic to the French Americas under the French flag, and the traffic to Brazil under the Portuguese and Brazilian flags. Only a few of these vessels were American, with an American master and crew. But this situation began to change in 1835, when Great Britain and Spain signed a treaty that for the first time specified a range of equipment that could provide grounds for detention. In other words, slavers without slaves on board could be detained. The immediate effect was that slave traders abandoned the Spanish flag and began to register their vessels as Portuguese, though a growing number sought registration under American colors.

The British introduced other measures in 1839 and 1845 that extended the so-called equipment clause to Brazilian and Portuguese slave traders, thus increasing reliance on the U.S. flag even further. For a few years a weird set of flags appeared on the African coast, with vessels frequently carrying more than one set of papers, each to be used as required. Many ships flew no flag at all.

The use of the U.S. flag ended only after the Civil War began. In 1862, with Southern politicians finally gone from national politics, the United States at last signed a treaty with the British providing for mutual right of search on the high seas, an equipment clause, and joint Anglo-American courts (called courts of mixed commission) for adjudicating detentions. The fact that those courts never heard a single case detracts not at all from their impact.

True, the slave trade continued for another five years, but at decreasing annual volumes. More important, there were only three recorded voyages under the U.S. flag after the 1862 convention—and, we should add, after the execution that same year of Nathaniel Gordon, the only individual to suffer the full penalty of the 1820 Act that made slave trading a capital offense. Compare this to 123 such voyages documented in the five years preceding the 1862 treaty. Secession, and a Union victory in the war that precluded any renewed trading under the Confederate aegis, made all the difference.

What Lincoln Meant to the Slaves

STEVEN HAHN

The enormous excitement and anticipation around the 1860 presidential election campaign spread into unexpected corners of the United States. During the months surrounding the contest, and especially after Americans learned of Abraham Lincoln's victory, reports circulated across the Southern states of political attentiveness and restlessness among the slaves.

Southern newspapers noted the slaves' attraction to "every political speech" and their disposition to "linger around" the hustings or courthouse square "and hear what the orators had to say." But even more significant, witnesses told of elevated hopes and expectations among the slaves that Lincoln intended "to set them all free." And once Lincoln assumed office and fighting erupted between the Union and the Confederacy, hopes and expectations seemed to inspire actions. Slaves' response to the election of 1860 and their ideas about Lincoln's intentions suggest that they too were important actors in the country's drama of secession and war and that they may have had an unappreciated influence on its outcome.

Scholars and the interested public have long debated Lincoln's views on slavery and how they influenced his policies as president. How committed was he to abolition? What was he prepared to do? Could he imagine a world in which white and black people lived together in peace and freedom? For many slaves, at least at first, the answer was clear: Lincoln's election meant emancipation.

On one Virginia plantation a group of slaves celebrated Lincoln's inauguration by proclaiming their freedom and marching off their owner's estate. In Alabama some slaves had come to believe that "Lincoln is soon going to free them all" and had begun "making preparations to aid him when he makes his appearance," according to local whites. A runaway slave in Louisiana told his captors in late May 1861 that "the North was fighting for the Negroes now and that he was as free as his master." Shortly thereafter a nearby planter conceded, "The Negroes have gotten a confused idea of Lincoln's Congress meeting and of the war; they think it is all to help them and they expected for 'something to turn up.'"

The slaves of course had no civil or political standing in American society on the eve of the Civil War; they were property subject to the power and domination of their owners and effectively "outside" formal politics. But they were unwilling to accept their assignment to political oblivion. Relying on scattered literacy, limited mobility, and communication networks they had constructed over many years, slaves had been learning important lessons about the political history of the United States and the Western Hemisphere. They heard about the Haitian Revolution and the abolition of slavery in the British West Indies; they knew of a developing antislavery movement in the Northern states and of slaves escaping there; and they heard of a new Republican Party apparently committed to ending their captivity.

Some slaves discovered that John C. Frémont was the first Republican candidate for president in 1856, and, like William Webb, a slave in Kentucky and Mississippi, they held clandestine meetings to consider what might come of it. But it was Lincoln, four years later, who riveted their imagination. Even as a candidate he was the topic of news and debate on countless plantations. In the view of one slaveholder, slaves simply "know too much about Lincoln . . . for our own safety and peace of mind." News spread quickly, recalled Booker T. Washington, who grew up in western Virginia: "During the campaign when Lincoln was first a candidate for the presidency, the slaves on our far-off plantation, miles from any railroad or large city or daily newspaper, knew what the issues involved were."

Of course the slaves' expectations that Lincoln and the Republicans were intent on abolishing slavery were for the most part misplaced. Lincoln's policy in 1860 and 1861 was to restrict the expansion of slavery into the federal territories of the West but also to concede that slavery in the states was a local institution, beyond the reach of the federal government. At the very time that slaves were imagining Lincoln as their ally, he was assuring slaveholders that he would uphold the Constitution and the Fugitive Slave Law and make no moves against them and their property.

Yet slaves were fortified in their beliefs by the dire predictions many slaveholders were making and by the secessionist movement that led to the creation of the Confederacy. They knew as well as anyone in the country that the likelihood of civil war was growing, and by sharing information and interpreting the course of political events, they readied themselves to act—not only to escape their bonds but to do their part to make the war about their freedom, whether the North wanted it that way or not.

Thus the case of Harry Jarvis. Born a slave on the eastern shore of Virginia, Jarvis took to the woods for several weeks after the Civil War began, where he survived owing to fellow slaves who brought him news and food. Then, seizing an opportunity, Jarvis headed to Fort Monroe, thirty-five miles away, where Union troops were stationed, and asked the commanding general Benjamin Butler "to let [him] enlist." Although Butler rebuffed Jarvis and told him "it wasn't a black man's war," Jarvis stood his political ground: "I told him it would be a black man's war before they got through."

Like many other politicized slaves, Jarvis seems to have understood the stakes of the Civil War far better than the combatants themselves. And by testing their expectations, they began to reshape federal policy. By the time of the first Battle of Bull Run, General Butler had declared fugitive slaves within Union lines to be "contrabands of war," and

A wood engraving of "contraband" slaves escaping to Fort Monroe, Virginia. Library of Congress Prints and Photographs Division, LC-DIG-ppmsca-35556.

Congress soon confirmed the designation. Before too much longer, as Northern armies moved into the densely populated slave plantation districts of South Carolina and the lower Mississippi Valley, slaves crossed the Northern lines by the thousands, at once depriving the Confederacy of needed labor and forcing the Lincoln administration to reevaluate its position on slavery.

By early fall of 1862 Lincoln had decided to issue an emancipation proclamation and enroll African Americans in the Union Army and Navy. Bold initiatives these were, revolutionary in effect and wholly unimagined when the war began—except by the slaves whose actions helped bring them about. Lincoln's political sensibilities had finally caught up to theirs.

William Webb's World

Susan Eva O'Donovan

William Webb was a typical Southerner. He was born in Georgia in the late 1840s, but like hundreds of thousands of Americans he rode the expansion of cotton westward, carried as a teenager first to Mississippi and then to Kentucky. Webb spent long days at work outdoors: driving wagons, hoeing cotton, harvesting tobacco. When he needed to raise cash, he sold homemade treats at camp meetings, those lengthy religious revivals popular among antebellum Americans. He started with ginger cakes, but when he realized that the

Slaves on a plantation near Beaufort, South Carolina. Library of Congress Prints and Photographs Division, LC-USZ62-67819.

Christians were not averse to something stronger he quickly switched to whiskey. It "paid the best," Webb admitted in a narrative he wrote years later.

That sense of inventiveness infused his personal life too. Single until 1867, Webb led an active social life in the years before secession. He enjoyed a good prank, especially if it cost powerful people their dignity. He made sure to reserve time for family and friends, holidays, and Sunday preaching. But Webb's life wasn't easy. Like nearly 4 million Southerners on the eve of the war, William Webb was a slave.

Webb resembled the vast majority of Americans in another important way: he could not tear his attention away from the escalating secession crisis. But unlike those who relied on the written word to monitor the fraught situation, Webb, who was illiterate, received his political news and engaged in political debate through conversation. Yet catch-as-catch-can chatter was not enough for someone who from an early age had dreamed of a more perfect union. Even before Webb left Mississippi for Kentucky in the late 1850s, he began fashioning his friends into home-grown political clubs, forums he hoped would facilitate a thoroughgoing debate about slavery, freedom, and the state of the nation, a debate that he insisted should include slaves.

Webb spoke often on political topics, but his real genius lay in mobilization. His success came in part from his daily labor as a hired-out slave, work that kept him moving from one master to another and that consequently made it easier for him to create and sustain a growing network of fellow slaves. But in his organizational scheme Webb also anticipated a hydra, a many-headed mystical creature that defied all attempts made to control it.

Webb's network creation was similarly protean: decentralized, a loose assembly of disparate groups. "You ought to single out some men to speak in different places, so that those who could not reach the place of meeting might be instructed in the great work that is going on in the land," he advised one group of acolytes. He advised another to appoint its own "king bee," a spokesman who in turn would "appoint a man to travel 12 miles, and then hand the news to another man, and so on, till the news reached from Louisiana to Mississippi." "[We need to] spread the faith," said Webb. "We can not do much unless we send word all over. We all must know, before we make a movement. . . . [We must] tell one another that we expec[t] to be free."

Webb and his nebulous network were no anomaly. The hydra they created raised its many heads throughout slaveholders' states. It spread word about Haiti, a nation that was the creation of slaves. It dominated late-night dinner conversation; it traveled along with marching columns of chained slaves, the infamous coffle lines that remain the iconic face of the domestic slave trade. The network thrived in the squalid confines of the South's county jails, places that enslaved inmates repeatedly remade into what Stokely Carmichael would later describe as "universit[ies] of social struggle and moral" change.

In west-central Georgia the network was centered in an enslaved blacksmith's shop. That was where Houston Hartsfield Holloway and his friends met to discuss "the Democratice partie the Whigg partie the no nothing partie the nulifires and the anteno nothing parties." As cover Holloway called his group a "reading club," but he could have easily called it a political club.

By the late 1850s this distended and ungainly congress had begun to colonize the South's great railroad projects, drawn along with thousands of slaves who had been hired away from their owners to grade roads, lay rails, and pound spikes. Ranging in population from dozens to hundreds, these peripatetic crews managed to more than triple the South's railroad mileage in less than ten years. They also contained enormous subversive potential.

Indeed, protested a Georgia slaveholder named Richard Lyon, large operations that gathered thousands of slaves who were strangers were nothing less than "regular convention[s] in which all the negroes . . . will be abley & fully represented." Lyon cringed when he saw slaves on the go. They were the stuff of a slaveholder's nightmare: the "Tackeys among us," said one in reference to the eighteenth-century Jamaican rebel. Out-and-about slaves talked too much, listened too much, learned too much, and remembered too much. But most of all, Lyon knew, the slaves on those crews would sooner or later go home, "their minds inflamed by the vicious with false & mischievious notions. . . . Can any sensible man doubt the result?" he asked, only half-rhetorically.

Should we respect Lyon's anxieties? As historians we are taught to never take our subject's words literally. At the same time, we are told to always take them seriously. If that's true, and I believe it is, then we need to pose a new set of questions about the disunion crisis, questions that take into account the William Webbs, the Houston Holloways, and all the slaves about whom Lyon fretted. In fact perhaps we should ask what really frightened that Georgia planter and his secessionist generation: Abraham Lincoln and a handful of arch-abolitionists, or the hydra that curled beneath slaveholders' feet?

A Capital under Slavery's Shadow

ADAM GOODHEART

Newspapers announced that the sale would take place in one week's time, on the very morning of Inauguration Day. At the precise hour that Abraham Lincoln rode down Pennsylvania Avenue to take his oath of office beneath the East Portico of the Capitol, a group of black people would stand beneath another columned portico just five miles away, at the Alexandria Courthouse.

"SHERIFF'S SALE OF FREE NEGROES," the ad read. "On the 4th day of March, 1861 . . . I will proceed to sell at public auction, in front of the Court House door, for cash, all FREE NEGROES who have failed to pay their tax for the years 1859 and 1860." It was a chilling reminder—in case any were needed—of the squalid realities lying almost literally in the shadow of the republic's glittering monuments.

The men and women in Alexandria were not being sold back into permanent bondage. They had fallen behind on paying the annual "head tax" that Virginia imposed on each of its adult free black inhabitants, and now their labor would be sold for as long as necessary to recoup the arrears. It is all too easy to imagine the deliberate humiliation thus inflicted on people who, in many cases, had spent long years in slavery before finally attaining their

Shackled slaves marching past the U.S. Capitol on their way to market, 1836. Library of Congress Prints and Photographs Division, LC-DIG-ppmsca-19705.

hard-won freedom. That scene at the courthouse door represented everything they had worked a lifetime to escape.

Across the Potomac, in the nation's capital itself, slavery and racial injustice were daily realities too. The labor of black men and women made the engine of the city run. Enslaved cab drivers greeted newly arrived travelers at the city's railway station and drove them to hotels, such as Gadsby's and Willard's, that were staffed largely by slaves. In local barbershops it was almost exclusively black men—many of them slaves—who shaved the whiskers of lowly and mighty Washingtonians alike. ("The senator flops down in the seat," one traveler noted with amusement, "and has his noble nose seized by the same fingers which the moment before were occupied by the person and chin of an unmistakable rowdy.")

Enslaved laborers toiled at the expansion of the Capitol. Enslaved servants attended their masters on the floor of the Senate, in the Supreme Court chamber—sometimes even in the White House. No fewer than ten of the first fifteen presidents were slaveholders: George Washington, Thomas Jefferson, James Madison, James Monroe, Andrew Jackson, Martin Van Buren, William Henry Harrison, John Tyler, James Polk, and Zachary Taylor. (However, Washington never lived in Washington, D.C., and Van Buren and Harrison both freed their slaves long before taking office.)

Even the slave trade, though supposedly outlawed in Washington more than a decade earlier, still operated there quite openly, with black men and women frequently advertised for sale in the newspapers and occasionally even sent to the auction block just a few hundred yards from the White House. The ban, passed as part of the Compromise of 1850, technically only forbade the importation of blacks into the District of Columbia to be sold out of state. The law permitted local masters to sell their own slaves, and there was little to keep them from being sent across the river to Alexandria, where slave trading flourished on an industrial scale and the unfortunate captives might easily be forced aboard a cramped schooner bound for New Orleans or Mobile. Nor was it an uncommon sight to see a black woman going door-to-door in the most fashionable neighborhoods of Washington, begging for small donations to buy her children out of slavery.

Here politicians from the free states—including the staunchest abolitionists—were constantly reminded that slavery was no mere theoretical abstraction. They found themselves immersed in slavery's presence from the moment they arrived in the capital. In February 1861 this was true of the newly arrived president-elect. Lincoln was very conscious of the fact that he was taking up residence in slave territory—indeed in a city just as Southern in many respects as Richmond or Nashville.

On February 27 Lincoln gave his first public speech in Washington, addressing a group of local dignitaries in a parlor at Willard's. He spoke as if he were a foreign head of state visiting an alien capital:

> As it is the first time in my life, since the present phase of politics has presented itself in this country, that I have said anything publicly within a region of the country where the

institution of slavery exists, I will take this occasion to say, that I think very much of the ill feeling that has existed and still exists between the people of the section whence I came and the people here, is owing to a misunderstanding between each other which unhappily prevails. . . . I hope, in a word, when we shall become better acquainted—and I say it with great confidence—we shall like each other the more.

Two days later, when Lincoln addressed a larger crowd gathered outside the hotel, he struck a similar note, telling his listeners, "[I hope to] convince you, and the people of your section of the country, that we regard you as in all things being our equals." He assured them he harbored no plans to "deprive you of any of your rights under the Constitution of the United States"—an obvious reference to their supposed right to hold slaves.

Lincoln had lived with slavery before, as a one-term member of Congress in the late 1840s. He and his wife had rented rooms in a boardinghouse owned by a Virginia-born lady, Ann Sprigg, who employed several hired slaves. (Despite this Sprigg's was known as "the Abolition house" for the political leanings of its occupants.) At that time slavery's worst atrocities were even more visible in Washington than they would be in 1861: coffles of slaves, shackled to one another in straggling single file, were marched past the Capitol on their way to Southern markets. In 1848 slave traders kidnapped Henry Wilson, an enslaved waiter at Sprigg's—a man Lincoln probably knew well.

In fact Representative Lincoln was so appalled by his experiences that in January 1849 he introduced a bill to completely, albeit gradually, abolish slavery in the District of Columbia. The law would have provided compensation to masters for emancipating their slaves, a scheme similar to the one eventually implemented in Washington (and attempted in Delaware) during Lincoln's presidency. The proposal was a topic of lively conversation at Sprigg's boardinghouse. "Our whole mess remained in the dining-room after tea, and conversed upon the subject of Mr. Lincoln's bill to abolish slavery," one congressman wrote in his diary. "It was approved by all; I believe it as good a bill as we could get at this time."

The proposal went nowhere in Congress. When President-elect Lincoln returned to Washington in 1861 after a twelve-year absence, all too little had changed. During the first week of March the same local newspapers carrying reports on his inauguration also ran an ad from a Louisiana cotton planter who announced that he was in town to purchase several dozen healthy slaves. "Any person having such to dispose of," the planter added, might write to him care of the District of Columbia post office.

What remained to be seen was whether the new president would maintain the vows he had made to the crowd at Willard's. Would he leave Washington just as he had found it, the capital city of a slave republic? Or would the principles that an obscure Illinois congressman had espoused in the dining room of Mrs. Sprigg's "Abolition house" reemerge, in more potent form, once he was in the White House?

Black or White?

DANIEL J. SHARFSTEIN

In February 1861, just weeks after Louisiana seceded from the Union, Randall Lee Gibson enlisted as a private in a state army regiment. The son of a wealthy sugar planter and valedictorian of Yale's Class of 1853, Gibson had long supported secession. Conflict was inevitable, he believed, not because of states' rights or the propriety or necessity of slavery. Rather a war would be fought over the inexorable gulf between whites and blacks, or what he called "the most enlightened race" and "the most degraded of all the races of men." Because Northern abolitionists were forcing the South to recognize "the political, civil, and social equality of all the races of men," Gibson wrote, the South was compelled to enjoy "independence out of the Union."

The notion that war turned on the question of black and white as opposed to slavery and freedom was hardly an intuitive position for Gibson or for the South. Although Southern society was premised on slavery, the line between black and white had always been permeable. Since the seventeenth century people descended from African slaves had been assimilating into white communities. It was a great migration that was covered up even as it was happening, its reach extending into the most unlikely corners of the South.

Randall Lee Gibson, 1870s. Library of Congress Prints and Photographs Division, LC-DIG-cwpbh-04007.

Although Gibson was committed to a hard-line ideology of racial difference, this secret narrative of the American experience was his own family's story.

Gibson's siblings proudly traced their ancestry to a prosperous farmer in the South Carolina backcountry named Gideon Gibson. What they didn't know was that when he first arrived in the colony in the 1730s, he was a free man of color. At the time the legislature thought he had come there to plot a slave revolt. The governor demanded a personal audience with him and learned that he was a skilled tradesman, had a white wife, and had owned land and slaves in Virginia and North Carolina. Declaring the Gibsons to be "not Negroes nor Slaves but Free people," the governor granted them hundreds of acres of land. The Gibsons soon married into their Welsh and Scots-Irish community along the frontier separating South Carolina's coastal plantations from Indian country. It did not matter if the Gibsons were black or white—they were planters.

The Gibsons were hardly alone in their journey from black to white. Hundreds of families of color had gained their freedom in the colonial era because they had English mothers, and within a generation or two they could claim to be white. Their claims were supported by law, which never drew the color line at "one drop" of African ancestry in the antebellum era. Most Southern states followed a one-quarter or one-eighth rule: anyone with a black grandparent or great-grandparent was legally black, and those with more remote ancestry were legally white. Antebellum South Carolina, though, never had a legal definition of race. "It may be well and proper," a state judge and leading defender of slavery wrote in 1835, "that a man of worth, honesty, industry and respectability, should have the rank of a white man, while a vagabond of the same degree of blood should be confined to the inferior caste." Preserving the institution of slavery mattered far more than preserving the purity of white "blood." As long as people who claimed to be white were productive members of society—in effect supporting the prevailing order—it made little sense to mandate a stricter measure of race.

When the Gibsons moved west in the 1790s, they had money and land and slaves but professed to know very little about their history, explaining a tendency toward dark complexion with vague accounts of Gypsy or Portuguese roots. They soon epitomized the manners and attitudes of the planter aristocracy. Randall Gibson grew up shuttling between a family mansion in Lexington, Kentucky, where his mother was from, and Live Oak, a sugar plantation in Terrebonne Parish, Louisiana, where his father had sought his fortune. He knew the family's slaves well and often asked after them in his letters home from Yale, referring to them always as "servants." Gibson's father, a Whig and longtime supporter of "the Great Compromiser," Henry Clay, gave significant responsibility to his slaves, hiring no outside overseers. Indeed Tobias Gibson repeatedly expressed dismay at the institution. "I am in conscience opposed to slavery," he wrote. "I don't like it and the older I get the worse it seems." Such sentiment provided an easy way for him to feel virtuous about his way of life; disliking slavery made him an enlightened master.

Enlisting in the Louisiana army represented a humbling new start for Randall Gibson. At Yale he had been lionized by his classmates, the flower of a select group of

Southerners walking in the footsteps of John C. Calhoun and Judah P. Benjamin. Gibson had thought of himself and his peers as the nation's great hope, an educated brotherhood that could guide the country through sectional crisis. The years that followed his graduation, however, were full of disappointment. He studied law, only to decide that he did not wish to practice. After traveling around Europe he bought a sugar cane plantation near his father's land southwest of New Orleans, but he could not make a profit and found the neighbors distasteful.

Almost as soon as Gibson returned to Louisiana from Yale he embraced an uncompromising Southern position on slavery, declaring his opinions to be "as decided as if I were a member of Congress." This was a predictable stance: without a fortune or connections to the primarily Northern-born merchant elite in New Orleans, Gibson could not afford to take an unpopular political stance. At the same time, he became convinced that "Southern society is based, its life and soul are staked, upon the inequality of the races, not only its aims, its expansion and progress, but its very existence."

Gibson's position that war was necessary to preserve white supremacy reveals how racism flourished at the prospect of abolition. When slavery served as a broad proxy of black and white, there was little need to dwell on the purity of "white blood" and the finer points of racial difference. Only freedom required a hard line on race, to preserve the existing order. As the abolitionist chorus swelled in the generation leading up to secession, Southerners responded, in one Virginian's words, by "rising up to promulgate the philosophical, sociological, and ethical excellence of slavery." In 1857 the Louisiana Senate considered a bill for the "prevention of marriages where one of the parties has a taint of African blood."

Had the bill passed, the racial status of countless whites would have been put in jeopardy. That it was proposed at all reveals a society that could not imagine such consequences. The South's traditional flexibility on questions of race—the ease with which families like the Gibsons were able to assimilate into white communities and the security that most people living as white had in their racial status—actually enabled white Southerners to embrace the idea of absolute, blood-borne racial difference.

If Gibson's ideology demanded secession, more practical considerations motivated him to enlist in the army. Well before the presidential election of 1860, Gibson expressed doubts that the Union would survive and urged the South to "prepare for every emergency," but his views did not bring the success that he craved. He ran for a seat at the state convention that would determine whether Louisiana would stay in the Union, but placed third out of four candidates. He had failed in business and politics. War seemed the only path left in a world that was bigger than cane fields and river levees. Ironically, when army life forced Gibson to confront the gap between his theories about race and how Southerners experienced it every day, the opportunity to serve trumped his ideology.

Soon after enlisting Gibson was promoted to captain of an artillery company and then elected a colonel in the 13th Louisiana Volunteer Infantry Regiment, ten companies totaling 830 men, mostly from New Orleans. They were, according to an aide, "as cosmopolitan a body of soldiers as there existed upon the face of God's earth. There were Frenchmen, Spaniards, Mexicans, Dagoes, Germans, Chinese, Irishmen, and, in fact, persons of every clime known to geographers or travellers of that day." They wore "jaunty zouave uniform[s]," drilled in English and French, sang songs in their native languages, speculated on their regiment's unlucky number, and lived a continuous "saturnalia" of gambling and drink.

Rather than dwell upon his recruits' racial origins, Gibson focused on turning them into soldiers. As he worked with his officers in camp, he refused to subscribe to the gentlemanly romance of war. While many in his regiment predicted a glorious Confederate victory before they had finished their training, Gibson devoted himself to the study of military tactics. Without any experience in war he knew that the army's true weakness was a lack of "military men by education," "scientific officers," and "West Pointers."

By late autumn the regiment was leaving Louisiana for the war's western front, marching as a band played "The Girl I Left behind Me." They reached Kentucky on the last day in November. Shrouded in snow and sleet they camped on frozen ground and waited for the fight.

Was Freedom Enough?

Gregory P. Downs and James Downs

Emancipation, the idea that lies like a pearl at the center of our understanding of the Civil War, seems simple: it means freedom, the end of slavery. That's how Booker T. Washington saw it. "Finally," he wrote in his landmark autobiography, *Up from Slavery*, "the war closed, and the day of freedom came. . . . Freedom was in the air and had been for months."

For a century and a half historians, like Washington, have explained the emancipation of 4 million slaves by contrasting their slavery with their newfound freedom. The nation's achievement, won with the blood of hundreds of thousands of men, was essentially a negative quality, an absence of an evil. For Washington, as for almost everyone who has wrestled with the story of the end of slavery, the idea of freedom did double historical duty: the word was simultaneously slavery's antonym and one of the keywords of the nation's history, embedded in its Bill of Rights. In becoming free, not only did slaves seem to make themselves more American, but the rest of the nation did too. Slavery had ended, and the paradox at the heart of American democracy had been resolved.

But contrast Washington's celebration of freedom with an account by Harriet Jacobs, a formerly enslaved woman turned reformer and author. She confronted the many meanings of freedom when she encountered dozens of liberated slaves in the line of houses known as Duff Green's Row in Washington in 1862. "Many were sick with measles, diptheria [*sic*], scarlet and typhoid fever," she wrote. "Some had a few filthy rags to lie on; others had nothing but the bare floor for a couch." As Jacobs attempted to comfort them, they looked up at her with "those tearful eyes" that asked, "Is this freedom?"

Slave pen, Alexandria, Virginia, early 1860s. Library of Congress Prints and Photographs Division, LC-DIG-stereo-1s04355.

In recent years Jacobs's question has been echoed by a growing number of historians. Was freedom, narrowly construed, enough? Was freedom simply a license, the right to make choices, however constrained, as white planters claimed? Or did freedom extend to the ballot box, to education, to equality of opportunity? And who defined freedom, and what did it mean to nineteenth-century African Americans, both under slavery and after the war?

In raising such questions historians have begun to place other concepts, like power and belonging, at the center of the story of emancipation. Instead of defining every aspect of postemancipation life as a new form of freedom, scholars have started to look more carefully at the importance of belonging to an empowered government or community in defining the outcome of emancipation. Rather than simply celebrating individual freedom, these works examine the enormous gap between rights on paper and the capacity to enforce those rights. In doing so they have cast a light on the key role of power and inclusion in shaping the post–Civil War world that emancipation made.

What is at stake in these works is not only how we understand the Civil War and the end of slavery but how we understand freedom itself. Reinforced by a hot war against fascism, a cold war against communism, and a forty-year critique of government from both the left and the right, freedom has come to seem the core American value. But at what cost? By underrating the importance of well-functioning bureaucracies for maintaining civil society, or by reinforcing views of government as freedom's enemy, has the freedom narrative obscured important aspects of what emancipation did and did not accomplish, even as it cast light on others?

Among the first contemporary scholars to raise these questions is Eric Foner. In *Reconstruction*, the most careful elaboration of the freedom narrative, he brilliantly defines the contest over emancipation and Reconstruction as a fight between competing versions of freedom. Others, including Thavolia Glymph in *Out of the House of Bondage* and Susan O'Donovan in *Becoming Free in the Cotton South*, emphasize the constraints on labor contained within freedom. In Steven Hahn's Pulitzer Prize–winning *A Nation under Our Feet* democratic power rather than freedom assumes center stage.

Newer work has taken these points even further. Much of it, including Kate Masur's *An Example for All the Land*, explores that troubled relationship between ex-slaves and the federal government. James Oakes likewise places the development of federal policy at the center of the story, demonstrating its role in the slow process of freedom. Other scholars study the conditions of freedom in the anarchic society that the federal government left behind in the postwar South. As ex-planters and ex-Confederates regained power, they stepped into the void and created campaigns of political, labor, and sexual terror—vividly rendered in Hannah Rosen's *Terror in the Heart of Freedom*—to force freed people into submission.

In turn many freed people began to use their newly minted status as citizens to tell the government in federal hearings the violent ways that freedwomen were sexually abused. Others, including Dylan Penningroth in *The Claims of Kinfolk*, emphasize freed people's reliance upon communal and kin group claims of power rather than individual freedom. Many scholars examine emancipation in a global context, placing the United States alongside the rise and fall of slavery in Latin America, the Caribbean, and even Egypt.

Asking hard questions about freedom helps scholars envision emancipation as a process rather than a shotgun moment of liberation. If understood as a practice, not a stroke of a pen, emancipation becomes a longer story, one that emphasizes the gulf between the federal government's plans and life on the ground in the postwar South. While it is possible to define those moments as the absence of freedom, it may well be that what ex-slaves suffered from was not a lack of freedom but a lack of power and belonging.

For example, in March 1868, three years after the end of the Civil War, a North Carolina ex-slave named Peter Price walked into the local office of the Freedmen's Bureau, a federal agency established to regulate the transition from slavery to freedom by enforcing labor contracts, adjudicating disputes, encouraging education, and, at times, distributing rations. Price's complaint was a common one: his landlord refused to turn over Price's share of the previous year's crop. Price found a receptive ear in Hugo Hillebrandt, a Hungarian revolutionary who had fought with Garibaldi in Italy before joining the Union cause as a federal agent. After listening to Price's story, Hillebrandt wrote an order demanding that the landlord turn over Price's share of the crop.

But when Price carried the order back to the farm, his landlord tore it into pieces, threw it on the ground, and declared that Price "might send ten thousand Yankees there and he did not intend to be governed by no such laws." As a judge of practical power, the landlord was right: Hillebrandt could not enforce his orders outside of his office. In desperation Price asked for help up the bureaucratic ladder, but without success. Some people, like Hillebrandt, would help him but could not; others perhaps could have but didn't.

While freedom and its limitations tell us something about cases like Price's, it may not tell us enough. In ways that cannot fully be contained by ideas of negative or positive freedom, ex-slaves like Price asked for and needed not just freedom but force. Self-sufficiency, much less equality, would depend on his inclusion in a group of people the government could commit to successfully assisting. As Price's case demonstrates, frameworks of defensible legal freedoms had limited meaning absent the ability to make themselves felt.

Americans have always found legal freedom alluring. We remember the Supreme Court's decision in *Brown v. Board of Education* but not the bayonets required to enforce it. So too with emancipation. As scholars wrestle with the centrality of freedom in defining emancipation, they open up new windows into the world the Civil War made and also wrestle with timeless (and timely) questions about the relationship between the individual, society, and the government.

Our Servants Do Pretty Much as They Please

ADAM ROTHMAN

Touring the United States for the *London Times*, the war correspondent William Howard Russell reached New Orleans late in May 1861 to find a city ablaze. Confederate flags flew from the public buildings and private homes. Soldiers paraded through the streets in smart columns of dash and pomp. Gentlemen at the St. Charles Hotel pored over the latest papers for news of the dawning war. The police were rounding up suspected abolitionists, and every night mysterious fires flared up around the city—set, it was rumored, by the slaves.

After hobnobbing with politicians, planters, and merchants, Russell observed that the Confederate elite "believe themselves, in fact, to be masters of the destiny of the world." But they soon discovered they were not even masters of their own homes.

New Orleans was a slave city: its fortunes depended on the slave-based sugar and cotton plantations of the lower Mississippi Valley, and the buying and selling of people was a big local business. More than thirteen thousand enslaved people (one out of every twelve residents) lived in the city itself in 1860, working as stevedores, carpenters, valets, cooks, and laundresses. Some were hired out and earned wages for their owners. Women made up a majority of adult slaves, performing "domestic" labor for masters and mistresses who could be just as abusive as any whip-wielding plantation overseer.

Yet daily routines took household slaves out to the city streets and shops, giving them the chance to socialize with friends and family and find refuge in hideaways outside their masters' gaze. Their skills as laborers and their networks of kinship and community would aid them when the Union Army arrived in May 1862, barely a year after the war began.

The Union occupation of New Orleans was also a liberation, if that is the appropriate word to describe the gnarled process of emancipation that took place there. Freedom did not arrive on board David Farragut's warships; the Union had not yet committed to a policy of emancipation. Nor did it arrive with the Emancipation Proclamation on January 1, 1863, which exempted the city and other territory once part of the Confederacy but no longer "in rebellion." And yet slavery began to crumble in New Orleans from the moment Union troops arrived. The letters and diaries of Confederates in New Orleans in the weeks and months after the Federals arrived were already filling with despair and rage at the loss of authority over their slaves. What was going on?

We tend to look back at emancipation as a series of official acts. But in many places, including New Orleans, it was the result of local initiative as much as Union policy. In occupied New Orleans slaves quickly recognized that the balance of power had shifted away from their owners, and they took advantage.

Many slaves, for example, ran away to the Union Army. Hundreds fled to Camp Parapet, a fortification just above the city, where the abolitionist commanding officer, Brigadier General John W. Phelps, welcomed them. Even those who were thought to be most loyal to their owners ran off. "There are many instances in which house-servants, those who have been raised by people, have deserted them," complained Clara Solomon, a teenager in the city.

Slave owners felt robbed by the Federals and betrayed by their slaves. Owners claiming to be loyal to the Union petitioned for the return of their human property, sparking a controversy on "the negro question" between Phelps and General Benjamin Butler, commander of the Department of the Gulf. The hard-nosed Butler was famous for his ingenious policy of confiscating slaves as "contrabands of war" in Virginia, but he did not want to wreck Louisiana's sugar plantations or alienate white Unionists. He thought that Phelps had crossed the line by fomenting slave unrest. "We shall have a negro insurrection here I fancy," Butler confided to his wife.

Butler and Phelps clashed too over Phelps's arming of black soldiers at Camp Parapet. Phelps resigned, but Butler eventually came around to the wisdom of the policy. By the end of 1862 black men, both free and slave, were joining the Union Army in southern Louisiana in droves. When asked whether slaves would fight their masters, one man told a Union officer, "Just put the gun into our hands, and you'll soon see that we not only know how to shoot, but who to shoot." The recruitment of black soldiers ate away at slavery, especially in Louisiana, which was credited with supplying over twenty-four thousand black men to the Union Army, more than any other state.

A black man in New Orleans, ca. 1863. Library of Congress Prints and Photographs Division, LC-DIG-ppmsca-11202.

Less well known are the contributions of enslaved women to the hastening of emancipation. Barred from battle, enslaved women fought daily skirmishes with masters and mistresses in their own kitchens and courtyards. They talked back. They refused to be beaten. They ran away and returned with bayonets. "Our servants do pretty much as they please," protested Ann Wilkinson Penrose, whose son was off fighting in the Confederate Army. Penrose's torrential diary chronicles her family's loosening grip on their slaves after the arrival of the Union Army and offers a striking example of what the historian Thavolia Glymph calls "the war within" slaveholding households.

Simmering resentments boiled over on April 14, 1863. Penrose was angry at Becky, her cook. She went into the kitchen, slapped Becky, and "asked her how she dared to send in such bread & cakes." Becky took offense. "She started up, looked furiously at me, and exclaimed, 'don't you do that again, let it be the last time, or I'll just march out of this yard.'" Becky was told to hush or else a policeman would be called in. As Penrose recounts, Becky retorted that "she might send for whom she pleased she didn't care."

Penrose didn't send for a policeman; her family decided it wouldn't do any good. The police were now on the slaves' side, they believed. Becky's defiance—and Penrose's inability to punish her for it—signaled the demise of slavery in New Orleans. The institution crumbled there not from a single dramatic blow or stroke of a pen but from the slow accumulation of resistance by slaves like Becky.

The law eventually caught up with the facts on the ground. Early in 1864 Union general Nathaniel Banks, who had replaced Butler as commander of the Department of the Gulf, recognized that Louisiana's state constitutional provisions and laws concerning slavery were "inconsistent with the present condition of public affairs" and declared them "inoperable and void."

Finally, in September 1864, more than two years after the arrival of Union troops, Louisiana's all-white electorate ratified a new state constitution that formally abolished slavery in the state. Heartened by the summer's debates over emancipation, one black soldier predicted, "Under God, this will yet be a pleasant land for the colored man to dwell in."

The Grove of Gladness

BLAIN ROBERTS AND ETHAN J. KYTLE

As dawn broke across a cloudless New Year's Day sky over the South Carolina Sea Islands, Charlotte Forten, a black Pennsylvania missionary who had gone south to teach local freed people, set out for Camp Saxton, a waterside settlement on Port Royal Island, near the town of Beaufort. After a short ride in an old carriage that was pulled by "a remarkably slow horse," Forten boarded a ship for the trip up the Beaufort River.

The Emancipation Day celebration at Camp Saxton, South Carolina, January 1, 1863. Library of Congress Prints and Photographs Division, LC-USZ62-88808.

A band entertained the white and back passengers on the warm winter morning as they steamed toward the headquarters of the 1st South Carolina Volunteers, a regiment made up of former slaves. By midday a crowd of thousands—comprising not only teachers like Forten but also Union soldiers, Northern ministers, and ex-slaves—had gathered in the largest live-oak grove Forten had ever seen. Located on a plantation a few miles outside of Beaufort, Camp Saxton was, according to Thomas D. Howard, another Northern missionary teaching in the Sea Islands, "ideal for the occasion."

Why had they come? It was New Year's Day 1863, yes, but more important, it was the day that Abraham Lincoln's Emancipation Proclamation was scheduled to take effect. It was, in other words, the moment in which Sea Island bonds people—indeed nearly all of the more than 3 million slaves who resided in rebellious Southern states—were to be officially declared "thenceforward, and forever free."

Critics have long dismissed the Emancipation Proclamation as a minor document. It had, they say, no immediate impact on or did not apply to the vast majority of American slaves. By freeing bonds people living behind Confederate lines while exempting slaves who resided in the four loyal border states as well as in Tennessee and Union-occupied portions of Virginia and Louisiana, the president promised liberty only where he could not deliver it. The Emancipation Proclamation "is practically a dead letter," wrote the conservative *New York Herald* on January 3, 1863, "and for the present, at least, amounts to nothing as a measure of emancipation."

Such criticism, however, overlooks several important facts about the Emancipation Proclamation. For one, it fused together the preservation of the Union and the destruction of slavery, at least in Lincoln's mind. The president had spent the first year of the war insisting that he would not touch slavery where it already existed. His only goal was to restore the nation as it was. Now Lincoln committed the United States to the idea that the preservation of the Union demanded an end to the institution of slavery. Most Confederate slaves would not realize emancipation on January 1, but, with their future linked to the formidable Union Army, they would not have to wait long.

What is more, some bonds people did not have to wait at all. The *New York Herald* admitted as much, conceding that "a few hundred slaves, here and there within the lines of our armies," had been liberated on Emancipation Day. In fact Lincoln's proclamation formally freed tens of thousands of slaves in Union-controlled areas of Arkansas, Florida, Mississippi, and North Carolina—as well as the South Carolina Sea Islands.

At Camp Saxton and elsewhere, then, the first of January signaled something more than a promise: the Emancipation Proclamation was a tangible move toward the imminent death of an institution that had thrived in the region since the seventeenth century.

Emancipation Day ceremonies—which occurred across the North and Union-occupied South, from New Orleans to the nation's capital—testified to the thrill of the news. Four thousand blacks paraded through the streets of Norfolk, Virginia, while runaway slaves, free blacks, and leading abolitionists like William C. Nell and Frederick

Douglass held a day-long observance at the Tremont Temple in Boston. Douglass later described the meeting as "one of the most affecting . . . occasions I ever witnessed."

None of the celebrations, however, matched the ceremony at Camp Saxton. "When some future Bancroft or Motley writes with philosophic brain and poet's hand the story of the Great Civil War," wrote Thomas Wentworth Higginson, colonel of the 1st South Carolina Volunteers, "he will find the transition to a new era in our nation's history to have been fitly marked by one festal day,—that of the announcement of the President's Proclamation, upon Port-Royal Island, on the first of January, 1863." The Massachusetts abolitionist presided over the day's events from his perch on a platform erected at the center of the plantation grove. It was a remarkable scene, he later recalled: "The moss-hung trees, with their hundred-feet diameter of shade; the eager faces of women and children in the foreground; the many-colored headdresses; the upraised hands; the neat uniforms of the soldiers; the outer row of mounted officers and ladies; and beyond all the blue river, with its swift, free tide."

Sitting next to Higginson on the platform were a dozen Union officers, musicians, and dignitaries, mostly white. They stared out at a sea of black faces, many of whom were now Union soldiers. It was a stark reminder that even emancipation celebrations could not entirely escape the racial hierarchy of the day.

But at times they did, as these were no ordinary commemorations. In fact just a few hours earlier the racial dynamic captured on stage had been symbolically challenged. As a ship full of emancipated slaves arrived at Camp Saxton, Northern soldiers, teachers, reformers, and reporters—most of whom were white—gave way to the newly arrived crowd. "For one day, the tables were turned," wrote Thomas D. Howard to the *Christian Inquirer*. "You know who have to wait, according to the general rules." But "on the 1st of January, 1863, the steamer Boston was the boat of the colored people. The white passengers patiently waited until the small boats had carried them to the shore of their grove of gladness." "Let them go first," said one white passenger, "the day will be too short for them."

The program began just before noon with a musical selection, a prayer, and a recitation of the preliminary Emancipation Proclamation—the final version was not sent out until later that day—by a local planter who had freed his slaves a quarter-century earlier. On paper Lincoln's proclamation may have had, in the historian Richard Hofstadter's famous description, "all the moral grandeur of a bill of lading," but when read aloud to the crowd at Camp Saxton—who repeatedly interrupted the recitation with loud cheers—it was plenty powerful.

The real emotional chord that day, however, was struck by the freed people themselves when, midway through the program, they broke out in an impromptu rendition of "My Country 'Tis of Thee." Just as Higginson formally accepted the regimental colors— a silk American flag and a regimental banner made of a lightweight wool fabric called bunting—from Reverend Mansfield French of New York, "there suddenly arose, close beside the platform, a strong but rather cracked & elderly male voice, into which two women's voices immediately blended, singing as if by an impulse that can no more be quenched than the morning note of the song sparrow."

Soon hundreds of voices joined in. The singing eventually spread to the white officers and missionaries seated behind Higginson on the platform, before the colonel curtly commanded, "Leave it to them."

At the end of the song sobbing men and women erupted in applause. An army surgeon, Seth Rogers, wrote that the freed men and women "sang it so touchingly that every one was thrilled beyond measure," while Forten deemed it "a touching and beautiful incident." Higginson was more effusive. "I never saw anything so electric; it made all other words cheap," he observed in his journal. "Art could not have dreamed of a tribute to the day of jubilee that should be so affecting; history will not believe it." It was "the key note to the whole day."

Just one day earlier Higginson had wondered whether locals even cared about Emancipation Day. "They know that those in this Department are nominally free already," he noted, "and also they know that this freedom has yet to be established on any firm basis." But the ceremony at Camp Saxton put an end to such doubts. "Just think of it," Higginson wrote that evening, "the first day they had ever had a country, the first flag they had ever seen which promised anything to their people,—& here while others stood in silence, waiting for my stupid words these simple souls burst out in their lay, as if they were squatting by their own hearths at home."

The spontaneity of the moment seemed to inspire the colonel, who offered lengthy off-the-cuff remarks from the platform. "I have for six weeks listened to the songs of these people," he told the crowd, songs that more often than not evoked "sadness and despair." Higginson had never heard them utter this hopeful hymn. "How could they sing it before to-day? Was it their country? Was it to them a land of liberty? But now, with this flag unfurled, 'the day of jubilee has come.'"

Higginson then called the regiment's color guard, Sergeant Prince Rivers and Corporal Robert Sutton, to the front of the stage. After presenting the Stars and Stripes to Rivers, Higginson reminded his sergeant that it was his solemn duty to defend the flag with his life. "Do you understand?" asked the colonel. Yes, sir, responded Rivers. Next Higginson presented the bunting flag to Sutton and ceded the platform to his men.

Rivers, a freedman whom Higginson compared to the Haitian rebel leader Toussaint L'Ouverture, spoke first. He repeated his pledge that he would "die before surrendering" the flag, adding that he hoped "to show it to all the old masters." Sutton focused his remarks on the emancipations that had yet to come. There was not a single person here, he told the assembled freed people, "but had sister, brother, or some relation among the rebels still." The ex-slave insisted that "he could not rest satisfied while so many of their kindred were left in chains," then urged the 1st South Carolina to "show their flag to Jefferson Davis in Richmond." The audience showered both soldiers with shouts of approval.

The program continued with another hour of speeches and songs before the large group retired to crude tables to enjoy a feast of barbecued oxen, hard bread, and molasses-sweetened water.

Then, in a fitting coda to the day's events, the 1st South Carolina Volunteers demonstrated their newfound freedom in an expertly executed dress parade, their bright red trousers, which Higginson hated, the only reminder that the former slaves were any different from the hundreds of thousands of white Americans who wore Union blue.

At 4 p.m. the crowd began to make their way home from Camp Saxton. They boarded the *Flora*, which headed north toward St. Helenaville, and another ship, the *Boston*, which sailed south for Hilton Head. Music filled the air as the black men and women, leaving "their grove of gladness," in Howard's apt phrase, once again broke into song. "The singing," he wrote, "seemed to come from free hearts."

When Freedom Came to Charleston

BLAIN ROBERTS AND ETHAN J. KYTLE

Nearly two dozen fires burned out of control across Charleston, South Carolina, on February 18, 1865, as the Union Army moved into the city where the Civil War had begun four years earlier. A brutal 545-day siege, the longest in American history, had reduced much of the city to rubble and driven away most wealthy residents, while General William T. Sherman's march through the heart of South Carolina—which threatened to cut off Charleston's supply line—had prompted Confederate forces in the city to set fire to cotton supplies and munitions and then evacuate.

But the Union soldiers who advanced into Charleston were welcomed with open arms—and not just because they helped put out the flames. Thousands of former slaves thrilled at the sight of their liberators, most of whom were members of the 21st U.S. Colored Troops. "The negroes cheer us, bless us, dance for joy when they see our glorious flag—pray for us, fight for us, 'can't love us enough,' as they beautifully express it," wrote James Redpath, a correspondent for the *New-York Tribune*.

Over the next few months, as the Civil War ground to a halt, Charleston was transformed from the birthplace of secession into the graveyard of slavery. In parades, commemorations, and demonstrations local freed men and women joined with the occupying force to mark Union victory and the end of the peculiar institution. Although the city had been practically burned to the ground, revelry reigned. Each week brought yet another "festival of freedom," as the black abolitionist William C. Nell dubbed such pageants.

Before the war Charleston had been the capital of American slavery. Nearly half the slaves transported to what would become the United States first stepped foot on American soil on nearby Sullivan's Island, the Ellis Island of black America. After American participation in the international slave trade ended in 1808, Charleston continued to be a vibrant market for slaves traded locally, as well as for those sold to the burgeoning cotton plantations of Mississippi and Louisiana.

And it wasn't just the buying and selling of human beings that made slavery so central to the city. For much of its early history Charleston had a black and enslaved majority, and in the decades leading up to the Civil War most white households owned at least one slave. Little wonder that Charleston played host not only to the 1860 South Carolina Secession Convention, which broke up the Union in the defense of slavery, but also to the opening salvo of the war with the 1861 firing on Fort Sumter.

This history was no doubt on the minds of black Charlestonians as they observed the liberation of the city four years later. Just hours after Charleston fell, hundreds of newly emancipated men, women, and children rejoiced when a company from the 54th Massachusetts marched across the Citadel Green, a park at the center of Charleston. "Shawls, aprons, hats, everything was waved," wrote C. H. Corey, a Northern minister accompanying the troops. "Old men wept. The young women danced and jumped, and cried, and laughed" in an outpouring of emotion that brought even the soldiers to tears.

Three days later the all-black 55th Regiment, Massachusetts, arrived, singing "John Brown's Body" to the African American crowds that cheered them on. "Imagine, if you can, this stirring song chanted with the most rapturous, most exultant emphasis, by a regiment of negro troops, who have been lying in sight of Charleston for nearly two years—as they trod with tumultuous delight along the streets of this pro-Slavery city," Redpath wrote. Some of the men in the 55th "had walked those streets before as slaves,"

Members of the 55th Massachusetts marching through Charleston, South Carolina, in February 1865. Library of Congress Prints and Photographs Division, LC-USZ62-105560.

noted Charles C. Coffin, a *Boston Daily Journal* correspondent. But now they were free, "soldiers of the Union, defenders of its flag."

Freed people assembled again on February 27 to receive the rest of the 54th Massachusetts. "On the day we entered that rebellious city, the streets were thronged with women and children of all sizes, colors and grades—the young, the old, the halt, the maimed, and the blind," observed John H. W. N. Collins, a black sergeant. "I saw an old colored woman with a crutch—for she could not walk without one, having served all her life in bondage—who, on seeing us, got so happy, that she threw down her crutch, and shouted that the year of Jubilee had come." One week later five thousand African Americans filed through the city in a show of affection for President Lincoln after his second inauguration.

Perhaps the largest festival of freedom was held on Tuesday, March 21, when a crowd of ten thousand gathered at Citadel Green. For decades the park had served as a parade ground for the adjacent South Carolina Military Academy, also known as the Citadel. But now the grounds where white cadets, charged with protecting the city against a slave insurrection, had regularly conducted public exercises became the gathering point for a parade of black Union soldiers and countless other black marchers. According to Redpath, the assembled viewed the procession as "a celebration of their deliverance from bondage and ostracism; a jubilee of freedom, a hosannah to their deliverers."

The parade started at about 1 p.m. under rain-filled skies and took several hours to wind its way down King Street to the Battery and then back to Citadel Green. Led by various dignitaries on horseback, a marching band, and the 21st U.S. Colored Troops, the procession also included local tradesmen, fire companies, and nearly two thousand newly enrolled schoolchildren singing songs like "John Brown's Body."

Most striking was a large mule-drawn cart bearing a sign that read, "A number of negroes for sale" and carrying a faux auctioneer's block and four African Americans—one man, two women, and a child—all of whom had been sold at some point in their lives. The man playing the role of auctioneer cried out to the crowd along the parade route, "How much am I offered for this good cook? . . . She can make four kinds of mock-turtle soup—from beef, fish or fowls. . . . Who bids?" Behind the auction cart trailed a simulated slave coffle of some sixty men, "tied to a rope—in imitation of the gangs who used often to be led through these streets on their way from Virginia to the sugar-fields of Louisiana."

The participants in this carnivalesque display intended to ridicule the system under which so many in Charleston—and the rest of the South—had suffered for so long, and the show did in fact, as one observer noted, produce "much merriment." Yet it touched a little too close to home for some. "Old women burst into tears as they saw this tableau," Redpath reported, "and forgetting that it was a mimic scene, shouted wildly, 'Give me back my children! Give me back my children!'"

Following the auction cart and slave coffle came an unambiguously comic feature of the tableau: a hearse carrying a coffin labeled "Slavery," which elicited laughter among the audience. A decade earlier Boston abolitionists protesting the rendition of runaway slave Anthony Burns had suspended a large black coffin, with the word *Liberty* painted in white, along the route by which Burns was marched back into bondage under armed guard. Now the tables were turned, and the funeral procession was for slavery, not liberty.

Scrawled in chalk on the hearse were the inscriptions, "Slavery Is Dead," "Who Owns Him," "No One," and "Sumter Dug His Grave on the 13th of April, 1861." A long train of female mourners dressed in black followed behind the coffin, their smiling faces the only tell of their true sentiments. "Charleston never before witnessed such a spectacle," concluded the *New York Times* correspondent of the day's events.

The festivities fueled the frantic chatter of upcountry slaveholders. Charleston expats traded stories—some true, others false or exaggerated—of interracial balls, plots of black insurrection, and the theft and wanton destruction of private property. In Columbia, Emma LeConte seethed in her diary that Charleston recently "had a most absurd procession described in glowing colors and celebrating the Death of Slavery." It was a world turned upside down. "Abolitionists delivered addresses on the superiority of the black race over white—Adam and Eve were black, so were Cain and Abel, but when the former slew his brother, his great fright turned him white!"

Despite their anger and unease, most whites back in Charleston scrambled to demonstrate their allegiance to the United States by taking the loyalty oath. Surrounded by black soldiers and their former slaves, the few Confederate sympathizers who remained were too chastened to protest any of the celebrations that spring. The *New York Times* reported that the "slavery is dead" parade "was by no means pleasant to the old residents, but they had sense enough to keep their thoughts to themselves."

Northerners marveled at the new climate in Charleston. "I have given utterance to my most radical sentiments to try their temper, and have not even succeeded in making any one threaten me by word, look or gesture," insisted Charles C. Coffin in late February. "William Lloyd Garrison or Wendell Phillips or Henry Ward Beecher can speak their minds in the open air . . . without fear of molestation."

A couple of months later Garrison and Beecher would do just that. On April 14, 1865, exactly four years after Major Robert Anderson had surrendered Fort Sumter to Confederate general P. G. T. Beauregard, the two Northern abolitionists joined thousands of former slaves and Union soldiers, including Anderson himself, at a ceremony to commemorate the return of the American flag to the small island fort. "No more war! No more accursed secession! No more slavery, that spawned them both!" Beecher intoned to an uproar of applause.

These festivals continued throughout the year. Black Charlestonians inaugurated Decoration Day (May 1), observed the Fourth of July, and celebrated the anniversaries of West Indian emancipation (August 1) and Lincoln's final Emancipation Proclamation (January 1). It was all a fitting reminder of how much had changed since 1861: the capital of slavery had become the citadel of freedom. As one abolitionist newspaper, the *National Anti-Slavery Standard*, observed in March, "Historical justice and poetical justice sometimes coincide in the annals of mankind, but rarely so exactly as in the example of the city of Charleston."

3. Women and the Home Front

Introduction

NICOLE ETCHESON

The historian Edward Pessen once asked, in the title of a landmark essay, "How Different from Each Other Were the Antebellum North and South?" Not as different as we might think, he believed: Both were largely rural and agricultural, where small farms emphasizing self-sufficiency were the norm. The patterns of economic stratification were similar in both regions. Both were primarily Protestant, believed in a gender system that assigned separate spheres to men and women, and were committed to white supremacy. Even in the North free blacks were not considered equal to whites: their voting rights were circumscribed, they were segregated by occupation and residence, and they were forbidden to migrate into certain states.

Historians have written a great deal more about the Southern home front than the Northern, for the obvious and sensible reason that the Southern home front was the site of the war. Southern civilians saw battles fought on their doorsteps, fled in the advance of armies, suffered under occupying forces, and had their social order overturned by the emancipation of the slaves.

And yet even their experiences of war, aside from the battlefield, were similar. Northerners and Southerners alike felt the class implications of the war: In the South men of the slave-owning aristocracy fought alongside non-slave-owning yeoman farmers; in the North wealthy Boston Brahmins served in the army alongside midwestern farmers and immigrant laborers. The Union and the Confederacy called on women of all classes to sacrifice for the war effort.

Wealthy men fought for both armies. One study of Mississippi shows that two-thirds of the state's wealthiest slave owners served in the Confederate Army. Robert Gould Shaw, the white colonel of the black 54th Regiment, Massachusetts, was perhaps the most famous aristocratic New Englander to die for the Union. But the structure of Confederate and Union draft laws gave credence to the charge that it was "a rich man's war and a poor man's fight." Common laborers and farmers could ill afford to hire a substitute or pay the $300 commutation fee in the North to escape the draft.

The hardships of war bore particularly harshly on poorer women, North and South. Yeomen Southern women not only began to urge their husbands to desert but also broke into stores in bread riots. In the North many women who were unable to provide for themselves and their families owing to an absent breadwinner turned to almshouses and poor relief. Lydia Bixby, a working-class widow, received a poetic condolence letter from President Abraham Lincoln, praising her sacrifice of her five sons. She made the loss of her sons public not to become a model of a "true-hearted Union" woman but to receive the relief money paid to soldiers' parents.

The working class in both regions included many who had been born abroad. Massive immigration, principally from Ireland and the German states, characterized the pre–Civil War period. In both North and South anti-immigrant sentiment was strong. Irish American soldiers who fought for the Confederacy were nonetheless looked down upon by other Southerners as barbaric and uncultivated. After the Union's Eleventh Corps, which included a large contingent of German American soldiers, fled from an unexpected flank attack at Chancellorsville, its members were unjustly vilified as cowards and compared to sheep. The New York City Draft Riots of July 1863 revealed the depth of immigrant anger against native-born, Protestant elites, who were the targets of the largely Irish Catholic mob. The rioters broadened their attacks to include not just agents of the Republican Party and the federal government, which had created the draft, but also Protestant missions and charities.

Catholics were less likely than Protestants to emphasize antislavery as a moral cause, viewing abolitionism as socially disruptive and slavery as "one of those intractable human conditions to be borne patiently for the sake of eternal reward," according to the historian Mark A. Noll. But both Catholics and Protestants supported the war effort. Mary Livermore, who volunteered for the Sanitary Commission, noted that Protestant and Catholic women together "scraped lint, and rolled bandages, or made garments for the poorly clad soldiery." Catholic nuns nursed soldiers, alleviating some nativist prejudice against their faith by their good works.

Both sections suffered from racial as well as ethnic tensions. In the North African-American leaders such as Frederick Douglass, in concert with their white allies, lobbied President Lincoln to adopt emancipationist war aims. But many Northern whites adamantly rejected such an expansion. A faction of the Democratic Party adopted the motto "The Union as it was and the Constitution as it is," rejecting the creation of a Union without slavery and a Constitution containing emancipation. Antiwar Democrats called upon the North to consider only "the welfare, peace, and safety of the white race, without reference to . . . the condition of the African" in reaching a settlement of the war. And antidraft rioters in New York City singled out black victims, sexually mutilating some of their corpses and even razing an orphanage for black children.

In the Confederacy white supremacy may have been unchallenged as the ruling ideology, but it was equally difficult to enforce. Blacks were not supposed to have a political identity in the Confederacy, but their cooperation was essential to the war effort—yet often denied. Slaves ran away to the Union lines, providing their labor and knowledge of the terrain to the enemy. They challenged authority on the plantations as white control weakened. Even when slave labor contributed to the Confederate war effort, some Confederates worried that slaves might not give their best efforts, for example, to build fortifications intended to hold back their potential liberators. A Confederate commander in Florida even court-martialed slave laborers for treason, despite their master's objection that slaves were incapable of a political allegiance that could be betrayed.

On both Northern and Southern home fronts race relations were being renegotiated. After the war James A. Garfield would ask, "What is freedom? Is it the bare privilege of not being chained?" It must be more than that, Garfield thought, and a freedom that gave blacks more than liberation from their chains inherently threatened Northern, as well as Southern, assumptions of white superiority. In 1862 Democrats in western Indiana voiced fears that emancipation would bring competition from black laborers. Indeed, between 1860 and 1870 the black population of Indiana more than doubled, to more than twenty-four thousand. The Fourteenth and Fifteenth Amendments to the Constitution, which gave African Americans citizenship and black men the vote, forced many Northern states to accept black testimony in court, to allow blacks to vote, and to accord blacks a greater measure of political and civic equality than had been imaginable before the war.

White women who sought a change in their status were less successful in exploiting the conflict to that end than were African Americans. Both the Union and the Confederacy needed the help of their women. As the historian Drew Gilpin Faust has noted, nineteenth-century white women were familiar with calls for sacrifice. Now they were called upon to run farms—and in the South to manage slaves—to nurse the wounded, and to take on jobs making munitions or as clerks in government offices. Most of all they were asked to sacrifice the men they loved. Faust credits Southern women's increased resistance to sacrifice as a "factor in explaining Confederate defeat." Not everyone agrees; the historian Nina Silber argues that the government successfully channeled Northern women's efforts into a support for the war that did not challenge male authority.

Certainly advocates of woman's rights, such as Elizabeth Cady Stanton and Susan B. Anthony, found the war frustrating. Stanton determined that the best course was to subordinate women's issues to emancipation and black rights. She later conceded that this strategy was "a blunder," but during the war she led the Women's National Loyal League in a campaign to secure signatures on a petition in favor of a constitutional amendment to end slavery. She expected women to be rewarded for supporting the war effort with equal rights. Instead the Fourteenth Amendment referred to "male citizens," and the Fifteenth enfranchised black men but not women.

The war brought irrevocable change to the home front. By its end both sections had suffered devastation. Although the physical destruction was much greater in the South than in the North, in both sections there were many vacant chairs and empty sleeves. Class and ethnic divisions too had been exposed. Women now found greater roles in the public sphere than they had previously known. And the black man now possessed full citizenship in the land of his birth, the land where only recently the vast majority of his people had toiled as chattel.

Women at War

ELIZABETH R. VARON

What do women have to do with the origins of the Civil War? Growing up in Virginia in the 1970s I often heard this answer: nothing.

Much has changed since then. A new generation of scholars has rediscovered the Civil War as a drama in which women, and gender tensions, figure prominently. Thanks to new research into diaries, letters, newspapers, and state and local records, we now know that women were on the front lines of the literary and rhetorical war over slavery long before the shooting war began. They were integral to the slave resistance and flight that destabilized the border between North and South. And they were recruited by both secessionists and Unionists to join a partisan army, with each side claiming that the "ladies," with their reputation for moral purity, had chosen it over its rivals. So what do women have to do with the origins of the war? The answer is: everything.

Some of the women most involved in these political developments are well known to scholars and the general public. But countless others are still obscure. For example, we all know about Harriet Beecher Stowe's contribution, her best-selling 1852 novel *Uncle Tom's Cabin*, to the antislavery cause. But how many Americans know that Stowe's book escalated a long-standing literary war over slavery? *Uncle Tom's Cabin* not only inflamed the proslavery press in the South, but it also prompted a concerted response from white Southern women writers like Mary Eastman and Louisa McCord, who countered Stowe with their own rose-colored fantasies about the purported gentility and harmony of plantation life. Works like Eastman's *Aunt Phillis's Cabin; or, Southern Life as It Is*, published the same year as Stowe's book, were widely hailed in the proslavery press and are the literary antecedents to that most enduring volley in the ongoing literary war over slavery, Margaret Mitchell's 1936 revival of the plantation-fiction genre, *Gone with the Wind*.

We all know the name of Harriet Tubman and recognize her role in leading the Underground Railroad in the 1850s. She was a remarkable, heroic individual. But she was not alone; new work in the historical record permits us to recover the names and stories of scores of female fugitives from slavery and of female Underground Railroad operatives, white and black, Northern and Southern, who fought their own campaign along the border of the free and slave states.

Their stories may be forgotten today, but they were national news back then. When the slave Jane Johnson was rescued from her master, a prominent Southern politician, by the Underground Railroad in Philadelphia in 1855, her case became a national cause célèbre. To the antislavery press she represented the slave's natural yearning for freedom and the courage and dignity of enslaved women. To the proslavery press she represented the faithlessness of Northerners, who, in defiance of the 1850 Fugitive Slave Law, refused to act as slave catchers.

Moreover gender tensions over competing definitions of manly and womanly comportment worked to escalate the sectional conflict. Attacks on the manhood and womanhood of one's political opponents—the charge that they were not "true" men and women—were a staple of antebellum politics, and such attacks, which became more pointed in the 1850s, greatly eroded the trust between the North and South. Indeed by the eve of war many Northerners and Southerners had come to believe that the gender conventions of the two regions were antagonistic and incompatible.

Defenders of slavery and "Southern rights" charged that Northern society, with its bent for social reform, was fundamentally hostile to the hierarchical, patriarchal social order of the slave South. As the proslavery *Richmond Enquirer* put it in 1856, in a typical accusation, antislavery Northerners who supported the new Republican Party threatened all of the pillars of traditional society: they were "at war with religion, female virtue, private property, and distinctions of race."

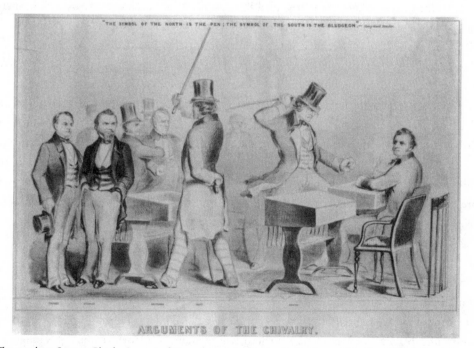

The attack on Senator Charles Sumner of Massachusetts by Representative Preston Brooks of South Carolina. Library of Congress Prints and Photographs Division, LC-USZ62-38851.

Gender politics made it into Congress as well. In 1856 Preston Brooks, a representative from South Carolina, savagely beat Senator Charles Sumner on the floor of the Senate with a cane after Sumner "insulted the honor" of the South with a speech on slavery in Kansas. On its face this seems the perfect illustration of the maxim that politics was a man's world. But when put in its context the incident illustrates how gender aspersions and images of women were central to the slavery debates. Sumner's speech had dubbed the forceful incursions by Southern settlers in the West and their bid to establish a proslavery regime the "rape of a virgin territory." Such sexualized imagery fueled the abolitionist critique of Southern men as rapacious and uncivilized and of Southern society as saturated by violence against women. The "bully Brooks," the Northern press charged, had "disgraced the name of man"; "there is no chivalry in a brute," a Boston newspaper put it succinctly.

Proslavery forces who rallied around Brooks, by contrast, claimed that Sumner's defenseless capitulation to Brooks's blows proved that Northern men were weak and submissive, slave-like in their subservience. This fueled the proslavery critique of the North as a world turned upside down, in which "strong-minded" abolitionist women and radical free blacks had raised the specter of social equality and effected the erosion of the patriarchal family and of male authority.

Even as they imputed gender transgressions to their opponents, antebellum politicians routinely called on women to join the ranks of political parties and movements. Of course women could not yet vote; nonetheless elite and middle-class women—to whom Victorian culture ascribed a penchant for piety and virtue—had a distinct role to play in electoral politics, both in influencing and mobilizing male voters and in lending an aura of moral sanctity to political causes.

It is no wonder, then, that during the secession crisis champions of the Union and of Southern nationalism alike claimed the "ladies" were on their side. During the election campaign of 1860 and the subsequent secession convention debates in the South, women attended speeches, rallies, and processions; contributed their own polemics to the partisan press; and, fortunately for historians, left a treasure trove of firsthand accounts of the deepening crisis. These accounts—letters, diaries, memoirs, poems, and stories—furnish moving and astute analyses of the agonies of secession.

Such sources are the most powerful argument for recognizing the centrality of women to the story of the war's causes. For example, there is no more chilling account of how it felt to be a Southern Unionist in the midst of secession fever than that of Elizabeth Van Lew of Richmond, Virginia. Van Lew was a native-born white Southerner, but one who harbored a loathing for slavery and a belief that her state, as the mother of the Union, should represent moderation and compromise. As she watched a secessionist procession snake through the streets of Richmond in the wake of Virginia's vote to join the Confederacy, she knew the time for compromise had passed. "Such a sight!" Van Lew wrote. "The multitude, the mob, the whooping, the tin-pan music, and the fierceness of a surging, swelling revolution. This I witnessed. I thought of France and as the procession passed, I fell upon my knees under the angry heavens, clasped my hands and prayed, 'Father forgive them, for they know not what they do.' "

For Van Lew secession was a kind of collective madness that had descended on the South. Although she could easily have sought refuge in the North, she chose to stay in Richmond during the war so that she could put her political principles on the line as the leading Union spy in the Confederacy. Her Richmond home was the nerve center of an elaborate interracial espionage ring that funneled critical information to Grant's army.

Like Stowe and Tubman, Van Lew was remarkable—but not anomalous. The nation's archives and attics contain the stories of countless other such women, who offer eloquent testimony of the war's causes and meaning.

The challenge that remains for scholars working in this field is to popularize the notion, among general readers and some skeptics in the ranks of academic historians, that women and gender were central, not merely tangential, to the story of the sectional alienation and strife. The stakes are high: the better we understand how women figured in antebellum politics, the better we'll understand the wartime relationship between home front and battlefront and the tangled process by which Americans have defined patriotism and citizenship ever since.

Laugh During Wartime

JON GRINSPAN

Americans remember the Civil War for the carnage it caused, the people it liberated, and the nation it rebuilt. Rarely do they remember it for the comedy it inspired.

Yet many considered the early 1860s to be a golden age of practical joking. Throughout the conflict soldiers and civilians, Union and Confederate, laughed at "the

A Union cartoon mocking Governor Henry Wise and his sons and other "First Families of Virginia" as "Fleet-Footed Virginians," presumably in retreat from Northern armies. Library of Congress Prints and Photographs Division, LC-USZ62-53597.

comedies mixed up with our country's tragedy," in the words of one observer. From prisoners of war to members of Congress, Americans joked about serious subjects, meeting disastrous events with goofy gags. Northerners mocked recruiting officers as lascivious pimps. Southerners caricatured zealous gangs of excessively helpful nurses who swarmed tired officers. Newspapers on both sides printed grisly amputation puns with titles like "An 'Off-Hand' Joke." Americans met their brutal war with bold and honest comedy.

The United States already had an international reputation as a land of iconoclastic tricksters, and the fighting sharpened their wits even further. Young women larded letters to their enlisted sweethearts with the latest jokes told back home, and nurses slipped books by their favorite humorists under the pillows of recuperating soldiers. Though many joked, veterans led the way. The army, some humorless civilians warned, is "deficient in reverence, and likes a laugh at anybody's expense."

Newspapers passed along much of the humor, often overseen by dedicated "funny editors," who filled their pages with war-themed jokes. They "scissored" puns and anecdotes from other publications and passed them off as their own. The best bits went viral, popping up from North Carolina to South Dakota. Papers freely floated between the Union and the Confederacy, further seeding the newest round of jokes behind the respective battle lines. Armies left trails of funny pages in their wake, and civilians seemed fascinated by whatever was making their former countrymen laugh.

Most of the comedy during the first year of the conflict aimed at deflating puffed-up war talk. Comedians North and South met the initial alarm over secession with exaggerated panic. Northern newspapers printed false correspondences warning, in hysterical tones, that the little girls of Charleston, South Carolina, were organizing an invading army. Both sides mocked martial posturing, caricaturing volunteer companies made up entirely of self-appointed generals more interested in epaulets than muskets.

Confederates soon debuted their own style of an aggressively macabre humor. When the Union called for seventy-five thousand volunteers, rebel jokers published such advertisements as "75,000 Coffins Wanted." Bill Arp, a daring and popular Georgia humorist, penned false letters to President Lincoln, thoughtfully worrying that the Union's military strategy might be "too hard upon your burial squads and ambulance horses."

Abraham Lincoln was the war's most notorious jester, known for his backcountry yarns and goofy, self-deprecating style. Washington socialites complained that he simply would not stop telling jokes at their dinner parties. His cabinet—stiff, bearded, capable men, whom Navy Secretary Gideon Welles called "destitute of wit"—met his enthusiastic joking with blank stares and awkward sneezes; William P. Fessenden, the secretary of the Treasury, objected that comedy was "hardly a proper subject." Lincoln ignored them, introducing his plan for emancipation by reading aloud a routine by his favorite humorist. He often joked with citizens who sought his aid: when a businessman requested a pass through Union lines to Richmond, Lincoln chuckled that he had already sent 250,000 men in that direction, but "not one has got there yet."

As casualties mounted, Lincoln's humor touched off a battle that would define Civil War comedy. Starting in late 1861 a faction of reverential Northerners pushed back against joking about the conflict, particularly by the president. Lincoln's political opponents waved banners screaming "NO VULGAR JOKER FOR PRESIDENT!" Some Union soldiers, crushed by devastating defeat after devastating defeat, moaned that their comrades "are handed over to be butchered" while "Old Abe makes a joke." Even the president's supporters began to fret about Lincoln's "unfortunate habit of joking" at "the very crisis of our existence."

Lincoln's humor introduced a larger cultural struggle over how Northern society should address brutality. Victorian sentimentalists sought to suppress anything other than reverential mourning and denounced comedy as "fearfully out of season." By 1863 even the *New York Herald*, formerly a sarcastic paper in a sarcastic city, turned its back on humor, demanding, "Was Bull Run a joke? Was Fredericksburg a joke? Was Chancellorsville a joke? Does anyone laugh at the wholesale slaughter of brave men?" Faced with colossal defeats, disfigured veterans, and eroding confidence, many argued it was simply too soon for joking.

But a new wave of humor, emanating from the barracks and brothels on both sides, squelched the sentimentalists. As the war grew bloodier, American men and women actually increased the audacity of their comedy. Those who kept joking tacitly argued that bold, comedic truth-telling was exactly what their nation needed.

In fact Union and Confederate army camps generated the toughest comedy. At first their jokes were relatively tame. Some wondered how many court-martials a barrel of rum held. Others joked that draft exemptions were open only to "dead men who can establish proof of their demise by two reliable witnesses."

But the slaughter at Chancellorsville and Gettysburg introduced a new darkness. Soon, noted one wartime memoirist, "anything short of death is a capital joke." Many gags starred a battlefield surgeon, "Old Sawbones," who could amputate a gangrenous leg without removing the cigar from his mouth. Surgery provided "an inexhaustible source of amusement," often involving amputation puns and jokes about former butchers finding their true vocation in the medics' tent. Not even the dead could escape the laughter: a genre of burial humor satirized sneaky mourners who stole graves dug by other companies.

As the fighting built to a bloody climax, Civil War humor reached its comedic peak. The unprecedented severity of General William T. Sherman's march through Georgia and South Carolina challenged Americans' already dark humor. Arp, the Confederacy's most talented comedian, responded with a hilarious series in which he bragged about chasing Sherman's "fleeing" army to the sea. Arp's fictitious wife was just as myopic, hoping that the "kind-hearted" Sherman would take good care of the things his men pillaged from her home. The joking was not limited to comedians: one Georgia girl, already a refugee, sent teasing notes to local boys falsely warning that Sherman's avenging army was just outside of town.

This may sound callous to modern sensibilities, but there is an impressive honesty to it: the comedy of the Civil War preferred to directly engage suffering rather than hide behind stern reverence. While humor could not stop the onslaught of grand and terrible events, at least it helped Americans talk about them. Arp acknowledged as much in a published letter at the end of the war, explaining, "I must explode myself generally so as to feel better." The very irreverent Union president agreed. Weighed down by the "fearful strain that is upon me night and day," Lincoln quipped, "if I did not laugh I should die."

The Civil War's Rip Van Winkle

ALBIN J. KOWALEWSKI

Great fiction, we all know, has the uncanny ability to imitate the unpredictability and emotion of real life. So it's a testament to the Civil War's otherworldliness that real life imitated great fiction in the remarkable story of Isaac Israel Hayes, one of America's most famous early Arctic explorers.

It's unclear if Hayes ever read Washington Irving's classic short story, "Rip Van Winkle," or if he even knew the plot, in which the main character inadvertently sleeps through the American Revolution. But by the spring of 1862 Hayes would have easily identified with Irving's famously henpecked hero. Like Rip, Hayes one day ventured off

Isaac Israel Hayes. Library of Congress Prints and Photographs Division, LC-DIG-cwpbh-00491.

into the unknown, missed some of the most defining moments of his generation (in this case everything from Lincoln's election to the Battle of Ball's Bluff in late 1861), and returned to a country he barely understood.

Hayes didn't sleep through the opening of the Civil War, but he might as well have. The Pennsylvania native spent fifteen of the most important months in American history, from July 1860 to October 1861, looking for the North Pole between and above Greenland and Canada.

Because telegraphs and mail didn't run that far north, Hayes had no idea that the United States had been torn in two during his absence. He heard rumors of the conflict on his way home, but it wasn't until he finally anchored in Boston Harbor in late October 1861 that the war's terrible realness stopped him cold. Within moments of stepping ashore Hayes realized, "The country which I had known before could be the same no more." Quoting the Book of Exodus but also presaging the title of Robert A. Heinlein's sci-fi classic, he wrote, "I felt like a stranger in a strange land, and yet every object which I passed was familiar."

Hayes hadn't always longed for something so familiar. Born in 1832 and raised in a Quaker family in Chester County, Pennsylvania, he was a medical doctor by training but rather unexcited about the predictable rhythms of private practice. Instead he was drawn to the barrens of the Arctic, an unforgiving and mysterious world where a young man could prove himself, and even achieve renown. If nothing else, the northernmost frontier would give Hayes the opportunity to lead what he would soon call "a novel sort of life."

Equal parts science and adventure—with undertones of national ambition—Arctic exploration during the mid-nineteenth century captivated the world much as the space race would do a century later. The top of the planet was impossibly cold, dark, and often fatal. But Victorian explorers kept going back: first, in a renewed search by the British and others for the Northwest Passage; then in typically hopeless rescue missions for the crews that never returned; and finally, after much of the North American Arctic had been mapped, they began a dangerous, often obsessive race "to reach the north pole of the earth," as Hayes first proposed in early 1860, that would last into the twentieth century.

Few American or European scientists had ever made it above 80 degrees north latitude, but Hayes believed, like other explorers, that an "open polar sea" blanketed the very top of the world, a navigable ocean kept ice-free by a mixture of warm Gulf Stream waters, strong undersea currents, and prevailing surface winds. He had been a member of an earlier Arctic team led by Elisha Kent Kane in 1853–55 that claimed to have found evidence of the sea's existence, and now he desperately wanted confirmation. Anxious to go back, Hayes organized a follow-up expedition.

The small crew left Boston in early July 1860, vowing to cross the ice belt in the lower latitudes, reach the open sea, and sail straight to the North Pole. Hayes's ship was "snug, jaunty looking," he said, but whether it would survive the dangerous and unchartered waters in its future remained to be seen. Hayes named his ship the *United States*.

After they tacked up Greenland's west coast, dense pack ice forced them to make winter camp near Smith Sound above Baffin Bay. Hayes traded for sled dogs and provisions with the Arctic's native peoples; were it not for their guidance—they did, after all, live in the very place Hayes had come to discover—his expedition would have ended much differently. After a long and dark winter in which temperatures dropped to 68 degrees below Fahrenheit, Hayes and most of his crew survived into the spring.

Just days before the Confederacy opened fire on Fort Sumter, Hayes pushed northward in search of the open polar sea. Traveling by dogsled, he struggled across the Arctic's broken terrain and its fields of ice hummocks. In mid-May, at a latitude Hayes recorded as 81 degrees 35 minutes north, he observed veins of open water fanning out like a "delta" across what he believed was the polar basin. He took a few measurements, enjoyed the view, planted a flag, and turned around. Severe damage to his ship prevented him from attempting to sail to the Pole, as he had originally intended.

Hayes later said that he "led a strange weird sort of life" in the Arctic. The irony, of course, is that it would only get stranger and weirder when he went back home. In 1860 he had embarked as a celebrity; he returned over a year later a mere afterthought, ridiculed in print. "Surely," wrote the *Detroit Free Press* a short while after Hayes docked at Boston, "enough of treasure and valuable life have been spent in search of facts to substantiate somebody's theory about the polar regions, which, whether it is this way or that way, is of no practical importance to anybody in the wide world. Suppose the continent of land does run up to the north pole, or suppose it don't. Suppose there is an open sea there or suppose there isn't. What does it amount to? Who will go there on a pleasure voyage or a trout fishing?"

But if the country had no time for Hayes, the explorer found the war an all-consuming horror. He felt out of place in an America that now seemed more alien than the Arctic North, leaving him "sad and dejected," he said. Confident that he had found the open sea but disappointed at not having reached the Pole, Hayes found his existential anxiety come rushing back. In the spring of 1862, despite his Quaker beliefs, he accepted a commission as a surgeon in the Union Army and was quickly appointed director of the massive Satterlee Hospital, outside Philadelphia.

After Hayes died in 1881, follow-up expeditions challenged his findings and overturned his claim about the existence of the open polar sea. He largely faded out of memory. But recent studies, including a 2009 biography by Douglas W. Wamsley, have begun resuscitating his legacy. Not only had Hayes pioneered the use of photography in the Arctic, Wamsley and others note, but he had also helped establish the route that later explorers—including his better-known rival, Charles Francis Hall—would follow in subsequent expeditions to locate the Pole.

Hayes once wondered if his time in the Arctic had been "set down in a dream." In a sense he was right—and more like Rip Van Winkle than anyone had ever realized, if they realized it at all. Coming back to the States in 1861 had indeed been a rude awakening.

General Butler and the Women

ALECIA P. LONG

On June 11, 1862, the *New York Times* addressed the widespread controversy that had erupted in response to General Benjamin Butler's General Order No. 28, commonly known as "the Woman Order." On May 26 the *Times* quoted the New Orleans native and Confederate general P. G. T. Beauregard, who opined that the order, announced on May 15, gave occupying Union troops "the right to treat at their pleasure the ladies of the South as common harlots."

Two weeks later, seemingly in answer to Beauregard, the *Times'* New Orleans correspondent wrote, "Throughout the South it has been received with a shout of execration. Be that as it may, it has had the desired effect, and the soldiers ceased to be insulted." That assertion regarding the Woman Order's effectiveness was widely shared by historians until recently, when new evidence emerged showing widespread, if frustrated, resistance.

Benjamin Franklin Butler had varied careers, as a respected and prosperous litigator, a successful state and national politician, and an ambitious but deeply controversial Union general. Despite his many other accomplishments, Butler gained and has retained his historical notoriety as a result of the controversies generated during his occupation of New Orleans. The Woman Order is widely considered his most provocative act while in charge of the city from May to December 1862.

Butler issued the Woman Order a mere two weeks after Flag Officer David Farragut had arrived in the city and turned it over to Butler's administrative control. The city's

A cartoon from *Harper's Weekly* showing a pro-Butler view of the effects of his rule on New Orleans women. Library of Congress Prints and Photographs Division, LC-USZ62-65334.

angry and unrepentant rebel residents initially proved unwilling to submit to federal authority. Yet in short order Butler took matters in hand and later recalled that "from the second day we landed, we had the men of New Orleans" completely under control. This claim was an exaggeration: there would be numerous arrests and imprisonments and at least one hanging among the city's Confederate loyalists over the following six months.

But even Butler admitted that while the men had been quickly subdued, it "was not so with the women of New Orleans," especially its upper-class members, who continued to abuse and disrespect his men. The behaviors that Butler and his troops found so galling included ladies exiting streetcars and leaving churches when officers or soldiers entered, teaching and encouraging children to sing Confederate songs, displaying Confederate flags or pinning small Confederate flags to their clothing, and choosing to walk in the middle of the street or turning their backs to avoid acknowledging their occupiers. In a few cases women reportedly spat on officers or encouraged their children to do so.

In one incident Butler reported that a woman dumped a "vessel" of "not very clean water" on Farragut's head as he passed below her balcony. Many writers have suggested that this vessel was in fact a chamber pot.

To stem the tide of female disrespect Butler created an order that brilliantly manipulated the South's existing gender and class ideologies while also taking advantage of the city's well-known reputation for harboring and tolerating large numbers of prostitutes. General Order No. 28 read, "As the officers and soldiers of the United States have been subject to repeated insults from the women (calling themselves ladies) of New Orleans, in return for the most scrupulous non-interference and courtesy on our part, it is ordered that hereafter when any female shall, by word, gesture or movement, insult or show contempt for any officer or soldier of the United States, she shall be regarded and held liable to be treated as a woman of the town plying her avocation." The threat implied by the order inflamed Confederate passions, garnered criticism from elsewhere in the Union and abroad, and earned Butler lasting infamy throughout the South.

The order cut right to the heart of both the class privilege accorded and the gender expectations demanded from upright, respectable Southern ladies. Its sexualized implications also seemed clear to many observers at the time and accounted for much of the hysteria generated in response. Confederate leaders howled with indignation about the sexual threat inherent in the Woman Order. Louisiana's exiled governor and Confederate president Jefferson Davis both issued formal denunciations; Davis even placed a bounty on Butler's head and ordered his execution if he was ever captured. The predictable outrage in Confederate circles also spread to newspapers in France and England, where Butler's order was condemned on the floor of Parliament.

For his own part Butler denied that his order contained an implicit sexual threat, but he did defend it in his autobiography, claiming that the order "executed itself" because "the ladies in New Orleans forebore to insult our troops because they didn't want to be deemed common women, and all the common women forebore to insult our troops because they wanted to be deemed ladies, and of those two classes were all the women secessionists of the city." According to the general, "there was no case of aggression after that order was issued, no case of insult by word or look against our officer or soldier while in New Orleans."

He also claimed that "no arrests were ever made under it or because of it," but historical records contradict that claim. The best-known case is that of Eugenia Levy-Phillips, a Confederate loyalist and diarist who had settled in New Orleans after being expelled from Washington. On June 30, a full month and a half after Butler promulgated the order and three weeks after the *New York Times* reported that "soldiers had ceased to be insulted," Butler ordered Levy-Phillips incarcerated under harsh conditions at Ship Island, in the Gulf of Mexico, for two years in return for laughing while the funeral cortège of a Union officer passed beneath her balcony. (Butler eventually relented, and she was released from the island after only two and a half months.)

In July Butler ordered a second woman, Anne Larue, to Ship Island because she had worn Confederate colors, donned a secession badge, and handed out what Butler termed Confederate propaganda. Larue's actions nearly set off a riot, and, once arrested by Union troops, she refused to back down under questioning, including by Butler. When asked why she had taken actions he deemed treasonous, Larue replied that "she felt very patriotic that day." She too was sentenced to two years at Ship Island but was released after only three weeks.

Butler's offensiveness was not limited to ladies, nor was his administrative brilliance a match for his abrasiveness, inflexibility, and financial opportunism. Foreign consuls bristled at his imperious treatment and complained to Washington. These complaints, accompanied by rumors that Butler was using his position to gain personal financial advantage, led to his peremptory dismissal and replacement by Nathaniel Banks in December.

Scrapbooking the Civil War

ELLEN GRUBER GARVEY

Soon after the Civil War began, a Savannah, Georgia, resident named Henrietta Emanuel Solomons, or someone in her household, began to clip items from newspapers. She pasted her clippings over the sheets of a used-up ledger from the family grocery business until sometime in 1863, when she ran out of space. When she finished they covered 483 large pages.

Solomons's scrapbook may sound obsessive today, but it was a common practice at the time. More important, it is a window into the emotions of a loyal Southerner living through the war. The scrapbook's stiff pages are dense with stories about Confederate victories, poems, and news reports. They assure readers that enslaved people want to help the Confederacy and would refuse freedom. They tell of women knitting for soldiers and spying for the Confederacy—cross-dressed or in their own clothing. Some are full of rage against the tyranny of Lincoln.

Reading the war news in New York City. Library of Congress Prints and Photographs Division, LC-USZ62-112561.

A newspaper-clipping scrapbook like this does not give us the direct information or expression we expect from diaries. Instead it is a reminder that, like us, Northerners and Southerners living through the Civil War relied on the media to tell them what was happening at a distance and even across town. They looked to the media to support and express their feelings. And like twenty-first-century Web users sharing links, they saved items that mattered to them and sent them around to friends, family, or strangers.

Newspapers took a new place in people's lives during the war. Everyone was hungry for information about family and friends on the battlefields and for news of victories. Northern papers printed telegraphed reports from the battlefield. The "imperious" newspaper called to readers, Oliver Wendell Holmes Sr. wrote, summoning people to buy it "at unusual hours . . . by the divine right of its telegraphic dispatches." Union soldiers pounced on bundles of passed-along newspapers and paid high prices to newsboys who brought fresh papers to the camps, especially if they covered battles they had been in. Civilians rushed to read newspapers posted in the street.

Southern readers were as eager for newspapers as Northern readers, and at home Americans on both sides made scrapbooks from their newspaper reading. They knew they were living through momentous events, and they felt they were saving history. Northern scrapbooks, flush with clippings, carry stories headlined "BY TELEGRAPH" and include maps and an occasional engraving. Southern scrapbooks are a record of scarcity: the blockade kept out Northern newspapers; Southern publications had almost no illustrations; the printer's ink on the clippings is sometimes pale; and publications were desperate for paper to print news on. Southerners hoping to make a scrapbook might find even used ledgers like Solomons's hard to come by.

In Augusta, Georgia, Ella Gertrude Clanton Thomas wrote worriedly in her diary that newspaper clippings were displacing her diary entries and made it appear that she paid too much attention to events beyond the family circle. By July 1863 she lamented that she'd saved many more clippings beyond the two volumes she had already filled but could not get another book to paste them into.

Many newspaper scrapbooks proceed chronologically, like diaries. Others are arranged carefully by topic, or they group such items as obituaries or poetry. Solomons's and some other Confederate scrapbooks, however, reflect the fact that with paper shortages, Southern newspapers were in short supply and editions were recirculated for some time before a scrapbook maker felt free to cut them up. Her scrapbook returns repeatedly to the same Confederate victories, clipped from different papers and separated by many pages.

Solomons's choices of what to clip reveal how dramatically her attitudes toward enslaved people changed in two years. Early in the war she collected poems and stories about slaves so loyal to their masters that they refuse freedom. In the articles she saved, enslaved blacks captured by the Union are "very anxious to get back to their masters." In one poem, "Yankee Doodle, to the Georgia Volunteers," "Uncle Tom" asks to "jine de boys" in fighting the Yankees and gleefully narrates the Confederate victories at Bethel Church and Manassas (Bull Run). The poem offers the added bonus of being singable to "Yankee Doodle," thus recapturing a patriotic American tune for Confederate use.

In another poem, from 1861, "A Southern Scene from Life," the "little Missis" tells her "Mammy" that Lincoln means to free her, but Mammy explains that the difference between her coal-black face and the child's "red and white . . . soft and fine" skin "with yeller ringlets" self-evidently results in Mammy's slavery and the little girl's liberty and wealth. Mammy declares that she'll wait for freedom in heaven, and ends by insulting Lincoln.

Solomons was not the only white Southerner who wanted to believe that enslaved people hoped for a Confederate victory. The *Macon Telegraph* asserted that "A Southern Scene from Life," which was reprinted in other Southern newspapers, was the "versification of a conversation that actually took place" and praised it for its "truth and feeling." Other Southern scrapbook makers savored it too. One liked it enough to carry it around before pasting it, so that it was heavily frayed and partially torn, corrected by hand to make up for a tear.

But once the Emancipation Proclamation began circulating in the fall of 1862, a new strain appeared in Solomons's scrapbook, beginning with an anonymous bombastic poem, "For Abraham Lincoln. On Reading the Emancipation Proclamation." The poem worries that Lincoln "wou'st unband / the negro from his easy chain" and arm black people. Black figures are no longer asking to "jine de boys," nor do they denounce Lincoln; rather, with emancipation on the horizon, they are armed and turning into "brutal fiends, whose reeking knives / Would spare nor sex, nor youth, nor age." The result would be that "wholesale murder clot our land." Solomons's book presents the murders resulting from arming blacks as terrifyingly different from the bloodshed the war was already engaged in.

The Southern newspapers' reports of brutal black fiends were, of course, no more accurate than their reports of slaves cheerfully giving their lives to protect their masters. In collecting both strains Solomons hints at a Southerner's increasingly conflicted beliefs about what enslaved people might actually think and feel and what they might do if the Confederacy lost and the Emancipation Proclamation became effective.

Solomons's scrapbook contains no notes or pointed juxtapositions to suggest that she took any of these newspaper accounts with a grain of salt or thought they contradicted one another. But other scrapbook makers used their scrapbooks precisely to monitor and uncover the deceptions of the press—the press of the other side, of course.

Daniel Hundley, a Confederate officer and prisoner of the Union forces in Sandusky, Ohio, read the Northern newspapers he had access to with relentless skepticism. He bought a scrapbook in 1864 and proposed "to fill it with the newspaper history of the times, which if I can preserve it until the war is ended, will be of incalculable service to me" in showing the contradictions among stories. He escaped from prison, presumably leaving his scrapbook behind.

In William Mumford Baker's 1866 novel *Inside: A Chronicle of Secession*, on the lives of Union sympathizers living in a Confederate town during the war, everyone is hungry for newspapers. Union sympathizers furtively pass Northern newspapers to one another and fear they will be lynched if their leanings are known. Neither side wants to believe news of its side's reverses. Ferguson, a Union man, compiles a scrapbook just to follow the "inaccuracy" of the Confederate news reports. Saving items and comparing the fanfare around each assertion of a battlefield or diplomatic victory allows him to notice the nearly imperceptible way the story is later dropped.

Ferguson retrieves the assertions from oblivion and pastes them into a record meant for critical media analysis. "Yesterday's news is forgotten because to-day's news is so much more glorious; then, yesterday's rumor was false, it seems, but that of to-day is certainly true," he explains to a friend before he hides his scrapbook in a safe. Evidence of paying too close attention to how news is reported could be dangerous.

For her part Solomons did not forget yesterday's news. Instead she kept returning to it. Her scrapbook was an ideal newspaper, holding what she chose to pluck and remember from the swirling stream of the press.

The Civil War and the Fourth Estate

FORD RISLEY

Union general Joseph Hooker had never been shy around the press. He had been given the nickname "Fighting Joe" by newspapers during the Seven Days' campaign. The general did not like the name because he thought it made him sound rash, but all agreed it accurately described his command style. It also characterized the way Hooker talked to newsmen about many of his fellow commanders.

After the battle of Antietam, where his corps launched the first assault on Confederate troops, Hooker told one correspondent, "McClellan knows I am a better general than he ever dared hope to be," referring to George B. McClellan. Of General Fitz-John Porter, Hooker declared, "So help me God, I will never go into another battle where Porter commands the reserve."

After General Ambrose E. Burnside's infamous "Mud March" in January 1863, Hooker told a *New York Times* reporter that the president was an "imbecile" and said, "Nothing would go right until we had a dictator and the sooner the better." The *Times'* publisher, Henry J. Raymond, relayed the comments to President Abraham Lincoln, who told him he would gladly put up with the impetuous and egotistic general if he could defeat the rebels, something few of his commanders had found a way to do.

A few days later Lincoln named Hooker commander of the Army of the Potomac. In a fatherly letter Lincoln told him, "I have heard in such a way as to believe it, of you recently saying that both the Army and the Government needed a Dictator. Of course, it was not for this, but it spite of it, that I have given you the command. Only those generals

General Ambrose E. Burnside reading the newspaper. Library of Congress Prints and Photographs Division, LC-DIG-cwpb-01703.

who gain success, can set up dictators. What I ask of you is military success, and I will risk the dictatorship."

Hooker promptly made several high-level command changes, cleaned up camps, improved the food, and granted furloughs, all of which restored the morale of the troops. And initially he enjoyed cordial relations with many Union newsmen. But on the eve of the spring campaign in 1863, Hooker began having some of the same problems with the press that other commanders had experienced.

A newspaper published a story about the Surgeon General's office that contained information about the size and location of the Army of the Potomac. A furious Hooker complained to Secretary of War Edwin M. Stanton that the chief of the Secret Service "would have willingly paid $1,000 for such information" about Confederate forces.

Indeed during the first two years of the war an increasingly aggressive and competitive press published stories that infuriated military leaders on both sides. The Civil War was the first war widely covered by American newspapers. And in their zeal to report the greatest event of their lives, newsmen produced a decidedly mixed bag of stories.

On one hand, many reporters honestly and faithfully chronicled the fighting. Tireless correspondents went to extraordinary lengths to report stories, often on tight deadlines. However, other newsmen mistakenly, and in some cases recklessly, reported the conflict. Correspondents less concerned with the facts and more interested in rushing stories into print wrote damaging stories that hurt their side.

For decades, newspaper correspondents had generally written anonymously, most using a pen name or no name at all. Although the writer's name had appeared with stories as far back as the 1830s, the practice was not widespread. During the war, newsmen liked the custom of not using their names, believing the secrecy allowed them do their work better. As one reporter wrote, "The anonymous greatly favors freedom and boldness in newspaper correspondence. . . . Besides the responsibility it fastens on a correspondent, the signature inevitably detracts from the powerful impersonality of a journal."

However, commanders did not like the practice because newsmen often could not be held accountable for what they wrote. McClellan had complained to Stanton of reporters repeatedly "giving important information" about the army in their stories. "As it is impossible for me to ascertain with certainty who these anonymous writers are," he wrote, "I beg to suggest that another order be published holding the editors responsible for its infraction."

The best newsmen on both sides recognized that irresponsible correspondents sometimes wrote stories that hurt their side. In a letter to the *Savannah Republican*, Peter W. Alexander, one of the most skillful Southern correspondents, wrote, "The truth is there are correspondents who invariably magnify our successes and depreciate our losses, and who when there is a dearth of news will draw upon their imagination for their facts." But Alexander and others also argued for the necessity of a free press. "This is the people's war," he wrote. "Their sons and brothers make up the army. . . . And shall they not be allowed to know anything that is transpiring within that army? . . . Is the army to be a sealed book to the country?"

After the news leak Stanton told Hooker that the War Department would support any measure to control journalists. That same day the general issued General Order No. 48, requiring that all reporters with the Army of the Potomac "publish their communications over their own signatures."

Newsmen in the North reacted variously to the new requirement that their name appear on stories. A *New York Herald* reporter said, "It is discouraging for correspondents to have their names paraded before the public as authors of carefully written letters; for sometimes the letters are written on horseback or in woods, and often with the shells screaming to us to 'hurry up!'" But another correspondent remarked that including their name would make correspondents "exert extraordinary means to achieve success."

Hooker maintained that the order was not intended to prevent criticism of him by the press. "After any fight the reporters can open their fire as loudly as they please," he wrote later. As long as correspondents did not reveal critical military information to the enemy, the general said, they would be given "license to abuse or criticize me to their heart's content."

"Fighting Joe" would indeed be criticized after the Army of the Potomac was defeated once again at the Battle of Chancellorsville. An aggressive plan to attack General Robert E. Lee's far smaller army initially went well, but the brash Hooker lost his nerve after the initial contact with the rebels. He pulled his army back to a defensive position, and the audacious Lee split his army into two units. Daring Hooker to attack, Lee split his men again, and after a hazardous twelve-mile march, General Stonewall Jackson's troops routed the Federals.

In June Lincoln replaced Hooker as commander of the Army of the Potomac. After his departure some correspondents went back to writing stories anonymously. But the byline had been established and would eventually become a widespread newspaper custom.

Thanks to the recognition they received in covering the fighting, reporters increasingly were becoming the face of their newspaper with the public. And developing professional practices during the war made them more responsible for the accuracy and suitability of what they wrote. The byline was one of those traditions.

Making War on the Draft

NICOLE ETCHESON

One summer night in 1863 an angry mob surrounded the house of James Sill, the draft enrollment officer for Marion Township in Putnam County, Indiana. Sill had a list of eligible men whom he intended to draft into the army. The mob, dozens strong, was there to take it from him, by force if necessary.

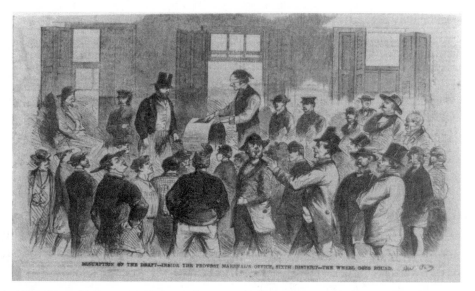

Blindfolded men drawing names for the draft in New York. Library of Congress Prints and Photographs Division, LC-USZ62-88856.

The Civil War was the first time in American history in which the government resorted to a draft. In the eyes of nineteenth-century Americans, drafts were incompatible with the liberties of a free people; European monarchs might conscript their armies, but Americans fought their wars with volunteers. Yet volunteering failed to keep pace with the two sides' manpower needs. The Confederacy instituted its draft in 1862. In July of that year the Union passed the Militia Act, which contained a provision allowing the secretary of war to draft militiamen. Congress did not pass its first draft law, the Enrollment Act, until spring 1863.

The Enrollment Act's primary goal was to stimulate volunteering. Each rural township and city ward had an enrolling officer responsible for compiling a list of men between the ages of twenty-five and forty-five. From those lists the provost marshal's office would determine each district's quota. If a community could meet its quota through volunteers, no draft would be held. As a result, once the quotas were announced, townships and cities would try to stimulate volunteering, often offering bounties. When the deadline for meeting the quota arrived, according to the historian Eugene C. Murdock, "the districts which had made their quota rejoiced in relief, while those that had failed stiffened themselves for a draft."

Enrolling officers like Sill thus found themselves on the front lines of the Union draft. It was Sill's responsibility to travel his district, collecting names and asking questions necessary to verify a man's age. (He was not required to verify anything other than age, even though marital status and disability affected one's eligibility for the draft.) Before the war Sill had enjoyed the respect of Marion Township, where he served as justice of the peace and notary public. But his support of the war had already proved costly, even before the mob showed up on his doorstep. Despite twenty-seven years of membership he had stopped attending his local Baptist church because of the congregation's antiwar sentiments.

Such sentiment was common in areas of the North like Indiana, where people had strong economic and family ties to the South, disliked the increasingly emancipationist aims of the war, objected to the Republican Party's economic agenda, and distrusted Lincoln's suspension of civil liberties in the name of preserving the Union. To them the Enrollment Act was merely another unconstitutional attack on the liberties of a free people.

In addition rural laborers like those in Putnam County were more vulnerable to the draft than city dwellers, according to the historian Tyler Anbinder. The Enrollment Act permitted men to avoid the draft by either purchasing a substitute or paying a $300 commutation fee. When the commutation fee was repealed in 1864, the price of substitutes became prohibitive. In Putnam County, for example, it rose to over a $1,000 by the end of the war. Farmhands often lacked the money for commutation or purchasing a substitute. Not only were rural residents too well known in their community to disappear, as might their urban counterparts, but men who did heavy farm labor would find it difficult to convince a doctor that they were physically unfit to serve.

Enrolling officers like Sill began to canvass their districts in the spring of 1863 just as the antidraft reaction was building. The historian Jennifer L. Weber calls Indiana "the most tense and violent state" as the draft went into effect, but resistance to enrollment also occurred in Illinois, Pennsylvania, Ohio, Wisconsin, and New Jersey. In mid-June Matilda Cavens wrote to her husband, a soldier from Putnam County, "The draft is being resisted all over the state." She mentioned several attacks on enrollment officers like Sill.

One Putnam County enrollment officer was informed by a committee of four men "that if he continued the enrollment . . . he would find himself a dead man before he got through." In another township the draft officer received a note signed "your friend," warning him, "If you don't lay aside the enrolling your life will be taken before to-morrow night." In yet another township the enrollment books were stolen, although there was suspicion that it was the enrolling officer himself who had destroyed them because he was "not all right on the war question." In Cloverdale the provost marshal's first choice for enrolling officer declined the job, probably because "vengeance is declared against the man who enrolls the militia of this township." And the Jefferson Township draft officer, confronted by a mob, was forced to surrender his papers.

In Sullivan County, Indiana, antiwar Democrats resolved to "resist the draft, by force of arms, if necessary." They considered the draft unconstitutional, "and they would not obey it." An assistant provost marshal in Indiana believed that, in Sullivan and Greene counties alone, there were 1,500 men drilling to resist the draft. Two enrolling officers were ambushed and killed in Rush County and another in Sullivan County. Weber found that the Provost Marshal General's Bureau reported thirty-eight enrolling officers killed and sixty wounded throughout the country.

Sill would fare better than many of his counterparts. One Sunday evening in June Sill's daughters, Candace and Harriet, were entertaining gentleman callers. Upon leaving the house the suitors encountered a mob of men. Candace reported that three hundred men surrounded the house, although later accounts put the number closer to fifty.

One of the suitors gave the alarm. Unknown to Sill, the women of his family had hidden the enrollment papers. Candace initially concealed them in a salt barrel, but then her mother, Elizabeth, moved them into another room. When the mob approached, Elizabeth grabbed the papers and ran out the back. She then stuffed them under a board the Sills had laid down as a path between the house and the outbuildings. Caught by two members of the mob, Elizabeth stood on the board while they searched her.

Meanwhile James Sill, with Candace at his side, confronted the men at the front of the house. Although Harriet had fled to a neighbor's house, Candace vowed not to leave her father's side, even though she thought it likely he would die "bravely defending the government papers." The mob gave Sill three minutes to produce the enrollment list or die. Candace recalled that she berated the men, calling them "every low thing I could think of for several minutes," while her father retrieved the papers. Of course he did not have the current list but instead produced one made for the previous year's militia draft. Sill threw the papers down at the feet of the mob. Candace held up a lantern and tried to see the men's faces. "One young man stepped forward," Candace recalled, "pulled his coat up over his head, took [the papers] from the floor and sprang back into the crowd saying 'We've got them; let's go.'"

Because Sill and his family recognized members of the mob, the military was able to make arrests. In September 1863 thirty-seven cases of conspiracy and resisting the enrollment in Putnam County were heard in the U.S. District Court in Indianapolis. Sill was a witness. The jury found the first defendant, Joseph Ellis, guilty, and the judge fined him $500. The defense attorney then asked the prosecution to drop the conspiracy charge in return for the remaining defendants' accepting a guilty verdict on the charge of resisting the enrollment. Three cases were dismissed, and the remaining defendants paid fines of up to $25. The governor of Indiana ordered a medal made to honor Elizabeth Sill, but she refused to accept it.

Some attacks on enrolling officers were spontaneous, as women defended their men from enrollment officers, just as Elizabeth and Candace Sill had protected James Sill and his papers. Men set dogs on enrolling officers who came to the house, and women sometimes tossed pots of hot water on them. In Boone County, Indiana, women threw eggs at an enrollment official. It was well known that the attacks on James Sill and other Putnam County enrolling officials had been planned in the law offices of a local judge, where a military company had been organized to resist the draft. The Copperheads were not through with Sill. At the beginning of 1865 he received an anonymous note threatening that his "harts blud shall pay dear" if he carried out another draft.

The New York City Draft Riots, in which over a hundred people died, became the most famous example of draft resistance in the North. That week of violence was, to that date, the most deadly riot in American history. But its history has overshadowed the widespread draft resistance that took place throughout the North, from Indiana and Illinois to Pennsylvania, Michigan, Minnesota, New Jersey, and Wisconsin. Even New Hampshire called its militia out to enforce the draft. As the historian Joan E. Cashin has written, "there was a great deal of small-scale violent resistance" to the draft. It had not seemed small-scale to the Sill family when their house was surrounded by a mob, but the attack on James Sill exemplified the nature of midwestern antidraft violence.

Going to the Fair

JENNIFER R. BRIDGE

Thousands of spectators assembled to watch a grand procession winding three miles long through Chicago on October 27, 1863. They cheered as columns of police, military companies, civic clubs, and religious organizations streamed past. One hundred wagons brimming with farm produce rolled along the unpaved streets. Army musicians played military airs, and marching groups of flag-waving children sang patriotic songs. Spectators jostled to catch glimpses of a carriage draped with tattered Confederate Army flags captured by federal troops.

The parade celebrated the opening of the Northwestern Sanitary Fair, a charity fundraiser organized by the female volunteers of the Chicago branch of the U.S. Sanitary Commission, a private relief agency supporting sick and wounded soldiers of the Union

The main hall at the Northwestern Sanitary Fair. Library of Congress Prints and Photographs Division, LC-DIG-pga-04317.

Army. The Commission's work included delivering the food, clothing, medicine, and other supplies enlisted men needed but were not provided by the federal government. The Chicago branch's stores were running low after caring for the wounded of the hard-fought campaigns of the summer of 1863—hence the fair. The "lady managers" of the Northwestern Fair hoped to bring Chicagoans and their neighbors together, promote patriotic commitment to the Union cause, and encourage the generous support of sick and wounded soldiers.

The fair was more than just a fundraiser; it offered a lens through which to view the Civil War–era popular culture. Indeed the fair's organizers had a more ambitious vision for their event than the traditional American charity bazaar, in which female members of a church congregation decorated a hall and invited members of their community to buy handicrafts and refreshments to benefit local causes. The Sanitary Fair's managers expanded their exposition to attract all who could afford to pay the 75-cent admission fee. They booked one of the city's largest assembly rooms for sale booths stocked with merchandise donated from supporters. McVicker's Theatre served as an art gallery, while a large temporary building called the Machinery Department exhibited the industrial products of the Northwest. One of the city's best-known theaters hosted concerts, lectures, and theatrical performances benefiting the fair.

The Chicago Sanitary Fair's organizers also adapted popular commercial entertainments to appeal to potential customers. The internationally famous attractions of living wonders, mechanical marvels, and historical artifacts of P. T. Barnum's American Museum, located in New York City, influenced the Chicago Fair's Curiosity Shop, including the largest display of war souvenirs and Americana yet seen in the North. In addition to entertaining visitors the fair's relic displays promoted Union nationalism. The Curiosity Shop's displays communicated extreme versions of sectional differences between "civilized" Northerners and their "barbaric" Southern enemy.

The Shop featured a long table with trophies captured from the "secesh" enemy (and described by the *Chicago Tribune*): "guns, cimeters [*sic*], bowie knives of all shapes, butcher-knives of most ferocious aspect, swords, balls, pistols, shells, campstools, etc.—every one of which had a history." To illustrate the assumed incompetence of Confederate women, there was a "secesh bed quilt," a present a Union officer received from a young Southern woman who "may have had an affection for young Federal officers, but she evidently had no taste for embroidery." Southern industry under slavery was demonstrated by "a secesh shoe, it being an effort of a secesh to produce that very necessary article. It shows very plainly that although the secesh may be smart on shackles, they are nothing on shoes." Slavery artifacts were displayed nearby, including a metal collar "which challenged the attention and roused the indignation of all," worn by a contraband slave.

The Curiosity Shop and other attractions at the 1863 Chicago Fair drew sixty thousand visitors over twelve days and raised almost $79,000 for the Sanitary Commission's cause. Its combination of traditional charity, modern entertainment, and sectional feeling was so successful that other Northern cities followed Chicago's lead. Each created its own novelties as civic boosters competed to raise the most money for the Union war effort. From New York to Iowa volunteers organized more than thirty fairs between 1863 and 1865. The largest of these exhibitions, New York's Metropolitan Fair and Philadelphia's Great Central Fair, raised $1 million in total for the cause.

Frequent fair attractions included live animal sideshows, like the 3,600-pound ox named General Grant, advertised as the largest bovine in the world. (He was butchered for a celebratory barbecue at the war's end.) A piece of black bread nicknamed "the Hundred Dollar Loaf" purchased by a soldier at the Battle of Gettysburg for 5 cents made the rounds of the East Coast sanitary fairs, raising $390 as it was sold and resold. Native American dancers and appearances by wartime celebrities like General William T. Sherman drew thousands of spectators. Crowds were thrilled by a mechanized miniature of the *Monitor* and *Merrimack* naval battle, complete with cannon sounds and puffs of smoke. Visitors strolled the winding paths of horticultural halls designed with water features, exotic plants, and wishing wells. Waiters dressed in colonial costumes served corn pudding and pumpkin pie to diners in New England–themed farmhouse restaurants.

Chicagoans copied many of the successful attractions pioneered by earlier exhibitions while planning the last major sanitary fair, in May 1865. The organizers of the exhibits could hardly keep pace with current events. New war trophies arrived daily to stock the fair's Temple of Relics. Volunteers added a wax figure of Jefferson Davis wearing a dress, illustrating the popular Northern myth that the president of the Confederacy was captured by Union troops disguised in his wife's clothing.

The contrast between the figure of Davis in women's clothes and the fair's exhibit of Abraham Lincoln items, including his boyhood log cabin home and souvenirs from his funeral, underlined for Northerners the contrasts between the characters of the so-called Belle of Richmond and their martyred Illinois Rail Splitter.

The Northern public's enthusiasm for the sanitary fair craze faded as the war drew to a close. In 1865, though thousands attended on the days when famous Union generals like Sherman and Ulysses S. Grant visited the fair, organizers raised only $325,000 in support of the Chicago Soldiers' Home, serving disabled Union Army veterans.

Albert Cashier's Secret

JEAN R. FREEDMAN

In the spring of 1914 a Civil War veteran named Albert Cashier arrived at an Illinois state hospital with symptoms of advanced dementia. As a young private Cashier had fought at the Siege of Vicksburg, where he and his comrades broke the spine of the Confederacy, and his name was inscribed on the Illinois victory monument there. He had lived out the intervening years in modest circumstances, working as a farmhand, a laborer, and, on occasion, a street lamplighter, one of the many former soldiers whose civilian lives never

Jennie Hodgers, aka Albert Cashier. Courtesy of the National Park Service.

achieve the glory of their wartime service. He was destined for the same obscurity in death, had it not been for a secret that the state hospital made public: Albert Cashier was actually a woman named Jennie Hodgers.

Little is known of Hodgers's early life; she was born in Ireland and came to the United States while still a young girl. No one knows exactly when or why she began to dress and identify as a boy, but long before the first shots were fired on Fort Sumter, she had abandoned skirts for trousers. On August 6, 1862, as Albert Cashier, he joined the 95th Illinois Infantry after a cursory medical examination that required recruits only to show their hands and feet.

Though the shortest soldier in his company, Cashier was one of the bravest. At Vicksburg he was captured while on a reconnaissance mission but escaped by attacking a guard, seizing his gun, and outrunning his captors till he reached his comrades. On another occasion, when his company's flag was taken down by enemy fire, he climbed a tree and attached the tattered flag to a high branch while snipers' bullets soared past him.

Albert was not the only Civil War soldier who was born a woman but identified as a man, finding ways to bathe and dress alone in that least private of environments, the military encampment. Historians have uncovered accounts of hundreds of women who passed as men to fight, some of whom, like Albert, had been passing long before the fighting started.

Cashier's fellow soldiers recalled him as a modest young man who kept his shirt buttoned to the chin, hiding the place where an Adam's apple should be. His comrades teased him because he had no beard, but this was an army of boys as well as men, and he was not the only beardless recruit in her company. He resisted sharing a tent with anyone but made close friends among his fellow soldiers; with one of them he briefly owned a business after the war. Despite his diminutive size he could "do as much work as anyone in the Company," one soldier attested.

Cashier served in General Nathaniel P. Banks's Red River Campaign in the spring of 1864, marching for miles in the Louisiana heat; by December of that year he was in Nashville, fighting with the Army of the Cumberland in its hard-won victory over John Bell Hood's forces. His final combat experience came during the siege of Mobile, Alabama, a fight that did not end until after Robert E. Lee's surrender at Appomattox Courthouse.

By all accounts Cashier never avoided danger—indeed at times he seemed to court it—but despite his frequent participation in combat he was never wounded severely enough to require medical treatment. A combination of good luck, good health, and skillful soldiering kept Cashier from the attention of those who might penetrate his disguise. Cashier served an entire three-year enlistment without anyone guessing his birth sex.

Albert Cashier mustered out of the service with the rest of his regiment on August 17, 1865, and went back to Illinois. Cashier could not read or write, but working steadily and honestly he made an adequate, if hardly affluent, living as a handyman, a farm laborer, and a janitor, turning his work-worn hands to whatever came his way, supplementing his income with a veteran's pension. People in the town of Saunemin, where Cashier eventually settled, may have wondered why the shy young veteran never married, but no one thought it strange for a man to live alone and make a living at any job he could find.

It all came crashing down when Cashier, elderly and enfeebled, entered the state hospital for the insane. There, once doctors discovered his birth sex, he was required to abandon the identity he had maintained for decades and live in the narrow hallway that early twentieth-century America had designed for women.

Officials at the Illinois state hospital forced Cashier, now forced to identify as a woman, to wear skirts for the first time in over fifty years; he found the garb restrictive and humiliating and perhaps more dangerous than the sniper fire he had outwitted so many years before. Unused to walking in the long, cumbersome garments deemed appropriate for his birth sex, he tripped and fell, breaking a hip that never properly healed. Bedridden and depressed, his health continuing to decline, he died on October 11, 1915, less than two years before women gained the right to serve openly—if minimally—in the U.S. Armed Forces.

By the time of Cashier's death the presence of female soldiers on both sides of the Civil War was well known and well documented. Their exact number is unknown because their service had to be clandestine, but the ones whose stories we know offer a fascinating glimpse of women who pushed against the boundaries of their Victorian confinement at a time when American women could not vote, serve on juries, attend most colleges, or practice most professions and who, when they married, lost all property rights in most states. Some women were discovered when they were wounded, others when they gave birth, still others when they were taken prisoner. Some women soldiers were discovered only when their bodies were being dressed for burial, and some were only discovered years after the fighting stopped.

The female Civil War soldiers were not the first American women to fight on the battlefield; Deborah Sampson of Massachusetts served for nearly two years during the Revolution before her sex was discovered in a military hospital. (After being honorably discharged Sampson received a veteran's pension for her service, which went to her children upon her death.) Nor would they be the last. But their service came at a crucial time: when the foundation of the Republic had shifted to allow an expansion of individual rights, when the very nature of freedom was being questioned and the bonds of restricted servitude were being broken, and when the unfulfilled promise that "all men are created equal" was tentatively held out to an expectant generation of American women who, almost twenty years earlier at Seneca Falls, had inscribed their gender onto Thomas Jefferson's ringing prose.

It would be many years before their sisters-in-arms would reap the benefit of their fledgling feminist agitation—in a world where the word *feminist* did not even exist. Like many pioneers, they sowed the seeds that they would not live to see burst into flower.

Blacks, Baseball, and the Civil War

GEORGE KIRSCH

The Civil War era revolutionized the still nascent game of baseball in America—and not just for whites. During the war black baseball clubs increased; in the postwar period they sought recognition and equal treatment by white clubs and state and national baseball associations. But as in so many parts of national life, those achievements were ultimately limited and soon foreshortened; while black players gained respect from some members of the ball-playing fraternity, racist stereotypes, discrimination, and segregation barred them from achieving equality on America's diamonds.

Black ballplayers shared in the baseball mania that began in the 1840s in Manhattan and Brooklyn and then spread, during the late 1850s and early 1860s, to dozens of cities and towns. During these years most Northern blacks were impoverished, but a few of the more privileged could afford the time and expense of baseball. African Americans founded their own clubs in cities from New York to New Orleans. Most of these clubs recruited members from the upper ranks of black society, especially artisans, shopkeepers, clerks, and teachers.

The start of the Civil War disrupted ball playing by both whites and blacks, but the following year brought a baseball revival. But if baseball playing by blacks increased, so

A black baseball team in Danbury, Connecticut, in 1870. Library of Congress Prints and Photographs Division, LC-DIG-ppmsca-11502.

did discrimination against them. Newspaper reporters used racist stereotypes to describe blacks playing baseball: on October 17, 1862, the *Brooklyn Daily Eagle* published a brief account of a match between the Unknowns and the Monitors. Its headline introduced the contest as a novelty: "A New Sensation in Baseball Circles—Sambo as a Ball-Player and Dinah as an Emulator." The reporter observed that everyone in the large crowd was "as black as the ace of spades."

But the report also gives some clues about the history and scope of black baseball. The reporter's comment that the spectators included "a number of old and well known players, who seemed to enjoy the game more heartily than if they had been the players themselves," suggests that baseball had long been a familiar pastime in African American communities. He added, "The assemblage included women and children: Dinah, all eyes, was there to applaud. . . . All appeared to have a very jolly time, and the little piccaninnies laughed with the rest."

Before, during, and after the Civil War black baseball was inextricably linked to the campaign for African American civil and political rights. On July 4, 1859, Joshua Giddings, a white antislavery Republican congressman from Ohio, showed his support for desegregation and equality in baseball by playing in a game with African Americans. During and after the war members of Philadelphia's Pythian Base Ball Club, an elite African American association, were activists in local and state campaigns for black equal opportunity. In 1863 the club's secretary, Jacob C. White Jr., and the shortstop and captain of its first nine, Octavius V. Catto, served on a committee that recruited soldiers for the Union Army and joined a local African American militia. During the late 1860s Catto campaigned for the desegregation of Philadelphia's streetcars and for blacks' right to vote. After voting on Election Day of 1871 he encountered Frank Kelly, a Democratic Party supporter; the two got into a fight, and Kelly shot and killed Catto.

In 1859 in Rochester, New York, Frederick Douglass Jr., son of the renowned abolitionist, played baseball with the integrated Charter Oak Juniors; after the war he was one of the founders of the Alerts Base Ball Club of Washington. Another son, Charles Douglass, third baseman for the Alerts, spent three years with the Freedman's Bureau before earning a position as a clerk in the Treasury Department. In 1869 he joined Washington's Mutual Club and became its corresponding secretary. In August of that year the Mutuals (with Charles Douglass on its first nine) headed north for a tour of upstate New York towns that had provided safe houses on the Underground Railroad.

The Thirteenth, Fourteenth, and Fifteenth Amendments, ratified after the war, redefined state and federal citizenship and extended civil and political rights, but they included no provisions for equality in private, voluntary activities. Nevertheless officers of the leading black clubs of Brooklyn, New York City, Philadelphia, and Washington sought equal treatment by the white ball-playing fraternity. Some of them were on good terms with white club officials and frequently obtained permission to use their grounds for feature contests. White umpires sometimes officiated at their games. The Pythians enjoyed harmonious relations with the officers of the city's powerful Athletics Base Ball Club, who gave them permission to use their field for major matches.

All of the premier white clubs that competed for unofficial state and national championships drew the line at interracial competition; according to the *Spirit of the Times* of Wilkes-Barre, Pennsylvania, the Athletics "would have nothing to do with the dark votaries of the bat and ball." (A few lesser-known white teams did, however, play black teams.) Exceptions included an 1869 match arranged by Colonel Thomas Fitzgerald, editor of another local paper, the *City Item*. The historic encounter attracted a large crowd that watched the Philadelphia Olympics rout the Pythians, 44–23. The *Spirit* praised the experiment, declaring, "Old-time prejudices are melting away in this country." It noted that interracial sporting contests were common in England and other countries, adding, "It is not considered outside our own territory a lessening of dignity nor in the least disparaging to white men that they contend with blacks." That journal hoped, "Now that the prejudice has been broken through here, it will be entirely swept away."

A few weeks later the Pythians defeated the City Item's first nine 27–17 at the Athletics' ball field. In September the Washington Olympics manhandled the black Alerts of that city on the grounds of the Washington Nationals 56–4 in front of a large assembly of men and women of both races, including federal government officials. The *Brooklyn Eagle* observed that the game provided

a striking illustration of the social change of the last eight years. . . . Until now when a question of color has arisen, it has been solely on a claim of equal civil and political rights for the negro. . . . It is not a political or civil right or a privilege of citizenship that a colored base ball club shall be permitted to challenge a white base ball club, and that the challenge shall be accepted. It is purely a voluntary matter, having nothing to do with any law of Congress or amendment to the Constitution. The peaceful way in which this new war of races is carried on is significant. How long is it since such a game as that proposed to be played to-day would have provoked a riot?

In September 1870 in Boston a white club and a black club, both called the Resolutes, competed for the right to use that name. The "colored" Resolutes triumphed, 25–15. The *New York Clipper* described the outcome as a victory for the "sons of Ham, who fought nobly for their cherished title, out-playing their fair-faced friends at every point in the game, especially in the field."

Despite these occasional interracial matches, white baseball clubs excluded black clubs from participation in tournaments and membership in state and national baseball associations. The sponsors of an 1870 Chicago amateur competition barred that city's Blue Stockings Base Ball Club, an African American organization composed mainly of hotel and restaurant waiters. The Blue Stockings thought that the white clubs feared the humiliation of losing to a black nine. The *Chicago Tribune* denied that allegation but conceded that the white teams included some young men of high social standing who "were not disposed to burlesque the tournament by the admission of a colored club of inferior capacity, even though the gate receipts should suffer thereby."

State meetings followed the same segregationist policy. In the fall of 1867 the Pythians sent White to Harrisburg to present the club's credentials to the Pennsylvania State Association of Base Ball Players. He reported to the members, "Whilst all expressed sympathy for our club, a few only . . . expressed a willingness to vote for our admission. . . . Numbers of the others openly said that they would in justice to the opinion of the clubs they represented be compelled, tho against their personal feelings, to vote against our admission." Supporters advocated a discreet withdrawal to avoid a humiliating rejection by ballot, and White reluctantly concurred. Similarly in 1870 the New York State Base Ball Association approved a motion that if any of the clubs admitted were found to be composed of people of color, their association membership would be voided. The *Clipper* objected and advised black clubs to establish "a National organization of their own."

The Pythians faced the same resistance at the national level. In December 1867 they applied for admission to the National Association of Base Ball Players. Its nominating committee "unanimously reported against the admission of any club which may be composed of one or two colored persons." It added, "If colored clubs were admitted there would be in all probability some division of feeling whereas, by excluding them no injury could result to anybody, and the possibility of any rupture being created on political grounds would be avoided."

By 1870 baseball was widely recognized as America's national pastime—and, like much of the national culture, was tightly segregated. While a few African American ballplayers joined professional clubs during the 1880s, another six decades passed before Jackie Robinson broke the color barrier and revived the campaign to achieve equal opportunity on America's diamonds.

4. The Battlefield

Introduction

GARY GALLAGHER

Anyone hoping to understand the military dimension of the Civil War should keep several basic points in mind. The first is the vast sweep of the fighting, which played out in three principal geographical arenas. The Eastern Theater, which included most of Virginia, parts of western Maryland, and the lower tier of counties in central Pennsylvania, witnessed by far the most concentrated combat: more men became casualties within just twenty miles of Fredericksburg, Virginia, than in any other Confederate state as a whole.

The Western Theater, in contrast, sprawled across several states and offered a moveable feast of military action. Early in the conflict it stretched southward from the Ohio River to the Gulf of Mexico and westward from the Appalachian Mountains to the Mississippi River. By the end of the conflict western armies had fought through Georgia and into the Carolinas, setting up a final scene at Durham Station, North Carolina, where General William Tecumseh Sherman accepted the capitulation of the last significant Confederate field army. The Western Theater contained crucial logistical resources, as well as New Orleans, the Confederacy's largest city and most important port, and Nashville, Memphis, Atlanta, and other vital centers of commerce and communication.

The third theater was descriptively named the Trans-Mississippi and encompassed the entire region that lay beyond the great river. Arkansas, Missouri, Texas, western Louisiana, Indian Territory (present-day Oklahoma), and the distant territories of New Mexico, Arizona, and Colorado figured in military planning for both sides, though operations west of the Mississippi River never rivaled in importance those in the Eastern or Western Theaters. U.S. armies gained early control in parts of this region, especially those closest to the Mississippi, while other parts, most notably Texas, experienced almost no Union incursions.

A second point to keep in mind is that despite the war's outcome, for much of its duration either side could have won. Neither the United States nor the Confederacy possessed a clear advantage in resources of high command. Graduates of West Point, who had served in subordinate roles during the war with Mexico, advanced to the top echelons of responsibility in both armies. These men had taken classes together at West Point, learned the same lessons under Generals Winfield Scott and Zachary Taylor in Mexico, and shared a military heritage stretching back to the Revolution and even earlier. Some inevitably applied their training and knowledge more effectively than others, and each side had its share of successes and failures. But on the whole the quality of generals proved very similar.

Superior economic capacity and manpower are well-known Union advantages. The loyal white population, from which more than 90 percent of Union soldiers would be drawn, outnumbered the Confederate white population by nearly 4 to 1. Enslaved labor allowed the Confederacy to mobilize a much higher percentage of its military-age white males (at least 80 percent, compared to about 50 percent for the United States), and border states sent 75,000 men into Southern armies. But approximately 100,000 black men and 105,000 white Unionists from the Confederacy fought in blue uniforms. Overall the United States mustered approximately 2.2 million men into the army, compared to 800,000 to 900,000 for the Confederacy.

But the balance sheet also included significant Confederate advantages. Most obviously conditions for victory favored the Confederacy. Confederate success required no projection of military power into the United States and no occupation of enemy territory; the Confederacy needed only to convince the Northern citizenry that subduing the rebellion would cost too much human and material treasure. In this struggle between two democratic republics, civilian populations would be the key—something perceptive political and military leaders on both sides realized. Whatever the real condition of armies in the field, the war would end when one side's civilians reached their breaking point. The American Revolution presented a powerful example of how a weaker combatant could prevail by exhausting a stronger one's will to persevere.

Other factors similarly favored the rebels. Spread over more than 750,000 square miles and served by a substandard transportation network, the Confederacy posed massive logistical obstacles to invading Federal forces. It is instructive to think of the Union's challenge regarding supplies in this way: every time the Army of the Potomac stopped for the night, it became the second-largest city in the Confederacy, behind New Orleans. Moreover a 3,500-mile Confederate coastline and open border with Mexico rendered an effective Union naval blockade virtually impossible. (On the negative side major rivers such as the Mississippi, the Tennessee, the Cumberland, and the James ran in the wrong direction from the Confederate perspective, offering Union forces attractive avenues of advance.)

Finally, fighting for home ground also gave Confederates an edge. Soldiers defending hearth and family typically display greater resolve than those seeking to conquer and occupy an opponent's territory.

In terms of overarching strategic goals, the Confederacy sought to counteract whatever moves the United States initiated, hoping to defend its borders and establish independence. Lincoln and his advisers confronted the far more daunting task of marshaling and projecting military power to compel the wayward states to return to the Union. For the most part the Confederacy stood on the strategic defensive, though always with an eye toward landing counterblows that would cripple the Union. The Lincoln government necessarily pursued an offensive strategy, and the president himself pressed commanders to apply superior Union resources relentlessly.

General in Chief Winfield Scott took the lead in devising a strategy to defeat the Confederacy. In the spring of 1861 he proposed a naval blockade of the Confederacy and a combined army-navy strike down the Mississippi River to split the southern republic into two pieces. Should the rebels continue to resist after the loss of key ports and control of the Mississippi, the United States might have to "conquer the seceding States by invading armies." Scott's blueprint, dubbed the "Anaconda Plan" because it sought to squeeze the life from the Confederacy, anticipated, in broad outline, how the war unfolded militarily. Beginning in 1861 Union naval and land forces began closing Confederate ports, and control of the Mississippi passed into Union hands by mid-1863. Intensive pressure against Confederate forces in Virginia, Tennessee, Georgia, and the Carolinas in 1864–65 finally settled the issue.

Still the success of that initial plan should not lead anyone to embrace what might be called the Appomattox syndrome. That flawed way of looking at the conflict begins with knowledge of U.S. victory, assumes that was the only possible outcome, and works backward looking for evidence of why the Confederacy failed. Stronger popular will in the United States did win out, but only after Confederate military successes bred political strife and created moments of despair in the loyal states that, as late as the summer and early autumn of 1864, almost settled the issue in favor of the rebels.

Perhaps the most important point to keep in mind about the military aspects of the war is the nature of the men who fought: it was a war waged by citizen-soldiers. Although members of slaveholding households were overrepresented among the Confederacy's enlisted men and officers, the armies largely mirrored their respective societies. Both sides eventually resorted to conscription, but a majority of Union and Confederate soldiers were volunteers and should not be confused with professional soldiers. Continuing the antimilitaristic American tradition rooted in opposition to British regulars during the colonial and revolutionary eras, the Civil War's citizen-soldiers, far from emblematic of a militarized nation-state, carried forward a republican tradition exemplified by George Washington and the Continental Army.

The memory of the nation's greatest military struggle remains evident at places such as Gettysburg and Shiloh, in the system of national cemeteries created to hold more than a third of a million Union dead, and in our national Memorial Day. But the most obvious legacy of the battlefield's verdict lies in the continuing presence of the American republic, salvaged by the soldiers who, as one Northern newspaper commented at the end of the war, "were our friends and brothers and sons, our fellow-citizens, our *people*."

Blue, Gray, and Everything in Between

MICHAEL O. VARHOLA

While the colors blue and gray are almost iconically associated with the opposing ground forces of the Civil War, early in the conflict many regiments reporting for duty on either side were much more colorfully attired. Some rebel troops wore blue; some Northern troops wore gray; units on both sides sported every shade of red, green, black, white, and even tartan; and uniform patterns were almost completely nonstandardized.

This discordant variety of military garb reflected not just diverse aesthetic sensibilities but in some cases ideological ones as well, and was a virtual barometer for the lack of strong central organization in either the Confederate or the Federal camp. Uniforms for volunteer units were produced not according to the specifications of national war departments but according to those of state militia authorities or even units themselves and were issued not from central quartermaster depots but from local storehouses, or even ordered from tailors by individuals.

These disparate supply systems were not well suited to clothing the many troops that would ultimately be called into service for the war or to supplying them for the extended period it would last. Even the centralized mechanisms that were in place early in the conflict did not reflect the organization that would be required to outfit the two great military machines that eventually faced each other.

As late as April 1861, for example, the Confederate quartermaster general was placing orders for regular army uniforms that included blue battle tunics. And the Confederate system of commutation, in which the government reimbursed volunteers for providing their own uniforms, ensured that many troops wore civilian clothes, in whole or in part, the first year or two of the war.

Some of the most familiar of the exotic uniforms were those worn by Zouaves—light infantrymen clad in baggy pantaloons, gaiters, braided jackets, sashes, and tasseled fezzes or turbans, clothing more typical of North Africa than North America. Such uniforms were in fact inspired by those first worn by French colonial troops in Algeria in the decade before the U.S. Civil War, and both the Union and the Confederacy had units that wore them.

While the Zouaves' colorful uniforms are well known, they were not unique in their diversity; atypical uniforms, many with an ethnic emphasis, were used by units on both sides. Some were patterned on those worn by various European troop types, especially skirmishers (e.g., French chasseurs, German jaegers).

The 79th New York Volunteer Infantry, the "Highland Guard," provides a particularly colorful example. Formed under the auspices of state militia authorities in 1858, it was essentially a Scottish American tribute unit that took its numerical designation and the tartan for its uniforms from the British military's 79th Regiment of Foot, the "Cameron Highlanders" (it was even backed in part by the brother of Secretary of War Simon Cameron). Beyond these cosmetic commonalities, however, it had no actual connection to the original Scottish unit and was more or less a privately funded social club.

The official uniform for the New York Highland Guard's soldiers included wool trousers patterned with the chiefly red-and-black plaid tartan of the Scottish 79th; a dark blue jacket with red cording and red cuffs, and collars with white piping; a dark blue boat-shaped Scottish cap called a glengarry, complemented with a plaid band; and low-quarter leather shoes with false buckles.

New York State Militia guidelines precluded unit members from wearing kilts, but they ignored these provisions and did so anyway when on parade, wearing nonstandard civilian-pattern versions in the same tartan as their trousers, holding them up with suspenders. They paired these with red and white-diced hose and sporrans—pouches worn with kilts that took the place of pockets—made of nappy white horsehide and accented with black tassels.

Members of the Garibaldi Guard parade past President Lincoln. Library of Congress Prints and Photographs Division, LC-DIG-ppmsca-31563.

Another New York unit distinguished by its couture was the 39th New York Volunteer Infantry Regiment, colloquially known as the "Garibaldi Guard" or the "Italian Legion." Many of its members were already combat veterans, followers of the revolutionary leader Giuseppe Garibaldi during the Second Italian War of Independence. They showed their commitment to Garibaldi's ideals by adopting blousy red shirts similar to those they had worn as soldiers in Italy. (There was also, interestingly, a Louisiana-based "Garibaldi Legion" of Italians that fought for the Confederacy and wore red jackets.)

Southern militia and volunteer units were just as likely to have atypical uniforms as their Northern counterparts and also included both Zouaves and other sorts of troops. A notable example of the former was Wheat's Special Battalion, a Louisiana infantry outfit made up largely of immigrants, street thugs, dockworkers, and military adventurers.

At the other end of the social spectrum stood the Washington Artillery, a New Orleans militia battalion that had been formed in 1838, fought in the Mexican-American War of 1846–48, and functioned as an exclusive men's club. Prospective members had to apply, pay a fee, and be accepted by an examination committee. The Washington Artillery dress uniform included a dark blue frock coat with red collar, sky-blue trousers (with a gold stripe along the outer seam for officers and a red one for enlisted men), and a red kepi with a blue band and a brass device consisting of crossed cannons and the letters "WA" (augmented with a pelican for officers). Enlisted men's uniforms also had red cuffs. Brass buttons, belt buckles, and epaulettes (gold for officers), emblazoned with various forms of pelican or the letters "WA" or "NO" as appropriate, buff-white leather accoutrements (black for officers), and white gloves and gaiters completed the ensemble.

The Clinch Rifles of Augusta, Georgia, was another unit formed by the social elite of its community. When the War between the States began, its uniform was patterned after the newest U.S. Army infantry uniform. Following the European tradition for infantrymen, however, the frock coat and trousers were forest green in color with gold braid trim, as was the forage cap, or kepi, worn by such troops even for dress purposes (and generally only in the field by regular units).

Soon after the first shots of the Civil War were fired, the exotic uniforms began to disappear; as the war escalated and then ground on for months, then years, these colorful outfits became increasingly rare. Many of them were not practical for combat, were too expensive or logistically difficult to maintain or replace, or were too easily confused with enemy uniforms (as was the case with the uniforms of the Washington Artillery).

Some units did maintain muted versions or elements of their original uniforms, especially those organized as Zouaves, whose uniforms had the benefit of being generally well-suited to hot weather and rough terrain. Predominantly, however, the realities of supplying great armies dictated that the opposing central governments overseeing the war effort issue clothing in the uniform styles and colors that are most often associated with them. Countless patterns converged into a much narrower range dominated by standardized frock coats, jackets, trousers, and forage caps, and the broad palette of colors was reduced, for the most part, to just two.

So the festive diversity of uniforms largely vanished, leaving the opposing ground forces clad primarily in the two familiar and iconic colors. And with the colorful pageantry went the idea that the war was a grand adventure, displaced by the brutal realization that it was something far more grim and industrialized, fought not by individuals but by monolithic forces of blue and gray.

The War Comes Home for Lee

Jamie Stiehm

Disunion hit home swiftly for Robert E. Lee, the Virginia colonel who spurned President Lincoln's offer to lead the Union forces just before the Civil War broke out. Lee, as everyone knows, went on to lead the Confederate Army. Less well known is that, soon after he sided with the South, he also lost his home.

The mansion, then known as Arlington House and today as the Custis-Lee Mansion, sits on a hilltop across the Potomac from Washington, amid what is now Arlington National Cemetery. The area around it was occupied by Union forces in May 1861, and soon after they decided to commandeer Lee's house itself. Orchards on the vast expanse of Arlington acres were clear-cut to make room for roads and telegraph poles. Union soldiers drilled on land that had been tilled by enslaved people for generations. A nameless number who died at the First Battle of Bull Run were later buried on the grounds in a not so subtle

The front of the Custis-Lee Mansion in Arlington, Virginia. Library of Congress Prints and Photographs Division, LC-H812-T-L07-020-B.

message that their blood was on Lee's hands (though he did not lead troops into the Civil War's first engagement). Lincoln himself rode over to the barracks and tents at Arlington to shore up soldiers' morale after the devastating Bull Run loss.

But the occupation's principal significance was its symbolism. Cherished land in Yankee hands was a Confederate nightmare—even more so when word got out that William Tecumseh Sherman was given his general's command in one of the mansion's parlors. The seizure struck a strikingly personal and visible blow to Lee, a figure fast developing a larger-than-life reputation in the South.

Arlington House was the center of Lee's prewar life: he and his betrothed were wed under one of its arches, and his wife gave birth to six of their seven children there. But the house had a national significance as well. Finished in 1818 it was built to honor the legacy of George Washington, an ancestor by marriage of Mrs. Lee. (Martha Washington was Mrs. Lee's great-grandmother, a fact she never let Yankees "thieves" forget.) Moreover Mrs. Lee's maiden name, Custis, was synonymous with great slaveholding wealth. She never got over the blow of packing and leaving her inherited family property, built by her father, George Washington Parke Custis. She, not her husband, owned the house; in fact the Confederate general's name was not on the deed. By law the property went directly from Mrs. Lee to the federal government, for the price of $26,800. As Mrs. Lee left for good that spring of 1861, she defiantly placed the house keys in the hands of a trusted slave, Selina Gray.

Lee was more resigned about the occupation of Arlington House than was his wife: "It is better to make up our minds to a general loss. They cannot take away the remembrances of the spot and the memories of those that to us render it sacred." To a daughter he wrote, "I should have preferred it to have been wiped from the earth, its beautiful hill sunk, and its sacred trees buried, rather than to have been degraded."

Union forces went about putting Arlington House and its grounds to practical use. The Freedman's Village, a thriving community and school for free blacks, was constructed on the Arlington estate in 1863. School was a radical concept in a time and place where enslaved people were rarely educated to become literate. Arlington, antebellum America's best address, became a symbol of emancipation. As if to prove the point, the brilliant Bostonian abolitionist Julia Ward Howe composed the searing verses of "The Battle Hymn of the Republic" after visiting the Arlington wartime encampment.

As Civil War casualties mounted, Lincoln's trusted military aide, Montgomery C. Meigs, decided to "encircle" Arlington house with bodies of war dead, deliberately burying some Union Army officers in Mrs. Lee's flower garden and the modest slave quarters. Each grave was but a few steps away from the front door. Meigs, a raging creative mind in a quartermaster general's uniform, actually knew Lee from a prewar army engineering project. In conversation with the president after the high-water mark of Gettysburg, Meigs was inspired to suggest Lincoln transform the beautiful plantation by the river into a place of remembrance, a "field of honor." Meigs's son died in the war, giving the thought a touch of personal pathos. The president, anguished about the rising death toll, immediately approved the idea. Meigs himself is buried at Arlington.

Seizing Arlington made sound military sense, largely for the property's strategic heights overlooking Washington. More important, banishing the antebellum Lee-Custis family from their perch was an extraordinary political move for Lincoln. He was, after all, a stranger to town and country up against a celebrated warhorse. Nevertheless it would take years, and hundreds of thousands of lives, for the president to win his fight. And yet to this day the argument goes on, frozen in neoclassical marble, as the lofty Lee mansion and the gleaming shrine of the Lincoln Memorial stare at each other from opposite sides of the Potomac.

The Boys of War

CATE LINEBERRY

With hopes of adventure and glory, tens of thousands of boys under the age of eighteen answered the call of the Civil War, many of them rushing to join Union and Confederate troops in the earliest days of battle. Both sides had recruitment rules that barred underage men from enlisting, but that didn't stop those who wanted to be part of the action: some enlisted without their parents' permission and lied about their age or bargained with recruiters for a trial period, while others joined along with their older brothers and fathers whose partisan passions overwhelmed their parental senses. Most of the youngest boys became drummers, messengers, and orderlies, but thousands of others fought alongside the men.

As each side scrambled to get troops into the field in the early days of the war, many of these boys went to battle with just a few weeks of training. It didn't take long for them to understand what they'd gotten themselves into. Elisha Stockwell Jr., from Alma, Wisconsin, was fifteen when he enlisted. After the Battle of Shiloh in April 1862, he wrote, "I want to say, as we lay there and the shells were flying over us, my thoughts went back to my home, and I thought what a foolish boy I was to run away and get into such a mess as I was in. I would have been glad to have seen my father coming after me."

While some regiments protected their boy recruits by sending them to the rear when fighting broke out, others expected them to work in the front lines as stretcher bearers. Harry Kieffer, a musician for the 150th Pennsylvania, wrote about his experience at Gettysburg: "[I am called] away for a moment to look after some poor fellow whose arm is off at the shoulder, and it was just time I got away, too, for immediately a shell plunges into the sod where I had been sitting, tearing my stretcher to tatters." A sixteen-year-old musician, John A. Cockerill, who was also at Shiloh, later wrote:

> I passed . . . the corpse of a beautiful boy in gray who lay with his blond curls scattered about his face and his hand folded peacefully across his breast. He was clad in a bright and neat

uniform, well garnished with gold, which seemed to tell the story of a loving mother and sisters who had sent their household pet to the field of war. His neat little hat lying beside him bore the number of a Georgia regiment. . . . He was about my age. . . . At the sight of the poor boy's corpse, I burst into a regular boo hoo and started on.

Perhaps the most famous boy of the war was John Joseph Klem, better known as Johnny Clem. At only nine years old and roughly four feet tall, Clem tried unsuccessfully to enlist with the 3rd Ohio in May 1861, soon after Lincoln first issued the call for volunteers. Clem left his father, brother, and sister in Newark, Ohio, to join; his mother had been killed in a train accident earlier that year. Undeterred by the rejection of the 3rd Ohio, Clem tried his luck with the 22nd Michigan, which allowed him to join as an unofficial drummer boy. Until he was added to the muster roll in 1863, the $13 he earned each month came from donations made by the officers of his regiment.

Clem became a celebrity for his actions at Chickamauga, Georgia, in September 1863. The 22nd Michigan was assigned to defend Horseshoe Ridge, but Confederate soldiers soon surrounded it. A Confederate officer spotted Clem, who was armed with a musket modified for his size, and demanded that he surrender. In the face of danger Clem shot

Johnny Clem, perhaps the most famous drummer boy of the war, shot a Confederate officer who had ordered him to surrender. Courtesy of the Massachusetts Commanders Military Order of the Loyal Legion and the U.S. Army Military History Institute.

the officer and ran, making his way back to Union lines. Though he escaped unharmed, 389 of the 455 men who made up the 22nd Michigan were captured, wounded, or killed in the battle.

Sixteen days later Confederates captured Clem while he was riding on a wagon train carrying provisions to nearby Chattanooga, Tennessee. He was paroled after just three days and sent to Camp Chase, Ohio, where he was exchanged as a prisoner of war. On his way back to his regiment Clem told his story to General William S. Rosecrans, who had been relieved of his command of the Army of the Cumberland following the Union defeat at Chickamauga. Impressed with the boy's actions, Rosecrans informed the press. The *Columbus Daily Express* wrote, "The little fellow told his story simply and modestly, and the General determined to honor his bravery." How modestly Clem told his story is debated, but people in the North embraced it. The "Drummer Boy of Chickamauga," who had been promoted to sergeant, was now a Union hero. The daughter of Treasury Secretary Salmon P. Chase asked her father to honor Clem with a medal, which Clem wore in at least one of the many pictures taken by photographers hoping to profit from the young boy's newfound celebrity.

As his fame grew, Clem continued to serve in the Union Army. He mainly carried dispatches, suffering two minor wounds in Atlanta. Despite stories that claim Clem's drum was destroyed at Shiloh, giving him the nickname "Johnny Shiloh" and inspiring the song "The Drummer Boy of Shiloh," it's unlikely he was ever there.

On July 6, 1864, the War Department forbade any officers to enlist any soldier under sixteen or face severe penalties. Almost a month later Lieutenant Colonel Henry Dean of the 22nd Michigan requested that Clem—who had changed his name during the war from John Joseph Klem to John Lincoln Clem in honor of the president—be released from service so that he "may have a better opportunity for educating himself."

While awaiting his discharge, Clem went to Carlinsville, Illinois, where he started school. But the war remained very much on his mind; in a letter to Captain Sanford C. Kellogg, an officer in his former unit, in September he wrote, "I am going to school here and am very much pleased with the institution and my schoolmates. Please tell my Colonel to write to me as soon as he can. . . . How is Georgie Lutz getting along? Who has my little pony now? . . . If any of the officers are willing to write to me I would be very much pleased to hear from them."

Clem graduated from high school in 1870 and was nominated to West Point by President Ulysses S. Grant. He failed the entrance exam several times, but Grant nevertheless appointed him a second lieutenant in the army. After serving forty-three years in the military, Clem retired with the rank of major general—the last Civil War veteran to actively serve in the army. He died in 1937 and was buried at Arlington National Cemetery.

Though he became one of the most famous drummer boys of the war, Clem was just one of thousands of young men who proved to be as brave as the men in their regiments. At least forty-eight boys under eighteen—eleven of whom were under sixteen—received the Congressional Medal of Honor for their extraordinary valor in action. The youngest were mostly drummers: Willie Johnston, eleven, was the only drummer in his brigade to hold on to his instrument during the Peninsula Campaign's heavy fighting; Orion Howe, fourteen, was a drummer who, despite being severely wounded, remained on the battlefield at Vicksburg, Mississippi, until he had reported that troops needed more cartridges; and William Horsfall, fourteen, was a drummer who saved the life of a wounded officer lying between the lines at Corinth, Mississippi. John Cook, fifteen, was a bugler who volunteered to act as a cannoneer under enemy fire at Antietam, Maryland, while Corporal Thomas C. Murphy, sixteen, who was born in Ireland, voluntarily crossed the line of heavy fire at Vicksburg carrying a message to stop the firing of one Union regiment on another.

These and the other boys who served, whether as drummers, orderlies, or soldiers, risked their lives alongside men twice their age and, sometimes, size. Some became prisoners of war, while others were killed in the thick of battle or died from diseases that ravaged even the strongest men. Those who were lucky enough to survive were often left with a lifetime of haunted memories.

The Purchase by Blood

CAROL BUNDY

Two cousins, on the field at battle's start, catch each other's eye, salute, and then—"when next I looked," Oliver Wendell Holmes Jr. writes of his cousin, James Jackson Lowell, "he was gone." At Cedar Mountain, Captain Henry Sturgis Russell is captured because he has stayed to tend the wounds of his friend, Major James Savage. But once in Confederate hands the two are parted: Russell is exchanged, while Savage begins the slow decline that will end in his lonely death at the hands of incompetent surgeons in a Confederate hospital.

At Antietam, Lieutenant Colonel Wilder Dwight, a lawyer in his civilian life, is mortally wounded and trapped between the lines, forced to lie there alone and exposed as the battle rages. Pulling from his pocket the letter he had begun that morning to his mother, Dwight continues to write, and does so until Rupert Sadler, a man whom Dwight had acquitted from a murder charge before the war, finds the courage to run out with water and join Dwight in no man's land.

Soldiering, particularly in the Civil War, was not a solitary act but something done in community. Because regiments were raised within very limited geographical areas, men marched off to war surrounded by workmates, childhood friends, relatives—cousins and brothers. This produced great solidarity within the ranks, and the attendant sense of community did much to maintain morale. But such homogeneous regiments also meant that losses in battle were felt disproportionately within the civilian population.

These soldiers—Lowell, Holmes, Russell, Savage, and Dwight—were part of the elite community surrounding the 20th Massachusetts and the 2nd Massachusetts Infantry, two regiments loaded with the sons of Boston's bluest blood. Like the young British aristocrats who left the playing fields of Eton and Harrow for Ypres and the Somme, the officers of the 20th and 2nd Mass Infantry clung to almost medieval notions of valor and fell in battle in disproportionately high numbers. Of two thousand Union regiments, the 20th Mass ranks fifth in losses sustained. At the Battle of Ball's Bluff the 20th Massachusetts lost thirteen out of twenty-two officers. Less than a year later, at Cedar Mountain, Virginia, an equally insignificant location, the 2nd Mass lost sixteen out of twenty-three officers.

The losses sustained in these two minor engagements brought home the cost of war to the wealthiest and most influential families in Massachusetts. By the end of 1862 these families understood the national anger at the corruption of the war effort, at the incompetence of politically appointed generals, and at the pernicious mix of human weakness, stupidity, and bloody-mindedness that had so successfully exacted its pound of flesh. For most the calculus was made at the ubiquitous funerals. "Are we paying too heavy a price?" asked Reverend George Putnam, while Reverend Cyrus Augustus Bartol titled one of his funeral orations "The Purchase by Blood."

If wealth, influence, and power did not offer immunity from the fundamental absurdity of war, it did permit a determined effort to try to give meaning to what was senseless slaughter, to purchase something with all that loss. In the case of Ball's Bluff, the death of one of the young officers, Lieutenant William Lowell Putnam, came to symbolize not only the tragedy of war but, increasingly, the martyrdom necessary to achieve emancipation. Although born into a wealthy Boston family with the strongest interest in the cotton economy, young Putnam belonged to a staunchly abolitionist branch of that family. After his death the family circulated his letters that passionately advocated the need to eradicate the slave culture.

Although in this early period of the war Union soldiers fought to preserve the Union and the issue of slavery took a backseat, as the war went on and as the death toll mounted, as it became clear that any hope of a mediated settlement was futile, and as Boston prepared itself for the next phase of war—harsher and more punishing—the issue of slavery returned. For the pragmatic it was a war measure. But it also offered a cause worthy of such deaths. "Not merely for country, not merely for humanity, not only for civilization, but for the religion of our Lord itself," or so insisted Governor John Albion Andrew in April 1863 at the flag presentation of the 54th Regiment as he offered to its colonel, Robert Gould Shaw, a white silk banner embroidered with a golden star, a golden cross, and the inscription IN HOC SIGNO VINCES: "By this sign thou shalt conquer." This had been the vision of Constantine on the Milvian Bridge—the moment of the emperor's conversion to Christianity.

As Governor Andrew admonished the 54th to "follow the splendid example" of Lieutenant Putnam, Colonel Shaw had a vivid memory of the young officer he had found the day after Ball's Bluff when he, along with other officers of the 2nd Mass, arrived at

Robert Gould Shaw. Library of Congress Prints and Photographs Division, LC-DIG-ppmsca-10886.

Edward's Ferry to visit the wounded, from whom they heard firsthand accounts of the battle. Putnam's guts had been shot away, and nothing could be done but to give him morphine. Shaw's cousin, Lieutenant Henry Sturgis, had carried Putnam from the battlefield, down the steep bluff to the river's edge. Norwood Penrose Hallowell, a lieutenant colonel in the 54th Mass, had lashed together the raft on which Putnam had been poled across the Potomac. The very youthful Cabot Jackson Russell, now a captain in the 54th, was a younger cousin who, after Putnam's death, had been sent on a western expedition to prevent him from enlisting. He telegraphed his father from Nevada after the death of yet another cousin, "Now I will have to fight." And so it went, an endless web of connections.

Governor Andrew's pointed reference to Lieutenant Putnam brought back to the officers of the regiment, and also to the crowd gathered, intensely personal and profound memories, memories that mixed childhood with war, innocence, and the loss of innocence, and came to embrace the experience of loss more generally. Shaw, for example, had been detailed to recover the bodies of the fallen soldiers of the 2nd Mass at Cedar Mountain. His experience traveling over that battlefield, stepping about "among heaps of dead bodies, many of them ... friends and acquaintances," had inured him to any ordinary squeamishness. It was this callousness that led him to write, "I long for the day when we shall attack the rebels with an overwhelming force and annihilate them. May I live long enough to see them running before us hacked to little pieces."

Of course Shaw did not live that long. Nor did most of his friends among the city elite. And for those who did survive the war, even the heroes among them, victory would always have the inevitable taste of ash. They had all been changed by war, as had their world. Gone was the old idealism, and in it its place was a harder, grittier knowledge of life as brutal and indifferent, mixed with deep guilt and regret and the sense that nothing so terrible and so utterly transformative would happen again, at least to them.

Over the 150 years that have passed, their faces stare out at us—at once cavalier, innocent, doubtful, but most of all young. We search them for clues: wondering how they found the courage to do what they did, whether it was wisdom or innocence that motivated them, and how to reconcile ourselves to their hard fate.

The Fighting Second

LAWRENCE A. KREISER JR.

The creation of army corps during the early winter of 1862 represents one of the greatest, if lesser known, organizational accomplishments of the Union Army. The sheer numbers were staggering. By the end of March the Army of the Potomac, the premier Union military force in the Eastern Theater, had swelled to 120,000 men. By comparison the American army that captured Mexico City during the Mexican War—the nation's last major conflict—had numbered only about fourteen thousand soldiers.

Such an immense force required new levels of military organization. In an effort to streamline the Army of the Potomac, President Lincoln ordered its twelve divisions, stationed in and around Washington, into four corps: the First, Second, Third, and Fourth. The corps as a unit type was already well understood in Europe; Napoleon had grouped his infantry, cavalry, and artillery into corps during the early 1800s, greatly increasing the French Army's operational mobility. These units formed the largest organizational blocks within individual armies and would serve as the primary means for field commanders to control their forces in the enormous battles that were to come.

By the end of the Civil War the Union had created nearly forty-five army corps, but none achieved the distinction of the Second Corps of the Army of the Potomac. In just over three years the Second Corps, which began with about eighteen thousand men, suffered more casualties than any other Union command of comparable size. It served in such key battles as Antietam, Fredericksburg, Gettysburg, the 1864 Overland Campaign from the Wilderness through Cold Harbor, and the Siege of Petersburg. Its senior commanders— the major generals Edwin Sumner, Darius Couch, Winfield Scott Hancock, and Andrew Humphreys—ranked among the best combat commanders ever fielded by the Union Army. Even today it stands as one of the finest American fighting units ever constituted.

The quality of the Second Corps was evident at every level, but especially in the individual soldiers. Countless letters and diaries speak to soldiers' bravery through an unremitting series of brutal battles. But also evident is a deep commitment to the Union.

Edwin V. Sumner, the first commander of the Second Corps. Library of Congress Prints and Photographs Division, LC-DIG-cwpb-04626.

Soldiers in the Second Corps knew that the United States would endure even if the Confederacy established itself as an independent political entity, but they believed the freedoms guaranteed white Americans by a republican form of government would suffer a fatal blow. They were, one wrote, fighting to protect "our great and free government" and the "best government that ever was instituted."

Jonathan Stowe, a farm laborer, enlisted in the 15th Massachusetts—one of the hardest-fighting regiments in the Second Corps—during the autumn of 1861. Stowe wrote that Southerners who took up arms against a freely elected government were not only "my country's enemy" but "base traitors to humanity and the world." He made the ultimate sacrifice one year later, when he was mortally wounded at Antietam.

In the spring of 1864 Lieutenant Josiah Favill admitted that he and many other soldiers were homesick. Yet maintaining the Union came above all else, and "until the work is done this army will never lay down its arms."

At first glance not all of the soldiers of the Second Corps seemed destined to become among the most redoubtable fighters in the Union Army. Many of them came from Democratic homes and ethnic communities that gave little support to the expansion of Federal war aims to include emancipation. Private William Smith of the 116th Pennsylvania, a largely Irish regiment recruited in Philadelphia, argued that fighting to free the slaves was a betrayal of why he had gone to war. "To hell with the Niggers," he concluded. After the Second Corps was badly bloodied in the fighting around Fredericksburg, Virginia, in late 1862, a New York private fumed that the loss of life was because of the "accursed Nigger. It is all fudge and I am mad."

And yet what modern-day Americans must grasp, amid the harshness of such racial attitudes, is that the soldiers of the Second Corps saw the fighting through. Many of these men reenlisted during the winter of 1863–64, when their three-year term of service was about to expire. That fall, in fact, they overwhelmingly voted for Abraham Lincoln and the continuation of the war in overwhelming numbers. Without such resolve, whether the Union even would have won the war, let alone destroyed the institution of slavery, remains open to question.

The emphasis on union continued into the postwar era. Veterans of the Second Corps were active in commemorating their wartime sacrifices and accomplishments through the dedication of battlefield monuments, especially at Gettysburg. The site of ferocious fighting during the summer of 1863, Gettysburg marked a major Union battlefield triumph. Amid the chirp of birds and the sway of the breeze, survivors of the Second Corps reminded listeners that they had helped to render "this field hallowed ground, dear to every lover of liberty and the cause of free constitutional government."

Reflecting the move toward national reconciliation in the late nineteenth century, veterans of the Second Corps praised their former gray-clad adversaries as Americans "as brave as ourselves" and "foemen 'worthy of our steel.'" African Americans and their plight in the postwar South rarely intruded upon the good feelings, even as Second Corps veterans often patted themselves on the back for helping to bring an end to the institution of slavery. Talk flowed freely about slavery as a "foul blot wiped out forever" and America as a land "where all mankind are free." Yet the transition of millions of blacks from slavery to freedom simply was not these veterans' concern.

Pride in the Second Corps became almost boundless at battlefield reunions. Veterans sometimes blurred the truth to bring more credit to their units. But they recognized that association with the Second Corps brought prestige. The Second Corps was the "gallant old corps" and the "fighting corps" of the Army of the Potomac. Veterans likely would have been pleased when, on the fiftieth anniversary of the fighting at Gettysburg, Speaker of the House Champ Clark, elected from the former border state of Missouri, referred to soldiers of the Second Corps as "those unconquerable men in blue."

To a great extent he was right. The Second Corps demonstrated the wisdom of Lincoln's organizational innovation: men could be placed in immense operational units and still develop a strong sense of cohesion, both with the unit and with its overall mission. More important, perhaps, is that this cohesion proved more powerful than the racial antipathies that ran through many parts of the Union Army, frustrations and outright hatreds that could otherwise have ripped the force apart long before its battlefield victories were complete.

Winning the Field but Not the War

James Q. Whitman

In the first week of May 1863 more than 133,000 Union soldiers squared off against more than 60,000 Confederates in the Battle of Chancellorsville. Though the battle swung back and forth for several days, it ended with a decisive Southern victory. And yet the war ground on for another two years, ending only when the devastation spilled off the battlefield, as Sherman and his army took the conflict to the farmland and cities of the South.

It is important to understand the change this pattern marked in military history. Victory in pitched battle (that is, staged and formalized) was not enough to end the Civil War—and that was an ominous sign for the wars of the future.

Pitched battles like Chancellorsville and Gettysburg are terrifying events for the soldiers who participate in them. But for society at large they are a blessing: they confine the horror of war to a single field, ideally for a single day. Strange though it may sound, a pitched battle functions as a kind of orderly legal procedure. It is a formal trial by combat, and when it works, it puts a quick and tidy end to conflict. The "verdict of battle" settles a war before it spins out of control.

All through the eighteenth century Westerners were proud to fight "civilized" wars, contained to single fields of battle, where professional, uniformed soldiers resolved international disputes by staging an orderly trial by combat without visiting violence on

The dead at the Battle of Antietam. Library of Congress Prints and Photographs Division, LC-DIG-ds-05174.

the surrounding population. Victory in eighteenth-century war came from the verdict of formal encounters like Saratoga and Yorktown, not from campaigns of devastation like General William Tecumseh Sherman's. Even in the Napoleonic Wars victory still came from pitched battles: Waterloo was enough to end Napoleon's career; there was no need for a March to the Sea. As recently as 1859 the Battle of Solferino was enough to end the Second Italian War of Independence, and in 1866 the Battle of Königgrätz would be enough to end the Seven Weeks' War between Prussia and Austria.

But the system of pitched battle broke down in the American Civil War. Five years later it would break down again in the Franco-Prussian War, when Helmuth von Moltke's Prussian troops mounted their own campaign of devastation, reducing the French cities one by one in bloody sieges because victory in pitched battle was no longer enough to end the war. Even the enormous Battle of Sedan, which resulted in the capitulation of the French emperor Napoleon III, was not enough to end the fighting, which went on for another eight months.

The collapse of the system of pitched battle was fatal for the South. During the first two years of the war Southerners hoped that victory on the battlefield would translate immediately to victory in the war. In their eyes they were fighting a second American War of Independence, and it was victory in pitched battle that had won the first War of Independence, most especially the Battle of Saratoga in 1777, which earned the American rebels the one thing they needed most: French recognition. European diplomatic recognition was still the grail for the South; everyone on both sides understood that the decisive battle was in some sense to be fought in the courts of London and Paris. Observers like Henry Adams watched the progress of the war anxiously in Europe, fearing that some Southern victory would count as its Saratoga. In the summer of 1862 the Second Battle of Bull Run almost did the trick.

But in the end the Europeans understood that victory in battle was not enough. More important, so did the Americans. Neither the North nor the South was prepared to accept the verdict of battle—not at the Second Battle of Bull Run, not at Chancellorsville, and not at Gettysburg. Instead both sides breached the limits of the battlefield and lurched together into the uncontained expanses of modern war.

Why did the system of pitched battle break down? Historians give two answers, neither of which can be right. Some argue that military technology drove the transformation. Muskets gave way to rifles. Railroads made it possible to move troops over vast distances. Armies grew in size. Yet these technological changes did not make it impossible to stage pitched battles. Battles like Solferino, Gettysburg, Königgrätz, and Sedan were still staged. Rifles were not necessarily more deadly than muskets, and troops still confronted each other as they had done in the eighteenth century. The trench warfare of World War I still lay generations in the future. There were pitched battles, and many of them. What changed was that the populations of America and France would no longer accept their verdicts.

Other historians argue that the system of pitched battle broke down because aristocratic culture broke down. An eighteenth-century battle, they maintain, was a kind of duel, fought between men of honor. In the nineteenth century the culture of dueling honor vanished, and the honor accorded to the results of pitched battle vanished with it. Yet the eighteenth century did not in fact regard battles as duels. Battles were lawful procedures, by which sovereigns proved their lawful claims. Duels were illegal. Nor did dueling culture die out in the nineteenth century. On the contrary the nineteenth century marked the high point of dueling culture in Europe, and it was nineteenth-century wars, not those in the eighteenth century, that were more often fought over points of honor.

The answer is more troubling than that. The system of pitched battle broke down because wars like the American Civil War and the Franco-Prussian War were fought over high ideals and because they were fought by republics, not monarchies. The wars of the eighteenth century were fought over carefully stated legal royal claims to territory, and were justified by carefully formulated legal briefs. They were staged in orderly ways intended to symbolize the glory and civilization of royal courts. But in the mid-nineteenth century the two American republics and the French Republic began to fight more bitter and more horrible wars, in the name of grander ideals. Hard though it is to accept, democratic idealism and widespread death began to march hand in hand.

Striking the Blow at Fort Wagner

GLENN DAVID BRASHER

"Today we recognize the right of every man . . . to be a MAN and a citizen," Governor John Andrew of Massachusetts proclaimed on May 18, 1863, to a crowd gathered around the 54th Massachusetts, the first African American regiment raised in the North. They fight "not for themselves alone," he insisted, but also for their race. Their military service would refute "the foul aspersion that they [are] not men," proving that African Americans deserved their nation's citizenship rights.

The regiment then proudly accepted its official flag, and Andrew told its commander, Colonel Robert Gould Shaw, to report to the Department of the South, which included the coastal areas of South Carolina and Georgia. The soldiers would thus begin their war against slavery deep in the institution's bowels. We are "on our way to Dixie," Corporal James Henry Gooding proclaimed, and "the greatest difficulty will be [for anyone] to stop [us]."

On May 28 the regiment marched through Boston to Battery Wharf as a crowd of twenty thousand lined the streets to watch. Detractors hissed, but supporters outnumbered the critics. Souvenirs were sold that included a quote from Byron: "Those who would be free, themselves must strike the blow." The sight of the handsomely dressed soldiers marching in perfect order, with the sun glinting off their meticulously polished bayonets and buttons, was thrilling. Leading the march from horseback was Shaw, and he

Storming Ft. Wagner, 1890. Kurz & Allison Art Publishers. Library of Congress Prints and Photographs Division, LC-DIG-pga-01949.

too made a lasting impression. The poet and abolitionist John Greenleaf Whittier recalled that Shaw looked as "beautiful and awful" as an avenging angel sent to lead the men. But no one was more impressed than Shaw's mother. "If I never see him again," she wrote, "I shall feel that he has not lived in vain."

After taking Beacon Street to Boston Common the regiment halted for speeches, then continued to the wharf and boarded ship. Reflecting later, Shaw wrote his new bride, Annie Shaw, "The more I think of the passage of the Fifty-fourth through Boston, the more wonderful it seems to me." He recalled that when first taking command he heard "sneering and pitying" remarks from those who did not believe blacks could be good soldiers. For Shaw the "perfect triumph" of the parade seemed a vindication.

Unfortunately the regiment's first action in the field encouraged the detractors. The 54th was sent to St. Simons Island, Georgia, and was coupled with another black regiment, the 2nd South Carolina. Comprising freed slaves, the regiment was led by Colonel James Montgomery, one of John Brown's Kansas cohorts. Shaw immediately admired the fiery abolitionist, although he "looks as if he had quite a taste for hanging people & throat cutting." On June 9 the regiments raided the small town of Darien, Georgia. Finding it practically deserted, the soldiers were ordered to "take out anything that can be useful in camp." Shaw was shocked when Montgomery calmly said, "I shall burn this town."

When Shaw balked, Montgomery argued that the South must be shown what "real war" involved. Shaw recalled Montgomery's insisting that slaveholders "were to be swept away by the hand of God, like the Jews of old." The town was set ablaze, with Montgomery himself lighting the final fire.

The event gnawed at Shaw. He felt that if the government ever deemed such tactics "a necessary policy," he would obediently comply. Yet because the town had offered no resistance or harbored any rebels, Shaw could not see any justification for the action. He was most concerned about its effect on the greater mission of his regiment. "I am not sure that it will not harm very much the reputation of black troops." As expected, Democratic newspapers soon argued that the event proved that African Americans were too "savage" to be soldiers.

Throughout June, Shaw hoped for an assignment that would win back the momentum generated by the Boston march. Unfortunately the regiment continued to be sent on small-scale raids. "These little miserable expeditions," Shaw complained, "are no account at all." He craved "a fair stand up [fight] such as our Potomac Army is accustomed to."

In July prospects brightened when the 54th joined Union forces gathering for operations against Charleston. The regiment camped at Beaufort, South Carolina, temporary home to many abolitionists who were helping to educate blacks behind Union lines. While there Shaw enjoyed talking with newly liberated African Americans and observing their religious "praise-meetings" and "shouts" that they "some times keep up all night." The 54th's men soaked in the admiration of the freed slaves. "They think now the kingdom is coming sure enough," Gooding noted.

Gettysburg news circulated in camp, and Shaw was jealous that his former regiment, the 2nd Massachusetts Infantry, was in the thick of the pivotal battle. While at Beaufort he kept the men busy with near-constant drilling and wrote letters requesting duty alongside white troops nearer Charleston. Happily, on July 8 the 54th was ordered to James Island, one of the many small islands ringing the city.

While on picket duty on July 16 about 250 of the 54th's men were attacked by 900 Confederates. The black troops gave the rebels "a warmer reception than they had expected," Gooding boasted. The 54th was forced back, but rallied, and then fought a perfectly executed delaying action, saving the 10th Connecticut Regiment from destruction. It was a small skirmish, but Union commanders took notice of the 54th's mettle and adherence to training while under fire. "The best disciplined white troops could have fought no better," the division commander, Alfred H. Terry, told the *New-York Tribune*. But the praise Gooding appreciated most came from the other enlisted men: "When a regiment of white men gave us three cheers as we were passing them, it shows that we did our duty as men."

The regiment was then ordered to Morris Island, requiring a night march in thick woods during a heavy thunderstorm. Reaching the beach on July 17, the regiment waited all day for transport while roasting under the unrelenting sun. The men were hungry and parched, but Shaw wrote, "It seems like old times in the Army of the Potomac."

Shaw sensed an opportunity coming but, while thrilled for his regiment, he had foreboding premonitions. He told a fellow officer that if he could have "a few weeks longer" with his new bride "I might die happy, but . . . I do not believe I will live through our next fight." Upon reaching Morris Island on July 18 the brigade commander, George C. Strong, informed Shaw that because of their performance on James Island they would be included in an assault that evening on Fort Wagner.

Federal commanders were determined to take Charleston, which required the recapture of Fort Sumter. This could not be done without first taking the sandy forts on the islands near Sumter. Most essential was Fort Wagner, but Union troops had been heavily repulsed when they first assaulted it. Naval artillery then pummeled the Confederate stronghold for a week, and it seemed time for another infantry attack.

Strong asked Shaw if he wanted the 54th to lead the assault. The young colonel knew his regiment had to seize the moment. If black troops played a prominent role in the capture of Charleston, the very birthplace of secession and the war, Darien would be forgotten and it would help accomplish everything his men were fighting to establish: liberty, citizenship, and manhood. Knowing it could cost his life, Shaw confidently told Strong yes, the African American men of the 54th would lead.

On the evening of July 18 Gooding noted, "We were marched up past our batteries, amid the cheers of the officers and soldiers." The drummer boy Alexander Johnson later recalled the men singing as they approached the fort. General Strong then rode up and reportedly shouted, "Is there a man here who thinks himself unable to sleep in that fort to-night?" The men shouted, "No!"

Shaw then exhorted the regiment, "Prove yourself men," ordering them forward as darkness fell. From a nearby hillside a *New-York Tribune* reporter noted the "terrible shower of shot and shell" that greeted the troops as they closed on the fort and "pushed their way" through it. A *New York Times* reporter claimed the soldiers advanced in silence until within two hundred yards of the fort and then "gave a fierce yell." Despite the "murderous reception" of artillery and small-arms fire, they continued forward, crossing a ditch that in some places contained four feet of water.

Working through the obstacles, the *Tribune* observed, they were hit by even more "grape and canister . . . from hand grenades, and from almost every other murderous implement of modern warfare." When they reached the fort wall, Gooding claimed that the color bearer was killed on the parapet and that "Col. Shaw seized the staff." Everyone agreed that in Shaw's last seconds he passionately beckoned the soldiers, "Forward!"

"When the men saw their gallant leader fall," Gooding wrote, "they made a desperate effort to get him out." But Shaw's death inspired another push, and many made it to the top.

The fight then became a confusing and savage hand-to-hand struggle. The *Tribune* noted that it was "a very dark night . . . and the enemy could be distinguished from our own men only by the light of bursting shell and the flash of the howitzer and the musket." Sergeant William Carney later recalled, "All around me were the dead and the wounded, lying one upon top the other." The soldier managed to grab the flag Governor Andrew had presented exactly two months earlier, and, as the *New York Times* observed, "he stood nobly on the glacis with his flag, endeavoring to rally the men." Frederick Douglass's son Lewis Douglass also made it inside the fort and recalled that the Confederate fire "swept us down like chaff . . . [but] still our men went on and on."

When the supporting regiments came up, Union forces somehow maintained a position in the fort for close to an hour, but it was a forlorn endeavor. Nearly every commissioned officer in the 54th was shot down by the time the order to withdraw was given, and the regiment suffered nearly 45 percent causalities. Despite serious wounds, Carney managed to bring the colors out and was cheered when he announced, "Boys, the old flag never touched the ground."

Burying the dead the next day, the Confederates did not afford Shaw's body the usual treatment given to officers, instead throwing it into a burial trench with his men. Yet Shaw's grieving parents believed it the most honorable resting spot for their son, never allowing any subsequent efforts to reclaim the body.

The attack failed, but Shaw and the 54th obtained immortality. Because the fight involved Charleston, it received more attention than recent actions by African American troops in the Western Theater, and in late July the story was a sharp contrast to reports of violence directed at blacks during the New York Draft Riots. Papers widely criticized the planning of the attack, but praised the 54th.

In an editorial seen in papers across the country, the *New York Times* exalted "the gallant negroes" and their "gallant Col. Shaw" and related Carney's heroic retrieval of the colors (which later earned him the Medal of Honor). The *Chicago Tribune* proclaimed that the regiment had proved its manliness when "fighting in that deadly breach till almost every officer had fallen and three hundred of its men lay dead." The *New York Herald's* reporter admitted having been a critic of black troops, but now he changed his mind: "I must [give] this regiment credit [for] fighting bravely and well." Even if they were "darkeys," he maintained, "the Massachusetts negro regiment is evidently made of good stuff." Shaw's men had helped prove that African Americans would heroically and manfully serve their country.

One correspondent visited the 54th's wounded in the hospital, and his report was widely published. The men grieved over "Father" Shaw but were determined to carry on. Despite amputations, bandaged wounds, and shattered limbs, the reporter noted, they were ready to try it again and insisted they would not quit fighting "till the last rebel be dead" or until "all our people get their freedom."

The war was tragically over for Colonel Robert Gould Shaw, but for the 54th Massachusetts and all other African American regiments eagerly recruited by the government in the wake of the Battle of Fort Wagner, the fight had just begun.

Life on the Battlefield

CAROLE EMBERTON

In Ambrose Bierce's short story "Chickamauga" a young boy emerges from his home, wooden sword in hand, and proceeds to kill imaginary enemies. He is unaware that a real battle—the namesake bloodbath that gives the story its title—is taking place just a short distance away. He is deaf and therefore can't hear the approaching gunfire or the groans of dying soldiers.

Intoxicated by his father's stories of vanquishing "savages" in his younger days, the young boy blissfully reenacts these heroic tales of conquest. The romanticism is so powerful that even when he stumbles across the horrors of the nearby battle—wounded bodies, bleeding, dying, drowning in a creek—he is unafraid and imagines he is their commander.

"He waved his cap for their encouragement," Bierce writes, "and smilingly pointed with his weapon in the direction of the guiding light—a pillar of fire to this strange exodus." Only when he sees that the pillar of fire is in fact his home and finds his mother's mangled body lying in the grass does the reality of war seep into his childish comprehension. Mute, the boy can make only "wild, uncertain gestures" and utter "a series of inarticulate and indescribable cries."

Most literary critics read "Chickamauga" as an allegory. The boy represents the young American nation, oblivious to the dangers of its long-standing romance with war and too eager to fight. Just as the boy had been "made reckless by the ease with which he overcame invisible foes attempting to stay his advance," Americans on both sides of the Civil War had naïvely believed that they would win quickly and with little bloodshed. Both the child and the nation had "committed the common enough military error of pushing the pursuit to a dangerous extreme."

Of course Bierce, who served with his Indiana regiment at Chickamauga but published the story in 1889, might also have been thinking about the rise in militaristic fervor at the end of the nineteenth century that peaked during the war against Spain. The story appears to serve as stinging commentary on America's ongoing war lust.

But what if we read the story more literally, as a commentary on the effects of the Civil War on civilians? Can this story help us imagine how families living near the battlefield at Chickamauga awoke to the realities of war as it made its way through their fields and yards?

According to the National Park Service, the park at Chickamauga contains one of the most pristine historic battlefields in the world. When the park was created in 1895, Congress noted, "No battlefield park of this quality and magnitude could be found in any other location in the world."

Very little had changed in the area in the preceding thirty years; the roads, fields, and forests remained mostly the same. Untouched and untrammeled, Chickamauga

Battlefield Park drew military personnel, dignitaries, and historians from across the globe to study the movement of troops during the fighting.

Yet there were some important elements missing. While the Park Service built reproductions of several civilian homes that were destroyed in 1863, these structures only hint at the texture of life within the local community on the Tennessee-Georgia border as the Union Army pushed deeper into the heart of the Confederacy.

In 1863 there were twenty-five farmhouses on the site of the battle. One of those houses belonged to Eliza and John Glenn, who lived, according to documents in the park's library, in a "one story double log" with their two children, four-year-old Avery and two-year-old Ella Nora. Years later Avery recalled that the house had two rooms and a kitchen along with a shed on one side and a porch on the front—a modest farmhouse, as were the other homes around Chickamauga Creek.

John Glenn built the house himself sometime around 1850 and was no doubt sorry to leave it when he enlisted in the Confederate Army in 1861. He went away to war like many of the local men, safe in the belief that they were defending those structures and the people sheltered inside their walls.

But it was not to be. War arrived at Glenn's home on the morning of September 19, 1863. Soon after the battle began, the house became the headquarters for the Union commander William Rosecrans, who advised Eliza that she should take her children and leave as the fighting drew near. With the help of a slave named John Camp, who had been given to her by her father when her husband left for war, Eliza loaded her children and a few belongings into a neighbor's wagon. The Glenns then made for a makeshift refugee camp about a mile west of the battle, where they waited until the firing had ceased.

As darkness fell on the first day of the battle Eliza returned to her home; all that remained was the chimney. John Glenn would not have the opportunity to rebuild his home; he died the next year in a Mobile, Alabama, hospital.

Other homes suffered similar fates. The house of George Washington Brotherton and his wife, Mary, survived the battle only to become a camp hospital for wounded Union soldiers. The Brothertons took refuge in the "canyon" along with Eliza Glenn and her children, but their daughter Adaline ventured back to the farm to find a few of her father's milk cows still alive. Planning to take the cows back to the refugees, Adaline instead gave the milk to the men lying wounded and dying in her front yard. Or so the story goes. Most likely Union officers would have confiscated the livestock and along with it Adaline's chance to be merciful.

Whatever the case, the Brotherton family would never be the same. Upon returning to the farm George and his son-in-law buried the bodies of Union soldiers who had been left in his yard as well as the dead animal carcasses that clogged his pond, all the while wondering about the fate of his two eldest sons, Thomas and Jim, both of whom were serving in the Confederate Army. Tom "knew every pig trail through the

The Brotherton House, Chickamauga, Georgia. Library of Congress Prints and Photographs Division, LC-DIG-det-4a23630.

woods" around the farm and served as a scout for General James Longstreet during the battle. Later, in a letter to Jim, Tom declared, "It's a sorry lad that won't fight for his own home." For Thomas Brotherton this was no abstract declaration of patriotism. Sadly he would never see his beloved home again. Captured in May 1864 near Dalton, Georgia, Thomas spent five months in a POW camp at Rock Island, Illinois. He took the oath of allegiance on October 28 and was released, but made it only to Indianapolis. Suffering from one of myriad "camp fevers," he died at Camp Morton, Indiana, on November 6. His name is engraved on a monument commemorating the Confederate dead buried in Crown Hill Cemetery, 430 miles and a lifetime away from the fields of Chickamauga.

In the end neither John Glenn nor Thomas Brotherton could protect the things and people they loved the most. War came, and as a young Indiana lieutenant witnessed those two days in northern Georgia, it spared nothing and no one in its path. The deaf-mute boy playing war may have been a figment of Bierce's imagination, but the writer no doubt looked into the face of despair and emptiness that day if he chanced upon Eliza Glenn or one of the other Chickamauga refugees. They must have resembled the little boy at the end of Bierce's story, standing motionless, with quivering lips, looking down upon the wreck.

Left Behind at Chickamauga

PAT LEONARD

For the title of his definitive book on the Battle of Chickamauga, the historian Peter Cozzens took three words from the diary of a Union soldier who fought there. "This terrible sound," as described by Private Alva Griest of the 72nd Indiana Infantry, did not refer to the ear-splitting cacophony that usually prevailed on a Civil War battlefield—the roar of cannons, the crack of muskets, and the shrieks of a charging enemy—but "a worse, more heart-rending sound" that haunted him for years afterward. Like every other soldier, Federal and Confederate alike, who spent the night of September 19, 1863, on the front lines, Griest was deeply affected by "the groans from thousands of wounded in our front crying in anguish and pain, some for death to relieve them, others for water. Oh, if I could only drown this terrible sound, and yet I may also lie thus ere tomorrow's sun crosses the heavens."

A fellow Hoosier, Sergeant Benjamin McGee, in writing the regiment's history nineteen years later, was even more descriptive: "The roar of the battle's bloody storm has ceased, and all is still save the waves that sob upon the shore—those waves are the shrieks of the wounded and dying—and these are more horrible and trying to our hearts than was the storm of battle. In this storm of groans and cries for help that come on the black night air, manly sympathy for comrades and enemy makes our hearts bleed, for we can give no help." By this point in the Civil War, bringing relief to the wounded had become a priority on the battlefield, especially when nightfall had ended a day's hostilities. At Chickamauga,

The Battle of Chickamauga. Library of Congress Prints and Photographs Division, LC-DIG-pga-01846.

however, several factors combined to make such assistance less timely than usual, and less effective when it did arrive.

First was the fluid nature of the battle itself, which required the hasty redeployment of divisions and even a whole corps (General George Thomas's Fourteenth Corps) as the conflict developed. On the Union side the medical director Glover Perin had selected an appropriate site for most of the division hospitals the day before, near the abundant waters of Crawfish Springs, but as the army continued to shift northward these hospitals (and in some cases individual units' ambulance corps) were left behind. Complicating matters was the fact that Crawfish Springs was away from, rather than along, the army's line of retreat, a fact that would have grave consequences on the battle's second day.

Another factor that worked against the wounded was the heavy undergrowth that dominated most of the field. All during the first day units advanced and then were driven back over the same patches of forest, thickets, and ripening farm fields, so that by nightfall the underbrush between the lines was carpeted with the dead and wounded of both armies. Rescue details blindly stumbled about in the gloomy no man's land, searching for fallen comrades, while often being fired upon by nervous pickets. Many of the fallen who might have survived were simply overlooked or deemed beyond reach and thus left to bleed or even freeze to death on the cold nights.

On the Confederate side yet another factor was at work: the rebel army was woefully short of ambulances to transport the wounded and of surgeons to provide treatment. And even though every available wagon, caisson, and limber was pressed into service to carry the wounded, the nearest railhead—from which they would be transported to hospitals in Atlanta or other cities—was anywhere from ten to twenty-five miles away. The wounded were compelled to endure an agonizing ride on crude roads and then to wait on the South's deficient rail system to retrieve them. As of September 25, five days after the battle, there were still twenty carloads of wounded rebels waiting to be moved. And once they were on their way, their miseries were further prolonged. More than ten thousand soldiers were shipped to Atlanta hospitals, which could accommodate at most only 1,800. Already debilitated by a meager diet and exhausted by days of marching and fighting, hundreds of men died from preventable diseases like scurvy or a lack of basic medical attention.

The Confederates did have one advantage, though: the countryside in which the battle took place was fiercely sympathetic to their cause. Area residents readily gave over their homes as field hospitals and helped provide whatever care and comfort they could to the injured men. One of the most noted examples took place at the home where the Confederate commander General Braxton Bragg had his headquarters. His hostess, Deborah Thedford, ministered so kindly to so many wounded men that she became known as the "Mother of Chickamauga." Two of the men carried into her home were her own sons, whom she had believed to be with Lee's army in Virginia. (They had been, until General James Longstreet's corps was sent west to support Bragg.) Her oldest son, William, died in her home on the battle's second day.

On that second day, September 20, the worst of Perin's fears were realized when a breakthrough by Longstreet cut off and then captured the Union's seven divisional hospitals at Crawfish Springs. Although many of the wounded and medical personnel had been able to escape and join a panicked retreat toward Chattanooga, many more—and most medical supplies and equipment—were left to fall into the enemy's hands. Dr. Konrak Sollheim, surgeon of the 9th Ohio, described the scene:

> An order arrived from the chief physician (Alonzo Phelps, XXI Corps). I was to take all the severely wounded with me in ambulances to Rossville.... The rest of the wounded, those not badly hurt, were to walk there. Too late! The battle already threatened the hospital.... Enemy infantry stormed at us, and the word was, Save yourself if you can! Chaos. Ambulances took the lead, some empty, others loaded with patients. Physicians followed afoot and on horseback.... Why should the enemy be at all concerned about our injuries, when he had suffered so many of his own?

Perin later reported, "In the confusion of the retreat, primary operations could not be performed to the extent desired; thus many cases of injuries of the knee and ankle joints subsequently proved fatal that might have been saved." He also estimated that 2,500 wounded, and dozens of surgeons, were left behind.

On a percentage basis the casualties suffered by both armies at Chickamauga were about equal (roughly 28 percent), but because—for one of the few times in the war—the Confederates had more men on the field, their total losses were greater. Union casualties were 16,170 (1,657 killed, 9,756 wounded, and 4,757 captured or missing), while the Confederates lost 18,454 (2,312 killed, 14,674 wounded, and 1,468 captured or missing). Chickamauga was the bloodiest battle in the Western Theater and second only to Gettysburg in the entire war.

Also contributing to the eventual death toll on the Confederate side, perhaps, was what Lieutenant General D. H. Hill described as the individual rebel soldier's loss of "dash" or "élan" after the barren victory. "He fought stoutly to the last," Hill later wrote, "but, after Chickamauga, with the sullenness of despair and without the enthusiasm of hope." As any health professional knows, patients with a positive mental outlook fare better than those who are despondent. After their commanders repeatedly failed to take advantage of opportunities to crush the Union Army, just before and just after the Chickamauga bloodfest, many of the soldiers in the ranks began to resign themselves to what the war's eventual outcome would be. It was a matter of time, and time was not on their side.

Humanity and Hope in a Southern Prison

PETER COZZENS

For more than the obvious reasons, Civil War soldiers in both armies despised military prisons. Not only were the inmates held against their will, but the hunger, filth, vermin, rampant disease, overcrowding, brutal treatment, and soul-crushing ennui made prison

The stockade at Cahaba Prison. Library of Congress Prints and Photographs Division, LC-DIG-ppmsca-33764.

camps slaughterhouses of slow death. Andersonville, the infamous Georgia prison, was the ultimate abattoir; during the summer of 1864 nearly one in three Union inmates died. In other Confederate prisons the average mortality rate was 15.5 percent; in Union prisons 12 percent.

There was one remarkable exception: the virtually unknown Cahaba Federal Prison, fifteen miles southwest of Selma, Alabama. At Cahaba the mortality rate was just 3 percent, a lower death rate than that among American prisoners in German stalags during World War II. According to federal figures, only 147 of the 5,000 prisoners interned at Cahaba died there.

What made Cahaba unique among Civil War prisons? Simple humanity. The prison commandant, Colonel Henry A. M. Henderson of Kentucky, understood Northerners. He had graduated from Ohio Wesleyan University and the Cincinnati Law School. Shortly after graduation and finding his true calling in the church, Henderson became a Methodist minister. When he assumed command of Cahaba in July 1863, a month after it opened, he pledged to run the prison with as much compassion as discipline and good order permitted.

Henderson didn't have a lot to work with. The prison was built around a partly completed, 15,000-square-foot cotton warehouse in the town of Cahaba on the west bank of the Alabama River. Within its brick walls 250 rough-timber bunks, capable of sleeping two men each, were built one atop of the other. An unfinished roof left 1,600 square feet in the center exposed to the elements. Confederate prison authorities built a twelve-foot-high wooden stockade around the warehouse, with allowance made for a small outdoor cooking yard. The prison's official capacity was five hundred by the time Henderson arrived, it already had climbed to 660, with latecomers compelled to sleep on the dirt floor of the warehouse.

The Kentuckian's first order of business was to improve sanitary conditions. Drinking water came from an artesian well that emptied into an open gutter, which in turn flowed two hundred yards through town before entering the northwest corner of the stockade. In his effort to depollute the water supply, Henderson had a willing ally in the prison surgeon, R. H. Whitfield. Making his case to the Medical Department, Whitfield said the water, in its course from the well to the stockade, "has been subjected to the washings of the hands, feet, faces, and heads of soldiers, citizens, and negroes, buckets, tubs, and spittoons, of groceries, offices, and hospital, hogs, dogs, cows, and filth of all kinds from the streets and other sources." Whitfield's graphic plea did the trick; quartermasters installed pipes to replace the open ditch, and clean water flowed into the prison.

To ensure it remained that way, the latrines—closed outhouses, not open filth holes in the center of camp, as at Andersonville—were built at the southeastern corner of the prison, where the water exited. Consequently dysentery was almost unknown at Cahaba; the majority of prisoners who died there seem to have entered the prison already in a weakened state.

Those who fell ill were well cared for at the prison hospital, located in a rambling, two-story hotel called Bell Tavern that the Confederacy had commandeered to serve both the guards and the prisoners. Whitfield treated Northerners and Southerners with equal consideration. Men died in the Bell Tavern hospital, but not for want of care.

Neither did they die for want of effort by Henderson, who in the autumn of 1864 found himself commandant of the most overcrowded of all Civil War prisons. That summer the Union's commanding general, Ulysses S. Grant, halted prisoner-of-war exchanges. As a result Cahaba's population surged to 2,151 in October, a number 600 percent above the prison's capacity. (Andersonville ran 330 percent above capacity at its peak.) Each man had only 7.5 square feet to call his own; those at Andersonville had 35 square feet of space, albeit squalid, per man.

Despite the ban on exchanges Henderson bypassed his own chain of command and proposed to the Union district commander, Major General Cadwallader C. Washburn, a special exchange of 350 of Cahaba's most debilitated inmates. Washburn forwarded the request, along with a letter praising Henderson's management, but General Grant denied the appeal.

Henderson persevered. With winter drawing near and the prisoners poorly clad, he suggested to Washburn that the Federals send a truce ship up the Alabama River to Cahaba with supplies. Henderson and Washburn overcame the reservations of their superiors, and in December a Union steamboat offloaded two thousand uniforms, four thousand pairs of socks, 1,500 blankets, medicine, and mess tins.

Henderson had done his best. But with overcrowding came a drop in rations, an inevitable course in a South scarcely able to feed its own troops by then. Prisoners wanted food more than supplies. Most of them bartered their new clothing to guards in exchange for victuals, and, reported Henderson sadly, the prisoners "were left with the same scanty clothing and ragged blankets in a climate particularly severe in winter."

Homesickness and ennui could kill men as effectively as disease, so Henderson and his subordinates did what they could to keep the men's minds occupied. "Every day on the arrival of the mail, one of them would bring in a late paper, stand up on a box and read the news," recalled Sergeant Melvin Grigsby of Wisconsin. "In many other ways, such as procuring writing material and forwarding letters for us, they manifested such kindly feeling as one honorable soldier will always manifest toward brother soldier, enemy though he may be, in misfortune."

Prisoners at Cahaba also were blessed with their own angel of mercy, Amanda Gardner, whose well-appointed home stood just outside the prison compound. There was no doubting her pro-Confederate convictions; Gardner had lost one of her two sons to Yankee bullets at the First Battle of Bull Run. But she had a reputation, a prison guard told Sergeant Grigsby, "of being one of the kindest-hearted and most intelligent women in town." Soon after Cahaba opened she began sending gifts of food that her young daughter slipped through cracks in the stockade walls with the connivance of friendly guards. When winter came she cut every carpet in her home into blankets to "relieve the suffering of those poor prisoners."

Most beneficial to prisoner morale was the generous use she made of a superb book collection her uncle had bequeathed her. Prisoners had only to send a note by a guard to Gardner or her daughter to borrow a book from her library. At Andersonville prisoners scuffled over dog-eared back issues of *Harper's Weekly* to alleviate the tedium. At Cahaba inmates enjoyed finely bound copies of the classics and a wide assortment of recent novels, as well as works of history, philosophy, science, and poetry. Word of Gardner's kindness spread beyond the prison walls to the Union lines; when a federal cavalry detachment realized they had captured her remaining son, they paroled him through the lines to her care.

Despite the best intentions of Henderson and Gardner, life at Cahaba was not easy. By late 1864 the average daily issue of rations fell to twelve ounces of cornmeal, eight ounces of often rancid beef, and occasionally some bug-infested peas. Prisoners were not starved, but they were hungry enough that thoughts of food permeated their dreams. "The same experience was often repeated," remembered an Illinois cavalryman, Jesse Hawes. "Go to the bed of sand at 9:00 p.m., dream of food till 1:00 or 2:00 a.m., awake, go to the water barrel, drink, and return to sleep again if the rats would permit sleep."

The rat population grew apace with that of the prisoners until they became a plague. They burrowed through the warehouse and swarmed over the cooking yard. "At first they made me nervous, lest they should do me serious injury before I should awake," said Hawes. "But after several nights' experience that feeling was supplanted by one of irritation that they should keep waking me up so many times that at length became nearly unbearable."

Harder yet to bear were lice, from which no prisoner was free. An Illinois private said that after his first night at Cahaba his uniform was so infested that it "looked more like pepper and salt than blue." Hawes agreed. Lice "crawled upon our clothing by day, crawled over our bodies, into the ears, even into the nostrils and mouths by night."

To compound the prisoners' misery, in early March 1865 the inmates of Cahaba faced a natural disaster of the first order. For several days rain had pounded the prison and inundated the surrounding countryside. On March 1 the Cahaba River, north of town, overflowed its banks. Water raced through Cahaba and swept into the stockade. Latrines backed up, and by nightfall prisoners found themselves waist-deep in ice-cold, fetid water.

Unfortunately for them Colonel Henderson was no longer at Cahaba. With the war winding down, General Grant had relented on prisoner exchanges. Confederate authorities detailed Henderson to organize exchanges at a neutral site in Vicksburg, leaving the prison under the command of Lieutenant Colonel Samuel Jones, a martinet who once threatened to run Gardner out of town because of her "sympathy for the damned Yankees." Refusing an appeal from his own guards to permit the prisoners to seek refuge on high ground outside the stockade until the waters receded, Jones left the Federals shivering in the water for three days. Then, as the water finally drained from the stockade, he told the incredulous inmates that they were to be paroled immediately. The war was all but over.

For four weeks steamboats plied the Alabama River with prisoners. Most were taken to Vicksburg, where they mingled with the skeletons in blue from Andersonville. Some 4,700 Union prisoners awaited transportation home. Some 1,100 were sick, nearly all of whom were from Andersonville. The Cahaba men, reported a Union department commander, Napoleon T. Dana, were in "excellent health."

But not for long. On April 24 the long months of humane work by Henderson ended in unspeakable tragedy. The Union paddle steamer *Sultana* left Vicksburg crammed with two thousand Union prisoners, more than half of them Cahaba men. The *Sultana* had faulty boilers and a legal capacity of 376 passengers. Three days after setting off up the Mississippi three of the four boilers exploded, and the *Sultana* sank. Three-quarters of the men onboard died.

General Dana took care to see that no harm came to Henderson while he was at Vicksburg, assigning a detachment of Indiana cavalry to act as the colonel's personal bodyguard. After the assassination of President Abraham Lincoln, not even a well-meaning Confederate like Henderson was safe within Union lines. So Dana spirited him across the Mississippi River into a camp of Texas Rangers.

Henderson went on to live a long and productive life. He served two terms as superintendent of public schools in Kentucky before returning to the clergy. The Reverend Doctor Henderson was pastor of the Jersey City Methodist Church when, on May 11, 1883, its most prominent member, Mrs. Hannah Simpson Grant, passed away. Her son, Ulysses S. Grant, entrusted funeral arrangements to Henderson and asked him to prepare an appropriate eulogy. It was a high tribute to Henderson's character that the former commanding general of the Union Army would place such trust in the one-time commandant of a Confederate prisoner-of-war camp.

Henderson died in Cincinnati in 1912. Obituaries incorrectly said he had been a Confederate general, omitting any reference to his duty at Cahaba. Not that it mattered. After the 1865 flood the county seat moved from Cahaba to Selma, and by the turn of the century Cahaba was a ghost town, the warehouse prison demolished for the bricks. The horrors of Andersonville and the notoriety of its commandant Henry Wirz would forever remain etched in American memory; memories of Colonel Henry A. M. Henderson's humanity were buried with the good reverend.

How Coffee Fueled the Civil War

JON GRINSPAN

It was the greatest coffee run in American history. The Ohio boys had been fighting since morning, trapped in the raging battle of Antietam, in September 1862. Suddenly a nineteen-year-old William McKinley appeared, under heavy fire, hauling vats of hot coffee. The men held out tin cups, gulped the brew, and started firing again. "It was like putting a new regiment in the fight," their officer recalled. Three decades later McKinley ran for president in part on this singular act of caffeinated heroism.

At the time no one found McKinley's act all that strange. For Union soldiers, and the lucky Confederates who could scrounge some, coffee fueled the war. Soldiers drank it before marches, after marches, on patrol, during combat. In their diaries *coffee* appears

A sketch of exchanged Union prisoners receiving rations aboard the ship *New York*. Library of Congress Prints and Photographs Division, LC-DIG-ppmsca-21716.

more frequently than the words *rifle, cannon*, or *bullet*. Ragged veterans and tired nurses agreed with one diarist: "Nobody can 'soldier' without coffee."

Union troops made their coffee everywhere and with everything: with water from canteens and puddles, brackish bays and Mississippi mud, liquid their horses would not drink. They cooked it over fires of plundered fence rails or heated mugs in scalding steam vents on naval gunboats. When times were good, coffee accompanied beefsteaks and oysters; when they were bad it washed down raw salt pork and maggoty hardtack. Coffee was often the last comfort troops enjoyed before entering battle and the first sign of safety for those who survived.

The Union Army encouraged this love, issuing soldiers roughly thirty-six pounds of coffee each year. Men ground the beans themselves (some carbines even had built-in grinders) and brewed it in little pots called muckets. They spent much of their downtime discussing the quality of that morning's brew. Reading their diaries one can sense the delight (and addiction) as troops gushed about a "delicious cup of black" or fumed about "wishy-washy coffee." Escaped slaves who joined Union Army camps could always find work as cooks if they were good at "settling" the coffee—getting the grounds to sink to the bottom of the unfiltered muckets.

For much of the war the massive Army of the Potomac made up the second-largest population center in the Confederacy, and each morning this sprawling city became a coffee factory. First, as another diarist noted, "little campfires, rapidly increasing to hundreds in number, would shoot up along the hills and plains." Then the encampment buzzed with the sound of thousands of grinders simultaneously crushing beans. Soon tens of thousands of muckets gurgled with fresh brew.

Confederates were not so lucky. The Union blockade kept most coffee out of seceded territory. One British observer noted that the loss of coffee "afflicts the Confederates even more than the loss of spirits," while an Alabama nurse joked that the fierce craving for caffeine would be the Union's "means of subjugating us." When coffee was available, captured or smuggled or traded with Union troops during casual cease-fires, Confederates wrote rhapsodically about their first sip.

The problem spilled over to the Union invaders. When General William Tecumseh Sherman's Union troops decided to live off plunder and forage as they cut their way through Georgia and South Carolina, soldiers complained that while food was plentiful, there were no beans to be found. "Coffee is only got from Uncle Sam," an Ohio officer grumbled, and his men "could scarce get along without it."

Confederate soldiers and civilians would not go without. Many cooked up coffee substitutes, roasting corn or rye or chopped beets, grinding them finely and brewing up something warm and brown. It contained no caffeine, but desperate soldiers claimed to love it. General George Pickett, famous for that failed charge at Gettysburg, thanked his wife for the delicious "coffee" she had sent, gushing, "No Mocha or Java ever tasted half so good as this rye-sweet-potato blend!"

Did the fact that Union troops were near jittery from coffee, while rebels survived on impotent brown water, have an impact on the outcome of the conflict? Union soldiers certainly thought so. Though they rarely used the word *caffeine*, in their letters and diaries they raved about that "wonderful stimulant in a cup of coffee," considering it a "nerve tonic." One depressed soldier wrote home that he was surprised that he was still living and reasoned, "What keeps me alive must be the coffee."

Others went further, considering coffee a weapon of war. General Benjamin Butler ordered his men to carry coffee in their canteens and planned attacks based on when his men would be most caffeinated. He assured another general before a fight in October 1864, "If your men get their coffee early in the morning you can hold."

Coffee did not win the war—Union material resources and manpower played a much, much bigger role than the quality of its java—but it might say something about the victors. From one perspective coffee was emblematic of the new Northern order of fast-paced wage labor, a hurried, business-minded, industrializing nation of strivers. For years Northern bosses had urged their workers to switch from liquor to coffee, dreaming of sober, caffeinated, untiring employees. Southerners drank coffee too—in New Orleans especially—but the way Union soldiers gulped the stuff at every meal pointed ahead toward the world the war made, a civilization that lives on today in every office break room.

But more than that, coffee was simply delicious, soothing—"the soldier's chiefest bodily consolation"—for men and women pushed beyond their limits. Caffeine was secondary. Soldiers often brewed coffee at the end of long marches, deep in the night while other men assembled tents. These grunts were too tired for caffeine to make a difference; they just wanted to share a warm cup—of Brazilian beans or scorched rye—before passing out.

This explains their fierce love. When one captured Union soldier was finally freed from a prison camp, he meditated on his experiences. Over his first cup of coffee in more than a year, he wondered if he could ever forgive "those Confederate thieves for robbing me of so many precious doses." Getting worked up, he fumed, "Just think of it, in three hundred days there was lost to me, forever, so many hundred pots of good old Government Java."

So when William McKinley braved enemy fire to bring his comrades a warm cup—an act memorialized in a stone monument at Antietam today—he knew what it meant to them.

Was the Burning of Columbia a War Crime?

THOM BASSETT

When General William Tecumseh Sherman's troops left Columbia, South Carolina, on the morning of February 20, 1865, about a third of it lay in ashes behind them,

The burning of Columbia, South Carolina, in February 1865. Library of Congress Prints and Photographs Division, LC-DIG-ppmsca-33131.

with thousands left homeless. Within weeks Southerners had begun to publish what they considered evidence of an orchestrated Northern atrocity. Ten years later the dispute remained so sharp that Sherman felt it necessary to defend himself in his memoirs by accusing Confederates of setting the city on fire themselves. Even today many neo-Confederate websites argue that the burning of Columbia was a Union war crime.

The truth is different: Columbia burned during the night of February 17–18, 1865, but not directly because of command decisions by either the Confederate or Union generals ostensibly in control. While the Northern generals deserve some blame, the burning of South Carolina's capital was in reality a result of confusion, misjudgment, and simple bad luck. It was, in sum, an accident of war.

By 1865 Columbia was one of the few places of refuge for Confederates fleeing the Union onslaught across the South. It also retained a vital importance to the war effort, serving as a nexus for one of the last rail systems that could still get supplies to General Robert E. Lee's beleaguered forces in Virginia. It was a production center too: the city produced swords, rifles, shoes, socks, and uniforms; the Palmetto Iron Works manufactured shells, Minié bullets, and cannon. Joseph LeConte, a chemistry professor at South Carolina College, provided indispensable war service by heading efforts to produce badly needed medicine and gunpowder.

In early January Sherman, encamped at Savannah, Georgia, decided to take Columbia during his planned march through the Carolinas. After sweeping aside the token resistance they met along the way, Sherman's troops arrived at the southern edge of Columbia on the morning of February 17. They drove off a handful of Confederate skirmishers, circled around the city, and entered it in force from the northwest.

What the soldiers found was a city almost ideally situated to burn. Columbia was bursting with highly flammable bales of cotton. Its location made it ideal for cotton trading and transport, and overproduction during the war as well as the Union blockade resulted in tremendous amounts of cotton being stored in all available warehouses, basements, and empty buildings.

To keep the cotton out of Union hands, on February 14 General P. G. T. Beauregard, who headed the defense of Columbia, ordered that the stored cotton be taken outside the city and burned. But there was too much cotton to move by carriage, so the Confederate officer in charge of the operation decided to move the bales into city streets, to be burned there. His order was published in Columbia's newspapers on February 15.

But early on February 17, mere hours before Union soldiers entered Columbia, Beauregard's subordinate Wade Hampton persuaded him to reverse the order out of concern that the flames of burning cotton in the streets might spread throughout the city. Around 7 a.m. Hampton issued an order not to fire the cotton, but it was too late. The Confederate withdrawal, then under way, was confused and chaotic. The chain of command had broken down, so the order was at best fitfully communicated to soldiers remaining in the city and private citizens. By the night of February 16–17, before any Union soldiers entered the city, cotton was already burning.

In at least two places witnesses saw cotton burning in Columbia, including on Richardson Street, the city's central cotton market. It's unclear whether these fires were started by looters in a city where order had dissolved, by soldiers following Beauregard's order, or by Union shelling. Nevertheless by 3 a.m., one Confederate officer recalled, "the city was illuminated with burning cotton."

Besides cotton Columbia held a remarkable amount of alcohol. Since early in the war Charleston merchants had shipped in vast stores of whiskey to save it from naval bombardment. Columbia also had a government distillery that produced several hundred gallons of whiskey a day, and a large quantity of medicinal supplies had been abandoned and left unguarded in the confusion.

As soon as Sherman's soldiers entered Columbia and began to march down Richardson Street, jubilant blacks and placating whites plied them with whiskey. This went on over the next several hours as unit after unit paraded through Columbia and then took up camp north and east of the city.

But this army wasn't the greatest threat that came in from the north. Since before dawn on the 17th, a strong wind had blown into the city. Around noon Sherman rode down Richardson Street and took note of the scene. Cotton bales were torn open. The wind had scattered the cotton thickly, catching it on buildings and tree branches. Sherman remarked that the result was like a Northern snowstorm. Southern witnesses agreed. The Columbian Mary S. Whilden, for example, noted the city's "peculiar appearance" from streets and trees being covered with the "most combustible material."

Still, by midafternoon relative calm had returned to Columbia. Union guards had been posted at major intersections, in front of public buildings, and at private homes that requested protection. Sherman told the mayor that the burning of war-related buildings would be delayed because of the high winds still blowing through the city. Federal troops worked with Columbia's fire department to control a few fires that had somehow broken out. Sherman appropriately assigned Major General Oliver Otis Howard provost duty command, and Howard resolved to remain in Columbia to keep a close eye on things.

As evening came on, though, the situation quickly deteriorated. Encamped troops had been straggling back into Columbia, seeking amusement and more of the easily available alcohol. Both soldiers and citizens were getting drunk and rowdy. Some Union officers ordered whiskey barrels to be smashed to keep them out of the crowd's hands, but no one paid them much mind. Howard ordered a fresh contingent of troops into the city, but they didn't arrive for almost two hours.

Several more fires broke out in the city, with no definite cause. Arson cannot be ruled out, but neither can the possibility of inadequately extinguished cotton bales from earlier in the day, brought back to life by the wind that now approached gale strength. The tipping point came around 8 p.m., when a fire started on Richardson Street. There is no conclusive evidence that establishes how it began, but it roared for several hours and caused most of Columbia's destruction. The fire ended only because the wind stopped around 3 a.m., allowing firefighting efforts to finally succeed.

There's no single, definitive account of how federal troops behaved during the conflagration. Union and Confederate eyewitnesses agree that many officers and men worked ceaselessly to protect lives and property. When the reinforcements Howard called in arrived, the officer in command immediately reassigned his men to fight the fire, not to clear the streets of disorderly factions. One brigade alone arrested 370 fellow officers and soldiers, along with civilians. But testimony from both sides also shows that at least a few others contributed willfully to the destruction by bayoneting fire hoses and carrying torches into private homes.

The command decisions from Sherman on down demonstrate at least the intention to act in accordance with the rules of war, even if they lost control of some of their men. But Southerners also contributed to the destruction. Black and white Columbians looted, rioted, and committed arson. And they plied Union troops with whiskey. If the burning of Columbia was a "carnival of destruction," as critics of Sherman have put it, some Southerners were themselves avid, gleeful revelers.

Furthermore the Confederate commanders Beauregard and Hampton may be criticized for failing to take control of Columbia's vast alcohol supply before abandoning the city. Their woefully inept evacuation of the city also left large amounts of highly flammable cotton in places most vulnerable to burning.

In 1872 an international commission assigned to adjudicate insurance claims arising from the fire determined that the destruction "was not to be ascribed to either the intention or default of either the Federal or confederate officers." This decision had legal consequences, but it didn't dislodge the prevailing Southern conviction that Columbia was intentionally burned by a horde of barbarians led by a demonic, vengeful general.

For his part Sherman forever insisted that the Confederates had simply burned down their own city. The least acceptable truth for everyone, it seems, is that even in a war where tremendous force had been concentrated and applied with often masterful skill for almost four years, sometimes the terrible destructive power of war was out of everyone's control.

5. The West and Native Americans

Introduction

BOYD COTHRAN

It was bitterly cold. So cold that the men's whiskey rations froze in their canteens. Steam rose from their horses as they labored down the valley toward the Shoshone village along Boa Ogoi, or Bear River, in what is today southeastern Idaho. Part of the 2nd California Volunteer Cavalry, the 220 Union soldiers commanded by Colonel Patrick Connor, were, at least in theory, out to arrest the Shoshone headmen Bear Hunter, Sanpitch, and Sagwitch. Three weeks earlier Shoshone raiders had killed a settler named John Henry Smith. Attributing the death to members of the local Shoshone band, the Utah Territory's chief justice, John F. Kinney, issued a warrant for the headmen's arrest and requested the military's assistance. Connor, under pressure from local settlers to pacify the Shoshone, saw the warrant as an opportunity to, as he would later report, "chaste them if possible."

Just as dawn was breaking over the valley on the morning of January 29, 1863, Connor and his California Volunteers attacked the Shoshone's winter village. There was no attempt to arrest the headmen peacefully. Connor's soldiers completely surrounded the village, cutting off escape, and then began shooting, bayoneting, and clubbing men, women, and children. The killing lasted for several hours, and the raping several hours beyond that. At the end as many as 384 Shoshone villagers lay dead.

The Bear River Massacre is rarely remembered today. Overshadowed by the battles in the far eastern theaters of the Civil War, American Indians and the West are often seen as peripheral to the main events of the war. Yet the events outside the Eastern Theater had ramifications that Americans are still struggling with.

The massacre that January morning marked the horrendous end to over a decade of intrusion and land loss for the Northwestern Shoshone. It was the deadliest day in all of the Indian Wars of the nineteenth century. And it was the direct result of shifts in American Indian policy during the Civil War. Yet despite its importance, the two are rarely connected.

February 20 the Council declared, "Any person or Persons, who may have been held in Slavery are, hereby, declared to be forever free." Why did Cherokee leaders change such a fundamental aspect of their emancipation plans?

Between Lincoln's endorsement of compensated emancipation in his annual address and the Cherokee's plan for compensated emancipation a watershed had occurred. On January 1, 1863, President Lincoln signed the Emancipation Proclamation. This action forever altered the parameters of freedom in the United States, and Lincoln would cease his offers of compensated emancipation. The Cherokee Nation had missed its opportunity to receive payment for freeing slaves. Strengthening ties with the Union would require the Cherokee to adjust to Lincoln's new emancipation policies.

The Cherokee, however, differed from Lincoln and his cabinet over one key issue. There was no serious discussion or consideration of freedmen's citizenship in the Cherokee Nation. Instead, on November 14 the Cherokee Council passed an act that explicitly denied citizenship to former slaves and required freed slaves remaining in the Nation to obtain work permits. The incorporation of the former slaves of Cherokee masters into the Cherokee citizenry would wait until the 1866 treaty between the Cherokee and United States.

In the aftermath of freedom the United States incorporated freed people into the body politic with constitutional amendments outlining their citizenship rights. In the 1866 treaty federal officials also required Cherokee leaders to grant former slaves and their descendants "all the rights of native Cherokees." This particular phrase is important because it did not explicitly state what these rights were, and it has been a source of tension between Cherokee leaders and the Cherokee Freedmen ever since.

Becoming Mark Twain

JIM McWILLIAMS

By early February 1863 Samuel Langhorne Clemens must have felt glad that he was more than eighteen months removed from any direct participation in the Civil War. No longer risking his life in a guerrilla war in northern Missouri, he was a newspaper editor in the Nevada Territory, causing some local scandals with his acerbic political commentary and tall tales. Although he occasionally wrote about the war raging back east, Clemens mainly focused his columns on mocking the territorial legislature or relating humorous anecdotes about the citizens of Nevada. Surely, though, he must have sometimes thought about his own war experiences in the summer of 1861.

Commercial traffic on the Mississippi River had ceased soon after war broke out, and Clemens, then twenty-five years old and a steamboat pilot for two years, decided in early June 1861 to join some friends in enlisting in the Marion Rangers, a unit of the Missouri State Guard from the Hannibal area. While his father had once owned a slave,

Samuel Clemens, who took the pen name Mark Twain. Library of Congress Prints and Photographs Division, LC-USZ62-28851.

and while he had spent many boyhood summer days surrounded by slaves on his uncle's farm, Clemens seemed to enlist more as a lark than for any political or ideological reasons. Indeed in the months before joining the Rangers, Clemens had expressed both pro-Union and anti-Union views as the states seceded and war approached. His rather flippant attitude toward the war would change, however, as the realities of army life in the field set in.

According to a fellow recruit, Clemens showed up for the Marion Rangers riding a mule and carrying a squirrel rifle and an umbrella. Disregarding his complete lack of military experience, his comrades elected him lieutenant, which made him second in command of the dozen or so men. According to Clemens's 1885 short memoir of his war experiences, *The Private History of a Campaign That Failed*, the Rangers would occasionally attempt a military drill, but they soon collapsed into horseplay and then forgot what little they had learned. Moreover Clemens discovered that his friends would refuse any orders that he gave, arguing that he was certainly not their superior.

Clemens also wrote in his memoir that it rained almost constantly and that he and the men lacked uniforms and arms and relied on local farmers for food and shelter. Every few nights, he noted, a rumor of approaching Union troops would send the Rangers, at top speed, in the direction opposite of the supposed Yankees. Those enemies never materialized, and the Rangers were soon filthy and hungry. Clemens related one particularly tragic nighttime incident when the terrified Rangers shot and killed an approaching figure on a horse they assumed to be a Union advance scout, but who turned out to be a passing stranger. (The incident is probably fictional, as no record of it, aside from Clemens's own memoir, exists.)

After two weeks in the field the Rangers heard a convincing rumor that a Union colonel, leading an entire regiment determined to destroy any Confederate irregulars in northeast Missouri, was heading toward Marion County. The Rangers quickly disbanded, most of the men slipping back into civilian life but a few joining the regular Confederate Army. Clemens returned to relatives in St. Louis and tried to keep out of sight, since Union general John C. Frémont governed the city under martial law that threatened insurrectionists with hanging.

On July 18, 1861, about a month after the Rangers had disbanded, Clemens started west with his older brother, Orion Clemens, who had just been appointed the territorial secretary of Nevada. Clemens intended to make his fortune by mining silver, but he soon discovered that journalism was not only easier physically but also paid more regularly. By late 1862 he was a full-time newspaperman in Virginia City, and on February 3, 1863, he decided to sign an article with the name "Mark Twain," an old river expression that meant "two fathoms." Within two years his new name would be famous across the country.

Coincidentally, some years later Twain discovered that the commanding officer of that regiment ordered to destroy Confederate irregulars was none other than Colonel Ulysses S. Grant, an ex-army officer who had recently resumed his military career after being cashiered for drunkenness in 1854. Grant had spent the years immediately before the war in the St. Louis area, where he and his wife had reportedly socialized with William and Pamela Moffett, Twain's brother-in-law and sister. Many years after the war, and following his presidency, Grant would begin a friendship with Twain, who would later offer his own company to publish the president's memoirs. The collaboration was a success, and *The Personal Memoirs of U. S. Grant* became a best seller in late 1885, although Grant himself died in July 1885, shortly after completing his final draft.

In *The Private History of a Campaign That Failed*, Twain summed up his wartime experiences: "It seemed an epitome of war; that all war must be just that—the killing of strangers against whom you feel no personal animosity; strangers whom, in other circumstances, you would help if you found them in trouble, and who would help you if you needed it. My campaign was spoiled. . . . I could have become a soldier myself if I had waited. I had got part of it learned; I knew more about retreating than the man that invented retreating."

6. Law and Rights

Introduction

JOHN FABIAN WITT

Law has always had an awkward place in the history of the Civil War. For nearly three quarters of a century the Constitution of 1787 had held together a legal entity called the United States, divided though it was by region and slavery. But in April 1861 the guns of Charleston Harbor signaled the collapse of the legal regime the Framers had patched together in Philadelphia.

It should be no surprise, then, that scholars have given short shrift to the war's legal aspects. Though Lincoln's willingness to suspend habeas corpus was at the time a matter of national scandal, scholars have long considered it and other developments a sideshow. No one expressed this better than the historian Charles Francis Adams Jr., himself a Civil War veteran. Looking back on the war fifty years later, Adams characterized its legal controversies as "unintelligible" and "ludicrous," a "solemn farce" in the midst of a deadly serious conflict. Subsequent historians have typically followed suit. Until the last third of the twentieth century historians derided Lincoln as a lawless tyrant; more recently they are likely to cheer the president for his pragmatic willingness to disregard lawyers' sacred cows when common sense so required. Either way, the law seemed irrelevant to the action.

Two thousand years ago Cicero asserted that in times of war the law falls silent. It has been exceedingly difficult for Americans to hear the voice of the law over the din of a war that killed 750,000 people. Nonetheless the law spoke, dictating the course of important junctures in the conflict. It was, after all, the law of the Constitution that shaped the path to war from at least 1820 onward. None of the controversy over the admission into the Union of the western states as either free or slave makes sense without the constitutionally created balance of the Senate's votes: two per state. Secession was a legal act too; the Confederate States of America wrote a constitution of their own (one that looked remarkably like the Constitution of 1787, with a few pro-slaveholder amendments). And once secession began, Lincoln's authority, his tools, and his dilemmas were built on the blocks of law and the Constitution. It was law that told Americans who was the president; it was law that constituted the Congress; and it was law that defined what Lincoln meant when he said that reestablishing the legal entity known as the Union was the war goal of the North. Law, it turns out, did not disappear when the shooting started. To the contrary, legal institutions defined the field. It told people who was who.

This is not to say that the Civil War did not put many pieces of the prewar legal order under enormous stress. Of course it did. Some legal rules and institutions simply burst asunder. The widely held assumption that only Congress could suspend the writ of habeas corpus gave way for the war's first two years. In the summer and fall of 1862 perhaps the most important consensus in the antebellum Constitution—that the federal government lacked authority to abolish slavery in the states—gave way in the face of Congress's Second Confiscation Act and Lincoln's Emancipation Proclamation. In less well-remembered areas such as the law of the blockade, the Lincoln administration unilaterally reversed long-standing U.S. positions on the freedom of neutral merchant shipping on the high seas.

The hardest part in thinking about the role of law in the conflict is to see that even these moments—when the law seemed to be pressed to its limits or simply violated—offer evidence for the continuing significance of the law. The Lincoln administration's controversial decisions sometimes contorted the law. But flouting the law did not come cheap. Decisions to suspend the writ of habeas corpus, emancipate slaves behind rebel lines, and issue controversial blockade orders all exerted political costs. They were ways in which the administration spent political capital. And legal obstacles increased the price of those policies, often substantially if we can go by the extent to which opponents cited and relied on the law in their criticisms.

Consider the Union's piracy prosecutions. In the fall and winter of 1861–62 the Lincoln administration sought to prosecute as pirates all captured seamen aboard private vessels designated by the Confederacy as "privateers": privately owned vessels commissioned by one nation-state to fight against an enemy in wartime. The Union position was that the Confederacy was not a nation-state at all but a criminal conspiracy. And so its "privateers" were not entitled to be treated as legitimate combatants. They were pirates and punishable as such. The difficulty for Lincoln was that the Union had assembled a blockade off the Southern coastline. The blockade was an act of war for legal purposes, which implied that the Confederacy was the equivalent of a nation-state. The Union, in short, wanted to have it both ways. And for a little while it seemed as if it might work. But in one case involving a captured Confederate privateer, a charismatic lawyer named Algernon Sydney Sullivan pointed out the inconsistency to the jury—and the jury refused to convict, despite the fact that the defendant was fighting against the very Union that had impaneled them. The costs of the inconsistency were made clear, and the Union abandoned its piracy prosecutions for the duration of the war.

Emancipation too signaled the continuing significance of the law. At the time even many critics in the North condemned acts like the Emancipation Proclamation as illegal.

But in retrospect the limits of emancipation seem more salient. The order Lincoln issued on January 1, 1863, applied only behind rebel lines. That it excepted the border states made political sense: Lincoln could not afford to lose the support of the fragile Union coalitions of Missouri, Kentucky, and Maryland. But why exempt those parts of secessionist states under Union occupation? One central reason was the source of Lincoln's authority to issue the Proclamation in the first place. Emancipation, Lincoln explained, was an act warranted by "military necessity." As such it applied only where Union armies had not yet been victorious. Antislavery critics ever since have complained that the proclamation by itself therefore freed not a single slave. That may be true—it's complicated. But that's the point: Lincoln acted according to the law, as limiting as it was.

One last example is irresistible. Why, one wants to know, were there no prosecutions for treason after the war? Never in American history has widespread treason been more apparent. And the Union was in a powerful position to punish secession as treason: in the summer of 1865 virtually all of the Confederacy's high-ranking officials were held in Union custody. Jefferson Davis, the president of the Confederacy, moldered in Fortress Monroe. In fact Davis was indicted for treason not once but twice! And yet not a single treason trial ever took place.

Historians cite any number of reasons. There was the risk of a deadlocked jury in Virginia, which, as the place where the crime had been committed, would be the site of the trial. (Such a jury, composed of men sympathetic to Davis, might even acquit.) There was the difficulty of getting the reluctant chief justice, Salmon P. Chase, to preside. And there was already an emerging desire to let bygones be bygones, to move on.

But the central difficulty in any prosecution of Jefferson Davis was that, having treated the Confederacy during nearly four years on the battlefield as the equivalent of a nation-state, it was costly to toggle back to treating it as a criminal conspiracy. The Union had treated the South's soldiers as legitimate combatants. It had erected a blockade as if the Confederacy were its own country. And so in 1865 it turned out to be exceedingly difficult to switch the basic premises of the conflict and pretend it had been something other than a war.

Here, then, is the payoff from attending to the law of the Civil War. It reveals that the conflict was not a total war at all, at least not if a total war is one in which there are no rules but only a lawless anarchy. On the contrary the law fundamentally shaped the course of the war, just as much as politics and the battlefield did.

States' Rights, but to What?

PAUL FINKELMAN

On December 20, 1860 South Carolina declared its independence from the United States. The move had been in the offing since early November, when Abraham Lincoln's election led the state's leaders to fear that Washington would begin to restrict slavery in the territories and in their own state. That was the proximate cause, at least; there was more to it. Beyond the election South Carolina was no longer happy in a union with the free states, where Northern opponents of slavery were allowed to openly denounce the "peculiar institution" in Congress and in their home states.

It's true, then, that South Carolina seceded over states' rights, though, as neo-Confederates are loath to admit, the specific right in question concerned the ownership of human chattel. One of the South's persistent complaints was that the Northern states would not vigorously cooperate in the return of fugitive slaves and that the free states allowed antislavery organizations to flourish.

In other words, for South Carolina, slavery and states' rights were not mutually exclusive; in fact they were the same thing. Today too few people understand the intricate legal history that connects slavery to states' rights—and as a result a needless debate continues, 150 years after secession began.

As most people know, until the adoption of the Thirteenth Amendment in 1865 owning slaves was constitutionally protected. But the Constitution also protected the slave owners' right to have escaped slaves returned: the Fugitive Slave Clause of Article 4, Section 2 of the Constitution declares that "No Person held to Service or Labour in one State, under the Laws thereof, escaping into another, shall, in Consequence of any Law or Regulation therein, be discharged from such Service or Labour, but shall be delivered up on Claim of the Party to whom such Service or Labour may be due."

The clause was awkwardly phrased and deliberately constructed to mislead readers; the delegates to the Constitutional Convention purposely did not use the term *slave* in the Constitution. Its language seemed to imply that the return of fugitive slaves would be entirely a matter of interstate relations. That made sense at the time: slavery was legal in eleven of the thirteen states; only Massachusetts and New Hampshire had ended the institution. Pennsylvania, Rhode Island, and Connecticut had passed laws to gradually end slavery, but all three had legislation authorizing the return of fugitive slaves.

Despite the ambiguous language of the constitutional clause, in 1793 Congress passed the first Fugitive Slave Law, which regulated the return of runaway slaves and authorized both federal and state judges to enforce it. The standards in this law were weak, and many Northerners feared it would lead to kidnapping.

The federal government got involved at an opportune time because the slave-owning consensus at the state level was fracturing. By 1804 New York and New Jersey had passed laws to gradually end slavery, while the new Northern states, Vermont and Ohio, had banned slavery outright. Moreover, starting in the 1820s most Northern states passed legislation known as "personal liberty laws" to protect free blacks from kidnapping. These laws also made it more difficult for Southerners to recover their fugitive slaves because, in addition to the federal requirements regulating the removal of alleged fugitives, they had to fulfill state rules as well.

In 1842 the U.S. Supreme Court weighed in with its decision in *Prigg v. Pennsylvania*. The Court ruled that the personal liberty laws violated a master's constitutional right to reclaim a runaway slave. The Court went further, holding that a master did not even have to bring a fugitive before a judge but had a common law right to recapture a runaway as long as it could be done without a breach of the peace. In an attempt to create a uniform national law, the Court also held that Northern judges had a constitutional and moral obligation to enforce the 1793 law (though, because they were not paid by the federal government, they could not be required to do so).

Southerners, of course, saw the ruling as a vindication of a constitutional right. But Northerners, incensed by this overwhelming federal protection of slavery, saw it as a license for kidnapping. As a result, with few federal judges in the nation and no national system of law enforcement, Southerners had an unqualified right to seize their fugitive slaves wherever they found them. But they could not necessarily count on any law enforcement from Northerners to help them.

Their fears were soon realized: eight months after the *Prigg* decision a Virginia master was forced to leave a slave, George Latimer, in Boston in exchange for a sum that was far less than Latimer was worth, because local law enforcement officials would not keep in him in jail long enough for a court to order his return to Virginia. Less than a year later Massachusetts passed the "Latimer Law," which prohibited the use of state jails and the participation of state judges in the return of fugitive slaves. Most of the other Northern states soon passed similar laws.

This led to Southern demands for federal guarantees that they could recover their runaway slaves, culminating in the infamous Fugitive Slave Law of 1850. The law allowed for the appointment of a federal commissioner in every county of the nation with the power to hear fugitive slave cases and order the return of an alleged fugitive. It was the country's first federal law enforcement bureaucracy and the first instance of a federal law enforcement presence at the local level.

The law was dramatically unfair: it denied alleged fugitives a jury trial, access to the writ of habeas corpus, and, most astounding of all, the right to testify at the hearing. Anyone interfering in the return of a fugitive slave could face six months in jail and a $1,000 fine, an enormous sum in the 1850s.

The worst part of the law was the procedure for paying commissioners. They received $5 if they determined that the alleged slave was in fact a free person, but they got $10 if they decided the person was a slave. Congress had reasoned that if a commissioner found for the slave owner he would have to fill out a great deal of paperwork and thus need greater compensation. But for the vast majority of Northerners this seemed like a crude attempt to buy justice.

The Fugitive Slave Law was never as effective as Southerners wanted, but over the next decade about 350 slaves were returned under it. Only a dozen or so were rescued by mobs across the North; while most Northerners opposed the law, few were willing to openly defy it. But where they did—in Boston, Syracuse, Oberlin, Milwaukee, and elsewhere— the rescues made headlines as they undermined the credibility of the national government and sent a powerful message to the South.

The standards in the Fugitive Slave Law were weak, and many Northerners feared it would lead to kidnapping. Library of Congress Prints and Photographs Division, LC-USZ62-1286.

In short, during the decades leading up to the 1860 election Northerners and Southerners battled over whether, and how, the states or the federal government would control the future of slavery. In this period the Southerners almost always won. But for South Carolinians, Lincoln's election appeared to be a takeover of the federal government by opponents not just of slavery but of the fugitive slave laws that they believed maintained the delicate balance between pro- and antislavery sentiments.

Even though Lincoln was on record insisting he would enforce all federal laws in both regions, they had something of a point. In its "Declaration of the Immediate Causes Which Induce and Justify the Secession of South Carolina from the Federal Union," the state declared that the

> ends for which this Government was instituted have been defeated, and the Government itself has been made destructive of them by the action of the non-slaveholding States. Those States have assumed the right of deciding upon the propriety of our domestic institutions; and have denied the rights of property established in fifteen of the States and recognized by the Constitution: they have denounced as sinful the institution of slavery; they have permitted open establishment among them of societies, whose avowed object is to disturb the peace and to eloign the property of the citizens of other States. They have encouraged and assisted thousands of our slaves to leave their homes; and those who remain, have been incited by emissaries, books and pictures to servile insurrection.

The South Carolinians put their argument in constitutional terms, claiming secession was both justified and necessary because "a geographical line has been drawn across the Union, and all the States north of that line have united in the election of a man to the high office of President of the United States, whose opinions and purposes are hostile to slavery. He is to be entrusted with the administration of the common Government, because he has declared that that 'Government cannot endure permanently half slave, half free,' and that the public mind must rest in the belief that slavery is in the course of ultimate extinction."

In other words, the Palmetto State asserted that slavery was threatened because the North no longer followed the Constitution, which protected states' rights to maintain the institution of slavery and protected the rights of individual Southerners to retrieve fugitive slaves. The South Carolinians wrote:

> But an increasing hostility on the part of the non-slaveholding States to the institution of slavery, has led to a disregard of their obligations, and the laws of the General Government have ceased to effect the objects of the Constitution. . . . [They] have enacted laws which either nullify the Acts of Congress or render useless any attempt to execute them. In many of these States the fugitive is discharged from service or labor claimed, and in none of them has the State Government complied with the stipulation made in the Constitution. . . . Thus the constituted compact has been deliberately broken and disregarded by the non-slaveholding States, and the consequence follows that South Carolina is released from her obligation.

Not all Southerners supported secession; those who opposed it argued that slavery was safer in the Union because they believed the national government could never free the slaves. As Charles Cotesworth Pinckney, the adamantly proslavery leader of the South Carolina delegation to the Constitutional Convention, bragged to his state's legislature, "We have a security that the general government can never emancipate them, for no such authority is granted and it is admitted, on all hands, that the general government has no powers but what are expressly granted by the Constitution, and that all rights not expressed were reserved by the several states."

But these arguments fell on deaf ears. South Carolinians no longer trusted the national government, the free states, or the Constitution. In that sense secession was most definitely about states' rights. But it is vital to remember just which rights South Carolina was committed to defending.

Freedom and Restraint

JOHN FABIAN WITT

On September 22, 1862, Abraham Lincoln announced the Emancipation Proclamation, promising to free the slaves in any state still in rebellion on January 1, 1863. Americans have celebrated Lincoln's proclamation, and argued about its meaning, ever since. But there's a surprising legacy that few Americans know anything about, one that historians have overlooked even though it shows just how thoroughly American ideas of freedom reshaped the globe. Emancipation touched off a crisis for the principle of humanitarian limits in wartime and transformed the international laws of war. In the crucible of emancipation Lincoln created the rules that now govern soldiers around the world.

Ever since 1775, when the royal governor of Virginia offered freedom to slaves who would turn against their revolutionary masters, American soldiers and statesmen held that freeing an enemy's slaves was anathema to civilized warfare. George Washington and the Continental Congress complained bitterly when British forces carried away slaves when they left New York in 1783.

In the War of 1812 British raids along Chesapeake Bay encouraged thousands of slaves to escape to freedom. For more than a decade after the war ended the American government pursued compensation from the British, contending that the laws of war protected slave owners from enemy depredations.

The irony of a humanitarian law that protected slave owners rather than slaves was not lost on European critics. But Americans argued that to seize an enemy's slaves was to make war on civilian economic resources.

White Southerners further argued that arming an enemy's slaves invited terrible atrocities by freed people against their former masters. Nineteenth-century Americans knew that the servile rebellions of antiquity had involved horrific violence: the Haitian Revolution in the 1790s led to the slaughter of white slaveholders, while several abortive slave revolts in the American South showed that the pent-up violence of slavery could explode in bursts of nightmarish terror.

It was no surprise, then, that Southern whites reacted to Lincoln's proclamation with fury. Jefferson Davis, the president of the Confederacy, condemned it as barbaric and inhumane, and he swore never to recognize black Union soldiers as entitled to the treatment afforded to prisoners of war. Instead he promised to punish them and their white officers as criminals, subject to enslavement or execution. The Union pledged to retaliate in turn. It soon seemed that efforts to limit the war might collapse altogether.

The South's threats forced the Union to restate its position on the laws of war. In December 1862, three weeks before the final emancipation order was to go into effect, and just as criticism of emancipation was reaching its height, Lincoln's general in chief, Henry W. Halleck, commissioned a pamphlet-length statement of the Union's view of the laws of war.

Drafted by the Columbia professor Francis Lieber and approved by Lincoln himself, the code set out a host of humane rules: it prohibited torture, protected prisoners of war, and outlawed assassinations; it distinguished between soldiers and civilians, and it disclaimed cruelty, revenge attacks, and senseless suffering.

Most of all the code defended the freeing of enemy slaves and the arming of black soldiers as a humanitarian imperative, not as an invitation to atrocity. The code announced that free armies were like roving institutions of freedom, abolishing slavery wherever they

The First Reading of the Emancipation Proclamation before the Cabinet, engraved by A. H. Ritchie. Library of Congress Prints and Photographs Division, LC-DIG-pga-03452.

went. And it defended black soldiers by insisting that the laws of war made "no distinction of color"—indeed mistreatment of black soldiers would warrant righteous retaliation by the Union.

The pocket-size pamphlet quickly became the blueprint for a new generation of treaties, up to the Geneva Conventions of 1949. Strong nations like Prussia and France had long suspected that law-of-war initiatives were little more than maneuvering by weaker countries and closet pacifists hoping to make war more difficult. Lincoln's code broke that diplomatic logjam: it contained no hidden European agenda, and no one could accuse the Lincoln administration of trying to hold back strong armies.

To the contrary the code had been devised just as Lincoln abandoned what he called the "rose-water" tactics of the war's first year in favor of the much more aggressive strategy signaled by emancipation.

And it set in motion the great paradox of the modern laws of war. These laws arose out of the greatest moral triumph of modern political history—emancipation—and they aimed to place outer limits on war's destruction. In a sense they succeeded: the feared terrors of a mass slave insurrection never came to pass.

But by authorizing freedom the new code also licensed a powerful and dangerous war strategy. It was a tool of the Union war effort, like the Springfield rifle and the Minié ball. That is why the Lincoln administration issued it, and that is why the most powerful states in the European world signed on to versions of it in the decades that followed.

The rules of armed conflict today arise directly out of Lincoln's example. They restrain brutality, but by placing a stamp of approval on "acceptable" ways to make war, they legitimate terrible violence. The law does not relieve war of all its terrors; it does not even purport to. But it stands as a living reminder, a century and a half later, of how thoroughly the most significant moment for the United States still shapes our moral universe.

The Lieber Code

RICK BEARD

In October 1861 a legal scholar and historian named Francis Lieber presented the first in a series of lectures entitled "The Laws and Usages of War" at the Columbia College's new law school in New York City. Though the talks, which ran through the following March, were long and often rambling, each drew up to a hundred people and afterward appeared in the *New York Times* and other newspapers around the country. The public, eager for insight into how the worsening war would and should be fought, devoured his every word.

Lieber was an unlikely public intellectual. He had arrived in the United States from Prussia in 1827. Unable to secure a permanent teaching post at a Northern university, he had spent over twenty apparently uncomfortable years teaching at South Carolina College (now the University of South Carolina), where his decidedly unsympathetic views on states' rights and slavery made him an outlier among his Southern colleagues. His decision to relocate to New York City in 1857 proved fortuitous. Columbia College, in the midst of expanding its faculty, appointed him a professor of history and political science, and in 1860 the law school named him professor of political science. Lieber retained his affiliation with Columbia until his death in 1872.

Lieber's popular lectures mirrored his belief that the laws of war needed to reflect the legitimacy of the combatants' war aims. Much of nineteenth-century thought defined a rigid set of rules with which to regulate armed conflict—the means—while devoting little if any consideration to the conflict's ends. In Lieber's calculus, ends could not be separated from means; the ends were the essential determinants of a military action's justification.

In the spring of 1862 Lieber renewed an acquaintance that would provide him with an unparalleled opportunity to put his theories into practice. While in St. Louis searching desperately for one of his sons, Hamilton, who had been wounded at Fort Donelson in February, Lieber turned to Union general Henry Halleck for help. The two had met briefly seventeen years earlier and found common ground in a shared distaste for the peace societies active in the 1840s. Halleck, a successful lawyer before the war, had himself earned a reputation as a political theorist when, in 1861, he published *International Law, or, Rules Regulating the Intercourse of States in Peace and War*.

After Halleck was named general in chief on July 23, 1862, Lieber sent him a letter congratulating him on his "high appointment" and alerting him, "I am now studying

Francis Lieber. Library of Congress Prints and Photographs Division, LC-DIG-cwpbh-01402.

for myself the very important question of Guerrilleros." Halleck's response a week later solicited Lieber's views on guerrilla warfare, a topic he noted "has now become an important question in this country."

The result was "Guerilla Parties Considered with Reference to the Laws and Usages of War," a 6,000-word report, replete with historical examples, which Lieber sent to Halleck in mid-August. The Union commander in chief responded enthusiastically and almost immediately: "I have hastily read your essay and highly approve it. I return it . . . with an order for 5,000 copies."

Lieber argued that three functional factors distinguished a soldier, who was entitled to all the protections of the laws of war, from a guerrilla, who was not: the presence of uniforms, an organized command structure, and the capacity to manage prisoners of war. Such factors trumped the more traditional consideration of a formal commission from one of the belligerent parties.

Halleck distributed Lieber's essay among his generals, many of whom embraced it immediately. The policies implicit in the document afforded Union field officers considerable discretion when handling enemy guerrillas; taken to its logical extreme, Lieber's formulation justified the summary execution of Confederate guerrilla fighters who fell into Union hands. While some Union commanders did carry out battlefield judgments, Lieber himself shied away from endorsing these acts, fearing they would initiate an endless cycle of retaliation. And although Lincoln came to endorse such executions, he did so reluctantly and more often than not commuted death sentences when the opportunity presented itself.

In addition to his work on guerrilla warfare, that same August Lieber prepared a memorandum at the request of Secretary of War Edwin M. Stanton on the "military use of colored persons." In it he argued that "the acknowledged law of war" admitted the use of slaves in armies. Lieber also maintained a regular correspondence with Halleck and with several members of the Lincoln administration throughout the late summer and fall of 1862.

As the date for Lincoln's issuance of the Emancipation Proclamation drew ever closer, the questions of slavery, its relationship to the laws of war, and how the newly freed slaves would act became increasingly fraught subjects. Confederate leaders, who had long felt the threat of potential slave revolts, were beside themselves at Lincoln's decision to recruit and train African American troops. Jefferson Davis ordered that former slaves fighting for the Union and their officers were to be treated as criminals and prosecuted by state authorities. Even those presumably inclined toward emancipation urged caution. Charles Francis Adams Jr., a captain in the 1st Massachusetts Cavalry and the son of Lincoln's minister to Britain, warned that "emancipation would force millions of irresponsible barbarians into society," where they would exact "just vengeance for their own wrongs."

In November Lieber wrote Halleck to urge the appointment of "a committee . . . to draw up a code . . . in which certain acts and offences (under the Law of War) ought to be defined and, where necessary, the punishment be stated." Scarcely a month later Halleck and Stanton called Lieber to Washington, where, on December 12, they appointed him to work with a small board of advisers to revise the 1806 Articles of War.

Lieber's fellow committee members included Major General Ethan Allen Hitchcock, the Union's commissioner for prisoner exchanges; Major General George Cadwalader, one of the first Union officers to question how the Union was to respond to slave uprisings in the South; Major General George L. Hartsuff, who had been wounded at Antietam; and Brigadier General John Henry Martindale, the military governor of Washington. The four left Lieber alone to draft the new set of instructions for the Union Army. He immediately plunged into the task, spending Christmas in Washington and returning to New York to complete the work in January 1863.

Hitchcock and his colleagues basically accepted Lieber's work without change. Only Halleck engaged in any meaningful editing, combing through the more than a dozen articles that addressed some aspect of slavery, emancipation, and the arming of former slaves to ensure that nothing in the new code undermined Lincoln's emancipation policies. On April 24, 1863, the president issued the finished code as "Instructions for the Government of Armies of the United States in the Field," General Order No. 100.

The code's 157 articles, broken into ten sections, addressed a staggering array of topics: from martial law to the protection of persons, religion, and the arts and sciences;

from the treatment of deserters, women, prisoners of war, partisans, scouts, spies, and captured messengers to prisoner exchanges and flags of truce; from battlefield booty to parole, armistice, and assassinations.

Lieber, who had consistently decried the "namby-pamby" views of warfare he ascribed to many Enlightenment jurists, embraced (as did Lincoln) what the scholar John Fabian Witt has characterized as "tough humanitarianism." The basic foundation of his code, Witt contends, was that "virtually any use of force was permissible if required by military necessity," which produced "both a broad limit on war's violence and a robust license to destroy." The best wars lasted the shortest amount of time. "The more vigorously wars are pursued," wrote Lieber in the code, "the better it is for humanity. Sharp wars are brief."

The reaction to Lieber's code, particularly those articles addressing slavery, fell out along predictable lines. Confederate secretary of war James Seddon fulminated that the articles were intended "to subvert by violence the social system and domestic relations of the negro slaves in the Confederacy and to add to the calamities of war a servile insurrection." Supporters of the Lincoln administration saw the code instead as a complement to the Emancipation Proclamation and a means of preventing the sort of slave insurrection that its critics predicted. More immediately it represented a response to Southern threats to prosecute black soldiers and their white officers as criminals.

Historians disagree about the meaning of Lieber's code for the remaining years of the Civil War. Surely it provided a starting point for negotiation on many issues, and it secured the moral high ground for Union leaders denouncing such Confederate depredations as the massacre of black troops at Fort Pillow. While many critics might well contend that General William Tecumseh Sherman's 1864 campaign gave the lie to any ameliorative impact of the Lieber Code on the Union Army, his actions might better be viewed as, in Witt's analysis, "the practical embodiment of the code's unsettling critique of the orthodox laws of war." Of equal importance is the long afterlife enjoyed by Lieber's work; it became a core text in the modern laws of war recognized worldwide, and many elements of his code continue to inform our public debate on how best to respond to a new form of warfare in both an effective and a moral manner.

Rape and Justice in the Civil War

CRYSTAL N. FEIMSTER

President Lincoln's General Orders No. 100, also known as the Lieber Code of 1863, set clear rules for engaging with enemy combatants. But the code also clarified how Union soldiers should treat civilians, and in particular women. Largely forgotten today, the Lieber Code established strict laws regarding an issue that was everywhere and nowhere in the consciousness of the Civil War: wartime rape.

Three articles under Section 2 declare that soldiers would "acknowledge and protect, in hostile countries occupied by them, religion and morality; strictly private property; the persons of the inhabitants, especially those of women" (Article 37); that "all robbery, all pillage or sacking, even after taking a place by main force, all rape, wounding, maiming, or killing of such inhabitants, are prohibited under the penalty of death" (Article 44); and that "crimes punishable by all penal codes, such as . . . rape, if committed by an American soldier in a hostile country against its inhabitants, are not only punishable as at home, but in all cases in which death is not inflicted the severer punishment shall be preferred" (Article 47).

Together the articles conceived and defined rape in women-specific terms as a crime against property, as a crime of troop discipline, and as a crime against family honor. Most significant, the articles codified the precepts of modern war on the protection of women against rape that set the stage for a century of humanitarian and international law.

Such explicit prohibition was necessary because, even after the code was in place, sexual violence was common to the wartime experience of Southern women, white and black. Whether they lived on large plantations or small farms, in towns, cities, or contraband camps, white and black women all over the American South experienced the sexual trauma of war.

Execution of a Union soldier for rape. Library of Congress Prints and Photographs Division, LC-DIG-ppmsca-11172.

Union military courts prosecuted at least 450 cases involving sexual crimes. In North Carolina during the spring of 1865 Private James Preble "did by physical force and violence commit rape upon the person of one Miss Letitia Craft." When Perry Holland of the 1st Missouri Infantry confessed to the rape of Julia Anderson, a white woman in Tennessee, he was sentenced to be shot, but his sentence was later commuted. Catherine Farmer, also of Tennessee, testified that Lieutenant Harvey John of the 49th Ohio Infantry dragged her into the bushes and told her he would kill her if she did not "give it to him." He tore her dress, broke her hoops, and "put his private parts into her," for which he was sentenced to ten years in prison. In Georgia, Albert Lane, part of Company B in the 100th Regiment of Ohio Volunteers, was also sentenced to ten years because he "did on or about the 11th day of July, 1864 . . . upon one Miss Louisa Dickerson . . . then and there forcibly and against her will, feloniously did ravish and carnally know her."

Black women were in even more danger. Rape was one of the many horrors of slavery, though whites rarely recognized it as such. Interestingly it was only in the context of war that Southern whites for the first time were forced to acknowledge the rape of black women. In the spring of 1863 John N. Williams of the 7th Tennessee Regiment wrote in his diary, "Heard from home. The Yankees has been through there. Seem to be their object to commit rape on every Negro woman they can find." Many times troops and ruffians raped black women while forcing white women to watch, a horrifying experience for all and a proxy rape of white women. B. E. Harrison of Leesburg, Virginia, wrote a letter to President Abraham Lincoln complaining that federal troops had raped his "servant girl" in the presence of his wife. General William Dwight reported, "Negro women were ravished in the presence of white women and children." Just as the rape of white women implied that Southern men were unable to protect their mothers, wives, and daughters, the rape of slave women told whites they could no longer protect their property.

A close examination of cases involving the rape of black women reveals that, while black women may have been particularly vulnerable to wartime rape, the Lieber Code brought them for the first time under the umbrella of legal protection. In fact some black women were able to mobilize military law to their advantage.

In the summer of 1864 Jenny Green, a young "colored" girl who had escaped slavery and sought refuge with the Union Army in Richmond, Virginia, was brutally raped by Lieutenant Andrew J. Smith, 11th Pennsylvania Cavalry. Thanks to the Lieber Code, though, she was able to bring charges against him and even testify in a military court. "He threw me on the floor, pulled up my dress," she told the all-male tribunal. "He held my hands with one hand, held part of himself with the other hand and went into me. It hurt. He did what married people do. I am but a child." That a former slave, and an adolescent girl at that, could demand and receive legal redress was revolutionary. Despite his attorney's argument that Green had consented, Smith was discharged from the army and sentenced to ten years of hard labor.

This was not an isolated instance or a random judge's opinion. The effect of the Lieber Code was almost immediate, as was agreement on the part of high-ranking officials. In reviewing Smith's sentence General Benjamin Butler—notorious for his Women's Order in New Orleans that threatened rape of women who resisted occupation by insulting Union soldiers—supported the guilty verdict. In summarizing the case he explained, "A female negro child quits Slavery, and comes into the protection of the federal government, and upon first reaching the limits of the federal lines, receives the brutal treatment from an officer, himself a husband and a father, of violation of her person."

Unwilling to entertain pleas for mercy on Smith's behalf, Butler declared the officer lucky to walk away with his life. "A day or two since a negro man was hung, in the presence of the army, for the attempted violation of the person of a white woman," he argued. "Equal and exact justice would have taken this officer's life; but imprisonment in the Penitentiary for a long term of years, his loss of rank and position—if that imprisonment be without hope of pardon, as it should be—would be almost an equal example." Abraham Lincoln also reviewed the case and wrote, "I concluded [to let Smith] suffer for a while and then discharge him."

Southern women's wartime diaries, court-martial records, wartime general orders, military reports, and letters written by women, soldiers, doctors, nurses, and military chaplains leave little doubt that, as in most wars, rape and the threat of sexual violence figured large in the military campaigns that swept across the Southern landscape. Nonetheless the Lieber Code made it possible for women to seek justice in military courts and eventually established the modern understanding of rape as a war crime.

Lincoln Answers His Critics

DOUGLAS L. WILSON

Today we widely understand that Abraham Lincoln's use of presidential war powers was indispensable to his success. But one of his biggest problems at the time was convincing the Northern public that suspending habeas corpus and other restraints on civil liberties was both temporary and constitutional and that their enforcement was necessary to win the war.

There was of course no convincing his strongest opponents, the Peace Democrats, who regarded the Union's military efforts as the effective cause of the rebellion. But even among many of his supporters the steady employment of presidential war powers from the first days of the war—especially the suspension of habeas corpus and the detention of civilians—raised the specter of dictatorship.

These issues came to a head in May 1863, when Union officers under General Ambrose Burnside, the commander of the Department of the Ohio, arrested a former congressman named Clement Vallandigham, a leading Copperhead, for defying an order forbidding the public expression of sympathy with the enemy. Tried and convicted by a military commission and sentenced to prison for the duration of the war—and eventually exiled—Vallandigham became an instant martyr.

The public outcry was immediate and general. How could the administration justify the arrest and imprisonment of a politician, especially by the military, for criticizing its policies? Even Lincoln was skeptical, though he was in no position to criticize the arrest. The situation was aggravated by the recent passage of an unpopular draft law and the stubbornly discouraging course of the war. Looking back on Lincoln's presidency, his secretaries and biographers declared, "No act of the Government has been so strongly criticized, and none having relation to the rights of an individual created a feeling so deep and so widespread." The great Lincoln scholar James G. Randall pronounced the Vallandigham affair "the cause célèbre of the Lincoln administration."

Lincoln's way of confronting this crisis tells us a great deal about the man, his unorthodox methods, and the success of his presidency. His response took the surprising form of a public letter, though it was not a spontaneous reaction to the event that prompted it. An Iowa congressman, James F. Wilson, related what Lincoln told him several months later about the preparation of the letter: "Turning to a drawer in the desk at which he was sitting and pulling it partly out, he said: 'When it became necessary for me to write that letter, I had it nearly all in there,' pointing to the drawer, 'but it was in disconnected thoughts, which I had jotted down from time to time on separate scraps of paper.'"

The occasion Lincoln chose for offering his defense was a petition of protest from a group of loyal Democrats meeting in Albany, New York, and chaired by the former congressman Erastus Corning. The tenor of the meeting reflected the angry words of New York's Democratic governor Horatio Seymour, who charged that if Vallandigham's prosecution was "approved by the Government, and sanctioned by the people, it is not merely a step toward revolution—it is revolution; it will not only lead to military despotism—it establishes military despotism." Lincoln's response was addressed to them but released to the public.

Lincoln's letter begins shrewdly. Because the petitioners pledge loyalty and support for the administration "in every constitutional, and lawful measure to suppress the rebellion," clearly their differences with him are not so much about ends as about "the choice of means." He then stresses that the petitioners have not taken into account that the Constitution makes provision for exceptional circumstances. "Ours is a case of Rebellion—so called by the resolutions before me—in fact, a clear, flagrant, and gigantic case of Rebellion; and the provision of the constitution that 'The previlege [sic] of the writ of Habeas Corpus shall not be suspended, unless when in cases of Rebellion or Invasion, the public Safety may require it' is the provision which specially applies to our present case."

Lincoln then proceeds to use this constitutional distinction to emphasize the difference between what is allowable in times of rebellion or invasion that would not be allowable in ordinary times. Vallandigham was arrested, Lincoln writes,

> because he was laboring, with some effect, to prevent the raising of troops, to encourage desertions from the army, and to leave the rebellion without an adequate military force to suppress it. He was not arrested because he was damaging the political prospects of the

Erastus Corning. Library of Congress Prints and Photographs Division, LC-DIG-cwpbh-02783.

administration, or the personal interests of the commanding general; but because he was damaging the army, upon the existence, and vigor of which, the life of the nation depends. He was warring upon the military; and this gave the military constitutional jurisdiction to lay hands upon him. If Mr. Vallandigham was not damaging the military power of the country, then his arrest was made on mistake of fact, which I would be glad to correct, on reasonably satisfactory evidence.

This is the heart of Lincoln's case, but it sets the stage for the highlight of his letter, the part that may have turned the tide of public opinion in his favor and certainly proved its most memorable moment. Against the claim that Vallandigham was simply expressing his political differences with the administration, Lincoln insists that in "warring upon the military" the former congressman was attempting to undermine military discipline and to encourage a willingness to desert, an action that was punishable by death. "Must I shoot a simple-minded soldier boy who deserts," Lincoln demands, "while I must not touch a hair of a wiley agitator who induces him to desert?"

We can be sure that another of the scraps in Lincoln's desk drawer was a note on General Andrew Jackson's handling of the issue of habeas corpus after winning the Battle of New Orleans, for it served Lincoln's purposes perfectly. Forced to defy a court to maintain martial law, Jackson, the legendary hero of the Democrats, answered the summons of the same judge after martial law was lifted and paid a fine of $1,000, an amount that was gratefully remitted by Congress thirty years later. Lincoln writes, "The permanent right of the people to public discussion, the liberty of speech and the press, the trial by jury, the law of evidence, and the Habeas Corpus, suffered no detriment whatever by that conduct of Gen. Jackson, or its subsequent approval by the American congress."

Lincoln's masterful letter to Corning contains many other fine touches and must be read in its entirely to be properly appreciated. Published on June 12, 1863, to great acclaim, the letter was so popular that it was reprinted as a pamphlet and eventually reached as many as 500,000 readers. What is all the more remarkable is that Lincoln did not agree with Burnside's decision to arrest Vallandigham but managed nonetheless to articulate and defend the constitutional rationale behind it. As the historian Mark E. Neely Jr. has written, "Burnside's unfortunate act caused Lincoln to fight on ground not of his own choosing, but he fought exceedingly well."

The Father of the Fourteenth Amendment

GERARD MAGLIOCCA

In September 1863 the Ohio politician John Bingham was at the lowest point of his career. He had once been among the fastest-rising stars in American politics. Nine years earlier he was among the first group of Republicans elected to the House of Representatives. Shortly after arriving in Washington, he established himself as one of the leading congressional voices against slavery. He was one of President Lincoln's most steadfast supporters and a key member of the House's pro-war caucus.

But things soon turned difficult. Bingham's Ohio district was redrawn after the 1860 census, support for the war was flagging in the North, and soldiers at the front were not allowed to vote with absentee ballots. As a result Bingham lost his seat in Congress during the 1862 elections.

Despite this personal and professional setback, Bingham remained confident about his future and of Union victory. The political views he espoused in Congress, he believed, would triumph; though currently unpopular, they would return to public favor in time— and with them his own career. He told Treasury Secretary Salmon P. Chase that the "limitations of the Constitution upon the States in favor of the personal liberty of all of the citizens of [the] Republic black & white [are] soon to become a great question before the people."

Bingham was right. Three years later he was back in the House, elected in the wave of pro-Lincoln sentiment that swept the country in the fall of 1864. Once there Bingham went to work. He took the lead in framing the Fourteenth Amendment to the Constitution, and he authored its guarantee that no state shall "deny to any person within its jurisdiction the equal protection of the laws." More than any man except Abraham Lincoln, John Bingham was responsible for establishing what the Civil War meant for America's future.

Bingham was born in Pennsylvania in 1815. His mother died when he was twelve years old, and he was sent to Ohio to live with his uncle. In 1835 he enrolled at nearby Franklin College, a haven for abolitionists led by a member of the Underground Railroad. One of Bingham's classmates at Franklin was Titus Basfield, an ex-slave who was one of the first African Americans to receive a college degree in Ohio. Bingham and Basfield became friends and corresponded regularly for the next forty years. It was highly unusual to attend a racially integrated school in the 1830s, and Bingham's relationship with Basfield almost certainly influenced his opposition to slavery and his belief in racial equality.

Prior to his election to Congress, Bingham practiced law in eastern Ohio and was active in the Whig Party. In 1848 he served as a delegate at the Whig National Convention and became a lightning rod by attempting to introduce a platform plank that would commit Whig candidates to resist any extension of slavery to the territories. While Bingham was not yet an out-and-out abolitionist—he supported the Compromise of 1850—he forged bonds with other leaders who would play a pivotal role in winning the Civil War. Edwin M. Stanton, a Democratic lawyer who became Lincoln's secretary of war, was one of Bingham's business competitors and a friendly political opponent. Salmon Chase, part of Lincoln's "Team of Rivals," was Bingham's mentor in the antislavery cause in Ohio. These three men would be at the center of the impeachment trial of President

John Bingham. Library of Congress Prints and Photographs Division, LC-DIG-cwpbh-00525.

Andrew Johnson in 1868, with Chief Justice Chase presiding over the Senate, Bingham giving the closing argument for the House, and War Secretary Stanton's dismissal by the president serving as the focus of the trial.

When the Kansas-Nebraska Act destroyed the Whig Party in 1854, Bingham seized his chance and was elected to Congress as a member of the new Republican Party. He rose to national attention during the debate over the statehood application of "Bleeding Kansas," displaying the talent that led many of his colleagues to describe him as the most eloquent member of the House. In a series of speeches over the next few years Bingham laid out his view that the Constitution was "based upon the equality of the human race. Its primal object must be to protect each human being within its jurisdiction in the free and full enjoyment of his natural rights." In a different speech he said, "You will search in vain in the Constitution of the United States . . . for that word white, it is not there. . . . The omission of this word—this phrase of caste—from our national charter, was not accidental, but intentional." He added, "Black men . . . helped to make the Constitution, as well as to achieve the independence of the country by the terrible trial of battle."

Bingham backed Chase for the Republican presidential nod in 1860, but he became one of Lincoln's most loyal supporters. He called the president "the saddest man I ever met," but said "few men could illustrate a point better than Lincoln by a homely story. There was always playful humor about him which seemed to be thoroughly incorporated in his nature, as a kind of offset against his constitutional sorrow and sadness."

When the secession crisis began, Bingham worried that Lincoln would not stand firm, as "the press is full of everything for compromise and carefully excludes every word said against compromise" under the slogan "compromise the Constitution, betray Liberty, and lose the African." As he told the House, "What just cause of complaint has the South, or any portion of her people, against this Government? There is none." The only injustice that could justify a revolt was that "wrong which dooms four million men and their descendants forever to abject servitude."

The Civil War transformed Bingham from a dissenter into a legislator. In the 37th Congress, from 1861 to 1863, he was instrumental in drafting bills to support the war effort, including the muster of the state militias, the admission of West Virginia, and the suspension of habeas corpus. He made an impassioned plea for the successful abolition of slavery in the District of Columbia, commenting that the legislation "illustrates the great principle that this day shakes the throne of every despot upon the globe, and that is, whether man was made for government or government made for man."

While Bingham was a civil libertarian who argued after the war that the entire Bill of Rights should be extended to the acts of state governments, during the war he argued that the First Amendment did not protect any man who "encourages armed rebellion against the Constitution and laws of the Republic." Likewise he said that the Fifth Amendment's guarantee that "no person shall be deprived of life, liberty, and property, without due process of law" was the "law of peace, not of war. In peace, that wise provision of the

Constitution must be, and is, enforced by the civil courts; in war, it must be, and is, to a great extent, inoperative and disregarded."

President Lincoln recognized Bingham's ability and offered him several jobs after the congressman was defeated in 1862. Bingham turned down a judgeship in Florida and a post as the administration's top lawyer at the Court of Claims, but Lincoln would not take no for an answer. In 1864 the president asked him to lead the prosecution of the surgeon general in a court-martial. Bingham hesitated because he knew nothing about military law, but Lincoln convinced him by saying that no "common lawyer understands martial or military law, but I think that you can learn it as soon as any man I know." When the president was assassinated, Bingham vindicated that faith by serving as one of the three military prosecutors of John Wilkes Booth's co-conspirators, giving the closing argument in one of the most sensational trials of the nineteenth century.

Bingham won back his congressional seat in 1864, and a year later he received a coveted position on the Joint Committee on Reconstruction, which was charged with setting the conditions for the South's return to the Union. In the 39th Congress he vied with Thaddeus Stevens for the leadership of the House and largely prevailed in his view that the rebel states should remain under military occupation until they agreed to ratify a new constitutional amendment.

Most significant, Bingham drafted the crucial language of the Fourteenth Amendment. It is Bingham who is responsible for the words "No state shall make or enforce any law which shall abridge the privileges or immunities of citizens of the United States; nor shall any state deprive any person of life, liberty, or property, without due process of law; nor deny to any person within its jurisdiction the equal protection of the laws."

This sentence would be the legal basis for the U.S. Supreme Court's subsequent decisions desegregating public schools, securing equality for women, and creating the right to sexual privacy. Bingham said that his text would also extend all of the protections of the Bill of Rights to the actions of state governments, which is largely, though not completely, the law today.

When the former Confederate states refused to ratify the Fourteenth Amendment, Bingham crafted a legislative compromise that ordered the Union Army to organize new elections across the South that would include African Americans. He told the House, "Unless you put [the South] in terror of your laws, made efficient by the solemn act of the whole people to punish the violators of oaths, they will defy your restricted legislative power when reconstructed."

Sadly, of course, this kind of bitter resistance was the norm until Dr. Martin Luther King Jr. led the civil rights movement to victory in the 1960s, but Bingham did his best to prevent that outcome. The new state elections organized under the Military Reconstruction Acts led to the ratification of the Fourteenth Amendment in 1868, and Bingham played a central role in shaping the Ku Klux Klan Act of 1871, which was intended to stop racist vigilantes and is now a cornerstone of civil rights law.

Bingham remained in Congress until 1873 and then served as the American ambassador to Japan for twelve years before retiring to Ohio. He died in 1900, largely forgotten.

Bingham's legacy is best summarized by a speech that he gave as a young man: "When the vital principle of our government, the equality of the human race, shall be fully realized, when every fetter within our borders shall be broken . . . and a noble mission fulfilled, we may call to the down-trodden and oppressed of all lands—come."

The Great Writ, North and South

FRANK J. WILLIAMS

During the Civil War both the federal and the Confederate governments had to deal with a pressing question far from the battlefield: how to balance the rights enshrined in their respective constitutions against effectively fighting the war.

This challenge was particularly sharp when it came to the writ of habeas corpus, considered the most important protection against the wrongful exercise of governmental power. The essentially similar ways in which Abraham Lincoln and Jefferson Davis, for all their many differences, limited their respective nations' citizens access to habeas corpus illustrates the thorny choices forced on leaders during wartime.

The federal government was thoroughly unprepared to grapple with the legal questions surrounding its response to secession in April 1861. Nevertheless, given his bedrock commitment to restoring the Union, Lincoln acted with remarkable dispatch, regardless of whether or not he was constitutionally empowered to do so. "It would not be easy," observed the historian James G. Randall, "to state what Lincoln conceived to be the limit of his powers."

Lincoln clearly considered control over habeas corpus—the constitutional principle that requires the government to justify an arrest before a judge—within those powers and exercised that power almost immediately. In the opening weeks of the war Maryland seethed with secessionist activity. To combat it, on April 27, 1861, Lincoln suspended the writ across the entire state. A Marylander named John Merryman was soon arrested on treason charges. He sought relief under the writ from the Supreme Court's chief justice Roger B. Taney, who was serving as a circuit judge, but the commander holding Merryman refused Taney's order to justify the detention in court.

Taney strongly condemned the administration's position in *Ex parte Merryman*, a ruling that Lincoln simply ignored for months. Finally, in a special message to Congress on July 4, 1861, the president claimed to possess authority to suspend the writ if necessary to protect the nation against the rebellion: "The whole of the laws which were required to be faithfully executed, were being resisted . . . in nearly one-third of the States. Must they be allowed to finally fail of execution, . . . are all the laws but one, to go unexecuted, and the government itself go to pieces, lest that one be violated?"

Chief Justice Roger B. Taney. Library of Congress Prints and Photographs Division, LC-USZ61-435.

In his chambers opinion Taney had asserted that under Article 1, Section 9 of the Constitution only Congress could suspend the writ. Lincoln's July message, strictly speaking, did not deny that. But Congress had been out of session when the war began, Lincoln said, and he wrote the message in the hopes that Congress would validate his actions retroactively. "These measures, whether strictly legal or not," he argued, "were ventured upon, under what appeared to be a popular demand, and a public necessity; trusting, then as now, that Congress would readily ratify them."

Lincoln sustained his position throughout the war and used it several more times. Before Congress finally passed legislation supporting the president's power over habeas corpus in March 1863 (many provisions of which the president later disregarded whenever he saw fit), Lincoln didn't hesitate to deal with what he considered threats to the national well-being. He issued orders that suspended the writ in parts of Florida under Union control, along the vital lines of travel between Philadelphia and Washington, and in large swaths of Missouri to help tamp down fearsome guerrilla warfare there. In September 1862, moreover, he declared the writ suspended nationwide in a wide range of cases.

But even after passage of the Habeas Corpus Act of 1863, Lincoln was willing to intervene independently regarding access to the writ. On the same day that Congress passed the act it also passed the Union's first national draft law. Resistance to conscription, which often relied on habeas claims, quickly became a serious impediment in the eyes of many to responsible execution of the war effort.

Perhaps no one was more taken aback by this resistance than Lincoln himself. By early September 1863 he had had enough of men resorting to the writ in state courts, particularly in Pennsylvania, to escape service in the army or navy. When the cabinet met on September 14 to discuss the matter, Attorney General Edward Bates would remember, Lincoln was angrier than he had ever seen him.

Lincoln proposed not only to suspend the writ for persons seeking relief from conscription; he also wanted to use federal military force against state officials, including judges, to enforce the suspension. After a closely divided cabinet debate, Secretary of State William H. Seward drafted a revised order that suspended the writ in draft cases for the rest of the war. Lincoln signed the order, and it was announced on September 17.

But what about Lincoln's nemesis, Jefferson Davis? A good deal of postwar scholarship and popular opinion have presented him as significantly more respectful of civil liberties in general and the writ of habeas corpus in particular than his Northern counterpart. This picture of Davis as the more principled defender of constitutional freedoms is due in large part to strenuous efforts by him and other ex-Confederates after the war to recast his wartime actions in a more favorable light.

In addition to the effects of Lost Cause mythologizing, the gap between Davis's rhetoric and the reality regarding access to habeas corpus in the Confederacy has misled many observers. On July 20, 1861, mere days after Lincoln defended his own suspension of habeas corpus, Davis thundered in a congressional message, "We may well rejoice that we have forever severed our connection with a government that thus tramples on all the principles of constitutional liberty, and with a people in whose presence such avowals could be hazarded."

But while asserting the superiority of the Confederacy in respecting fundamental liberties like habeas corpus, Davis countenanced violations of those same rights. Less than a month after denouncing Lincoln he pressured a political prisoner in Tennessee to end his criticism of the government as the price for release.

More tellingly, on February 28, 1862, five days after he was officially inaugurated as president, Davis signed legislation suspending the writ of habeas corpus approved by the Confederate Congress. This was the first of three such periods of suspension Davis signed, along with additional periods he requested from the Confederate Congress but did not receive.

Davis also adjusted his respect for habeas corpus to his larger wartime goals. As the latter necessarily shifted through the course of the conflict, so did the former. Early in the war, as part of his efforts to attract the border slave states to secede, Davis emphasized the Confederacy's supposed greater commitment to freedom.

This situational stand for freedoms like habeas corpus did not succeed in its direct aims, but it did bring additional benefits at least in the short term for the Confederacy. Davis's declarations that in the Union "upright men [are] dragged to distant dungeons upon the mere edict of a despot" helped strengthen white Southerners' fervor to defend their new nation.

Davis also hoped that his rhetorical defense of habeas corpus and other rights would lead to recognition by European nations, in particular Britain. He wasn't alone: as late as September 1862 a British observer could state that "if recognition should take place, it will be chiefly owing to the practical abrogation of the constitution" by the Lincoln administration.

By February 1864, however, as the Confederacy's fortunes darkened, Davis decided that the Confederacy's civil liberties must be sacrificed on the altar of military necessity, and he requested congressional approval for the suspension of habeas corpus. Calling the suspension "a remedy plainly contemplated by the Constitution," he justified the request as necessary to fight the "discontent, disaffection, and disloyalty" threatening to destroy the nation from within.

It is easy to be misled by some differences between Lincoln's and Davis's respective treatments of habeas corpus. Lincoln acted sooner than Davis to suspend the writ, and Davis's ability to execute his preferred policies was relatively more constricted by congressional and judicial action. However, at a more fundamental level both presidents subordinated respect for the writ to the imperatives of preserving their respective political entities and prosecuting the war.

Differences between their treatments of the writ can be traced to how they saw the abrogation of civil liberties contributing to the achievement of those goals, and not to any fundamental difference in political philosophy. Most important, Jefferson Davis was in practice no more committed to protecting the Great Writ than was Abraham Lincoln. Both men embraced the military and political realities confronting them in wartime.

The Nashville Experiment

WILLIAM MOSS WILSON

Emaline Cameron was among the thousands of refugees who poured into occupied Nashville, Tennessee, in 1863. While the strains of war may have contributed to her flight from her native Smithville, about fifty miles to the east, Cameron crossed Union lines to distance herself from an imploded marriage. James Hayes, known as Toy, had divorced her on the grounds that he was not the father of their eldest child. She admitted as much in court. While growing up she had worked as a chambermaid at the Smithville Hotel, which was run by her parents. After a boarder left the fifteen-year-old pregnant, they quickly married her off to the naïve Toy.

When Cameron got to Nashville there were many opportunities to clothe, feed, and entertain the garrison of Union soldiers, a demand for labor that far outstripped the city's prewar population. Family history reports that she chose the last sector: sometime after her arrival she "operated a house of prostitution." If true, my great-grandfather's great-grandmother participated in the first licensed and regulated sex trade in the United States.

Like other radical developments during the war, Nashville's experiment with legalized prostitution evolved as a practical solution to a military problem. Nearly one in ten Union soldiers were reported to have contracted gonorrhea or syphilis during the war; rates were even higher for troops garrisoned in and around cities. While these sexually transmitted diseases were hardly fatal, they increased demands on an already strained medical system. In Nashville, schools, hotels, storefronts, and even factories had been refashioned into hospitals to accommodate the thousands of wounded soldiers returning from the front. After the Battle of Stones River, federal hospitals were so overwhelmed that Brigadier General Robert Mitchell allowed wounded Confederate prisoners to be treated in the homes of known secessionists. Men with sexually transmitted diseases were an unnecessary added burden.

By June 1863 the large numbers of soldiers hospitalized in Nashville for venereal diseases led surgeons and regimental commanders to "daily and almost hourly" petition Brigadier General R. S. Granger, a local commander, "to save the army from a fate worse than . . . to perish on the battlefield." The first solution was to rid the city of its prostitutes. Deportation would prove no easy task; nearly every structure along the four blocks between Capitol Hill in downtown Nashville and the river wharves, known as "Smokey Row," was a house of prostitution, and other brothels were scattered about town.

In early July the case was assigned to Provost Marshal Lieutenant Colonel George Spalding, who led soldiers and police officers on a raid of the city's brothels, "heaping furniture out of the various dens, and then tumbling their disconsolate owners after." Under military escort several hundred women were dragged onto requisitioned steamboats. Captain John Newcomb of the *Idahoe* received his passengers only after vigorous protest. Newcomb feared for the reputation of his vessel, and correctly so—the *Idahoe* soon become known as the "Floating Whorehouse."

The following weeks revealed the limitations of the eviction policy. Armed guards in Louisville and later in Cincinnati refused to allow the female passengers of the *Idahoe* to disembark, and after the same scene was repeated at smaller ports, Newcomb had no choice but to return to Nashville. Moreover the day after the *Idahoe* departed for Louisville, the *Nashville Daily Press* complained that the only immediate effect of the removal was that black prostitutes filled the void left by their white colleagues:

Unless the aggravated curse of lechery as it exists among the negresses of this town is destroyed by rigid military or civil mandates, or the indiscriminate expulsion of the guilty sex, the ejectment of the white class will turn out to have been productive of the sin it was intended to eradicate. . . . No city . . . has been more shamefully abused by the conduct of its unchaste female population, white or black, than has Nashville . . . for the past eighteen months. . . . We trust that, while in the humor of ridding our town of libidinous white women, General Granger will dispose of the hundreds of black ones who are making our fair city a Gomorrah.

A hospital for federal officers in Nashville, Tennessee. Library of Congress Prints and Photographs Division, LC-B811- 2634.

Once deportation proved a failure, Granger and Spalding initiated a second, more radical solution. On August 20, 1863, Spalding released orders that required all of Nashville's prostitutes to register with the military government, which would in turn issue each woman a license to practice her trade. In exchange for a weekly fee of 50 cents, these women would receive a regular medical checkup and, if healthy, a certificate. Infected prostitutes would be hospitalized and treated at no additional charge. Failure to register would be penalized with a thirty-day sentence in a workhouse.

Shockingly, legalization did not draw the same vitriol from the press that had accompanied deportation. The City Council delivered de facto endorsement of military regulation on August 24, when Nashville's aldermen voted to "postpone indefinitely" legislation banning prostitutes "from riding in hacks with soldiers."

Nashville's prostitutes embraced the new scheme. More than three hundred licenses were issued in the first six months. By August 1864 Spalding had included black prostitutes in the program; of the more than five hundred licensed prostitutes in Nashville, fifty were black women. The women proudly flashed their credentials and prominently displayed their health certificates. Observers also noted a decrease in streetwalking in favor of less risky brothel work. Part of the licensing surge was attributed to an influx of prostitutes from Northern cities who perceived the increased safety and better working conditions provided by regulation.

Two hospitals were dedicated to treating sexual infections in Nashville: Hospital 11, for soldiers, and Hospital 15, also known as the Pest House, for prostitutes. The head surgeon, Robert Fletcher, claimed that after the first six months of regulation, when ninety-two women had been diagnosed with STDs, only thirteen of the nearly thirty-one thousand soldiers admitted to Hospital 15 had contracted their infections in Nashville. Dr. William Chambers, charged with medical inspections of the women, noted that regulations led to improvements in hygiene in addition to the decrease in new infections.

Chambers's work led him to a discovery that challenged the conventional wisdom of the day, which held prostitutes solely to blame for spreading sexual infection. In February 1864 a substantial spike in new visits to Hospital 15 accompanied the thousands of reenlisted soldiers returning from furlough. The following days brought a surge of new female patients to the Pest House. Chambers concluded that the returning soldiers must have brought the STDs with them and then infected his female patients.

Chambers's insight proved as fleeting as the wartime program, which did not survive his resignation in May 1865. Though the Union command at Memphis had borrowed from the Nashville experiment for a similar program in that city, civilian government in both cities quickly abandoned regulation of the sex trade at the close of hostilities.

While the Nashville experiment may not have had lasting social repercussions, it is possible that improved conditions in the dangerous profession delivered women like Emaline Cameron through the hardships of war. She survived her time in Nashville to return to Smithville, where she lived out her days in the home of her son.

Lincoln, God, and the Constitution

JOSEPH S. MOORE

On December 3, 1864, Abraham Lincoln proposed putting God in the Constitution. Preparing to submit his annual address on the state of the union, the president drafted a paragraph suggesting the addition of language to the preamble "recognizing the Deity." The proposal shocked his cabinet during a read-through. With his reelection secured and the political utility of such a move dubious, the most religiously skeptical president since Thomas Jefferson proposed blowing an irreparable God-size hole through the wall separating church and state. What was Lincoln thinking?

Recalling the meeting in his memoirs, Secretary of the Navy Gideon Welles wrote that the imprudent idea had been put in the president's head "by certain religionists," namely, the Covenanters. A tiny sect from Scotland that had resided in America since before the Revolution, they believed the Constitution contained two crippling moral flaws: its protection of slavery and its failure to acknowledge God's authority. With the Emancipation Proclamation poised to fix the one sin, they believed, why not correct the other? At their first meeting with Lincoln in late 1862 (it was much easier then for citizens to get an audience with the president) a group of influential Covenanters suggested doing just that.

In that first meeting Abraham Lincoln was quintessentially Abraham Lincoln—by turns respectful, humorous, and reflective. He regaled his guests with the rough-hewn ideas that became his second inaugural address. He observed that each side in the war prayed to the same God, read the same Bible, and invoked divine favor against the other; perhaps, Lincoln suggested, the war would ultimately decide which nation God chose.

The Covenanter ministers left their meeting emboldened. Thereafter they were instrumental in forming a coalition of denominations dedicated to acknowledging Christianity in the Constitution. This group, the National Reform Association, hoped to reference Jesus's authority just after "We the People" and before "in order to form a more perfect Union." They visited the president again in 1864 with an official request for action.

Lincoln is often remembered as a religious skeptic, at best, but throughout the war he showed exceptional shrewdness in wielding the political power of religion. As a young man he openly scoffed at Christianity and once wrote an essay examining all the falsehoods contained in the Bible. Open heresy proved politically perilous; he lost his first bid for a congressional nomination amid accusations that Christians could not vote for him in good conscience.

From that experience, and from his active participation in grassroots political organizing, Lincoln came to respect the ability of church networks to mobilize voters on moral issues. Thereafter he used religion to great effect in his political career,

Abraham Lincoln. Library of Congress Prints and Photographs Division, LC-DIG-ppmsca-19305.

casting his campaign platforms in stark moral terms, calling for more thanksgiving and fast days than any previous president, and meeting constantly with clergy. Those ministers returned from their audience at the White House preaching sermons that baptized the Union, the war, and the president with religious purpose. Cultivating relationships with religious leaders paid dividends when Lincoln won reelection in a landslide.

Even so, the sixteenth president paid more than lip service to religion. Raised by a Bible-thumping mother in a hard-drinking culture, he somehow managed to reject and have sympathy for both. He was a moralist and a fatalist and prone to bouncing between soaring hope and sinking melancholy. For all these reasons the president understood religion better and reverenced it more than many believers did, both as a political advantage and as a safe harbor for troubled souls in the midst of storms. Lincoln's own storms—the disintegration of the Union, the death of his young son Willie, and regular wartime casualty reports—heightened his belief in Providence and shook the skepticism of his youth. A distant, impersonal sense of divinity was replaced by the president's increasing conviction that God was concerned with the affairs of humanity. More important, Lincoln came to believe what he said in 1862—that this inscrutable God might actually choose sides.

In contemplating a religious amendment, then, Lincoln brought to bear his own conflicted sense about God and America. The nation was at war both with itself and with what he believed remained its ultimate destiny to be an example of free government to the world. With the Emancipation Proclamation, and soon the Thirteenth Amendment, Lincoln christened the Civil War with the moral name of abolition. Perhaps, if only briefly, he considered that Reconstruction would need a higher calling as well. Americans in the rubble of war would share little in common besides enmity. They might yet find unity in rebuilding a nation that possessed a divine destiny.

But Lincoln the philosopher was also Lincoln the lawyer; such a move would open a Pandora's box of divisive constitutional issues. The cabinet's very loud concerns were joined by some of his own. He struck the paragraph, and it was never mentioned again.

By suggesting it at all, though, the president put on display, however briefly, the exceptional power of the Civil War to remake American society. Just ten years before, most Americans might easily have conceived of a constitutional amendment invoking the name of God. Few would have predicted one eradicating slavery. Then the nation's greatest crisis proved capable of taking slavery out of the national compact but not of putting God in it. High-profile campaigns to Christianize the Constitution continued well into the twentieth century and even made their way into congressional committees. Still they never came closer to realization than that one paragraph read aloud by Lincoln in a cabinet meeting. Those brief words bespoke the limits of religion and reform in American government at the nation's most malleable moment.

How the Civil War Changed the Constitution

PAUL FINKELMAN

The most obvious constitutional result of the Civil War was the adoption of three landmark constitutional amendments. The Thirteenth ended slavery forever in the United States, while the Fourteenth made all persons born in the United States (including the former slaves) citizens of the nation and prohibited the states from denying anyone the privileges and immunities of American citizenship, due process of law, or equal protection of the law. Finally the Fifteenth Amendment, ratified in 1870, prohibited the states from denying the franchise to anyone based on "race, color, or previous condition of servitude."

These amendments, however, have their roots in the war itself and in some ways can been seen as formal acknowledgments of the way the war altered the Constitution. Other changes came about without any amendments. Thus the war altered the Constitution in a variety of ways. A review of some of them underscores how the Union that President Lincoln preserved was fundamentally different—and better—than the Union he inherited when he became president.

The first and most obvious change involves slavery. The Thirteenth Amendment was possible (as were the other two Civil War amendments) only because the war broke slavery's stranglehold on politics and constitutional development. The Constitution of 1787 protected slavery at every turn. Although the Framers did not use the word *slavery* in the document, everyone at the Constitutional Convention understood the ways in which the new form of government protected slavery. Indeed the word *slavery* was not used at the request of the Connecticut delegation and some other Northerners, who feared that their constituents would not ratify the Constitution if the word was in the document—not because the delegates objected to the word itself.

It would take many pages to review all the proslavery features of the Constitution, but here are some of the most significant ones. The three-fifths clause gave the South extra members in the House of Representatives based on the number of slaves in each state. Without these representatives, created entirely by slavery, proslavery legislation like the Missouri Compromise of 1820 and the Fugitive Slave Law of 1850 could never have been passed.

Equally important, votes in the Electoral College were based on the number of representatives in the House, and so slavery gave the South a bonus in electing the president. Without the electors created by slavery, the slaveholding Thomas Jefferson would have lost the election of 1800 to the non-slaveholding John Adams.

The domestic insurrections clause guaranteed that federal troops would be used to suppress slave rebellions, as they were in the Nat Turner Rebellion in 1831 and John Brown's attempt to start a slave rebellion in 1859.

Finally it took two-thirds of Congress to send a constitutional amendment to the states, and it took three-fourths of the states to ratify any amendment. Had the fifteen

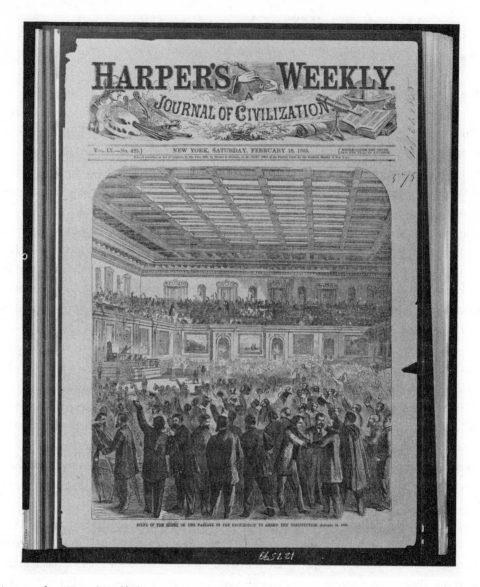

An image from *Harper's Weekly* showing the House of Representatives during the passage of the Thirteenth Amendment, January 31, 1865. Library of Congress Prints and Photographs Division, LC-USZ62-127599.

slave states all remained in the Union, to this day it would be impossible to end slavery by constitutional amendment, since in a fifty-state union it takes just thirteen states to block an amendment.

The political power of the slave states meant that the nation was always forced to protect slavery. Thus the South in effect controlled politics from 1788 until 1861. Slave owners held the presidency for all but twelve years between 1788 and 1850. All of the two-term presidents were slave owners. Three Northerners held the office from 1850 to 1860—Fillmore, Pierce, and Buchanan—but all were proslavery and bent over backward to placate the South.

It took the Civil War to break slavery's stranglehold on politics and fundamentally alter the nature of constitutional law and constitutional change.

The demise of slavery began with slaves running away and the army freeing them. But the key moment was the Emancipation Proclamation, which was the first important executive order in American history. In order to destroy slavery—and save the Union—Lincoln found new power for his office.

In another turn, secession and nullification ceased to be relevant constitutional questions. Since the beginning of the nation claims that states could nullify federal law or even secede had destabilized American politics and constitutional law. Sometimes Northerners made these claims, such as the disgruntled New Englanders who organized the Hartford Convention to oppose the War of 1812. But most claims of nullification came from the slave South. In 1798 Jefferson secretly wrote the "Kentucky Resolutions," while his friend James Madison wrote the "Virginia Resolutions"; both asserted the right of the states to nullify federal law.

From the earliest debates over the Union in the Second Continental Congress until the eve of the Civil War, numerous Southern politicians publicly advocated secession if they did not get their way on slavery and other issues. In 1832–33 South Carolina asserted the right to nullify the federal tariff, and then officially (although mostly symbolically) passed an ordinance to nullify the Force Law, which authorized the president to use appropriate military or civil power to enforce federal laws. At this time Georgia also brazenly declared that it did not have to abide by a federal treaty with the Cherokee. In 1850 Southerners held two secession conventions, which went nowhere. In the debates over what became of the Compromise of 1850, Senator John C. Calhoun of South Carolina asserted the right of the South to block federal law.

Some Northern opponents of slavery—most notably William Lloyd Garrison—argued for Northern secession because they rightly understood that slavery dominated the American government. But Garrison had few followers, and even many of them never accepted his slogan "No Union with Slaveholders." In the mid-1850s the Wisconsin Supreme Court declared the Fugitive Slave Law unconstitutional, but when the U.S. Supreme Court upheld the law the Wisconsin court backed off.

In short, nullification and secession were not new ideas in 1861, when eleven states left the Union, but had been part of the warp and weft of constitutional debate since the founding. But the Civil War ended the discussion. The question of the constitutionality of nullification or secession was permanently settled by the "legal case" of *Lee v. Grant*, decided at Appomattox Court House in April 1865. Grant had successfully defended the Constitution and the idea of a perpetual Union. Secession lost, and the United States won. The U.S. Supreme Court would weigh in on this in *Texas v. White* (1869), holding that secession had never been legal and that the state governments in the Confederacy lacked any legal authority.

A third change involved money and federal power. From the beginning of the nation there had been debates over whether the U.S. government could issue currency. Indeed before the Civil War there was no national currency, only bank notes issued by private or state banks. For two periods (1791–1811 and 1816–36) the federally chartered Bank of the United States circulated bank notes that functioned as a national currency. But Andrew Jackson vetoed the bank's recharter on the grounds that it was unconstitutional, and for the next twenty-five years the nation's economy was hampered by the lack of a stable, national currency.

The war changed this too. In order to finance the war, Secretary of the Treasury Salmon P. Chase developed a policy that led to the issuing of "greenbacks," and suddenly the constitutional issue was settled—not in court, but by the exigency of the conflict. The Supreme Court was perplexed by this new policy, and after the war the Court briefly declared that issuing greenbacks was unconstitutional but then quickly reversed that decision. Since then the dollar has emerged as the most important currency in the world. Although no longer backed by gold or silver, American currency remains "the gold standard" for international transactions.

Finally, the war also created a new set of rules—laws that are still with us—for when and how military tribunals or martial law can apply to civilians. For example, when the war began there were no federal laws prohibiting acts of sabotage or preventing civilians from forming armies to make war on the United States. Nor was there any national police force. Thus President Lincoln suspended habeas corpus along the railroad route from Philadelphia to Washington and used the army to arrest pro-Confederate terrorists, like John Merryman, who was tearing up railroads leading to Washington, D.C. and trying to organize a Confederate army in Maryland.

Again this was a matter of necessity, not ideology: Congress was not in session, and so Lincoln acted on his own authority. Indeed if Merryman had been successful, members of Congress would have been unable to reach Washington to meet. Congress later approved Lincoln's actions and authorized even more massive suspensions of habeas corpus. Thus the constitutional rule from the Civil War is that in a dire emergency the government may act to restrain people to preserve public safety.

But what happens when the immediate and pressing emergency is over? May the military still be used to arrest and try civilians? The answer from the Civil War is an emphatic no. During the war military officials in Indiana arrested Lambdin P. Milligan for trying to organize a Confederate army in that state. There was no combat in Indiana at the time, civil society was smoothly functioning, and even Milligan's allies were not blowing up bridges or destroying railroads as Merryman had been doing. Nevertheless the army tried Milligan and sentenced him to death. In 1866, in *Ex parte Milligan*, the Supreme Court ruled that the trial was unconstitutional. The military might arrest Milligan because of the emergency of the war (just as it had arrested Merryman), but the Court ruled that if the civilian courts were open, as they were in Indiana, it was unconstitutional to try a civilian in a military court.

This has generally been the law of the land ever since. In the aftermath of 9/11 the Supreme Court upheld the rule that civilians (even terrorists in the United States) could not be tried by military tribunals but only by civilian courts. The justices relied on *Milligan*.

When the war began, federal law denied African Americans virtually all constitutional rights. In *Dred Scott v. Sandford*, decided in 1857, Chief Justice Roger B. Taney ruled that blacks could never be citizens of the United States, even if they were treated as citizens in the states where they lived. This led to the oddity that blacks could vote for members of Congress and presidential electors in six states and could hold office in those states and some others, but they were not citizens of the nation. Federal law nevertheless supported Taney's rulings. For example, before the war blacks could not be members of state militias, serve in the national army, receive passports from the U.S. State Department, or be letter carriers for the post office.

During the war all this began to change. In 1862 Congress authorized the recruitment of blacks in the national army and in state militias. While most black soldiers were enlisted men, some served as noncommissioned officers, and a few served as officers. Martin Delaney held the rank of major. Just as striking, Eli Parker, a member of the Seneca Nation, served on Ulysses S. Grant's personal staff as a lieutenant colonel and was promoted to brevet brigadier general at the very end of the war.

The war also broke down racial, ethnic, and religious taboos and attitudes. Abraham Lincoln became the first president to meet with blacks and, in the case of Frederick Douglass, seek their advice. In 1864 and 1865 Congress gave charters to street railway companies that required that there be no discrimination in seating. Congress also changed the law that limited military chaplains to ministers of the gospel, thus allowing rabbis and Roman Catholic priests to become chaplains. During the war Congress created the office of recorder of the deeds for the city of Washington. The first officer holder was Simon Wolfe, a Jewish immigrant, but after that the office was held by African Americans for the rest of the century, including Frederick Douglass; Blanche Bruce, a former senator; and Henry P. Cheatham, a former congressman. In his last public speech Lincoln called for enfranchising black veterans and other members of their race. Five years later the Constitution would reflect that goal in the Fourteenth and Fifteenth Amendments.

Today we rightly look back at these two amendments, and the Thirteenth, as the most important lasting constitutional legacies of the Civil War. And that they are. But it is also important that we look at how America's understanding of the Constitution, especially as it related to racial and ethnic equality, changed during the course of the war and not simply as a consequence of it. Put differently: the Civil War amendments changed the Constitution, but even if, somehow, they had never happened, the war itself would have altered the way Americans saw one another and their government.

7. The Confederacy

Introduction

STEPHANIE MCCURRY

It is now quite possible, common even, to tell the story of the Civil War without much reference to the Confederate part. As it is now told, the history of the Civil War is the story of the Union in the war: of how a war for Union became a war for emancipation through the actions of Lincoln and the enslaved, the Union Army, and the Republican Party.

This is a mistake. The decision of seven Southern states to secede from the United States precipitated a reckoning with slavery that destroyed the first republic, transformed the United States, and set history on a new course. Confederate ambitions were not simply the indispensable trigger in the drama; far more than is commonly understood they set the parameters of what followed. The key reckoning with slavery came *inside* the Confederate republic, showing just how far wealth in slaves and cotton and a society built on violence and a thin basis of democratic consent could go in an age of modern nation building. The crucial question about the Confederacy, then, is not the military question of why it was defeated but the political question about what kind of nation Confederates aspired to build—and why they failed.

On December 20, 1860, precipitated by Lincoln's election—the first ever presidential victory with virtually no Southern votes—delegates to the South Carolina Secession Convention met and, by lunchtime on the first day, voted themselves out of the Union. Within weeks six other Lower South states had joined them. Existing originally as separate republics, by February 8, 1861, the seven had joined forces in the Confederate States of America.

The Confederate founders left no mystery as to their reasons: they believed that the institution of slavery was the basis of Southern wealth and power and that it was the indispensable foundation of a Christian republic such as the founders had envisioned. In Montgomery, Alabama, their first capital, they wrote a new constitution for their new proslavery state. Confederates left the Union because of slavery, because they believed it to be under threat, because they no longer had the political power to defend it within the Union, and because they would not contemplate giving it up. Theirs was a movement for national independence, to be sure, dedicated to the principle that all men were *not* created equal and to the enslavement of people of African descent into perpetuity. The Civil War was a test of those principles.

Secession was not easy to pull off. In some Lower South states secessionists squeaked out the win over strong Unionist opposition, in some cases even resorting to fraud. The eight Upper South slave states made no move until after the war began on April 12, 1861, when Confederate forces attacked Fort Sumter and President Lincoln called for 400,000 troops to put down the rebellion. Even then only four—Virginia, North Carolina, Arkansas, and Tennessee—joined the CSA.

In retrospect it is easy to view the Confederate cause as doomed from the start. But that makes it difficult to explain how it held on for four years. Nevertheless the challenges were considerable. The North had ten times the South's manufacturing capacity, and the Confederate population of 9 million was dwarfed by the Union's 22 million. But even that understates the problem, because in addition 40 percent of adult men in the Confederate states were enslaved and unavailable for military service.

It quickly became clear what such imbalances meant: the Confederacy would have to exert unprecedented and insupportable demands on its population and, notwithstanding its states' rights principles, build up a powerful central government to do what the private sector could not. Nearly 90 percent of its budget went to the War Department. In April 1862, only one year into the war, Jefferson Davis's administration was driven to adopt the first conscription act in American history. With adult slave men exempt, the slave republic had no choice but to mobilize a far higher proportion of white men to fill the ever-expanding ranks of its armies. When all was said and done the Confederate states had drafted over 75 percent of their white, military-age population.

Combined with the exemptions that the government was forced to make for slaveholders, and ones they could not afford to make for yeoman farmers, conscription quickly raised cries of "Rich man's war, poor man's fight." The cost of that decision was high; without an established political opposition, frustration over the costs of the war gave rise to a variety of political movements within the Confederate states, including food riots led by soldiers' wives in the spring of 1863.

The reckoning with slavery was even more direct. Confederate politicians had begun the war boasting of slavery as an element of strength and admitting no concern about slaves' allegiance or potential opposition. But by late 1863 some in high military circles were already acknowledging slavery as "one of our chief sources of military weakness," and slaves as the enemy within.

Behind that recognition lay the key drama of Confederate history: from the moment the war began, the 3.5 million people enslaved to Confederate masters mounted a wave of insurrectionary activity on the plantations that weakened their owners' nationalist commitment, thwarted every government effort to make their labor count militarily for the cause, and, in a dangerous, highly risky mass movement of people across the lines, transferred their military labor and service to the enemy.

It was in this context—a competition for the loyalty and service of slave men—that President Davis and General Robert E. Lee finally moved, against great opposition, in early 1865 to enlist slave men in the Confederate Army.

We now are well aware of how slaves' actions transformed a war for union into a war for emancipation. Less well known is how 3.5 million slaves' resistance to the proslavery agenda of the *Confederate* government pushed it down its own reluctant path to slave enlistment in direct repudiation of founding principles.

During the war the Confederates risked all and, in the end, lost all. In seceding to secure the future of slavery, Southerners arguably created the only set of conditions—war-borne and state-sponsored emancipation—under which slavery could be completely and immediately destroyed as an institution in American life. A proslavery vision of the future had been tried, and it had failed.

A Bad Document's Good Idea

JOHN J. MILLER

The Southerners who gathered in Montgomery, Alabama a century and a half ago saw themselves as the true inheritors of the original Founding Fathers. Indeed the Constitution they approved was more imitation than innovation. "We the people of the Confederate states," the preamble begins, "establish justice, insure domestic tranquility, and secure the blessings of liberty to ourselves and our posterity."

Despite the familiar ring, there are important differences. In trying to build their own version of a more perfect union, the secessionists protected "the right of property in negro slaves." In doing so they rendered their entire project suspect, both then and now.

Yet the authors of the Confederate Constitution were serious, learned men who thought hard about the principles of democratic government and sought ways to improve on the original document. They also came to their project with something that their forebears in Philadelphia lacked. In 1787 James Madison may have had clear notions about the operation of American government. The men of 1861, though, could draw from three score and fourteen years of actual experience.

And, in fact, parts of the Confederate Constitution improved on the original. One section gave the president the ability to delete parts of spending bills, for example. Today most governors possess the same authority. The Confederates' objectionable views on slavery should not automatically invalidate their opinions on unrelated matters. It's hardly racist to think that Americans would benefit if President Barack Obama also had a line-item veto on the budget.

The Confederate document contained another great idea that would certainly upgrade our own Constitution: it limited the president to a single term of six years. The lousy second-term president is one of the great curses of American history. When loyalists chant "Four more years" at party conventions, it's almost like they're hexing their subjects. From George Washington and Thomas Jefferson to Bill Clinton and George W. Bush, the disappointing presidential encore has become a dismal tradition. Given this pattern, even the most loyal Obama supporter must wonder whether reelection in 2012 was worth it.

Why do two-termers frequently finish on a bad note? Perhaps it's because they dash into office full of energy, goodwill, and political capital, then they grow tired and wear out their welcome. Midterm congressional elections usually erode their power and embolden their foes. Top aides often move on, replaced by second-stringers who lack the same level of commitment. When battered incumbents cross the finish line they're usually happy to go home.

For the original founders in 1787 the rules of presidential tenure were an open question. They considered proposals ranging from terms of three years to two decades, as well as reappointment by Congress rather than reelection by voters. In the end they settled on four years and unlimited eligibility for reelection thereafter. In *Federalist* Nos. 71 and 72 Alexander Hamilton argued that this struck the right balance between stability and

THE CITY OF MONTGOMERY, ALABAMA, SHOWING THE STATE HOUSE WHERE THE CONGRESS OF THE SOUTHERN CONFEDERACY MEETS ON FEBRUARY 4, 1861.

The Alabama State House in Montgomery, where delegates met to write the Confederate Constitution. Library of Congress Prints and Photographs Division, LC-USZ62-132567.

accountability. He was especially concerned about the former, warning against "the fatal inconveniences of fluctuating councils and a variable policy."

The Confederates didn't leave behind their own version of the *Federalist Papers*, but it's clear that they wanted to correct the earlier consensus. Hamilton's fears of instability concerned them less than the prospect of a mighty national government controlled by an energetic executive. They worried that presidents who could serve eight years or more would accrue too much power and threaten democracy.

Their answer was to create an office that was muscular enough to withstand congressional excesses but too weak to challenge the authority of the states. The line-item veto was a check on Congress. The single-term president was a check on the executive.

In time many other Americans came around to the Confederate way of thinking. The Twenty-second Amendment, ratified in 1951, formally limited presidents to two terms. It ended the prospect of the lifetime president, but it didn't solve the problem of the second-term letdown. The founding fathers of the stillborn Confederacy may have had it right: four years isn't enough, and two terms is too much.

Hastily Composed

ADAM GOODHEART

Like a feckless college student with a term paper deadline looming, Jefferson Davis apparently hadn't started seriously writing until the day before. Exhausted from a weeklong railway journey, he had stayed in bed in his suite at Montgomery's Exchange Hotel until after 10 a.m., then buckled down to work. Now, barely twenty-four hours later, standing in front of the Alabama State House's portico under a wintry sky, he unfolded a thin sheaf of paper and began to read his inaugural address in a strong, clear baritone: "Gentlemen of the Congress of the Confederate States of America, friends, and fellow citizens: Called to the difficult and responsible station of chief magistrate of the provisional government which you have instituted, I approach the discharge of the duties assigned to me with humble distrust of my abilities, but with a sustaining confidence in the wisdom of those who are to guide and aid me in the administration of public affairs, and an abiding faith in the virtue and patriotism of the people."

Davis had indeed been "called"—not exactly elected—to the presidency. Just ten days earlier delegates from six Southern states, meeting here in the Alabama capitol, had chosen him as the new Confederate nation's first chief executive. Like so many of the South's actions that winter—the secession meetings and ratifications, the drafting of a constitution—the decision had been taken in haste. Though several other men wanted the post, there had been almost no campaigning or debate: Davis's political and military experience were strong qualifications, certainly, but the most potent fact in his favor was probably that he had fewer enemies than his rivals.

Now he was not merely the Confederacy's "chief magistrate" but also its chief mouthpiece. Hitherto most statements on secession had come from individual states. But today it devolved upon him to explain to the world why the Deep South had announced its withdrawal from the Union. He said:

> Our present political position has been achieved in a manner unprecedented in the history of nations. It illustrates the American idea that governments rest on the consent of the governed, and that it is the right of the people to alter or abolish them at will whenever they become destructive of the ends for which they were established. . . . The impartial and

Jefferson Davis's inauguration as Confederate president at the Alabama state capitol, February 18, 1861. Library of Congress Prints and Photographs Division, LC-DIG-pga-01584.

enlightened verdict of mankind will vindicate the rectitude of our conduct; and He who knows the hearts of men will judge of the sincerity with which we have labored to preserve the government of our fathers in its spirit.

"Preserve the government of our fathers in its spirit": this was characteristic of the conservative tenor that pervaded Davis's address. By his lights, the Confederacy—though its manner of birth may have been unprecedented—was hardly novel in any significant respect. Its Constitution, he said, "differ[s] only from that of our fathers in so far as it is explanatory of their well-known intent, freed from sectional conflicts, which have interfered with the pursuit of the general welfare."

Members of his audience might have been forgiven for scratching their heads at this last, somewhat tortuous passage. But it was in fact a very delicate allusion to slavery: the founding fathers' "well-known intent" in Philadelphia in 1787 had been to protect slavery, Davis hinted, even if they had not quite made it explicit. Indeed the U.S. Constitution did not contain the word *slave*, whereas the Confederate version defiantly repeated it ten times, including in this crucial passage: "No bill of attainder, ex post facto law, or law denying or impairing the right of property in negro slaves shall be passed."

But unlike Davis's farewell speech to the Senate a month earlier, his inaugural speech included no clarion call to defend slavery and white supremacy. Even the South's favorite euphemism, "our domestic institutions," was left unuttered. The closest he came was in attesting that the desire to form a new nation was "actuated solely by the desire to preserve our own rights, and promote our own welfare." *Rights* and *welfare* obviously had very specific connotations in this context.

The closing lines were heavy with unintended irony:

It is joyous in the midst of perilous times to look around upon a people united in heart, where one purpose of high resolve animates and actuates the whole; where the sacrifices to be made are not weighed in the balance against honor and right and liberty and equality. Obstacles may retard, but they cannot long prevent, the progress of a movement sanctified by its justice and sustained by a virtuous people. Reverently let us invoke the God of our fathers to guide and protect us in our efforts to perpetuate the principles which by his blessing they were able to vindicate, establish and transmit to their posterity. With the continuance of his favor ever gratefully acknowledged, we may hopefully look forward to success, to peace and to prosperity.

And with that, having spoken for barely fifteen minutes, he concluded. The inaugural address had contained not a single memorable phrase or idea. Even Davis's admirers would rarely quote it.

The address was most notable for what it left out: any attempt to explain how a nation could possibly remain viable, let alone democratic, if it were founded on the principle that any constituent part might withdraw as soon as it found itself in the minority on an important political issue. This was the fundamental philosophical absurdity on which the whole Confederacy was constructed, like a grandiose classical edifice on a foundation of sand. The new president's failure to address it did not bode well. Indeed it was an early symptom of a fatal condition.

It is instructive to compare Davis's inaugural address and its method of composition with Abraham Lincoln's two weeks later. Lincoln had begun work on his speech not long after his election; by late January he had buckled down in earnest, hiding out in a small room in a shop belonging to his brother-in-law, where he would not be disturbed. He had asked his law partner, William Herndon, to procure copies of Henry Clay's 1850 address to the Senate; Daniel Webster's debates with Senator Robert Hayne of South Carolina; Andrew Jackson's statement against nullification; George Washington's farewell address; and the Constitution. Lincoln would continue working on the address over the course of six weeks, until the very morning of his swearing in.

The thinness of Davis's speech, and of his preparation, cannot be blamed merely on haste or inattention. Rather it betrayed an alarming void at the center of the self-proclaimed Confederate republic. The hard work that Lincoln had put into his message attested to his faith in the power and necessity of words, of arguments, of explanations, in a democratic system. By contrast the lackluster, shop-worn rhetoric of Davis and other leaders was not merely a failure of aesthetics but proof of the intellectual poverty and moral laziness undergirding their entire enterprise. It also revealed their lack of commitment to the essential democratic chores of persuasion and explanation.

The Confederacy was never truly much of a cause, lost or otherwise. In fact it might better be called an effect: a reactive stratagem tarted up with ex post facto justifications. This would soon be borne out in the practices of the two national legislatures. Over the next four years the Confederate Congress would transact nearly all its important business in secret, and even some of the most fervent secessionists would decry its lack of true accountability to the Southern public. (Robert Barnwell Rhett of South Carolina, a leading fire-eater in 1860 and 1861, would later blame the South's loss on the absence of any informed public debate within the Confederacy that might have held the Davis administration's policies up to scrutiny.) By contrast the Congress of the United States— notwithstanding all the bitter infighting that lay ahead—would never once go into closed session during the course of the war.

The most revealing words in the two contrasting inaugural addresses may have been those that came at the very beginning. Davis opened with "Gentlemen of the Congress of the Confederate States of America, friends and fellow citizens"—a catalogue of castes. Lincoln, though addressing an equally august assemblage, would begin his speech much more simply and democratically: "Fellow citizens of the United States."

The President and His General

PHIL LEIGH

In the pantheon of Confederate commanders the team of Robert E. Lee and his brilliant subordinate Thomas J. "Stonewall" Jackson stands at the fore. The two had developed a mutual admiration while serving together in the Mexican-American War. Later, during the Civil War, Jackson's lightning-fast brigades and audacious battlefield style provided Lee with an invaluable tool against often much larger Union forces.

But Lee benefited even more, perhaps, from a lesser-known symbiosis with the Confederate president, Jefferson Davis. Lasting from March 1862 until the end of the war, their tight-knit relationship was arguably one of history's great pairings of civilian and military leadership. It took Abraham Lincoln almost two years longer to form a similar relationship with Ulysses S. Grant, who became general in chief of the Union Army in March 1864.

It's easy to forget that Lee wasn't always the undisputed master of the Confederate military effort. When the war began Davis's closest generals were men like P. G. T. Beauregard and Joseph E. Johnston, both of whom led Southern forces at the First Battle of Bull Run.

But while that battle was a victory for the Confederacy, forcing the Union troops to retreat to Washington, Davis was criticized for not pushing the South's temporary advantage further. Evidently through carelessness Beauregard's battle report was leaked to a hostile newspaper, which suggested that Davis had vetoed a plan that would have captured Washington. It was a gross distortion, as Davis was himself surprised when no immediate pursuit followed the disorganized Yankee retreat. Similarly Johnston smoldered over trivia regarding his rank and dissatisfaction with an unwillingness of some civilian officials to retain conversational confidences. Consequently he became excessively secretive, thereby leaving Davis feeling uninformed.

Meanwhile, during the war's first winter, Lee was organizing defense along the south Atlantic coast. But in March 1862 Davis summoned him to Richmond as a presidential military adviser. Lee was already well-respected across the South, and as he conferred with the president that spring his star rose higher still.

Lee laid the foundation for Davis's confidence early. He helped avoid Richmond's near certain doom by urging Stonewall Jackson into action against the Union forces in the Shenandoah Valley, which made Washington vulnerable. It also prevented General Irvin McDowell's army near Washington from moving south to help General George McClellan's advance on the Confederate capital.

On June 1, after Johnston was wounded at the Battle of Fair Oaks, Davis replaced him with Lee, giving the general command of the largest Confederate Army. Lee ordered Jackson to join him near Richmond for a combined assault on McClellan instead of using Jackson to attack Washington directly. The result was the Seven Days' Campaign at the end of June 1862, one of Lee's greatest victories and the effective end to McClellan's Peninsula Campaign. Since the week's fighting was so close to Richmond, Davis visited the battlefields, came under fire, and slept with the army several nights—and thus saw his general's brilliance firsthand.

The fighting wasn't over; General John Pope, who had replaced McDowell in northern Virginia, was rapidly building up his forces, and Lee knew he had to act quickly, even if an attack meant leaving Richmond once again vulnerable. Davis supported Lee completely. That summer, in what became known as the Northern Virginia Campaign, Lee attacked Pope relentlessly across the state, culminating in a smashing victory at the Second Battle of Bull Run. Three days later the Confederates invaded Maryland. (Davis wanted to accompany Lee's army, presumably to be available should an opportunity for a negotiated peace arise. Lee advised against it, and eventually Davis deferred to the general's judgment.)

Although Lee was turned back in Maryland at the bloody Battle of Antietam, Davis remained confident in the general. It was a wise decision, because what followed was a new round of Union incursions into Virginia—and pivotal Confederate victories, again under Lee, at Fredericksburg and Chancellorsville in late 1862 and the spring of 1863. All the while Lee kept Davis up to date, and Davis followed his general closely, even as he lay seriously ill during Chancellorsville.

What was the source of their friendship? In part it was of course Lee's early success; though the South had more than a few excellent field commanders, none blended tactical brilliance and strategic clarity in a clutch better than Lee. Davis, who had gone to West Point and had once imagined becoming a Confederate general himself, clearly saw something of his martial ideal in his commander. But it also helped that Lee was punctiliously loyal to his president, even when he could arguably have claimed more popular acclaim than Davis. Where many serially victorious generals before him had let power go to their heads, Lee respected the notion of civilian control of the army and in particular the civilian who controlled it.

Their partnership, however, was tested when Grant put Vicksburg, Mississippi under siege in May 1863. Instead of sending more aid to the president's home state, Lee advocated a second invasion of the North. Even if Vicksburg were relieved, he told Davis, he believed the Confederacy was growing steadily weaker as the North gained strength. A quick victory on Northern soil near Lincoln's capital could lead influential Yankee easterners to recommend peace negotiations. Notwithstanding the fact that Davis's Mississippi home was only twenty miles from Vicksburg, he unselfishly sided with Lee. Confederate forces soon invaded Pennsylvania, a campaign culminating in the Battle of Gettysburg.

But in the forty-five days preceding Gettysburg the pair wasn't as fully synchronized as usual, partly owing to Davis's Vicksburg distractions. Their often perfect mutual understanding fell apart. When Lee requested reinforcements from departments below Virginia, Davis compromised with lesser substitutes. Lee's plan to threaten Washington from the south as well, which he had pushed on Davis, went unexecuted. In part as a result the Union was able to bring a large force to bear at Gettysburg, and Lee was defeated in the war's pivotal confrontation.

A cartoon showing Robert E. Lee and Jefferson Davis surrounded by Union generals. Library of Congress Prints and Photographs Division, LC-USZ62-92033.

Lee offered to resign. Replacement of a commander after a significant defeat, particularly a defeat that capped a daring and costly campaign, is standard operating procedure, and Lee could expect no less. And yet Davis, even while preoccupied by massive challenges implied by the twin disasters at Vicksburg and Gettysburg, refused. "To ask me to substitute you . . . by someone more fit to command," he replied, "is to demand an impossibility."

At least once Davis aided the partnership in a direct military context. While Grant engaged Lee fifty miles north of Richmond at Spotsylvania in May 1864, Davis directed General Benjamin Butler's 40,000-man army to attack Richmond's southern railroad supply line at the town of Bermuda Hundred. Although General Beauregard was advised to counter Butler, he did not comply. Finally Davis rode out to the threatened point and refused to leave until the Creole arrived. By acting promptly Butler might have captured Richmond a year before its time. Instead, thanks to Davis, he was bottled up on a peninsula with entrenched Confederates blocking the only land route out.

Lee's surrender at Appomattox in April 1865 ended the partnership without a defining punctuation mark. Ultimately the federal government left Lee unmolested, thanks to Grant's surrender terms—and the fact that Grant told President Andrew Johnson that he would resign if his terms were not honored.

Davis, however, was jailed for two years, amid calls for his execution. At his trial, to demonstrate Davis's culpability for all Confederate activities, the prosecutor summoned Lee. His object was to force the general to admit he was obliged to follow Davis's orders. Lee answered, "I am responsible for what I did." It was the last time the two saw each other.

The Birth of "Dixie"

Christian McWhirter

In a New York apartment on a rainy day in March 1859 Daniel Decatur Emmett sat down at his desk to write a song for his employer, Bryant's Minstrels, and its upcoming stage show. Then forty-four years old, Emmett had been composing minstrel songs—to be performed primarily by white actors in blackface—since he was fifteen. Looking out his window at the dreary day outside, Emmett took his inspiration from the weather. A single line, "I wish I was in Dixie," echoed in his mind. Before long it would echo across the country.

Few of us remember "Dixie" as antebellum America's last great minstrel song. We see it as most did two years after its creation—as the anthem of the Confederacy. And yet as phenomenally popular as it was in the North before the war, "Dixie" was slow to catch on in the South. Lacking the Yankees' enthusiasm for minstrelsy, most Southerners were unaware of the tune until late 1860. By sheer chance its arrival coincided with the outbreak of secession. As newly minted Confederates rejected the anthems of their old nation, they desperately sought replacements.

Indeed once it reached the South, "Dixie," despite being a song written by a Northerner, rose to prominence with exceptional speed. One songwriter recalled how it "spontaneously" became the Confederacy's anthem, and a British correspondent noted the "wild-fire rapidity" of its "spread over the whole South." The tune received an unofficial endorsement when it was played at the Confederate president Jefferson Davis's inauguration in February 1861. This was coincidental— it was recommended to a Montgomery, Alabama, bandleader who knew nothing of the tune—but the song's inclusion gave the appearance of presidential approval. The Confederate government never formally endorsed "Dixie," though Davis did own a music box that played the song and is rumored to have favored it as the South's anthem.

Repeated performances of "Dixie" by Confederates confirmed its new status. Even before Virginia seceded, the *Richmond Dispatch* labeled "Dixie" the "National Anthem of Secession," and the *New York Times* concurred a few months later, observing that the tune "has been the inspiring melody which the Southern people, by general consent, have adopted as their 'national air.'" Publishers recorded that sales were "altogether unprecedented"; when Robert E. Lee sought a copy for his wife in the summer of 1861, he found none were left in all of Virginia.

"Dixie" became so connected so quickly with the South that many Americans attributed its very name to the region. In fact the precise origin of the word *Dixie* remains unknown, though three competing theories persist: a benevolent slaveholder named Dix (thus slaves wanting to return to "Dix's Land"), Louisiana (where $10 notes were sometimes called Dix notes), or, most likely, the land below the Mason and Dixon line (the slaveholding South). Regardless, Emmett's tune made it part of the national vocabulary. During the Civil War soldiers, civilians, and slaves frequently referred to the South as Dixie and considered Emmett's ditty the region's anthem.

This popularity is remarkable, as little about "Dixie" recommends it as a national anthem. The melody lacks gravitas, and only the first verse and chorus express anything approximating Southern nationalism:

> I wish I was in de land ob cotton,
> Old times dar am not forgotten
> Look away! look away! look away! Dixie Land.
> In Dixie Land whar I was born in,
> Early on one frosty mornin',
> Look away! look away! look away! Dixie Land.
>
> Den I wish I was in Dixie,
> Hooray! hooray!
> In Dixie Land I'll take my stand,
> To lib and die in Dixie,
> Away, away, away down south in Dixie,
> Away, away, away down south in Dixie.

The Songs of War by Winslow Homer. Library of Congress Prints and Photographs Division, LC-DIG-ppmsca-23132.

The rest is unmistakably the work of a songwriter utilizing various minstrel clichés. The speaker is a slave who worries that his plantation mistress is being seduced into marrying "Will de Weaber," the "gay deceiber" who outlives her and inherits her plantation. Although the speaker expresses his desire to live in the South until he dies, the song provides little else to endear it to Confederate patriots.

Nevertheless a sort of inertia pushed the song's reputation higher and higher in the Southern mind. Confederates performed "Dixie" enthusiastically and remained devoted to it even when an alternative anthem, Harry Macarthy's "Bonnie Blue Flag," became available. The more Americans on both sides believed that "Dixie" was the Confederate anthem, the more it became so. This was especially true for soldiers, who were some of the first to embrace "Dixie" and increasingly associated it, amazingly, with sacrifices made for the war. One Confederate surgeon wrote that the song "brings to mind the memory of friends who loved it—friends, the light of whose lives were extinguished in blood, whose spirits were quenched in violence."

To be sure, many Southerners were well aware of "Dixie"'s obvious deficiencies. Most simply ignored these problems, though some tried to reconcile them with the Confederacy's history and objectives. The *Richmond Dispatch* stretched its credibility attempting to prove that the song was a parable for secession. It argued that "Will de Weaber" was not a minstrel stereotype but in fact Abraham Lincoln, who seduced the nation into voting for him, leading to the South's rebirth as the Confederacy. To conclude the author triumphantly asked, "Can any one now fail to see that, in the verses of this deservedly popular song, an epitome is given of the events which, since last November, have shaken this land?" Emmett surely disagreed, as he reportedly declared that had he known the Confederates would adopt "Dixie" as their anthem, "I will be damned if I'd have written it."

Other Southerners were more disturbed by "Dixie"'s apparently undeserved status and sought more extreme solutions. Many rejected it outright. "It smells too strongly of the [negro] to assume a dignified rank of the National Song," declared one malcontent, while another argued it was "absurd to imagine that Dixie, a dancing, capering, rowdyish, bacchanalian negro air," could be sung by "a nation of free men . . . with any respect for themselves." Others recognized that most of the song's appeal came from its catchy melody and simply drafted new lyrics. Numerous such revisions appeared throughout the war, but none achieved much success. Only one, by the Confederate Indian agent and general Albert Pike, enjoyed even a limited popularity and continues to appear occasionally in histories, songbooks, and public performances.

Even Lincoln recognized the song's power and, at the end of the war, attempted to reclaim "Dixie" as an American, rather than Confederate, song. "Our adversaries over the way attempted to appropriate it, but I insisted," he told a crowd of admirers in Washington, "that we fairly captured it."

Despite these efforts and the continued protestations of some Southerners, "Dixie" remained wedded to its Confederate identity. Although a simple minstrel ditty, 150 years of history have loaded the song with indelible political, racial, military, and social connotations. For better or worse "Dixie" was the South's anthem and will most likely remain so for generations.

The Drought That Changed the War

KENNETH W. NOE

In August 1862 two Confederate armies turned north from Tennessee, hoping to revive their nation's faltering hopes west of the Appalachians. And yet, despite a stunning victory at Richmond, Kentucky, the capture of Frankfort, the state capital, the installation of a Confederate governor, and a tactical victory at Perryville on October 8, by fall the two forces were limping back south. What happened?

Even as the two Confederate armies, one under Major General Edmund Kirby Smith (later elevated to a full general), the other under General Braxton Bragg, as well as a pursuing force under General Don Carlos Buell, raced north across central Kentucky on parallel paths in what many soldiers likened to a great foot race, the men were suffering—brought low not just by the summer heat but by vast dust clouds, increasingly short rations, and a growing dearth of potable water. Both armies had marched headlong into a drought.

General Edmund Kirby Smith. Library of Congress Prints and Photographs Division, LC-B813- 2013 A [P&P] LOT 4213.

Food shortages, inflation, and other hardships the Confederate plain folk suffered, as well as at least part of the disillusionment that grew out of those issues (the entire litany of the so-called "internalist" interpretation of Confederate defeat as a "rich man's war and poor man's fight") can be traced at least in part to the drought of 1862, its negative effect on Southern food production, and the choices the Jefferson Davis administration made when confronting the situation. The Confederacy simply had been born at the worst possible moment in the nineteenth century to launch an agricultural republic. Meanwhile Northern crops, especially midwestern wheat, boomed.

Months earlier Civil War soldiers would have found it hard to even imagine such a situation. The winter and spring of 1862 were unusually wet. High water and mud shaped campaigns in places as far apart as Fort Henry in western Tennessee and the bottomless swamps that Major General George B. McClellan encountered on the Virginia Peninsula. Wet conditions led to widespread wheat rust, a fungus that destroyed perhaps a sixth of the South's wheat crop. Flooding along the Mississippi and other rivers wrecked other spring crops in the field.

Then, in the early summer, the heavens closed, and drought conditions set in. Agriculture suffered. With the notable exception of Georgia, the corn crop of 1862 largely failed, and the *Montgomery Advertiser* pronounced the Confederacy's wheat crop all but ruined.

The armies confronted the great drought as well. The army of Union general Don Carlos Buell, sent from Corinth, Mississippi in July to take Chattanooga, had endured much as rivers fell to levels too low to permit the shipping of supplies, leaving the men dependent on railroads that soon proved easy prey for marauding rebel cavalry.

The "great foot race" north in late August and September proved more agonizing still. James Iredell Hall of the 9th Tennessee wrote, "The only water accessible was pond water and that was warm and muddy. The water we were compelled to drink, was so muddy that we could not wash our faces in it." A Confederate soldier in the 33rd Alabama remembered, "We obtained water under deep limesinks, some of these being partly full of water, and Federals had utilized some of the partly filled sinks as a place to butcher cattle and dumped offal into them, making the water unfit to drink."

The food situation was just as bad. In Tennessee and northern Alabama both sides already had encountered trouble filling their bellies. Part of Buell's decision to retreat from Chattanooga was his supply situation; elderly locals testified that 1862 was the driest summer in their memory. Pillaging and disorder increased as hungry soldiers took what their commissaries could not supply.

Bragg's plan depended upon living off the land as the Confederates marched north, a decision that quickly smashed into a dry reality: drought and the occupying federal army had left little for them to eat. Bragg changed course with every new rumor of ample foodstuffs ahead. On September 14, acting without orders, Brigadier General James Chalmers of Bragg's army and Colonel John Scott, commanding a detachment of Kirby Smith's cavalry, initiated an ill-advised attack on the entrenched federal garrison at Munfordville, Kentucky. Hoping to secure an easy victory, Chalmers had also heard that Munfordville contained large stores of wheat. Worried that the repulse would undermine Confederate sentiments in the Bluegrass State, Bragg veered his entire force to Munfordville and compelled the garrison to surrender.

But the delay allowed Buell to draw near. Briefly Bragg considered making a stand against Buell there, but instead returned to the march. Real hunger now appeared; Buell's men complained that they were reduced to half-rations, then quarter-rations, and when the hardtack they brought with them finally ran out, they received only wormy flour without the necessary utensils to make bread.

On September 22 Confederate forces halted at Bardstown, in the middle of the state, disappointing many Johnny Rebs who had assumed they were hurrying to take Louisville. Buell's exhausted men began arriving in that city on September 25, furious that their commander had allowed Bragg to come so far north without a fight. Indicative of the soldiers' collapsing morale, wild rumors circulated that the two generals actually were brothers-in-law who slept together nightly while making plans for another day's nonviolent marching. Some Hoosier troops were in fact so angry that they deserted by walking home across the drought-ravaged Ohio River.

On October 1, augmented by new recruits, Buell marched his army out of Louisville, determined to drive Bragg's smaller army from the state. Again the water crisis stymied the two armies. By October 7 at least one corps in the federal army was so dehydrated and so sick from pond-borne bacteria that it lurched into camp at the point of collapse and mutiny. Before dawn the next morning other elements of Buell's army moved forward in the darkness, determined to drive Confederates away from the precious springs of water they zealously safeguarded.

So opened the Battle of Perryville, Kentucky's largest battle, fought in the dusty hills just west of a town where the Chaplin River had all but run dry. Gaining a tactical victory, Bragg decided to retreat to Tennessee when he finally realized that he faced a numerically superior force, and he abandoned Kentucky entirely upon learning that his planned supply base was all but empty.

The drought that turned the war in the West would continue for another two years.

The Free Men of Color Go to War

TERRY L. JONES

As in all things, nineteenth-century New Orleans was a world apart from much of the rest of the South. When the Civil War began it had a large population of so-called free men of color, citizens descended from French and Spanish men and slave women.

Colonial-era slave codes granted them complete equality; the "hommes de couleur libre" could own land, businesses, and even slaves; they could be educated and serve in the military. They created a niche for themselves in the Crescent City's multicultural society and became important to Louisiana's defense, maintaining their own militia units that served in various Indian wars and against the British during the Revolutionary War.

After the United States acquired Louisiana in 1803, the status of the free men of color changed significantly. Louisiana's constitution of 1812 specifically restricted the right to vote to white men who owned property. The free men of color could still own property and serve in the militia, but they were left out of politics, and their status began to decline. Nonetheless they once again volunteered to defend their homes during the War of 1812 and bravely fought for Andrew Jackson at the Battle of New Orleans.

A week after civil war erupted in April 1861 some of New Orleans's free men of color offered to form military companies to protect the state against the Union. In an announcement published in the *Daily Picayune*, the men declared that they were prepared to defend their homes "against any enemy who may come and disturb its tranquillity." The *Daily Crescent* newspaper declared, "Our free colored men . . . are certainly as much attached to the land of their birth as their white brethren here in Louisiana. . . . [They] will fight the Black Republican with as much determination and gallantry as any body of white men in the service of the Confederate States."

Soon afterward hundreds of free men of color gathered in the street to show their support for the Confederacy. A regiment known as the Native Guards was formed and mustered into the state militia, but the Confederate government refused to accept them into the national army. All of the regiment's line officers were of African descent, although Governor Thomas O. Moore appointed a white officer to command it.

Popular history clams that many of the Native Guards were wealthy slave owners who were members of New Orleans's upper class, but that is not true. While a few might have been well-to-do and owned slaves, and some certainly were related to prominent citizens, the 1860 census shows that a vast majority were clerks, artisans, and skilled laborers— lower middle class at the time.

The black militia disbanded when Union forces occupied New Orleans in the spring of 1862. After the Battle of Baton Rouge in August, General Benjamin F. Butler, the Union's military governor of Louisiana, requested reinforcements to defend New Orleans, but none was forthcoming. In desperation Butler informed Secretary of War Edwin M. Stanton that he planned to raise a regiment of free blacks. On September 27, 1862, Butler mustered the 1st Louisiana Native Guards into Union service, making it the first sanctioned regiment of African American troops in the U.S. Army.

It has generally been assumed that the African Americans who joined Butler's Native Guards were the same ones who had served earlier in the state militia regiment by the same name. Butler in fact claimed that was the case. As a result historians have questioned the sincerity of the black militiamen who volunteered for Confederate service in 1861. Their supposed change in loyalty seems to indicate that their offer to fight for the South was made only to protect their economic and social status within the community; to not volunteer would make white neighbors suspicious and possibly lead to retaliation. Some Native Guards said as much to Butler and others.

FRANK LESLIE'S ILLUSTRATED NEWSPAPER

Entered according to the Act of Congress in the year 1863, by FRANK LESLIE, in the Clerk's Office of the District Court for the Southern District of New York.

No. 388—Vol. XV.] NEW YORK, MARCH 7, 1863. [PRICE 8 CENTS.

SCENES IN LOUISIANA.

OUR Artist has sent us some sketches which illustrate, in a striking degree, the novel phases of life, both military and civil, which the present struggle is evolving. The fact of black regiments being actively employed is not a novelty, since they have been for some time part of the British military system, which, with its usual common sense, avails itself of every aid in the pursuit of its objects. Our Artist says that among the cypress swamps of Louisiana negro soldiers are invaluable, and accompanies his sketch of the pickets of the First Louisiana native troops, guarding the New Orleans, Opelousas and Great Western Railroad, with some remarks which we quote:

"In this swamp in the wilderness the 'nigger soldiers' are eminently useful. The melancholy solitude, with the spectral cypress trees, which seem to stand in silent despair, like nature's sentinels waving in the air wreaths of gray funeral moss, to warn all human beings of the latent pestilence around, though unendurable to our soldiers of the North, seems an elysium to these sable soldiers, for the swampy forest has no horrors to them. Impervious to miasma, they see only the home of the coon, the possum and the copperhead, so that with 'de gun dat Massa Sam gib 'em,' they have around them all the essential elements of colored happiness, 'except ladies' society.'"

The Old Slave Laws.

In strange forgetfulness of the use to which the colored race may be put, the new régime has empowered Provost Marshal Col. French to put in force the old Slave Laws of Louisiana. Our Artist says: "The first result of the Emancipation Proclamation has been attended with a paradoxical effect, namely, a revival of the old Slave Laws of Louisiana. On the evening in question, all the negroes found in the streets after nine o'clock will ⸺

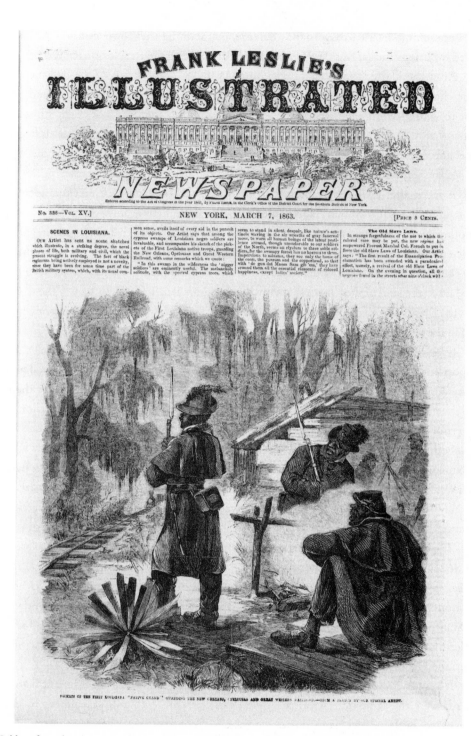

PICKETS OF THE FIRST LOUISIANA "NATIVE GUARD" GUARDING THE NEW ORLEANS, OPELOUSAS AND GREAT WESTERN RAILROAD.—FROM A SKETCH BY OUR SPECIAL ARTIST.

Soldiers from the 1st Louisiana Native Guard guarding the New Orleans, Opelousas and Great Western Railroad. Library of Congress Prints and Photographs Division, LC-USZ62-105562.

Military service records, however, call this assumption into question. Despite Butler's claim to the contrary, a vast majority of his Native Guards were not free men of color but slaves who had made their way into Union lines. James G. Hollandsworth Jr., a professor at the University of Southern Mississippi who wrote the definitive study of the Native Guards, found that only 108 of the 1,035 members of the Louisiana militia regiment, or about 10 percent, went on to serve in the Union's Native Guards. This would seem to indicate that a large number of the black militiamen were indeed sincere in their desire to fight for the South and defend their homes against invasion.

(That's very different, of course, from saying that a large number of African Americans voluntarily served in the rebel army, a claim made by some. The men of the first Native Guard had unique circumstances and motives that should be understood in their specific context, and not extrapolated to the entire black free and enslaved population. One extensive study of Louisiana's sixty-five thousand Confederate soldiers identified only fifteen who were known to be of African descent.)

While most of Butler's Louisiana Native Guards were runaway slaves, some were free men with connections to prominent white families. During an inspection the Native Guards' white colonel told another officer:

> Sir, the best blood of Louisiana is in that regiment! Do you see that tall, slim fellow, third file from the right of the second company? One of the ex-governors of the state is his father. That orderly sergeant in the next company is the son of a man who has been six years in the United States Senate. Just beyond him is the grandson of Judge_____ . . . and all through the ranks you will find the same state of facts. . . . Their fathers are disloyal; [but] these black Ishmaels will more than compensate for their treason by fighting it in the field.

Later the 2nd and 3rd Native Guards, likewise made up overwhelmingly of former slaves, were mustered into service. In July 1863 the three regiments were brigaded together in what became known as the Corps D'Afrique. All three regiments had white colonels, but the line officers in the 1st and 2nd regiments were black, while the 3rd Regiment had both black and white officers.

These Louisianans were the only black officers in the Union Army, but their racist superiors eventually purged most of them. To weed out incompetence all officers in the army had to pass an oral examination given by a board of experienced officers; those who failed either resigned or were stripped of their commission. Army examiners routinely failed black officers or harassed them to make them resign their commission. By war's end only two African American officers remained on duty in the entire army, and both were with the Louisiana Native Guards.

Like all African American soldiers who served in the Civil War, the Native Guards suffered from blatant discrimination. Not only were they paid less than white soldiers, but they were also issued inferior arms and rations, and white soldiers often insulted and harassed them.

As for the tsar, he too was peering across the ocean. In July his foreign minister sent a communiqué to the Russian envoy in Washington, expressing the strongest support of the Union cause yet offered by any European power: "For the more than 80 years that it has existed, the American Union owes its independence, its towering rise, and its progress, to the concord of its members, consecrated, under the auspices of its illustrious founder, by institutions which have been able to reconcile union with liberty. . . . In all cases, the American Union may count on the most heart-felt sympathy on the part of the [tsar] in the course of the serious crisis which the Union is currently going through." To this document Alexander added a notation in his own hand: "So be it."

The modern-day Russian historian Edvard Radzinsky, an admirer of Alexander, has called him "a reformer for a new kind for Russia—a two-faced Janus, one head looking forward while the other looked back longingly." In this respect, Radzinsky has suggested, the tsar resembled Mikhail Gorbachev. He might also have compared Alexander to Lincoln. Like the emperor, the president looked backward (toward America's founding principles) as well as forward (toward a new birth of freedom). He used radical methods (freeing the slaves) to achieve conservative goals (preserving the Union).

When, more than a year after Alexander's, Lincoln issued his own Emancipation Proclamation, it too was handed down as an executive decree from on high. (The president's opponents assailed him as an "autocrat," an "American Czar.") It too proclaimed only partial freedom. And perhaps unwisely Lincoln, unlike his Russian counterpart, provided neither compensation to the slaveholders nor land to the freedmen.

The tsar outlived the president, but he too would fall by the hand of an assassin. On March 1, 1881, nearly twenty years to the day after freeing the serfs, Alexander was riding through St. Petersburg in a closed carriage when two young radicals hurled bombs. The emperor, his legs torn to shreds and stomach ripped open, was carried back to his bedroom-study in the Winter Palace. He died just a few feet from the spot where he had signed his decree of liberation.

Bully for Garibaldi

Don H. Doyle

The tiny Mediterranean island of Caprera, near Sardinia, was not the sort of place to find an American diplomat in the late summer of 1861, but that's precisely where Henry Shelton Sanford landed late in the afternoon of September 8. It had been a long, involved trip: he came from Brussels to Genoa by train, secretly chartered a ship to avoid public notice, and, on the night of September 7, sailed through the Ligurian Sea to Sardinia. Landing late the next day, he hired a small boat to take him to Caprera, then walked more than a mile on a narrow path across the rocky, windswept island.

Sanford was used to such unconventional assignments; appointed minister to Belgium by Lincoln, he also served, unofficially, as head of American secret service operations in Europe, running spies, fostering propaganda, and planning covert activities. Now this deliberately anonymous man at this most isolated place was about to meet with one of the most famous people in the world.

He arrived at a rustic whitewashed house built in the style of a hacienda; the house, stables, and other structures enclosed a rough dirt courtyard inhabited by animals, including a donkey named Pio Nono in dubious honor of Pope Pius IX. Inside the rustic house, amid an array of barrels, saddles, and crude furnishings, Sanford waited to meet the "Hero of Two Worlds," Giuseppe Garibaldi.

For months the European and American press had been alive with rumors that Garibaldi, the celebrated champion of Italian unification, and his Red Shirt army were coming to lead the struggle for America's reunification. Since June a series of contradictory reports and denials and stony silence from Union officials left the world in suspense. "Garibaldi Coming to America!" and "Bully for Garibaldi . . . He Has Accepted," the headlines exclaimed. "Garibaldi Not Coming," another newspaper announced with equal certainty. Now Sanford had arrived with an offer, authorized by President Lincoln and Secretary of State William H. Seward, inviting him to serve as major general in the Union Army.

Sanford was dismayed to find the famed general "still an invalid," recuperating from a prolonged bout with rheumatoid arthritis. However, he knew as well as Lincoln and Seward did that, whatever value an aging Italian general who spoke no English might offer militarily, Garibaldi's mere "presence" and "gallantry," as Seward put it, would prove "eminently useful" to the Union cause.

The conversation began promisingly. "I will be very happy to serve a country for which I have so much affection," Garibaldi replied to preliminary inquiries. He had lived in exile in New York and considered himself a citizen of what he fondly referred to as his "second country." But what he wanted to hear, and what Sanford could not tell him, was that this would be a war against slavery.

In Garibaldi's mind victory over the Southern slaveholders would come swiftly. "The enemy is weakened by his vices and disarmed by his conscience," he told his comrades. From there they would go on to vanquish the slaveholders of the Caribbean and Brazil, where millions of "miserable slaves will lift their heads and be free citizens."

Garibaldi's question first arose when James W. Quiggle, outgoing American consul in Antwerp, Belgium, seized a chance at glory by writing an unofficial letter to him in June 1861. "The papers report that you are going to the United States to join the Army of the North in the conflict of my country," he wrote. "If you do, the name of La Fayette will not surpass yours. There are thousands of Italians and Hungarians who will rush to join your ranks and there are thousands and tens of thousands of Americans who will glory to be under the command of 'the Washington of Italy.'" Quiggle offered to join their ranks himself.

Henry Shelton Sanford. Library of Congress Prints and Photographs Division, LC-USZ62-130858.

Garibaldi responded, "I have had, and I have still, great desire to go . . . if your government would find my services of some use." But while willing to fight for America, he was not sure exactly what it was fighting for. "Tell me," he asked pointedly, "if this agitation is regarding the emancipation of the Negroes or not."

Quiggle sent his correspondence with Garibaldi to Seward on July 5, which should have arrived in Washington just before the First Battle of Bull Run on July 21, 1861. It was a day of humiliating defeat for the Union, marked by poor leadership and disorderly (some said cowardly) retreat by Union soldiers.

Earlier Quiggle's idea of bringing an Italian general to lead a Union Army might have been dismissed as a harebrained scheme, but after Bull Run Seward feared Britain or France might declare support for the Confederacy. He saw in Garibaldi an international hero whose charisma and leadership were desperately needed. After consulting with Lincoln, on July 27 Seward sent instructions to Sanford to meet with "the distinguished Soldier of Freedom" and enlist "his services in the present contest for the unity and liberty of the American People." "Tell him," he instructed Sanford, "that the fall of the American Union . . . would be a disastrous blow to the cause of Human Freedom equally here, in Europe, and throughout the world."

Garibaldi had fascinated journalists ever since the 1830s, when he was in exile in South America fighting for the independence of southern Brazil and Uruguay. When the revolutions of 1848 broke out across Europe, he returned to Italy and led a heroic defense of the Republic of Rome against French and papal forces. He was again exiled, to New York, but later returned to live in isolation on Caprera. Then, in 1860, he led a ragtag army of volunteers known as "the Thousand" in an invasion of Sicily to overthrow its Bourbon rulers. The whole world followed Garibaldi's Red Shirts as they vanquished a large professional army, swept across southern Italy, and entered Naples in triumph, all within four months. Precisely as the United States was coming apart, Italy proclaimed its new existence as a united nation. Garibaldi had made Italy; perhaps this remarkable general could help remake the United States.

Garibaldi was reviled by the pope and many crowned heads of Europe, but he enjoyed remarkable popularity among republicans and liberals everywhere. Women adored him; they wore dresses and blouses that imitated the Red Shirt regalia of the Garibaldini. Journalists celebrated the Garibaldi legend in print, shared intimate details of his personal life, and made his image, with his gray beard and mesmerizing gaze, familiar to everyone.

Sanford experienced Garibaldi mania for himself. The night before he left for Caprera, he witnessed throngs of people in the streets of Genoa shouting "Viva Garibaldi!" and singing the Garibaldi hymn. On the main square he viewed a wax effigy of their hero "mounted on a kind of altar surrounded by flags at which people are bringing candles by the hundreds to burn, as you have seen in the churches of patron saints." It was the first anniversary of Garibaldi's triumphant entry into Naples, and all across Italy there were similar demonstrations.

Now, face to face as the evening sun set over the Mediterranean, Sanford and Garibaldi discussed the terms of the offer and the purpose of the war. Garibaldi expected to be offered supreme command of all armed forces. He explained that, like the captain of a ship, he must have complete control and "would be of little use as a subordinate." This may have been lost in translation, but more likely it was the enthusiasm of Quiggle (whom Sanford blamed) or the blunder of his own advance messenger (which he obscured). Sanford's careful efforts to explain that the rank of major general "would carry with it the command of a large 'corps d'armée' to conduct in his own way" did little to persuade him.

But it was the purpose of the war that seemed to concern Garibaldi most. "Could slavery not be abolished?" he asked Sanford. If it was not being fought to emancipate the slaves, he told Sanford, "the war would appear to be like any civil war in which the world at large could have little interest or sympathy."

Since his arrival in Europe Sanford had been trying to tell Seward that Europeans expected this to be a war of liberation, without which they would as soon see the nation fall apart. But to Garibaldi's question Sanford could do no more than explain Lincoln's legalistic apology for the federal government's limited constitutional power to interfere with slavery in the states.

Late that night Sanford went to sleep in Garibaldi's house still hoping the general might agree to come view the American scene for himself before deciding. They spoke for hours the next morning, until Sanford finally accepted that he could give no satisfactory answer to Garibaldi's question. He left Caprera later in the day for his long journey back to Brussels.

For weeks the story continued to play in the international press, and even a year later rumors revived that Garibaldi might yet come to America. Eventually the story faded from the news, and from historical memory, resurfacing from time to time as little more than a bizarre curiosity of Civil War history.

It was much more than that, for Garibaldi's question anticipated a fundamental problem the Union confronted in trying to explain its cause to a puzzled world. Was this only a civil war, a purely domestic conflict in a quarrelsome democracy? Was the Union's goal nothing more than to put down rebellion and protect its sovereignty? Or was there something of real consequence to the world at large? The Union would have to find answers before other powers of the world decided to include the South among the family of nations.

Why Bismarck Loved Lincoln

Kenneth Weisbrode

We usually think of the Civil War as a uniquely American event, a war unlike any other fought in the Western world during the nineteenth century. And of course that's true, strictly speaking; no other country saw itself split in two over slavery. But that's not the only way to think of the war. Put a different way, the Civil War was just one of several wars for national unification—including fighting in Italy and Germany—on both sides of the Atlantic.

While countries like Britain and France were concentrating on expansion through colonization, the United States, Germany, and others were focused inward, developing—intentionally or not—the centralizing powers that have defined the modern state ever since. What seems like a particularly American event was really part of a much larger, and much more significant, historical trend.

As a war of national unification the Civil War represented a sharp historical break, a moment of crisis that would define the country's course for decades to come. Beforehand the notions of national unification and expansion had been indivisible; just fifteen years earlier the United States had defeated Mexico in a bloody war that brought vast territories under occupation and destroyed the delicate balance between slave and free states. Some people predicted the worst. "The United States will conquer Mexico," claimed Ralph Waldo Emerson in 1846, "but it will be as the man swallows the arsenic which brings him down in turn. Mexico will poison us." Ulysses S. Grant went so far as to declare the Civil War divine punishment for the Mexican conflict.

Indeed the Mexican War fueled an ongoing debate about how large the country should get. Canada, or parts of Canada, had been sought by eager expansionists virtually

Emperor Maximilian of Mexico. Library of Congress Prints and Photographs Division, LC-USZ62-17159.

since the two parts of British North America went their separate ways in 1776; spreading the plantation economy to Mexico and beyond—the so-called purple dream—had long animated the Southern imagination.

Even as the Civil War began, Mexico continued to fester and tempt interventionists. It announced in mid-July 1861 that it could not service its debts, having just ended its own civil war (called the Reform War), and so suspended payments to its European creditors. This was not unusual, but this time the country's creditors did more than reiterate demands for payment: the British, French, and Spanish governments joined forces in October to compel Mexico to pay; by the end of the year the city of Veracruz was occupied.

The British and Spanish soon reversed course, but Napoleon III of France, in league with Mexican reactionaries, persevered; he sought nothing less than a new Catholic empire in the Western Hemisphere under his auspices (thence the term *Latin* America). French troops occupied Mexico City and installed a Habsburg archduke, Maximilian, as emperor. He lasted until 1867 when, having lost the war against his opponents and even the backing of Napoleon, he was executed by a Mexican firing squad.

Here, then, was a major challenge to Washington, an act of aggression in the Western Hemisphere by European countries and thus a direct violation of the Monroe Doctrine. Some in Abraham Lincoln's administration may have urged him to strike, to invade Mexico and push the Europeans out before they dug in. But Lincoln rejected any such advice.

In part it was a matter of expediency; the Union had more pressing matters to its south to deal with. But it was also a resetting of the course of the American state. As Lincoln saw it, "older" powers like Britain, France, and Russia could go on to see imperial archipelagos flourish, but "younger" states should opt for geographic and political consolidation and centralization at home. Lincoln thus rebuffed the idea of conquering and colonizing Canadians and Mexicans in favor of building a new nation to the Pacific. It's no surprise that Lincoln would prefer this path; as a midwesterner his mental map extended more horizontally than vertically—east to west rather than north to south. But first he had to stop the American South from going its own way.

Lincoln wasn't alone in prioritizing centralization. Giuseppe Garibaldi and his fellow campaigners for Italy's unification—which had just been proclaimed in March—would have understood this, as would nationalists (sometimes called *unitarios*) elsewhere in the Western Hemisphere, notably in Argentina, Colombia, and Canada, whose confederation debate got going at about the same time. As a matter of fact Lincoln authorized a commission for Garibaldi in the Union Army. Garibaldi turned it down—evidently because freeing the slaves was not yet sufficiently high on the list of the Union's war aims—yet Lincoln's offer underscores the fellowship between America's war of unification and those taking place in other parts of the world.

Perhaps no one was more in tune with Lincoln than Otto von Bismarck, the minister-president of Prussia. Beginning in 1862 Bismarck unified Germany, but he explicitly rejected the idea of a *Großdeutschland*, or "Greater Germany" incorporating Austria, in favor of a *kleindeutsche Lösung*, or "Little German Solution" that preferred centralization over maximum territorial expansion. This may have been one reason why, after the Civil War ended, Bismarck reportedly sounded out Washington on an alliance. It made sense: Europe's rising industrial and military power seeking common cause with an American counterpart that seemed destined for the same.

Unifying states needed more than just will; they needed propitious events and conditions. In Germany's case it was the Crimean War—triggered, incidentally, by Napoleon III, following his 1851 coup—that made unification possible by putting an end to the Anglo-Russian condominium underpinning the European, and therefore global, balance of power. In the United States it was the country's "free" security (provided in large measure by the British Navy) that allowed for its territorial expansion and consolidation.

And so the old order gave way to a new, contested one on both sides of the Atlantic; unification would come in both places by force. If the Crimean War had set the stage for the wars of unification in Germany and Italy, and the Mexican War did so for the war of unification in the United States, then it's worth asking: If there had been no Crimean War, might there still have been an American Civil War? Probably so; civil wars by definition happen largely for internal reasons. But without the conflict in Europe, the American war would not have been the nationalist achievement of world-historical import, as Lincoln, Bismarck, and later generations understood it.

In other words, the Civil War—as significant as it is for American history—is even more important when viewed through a comparative, transatlantic lens. The fight for internal unification rather than expansion meant that never again would the United States seek to conquer and annex its neighbors. It would, along with Bismarck's Germany, be a new kind of state: centralized, rationalized, and mobilized to dominate the coming century.

Lincoln's PR Coup

AARON W. MARRS

In addition to the domestic challenge it presented, the fledgling Confederacy posed a foreign policy dilemma for Abraham Lincoln's administration. The Confederacy hoped to use its position as a crucial source of cotton to secure recognition from foreign powers and boost its legitimacy, and it sent commissioners abroad to sway other countries to support its cause.

In response Secretary of State William Seward threatened war against European countries who interfered in America's domestic conflict. But the administration wasn't the only branch to enter the foreign policy fray; in July 1861 Representative Samuel Sullivan Cox, a Democrat from Ohio, submitted a resolution calling on Lincoln to share with the House "all correspondence with the English, French, Spanish, and other Governments with reference to the right of blockade, privateering, and the recognition of the so-called confederate States." It passed with bipartisan ease, as did two similar resolutions submitted during the following weeks.

Lincoln hardly welcomed such extensive oversight; on July 25, the same day that Representative Timothy Howe, a Republican from Wisconsin, submitted the third of the resolutions, the president sent word to the House that the "correspondence called for" would not be forthcoming at that time. The reason for the delay is unclear; of the three resolutions, Cox's mentioned that the correspondence could be submitted "at the beginning of the next session of Congress," and the administration appears to have taken that as an opportunity to wait as long as feasible to release the documents.

Eventually, however, Lincoln complied. In doing so he not only provided his contemporaries and future Americans with an almost real-time, detailed look into the daily operations of the country's foreign policy apparatus in crisis, but he set a precedent for State Department transparency that is still followed today.

Because the resolutions passed with little or no discussion, we have little direct evidence for what Congress was thinking at the time. But we can infer a few things from the broader context. For one, such requests were hardly unprecedented; throughout the early republic the legislature had asked for (and the executive branch had supplied) diplomatic instructions and dispatches related to treaties, boundary disputes, and other foreign affairs. And of course the war made foreign policy an especially touchy subject; by examining the correspondence Congress surely hoped to see that Seward was instructing ministers to appropriately defend American interests and that the ministers were faithfully carrying out the instructions.

After months of delay Lincoln finally complied with the resolutions. On December 3, 1861, as the second session of the 37th Congress got under way, Lincoln sent a message to both houses of Congress. The message portion of this communication was quite brief, but attached to it was correspondence between the United States and its ministers abroad, bound together in one volume.

Lincoln's missive opened with a short discussion of foreign relations before turning to other domestic matters. He characterized the Confederate effort to gain recognition from foreign governments as sputtering and unsuccessful, noting, "The disloyal citizens of the United States who have offered the ruin of our country, in return for the aid and comfort which they have invoked abroad, have received less patronage and encouragement than they probably expected." After dismissing Confederate diplomatic efforts, Lincoln announced that he had submitted the requested correspondence, and he hoped that those who read it would see that his administration had "practiced prudence, and liberality towards foreign powers, averting causes of irritation; and, with firmness, maintaining our own rights and honor."

There followed 425 pages of correspondence between the government and its diplomatic ministers abroad. (The United States would not have proper ambassadors until 1893.) After a series of general circulars, the volume reproduced material on twenty-four countries, not only the major European powers but most of Latin America and even Egypt, the Hawaiian Islands, and Japan.

The material wasn't for Congress alone; the White House released it to the public as well. For those who could not get their hands on the volume itself, copies of its contents traveled quickly up and down the coast, published in newspapers.

By perusing the documents Americans could see how the Union defended its interests in countries large and small, near and far. Obviously, staving off Confederate agents was a key task for America's ministers. Seward wrote to Carl Schurz, the minister to Spain, that preventing the Confederacy from gaining recognition was "your chief duty, and no more important one was ever devolved by the United States upon any representative whom they have sent abroad."

Even in countries of lesser importance ministers were urged to be on the watch. Although Seward did not believe that the Confederates would attempt to gain recognition immediately from Denmark, he wrote to his representative there, "Political action even of the more commanding or more active States is influenced by a general opinion that is formed imperceptibly in all parts of the Eastern continent. Every representative of the United States in Europe has, therefore, a responsibility to see that no effort on his part is wanting to make that opinion just, so far as the true position of affairs in his own country is concerned."

Representatives abroad had an important public relations role to play, particularly when news traveled slowly across the Atlantic Ocean and rumors were rife. Seward's instructions encouraged ministers to not let discouraging news from America cloud foreigners' perceptions of the war effort. After the First Battle of Bull Run, in a letter marked "confidential," he wrote to Charles Francis Adams, the minister in London, "You will hear of a reverse of our arms in Virginia," and encouraged him to think little of it. "The vigor of the government will be increased, and the ultimate result will be a triumph of the Constitution," Seward wrote. "Do not be misled by panic reports of danger apprehended for the capital." Seward likewise wrote to William Lewis Dayton in France, "Treason was emboldened by its partial success at Manassas, but the Union now grows manifestly stronger every day." Foreigners could get their news from any number of sources, and ministers had to stand ready to put a positive spin on events.

The volume also exposed domestic readers to the administration's frustration with the willingness of the British to treat the Confederates as belligerents. This step granted the Confederates some credibility, even if it fell short of the full recognition they desired. In these documents Northern readers could see unbiased proof that this action did not go without protest. Adams proclaimed to the British that the Americans were "irritated" by the British treatment of Confederates as belligerents.

Old State Department Building, 1860s. Library of Congress Prints and Photographs Division, LC-DIG-ppmsca-34789.

Slavery is mentioned throughout the volume, although at this point in the war the rhetoric was more about the dangers of the political power of Southern slaveholders than the virtues of emancipation. Slavery certainly got credit for causing the war. Seward wrote to Dayton in France, "The attempted revolution is simply causeless. It is, indeed, equally without a reason and without an object, unless it be one arising out of the subject of slavery." Seward instructed the representative in Russia that although slavery had existed in all the states at the time of the American Revolution, "it was expected that under the operation of moral, social, and political influences then existing the practice of slavery would soon cease." The "cause" of the rebellion was the fact that the slave states, having suffered defeat at the polls in 1860, "took an appeal from the verdict of the people, rendered through the ballot-box, to the sword, and organized a revolution with civil war."

The decision to release the material won glowing praise. The *Baltimore Sun* reported on December 9 that the correspondence was "receiving that close attention from persons skilled in diplomacy and public law which belongs to its distinguished source and the magnitude of the subject in question." The *Sentinel* of Keene, New Hampshire, reported, "In the whole of this correspondence, the Secretary of State exhibits marked ability as a statesman and diplomatist."

By January 1862 the correspondence had reached the West Coast, where the *San Francisco Bulletin* reported that the diplomatic correspondence was "quite voluminous" and "highly interesting." Seward again came in for praise; his "high-toned" and "courteous" messages were "as nearly perfect models of diplomatic correspondence as are to be found on the pages of modern history." The correspondence with Adams and Dayton "have swept to the winds all the aspersions of those who have accused him of favoring a timid and wavering policy in dealing with the rebels." The volume attracted attention from abroad as well; shortly after its release, Lord Richard Lyons, British minister to the United States, sent a copy to Lord John Russell, the British foreign minister.

What can we learn from this volume of foreign affairs documentation released as the first year of the war drew to a close? First, it represents what the Lincoln administration wanted the American public to know about foreign affairs (as distinct from telling us in the modern day everything we might like to know about diplomacy during the Civil War). Judging by the newspaper response, Americans were pleased with how the federal government was acting. Publishing the documentation also exposed British and French actions toward the Confederates, which helped Americans direct their ire toward those two countries.

Second, the publication of the volume demonstrates the balance of powers between the executive and legislative branches during the mid-nineteenth century: although the executive branch bore responsibility for foreign policy, the legislative branch could wield significant power by demanding to see copies of the documentation.

Third, and perhaps most important, the volume illustrates an early attempt at government openness—and, given the exigencies of wartime, a surprisingly forthright attempt. The summer resolutions requesting the documents made an allowance for

Lincoln's assessment of the "public interest" in determining which documents not to submit to Congress, and we have no way of knowing what type of selection policy was in place. At the same time, the resolutions make clear that Congress expected to receive something; indeed diplomatic correspondence was released to Congress on an ad hoc basis throughout the early republic. But that it was done in a moment of clear crisis demonstrates that Lincoln's administration saw the value in getting the correspondence in the public's hands.

There is a consequence that likely no one in 1861 could have foretold: the State Department continues to publish edited collections of foreign affairs documentation, a century and a half later. Although the *Foreign Relations of the United States* series does not release documents as rapidly as Lincoln did, and so has become a historical look at American foreign relations rather than a contemporary publication of documents, the release of the volume in 1861 set a landmark democratic precedent: that the American government must, on a regular basis, keep the public informed about its foreign policy operations.

Holland's Plan for America's Slaves

MICHAEL J. DOUMA

In 1863 American blacks were not the only enslaved people with emancipation on their mind. On the northeastern coast of South America, in the Dutch colony of Suriname, some thirty thousand slaves also prepared for their day of freedom, which would arrive with the government's emancipation mandate of July 1, 1863, six months after Lincoln issued the Emancipation Proclamation.

As in the United States, a certain nervousness prevailed. The Surinamese planter class feared a resulting decline in agricultural production in the Dutch colony and hoped to recruit additional laborers from abroad to aid the postemancipation economy. Meanwhile many whites in the United States feared emancipation and a postslavery society for both economic and racist reasons. For many, including Congress and President Lincoln, colonization was a popular alternative.

It makes sense that in light of these twin anxieties, the Dutch and the Americans might try to work out some sort of grand, postslavery bargain. But it is only in recent years that evidence scattered across archives in Europe and the Caribbean has come to light documenting the resulting web of transatlantic diplomatic correspondence—including, most notably, a cache of documents from the Netherlands' national archives in The Hague showing that the Dutch made a serious attempt to acquire American freedmen.

The earliest correspondence took place well before the Emancipation Proclamation. In July 1862 the Netherlands approached the American government with a plan to colonize freed American blacks in Suriname, where they would serve five-year labor contracts before receiving free agricultural land and citizenship. Secretary of State William

Seward redirected the Dutch inquiry to Caleb Smith, the secretary of the interior. Smith responded with a terse but inconclusive phrase that reverberated across the Atlantic: "The Government is not, at present, prepared to make any arrangements to that end." For the moment the Dutch seemed to have lost their chance. Yet only a few weeks later Lincoln authorized Seward to direct the American minister in the Netherlands, James Pike, to enter into negotiations with the Dutch for exactly this purpose.

Pike and P. Th. van der Maesen de Sombreff, the Dutch minister of foreign affairs, hammered out the terms of convention over a drawn-out fourteen months, signing it in The Hague on December 15, 1863. The convention gave the United States the power to supervise all emigration and guarantee the civil rights of the emigrants. A treaty was sent to the U.S. Senate for ratification.

In Washington the Dutch minister to the United States, Theodorus Roest van Limburg, did not learn about the signing of the convention until a month and a half later, when a German acquaintance handed him a newspaper report. Roest van Limburg was justifiably upset and embarrassed. The average delivery time for mail from The Hague to Washington was sixteen days, yet news of a convention between the country Roest van Limburg represented and the country he was stationed in had reached him by newspaper well before official diplomatic correspondence. He had opposed the deal from the beginning, deeming it infeasible, which may be why he was left out of the loop.

By early 1864 the proper paperwork for the eventual ratification of the colonization treaty appeared to be set, though the Senate declined to establish a date for considering it (perhaps because Pike, who secretly supported a plan to redistribute freedmen domestically, offered only halfhearted support for the colonization plan).

To promote the effort the Dutch would need reliable reports about the character of the freed slaves and the prevailing conditions in the United States. They would also need recruiting agents on the ground. With the hope that the treaty would eventually be ratified by the Senate, the Dutch Ministry of Colonies urged Roest van Limburg to prepare his consuls for action. A series of royal decrees in the Netherlands also established regulations and instructions for supplying free laborers to Suriname, copies of which were sent to Roest van Limburg.

Despite being shunted aside during the negotiations, Roest van Limburg dove into the project, readying his network of subordinate diplomats—a dozen unpaid, generally underappreciated consuls stationed in major American port cities. In response to an inquiry from his superiors in The Hague, he proposed Baltimore, New Orleans, New York, and Philadelphia as possible ports of embarkation for freed blacks bound for Suriname. Yet when he asked the respective consuls about the suitability of these possible jumping-off points, he discovered that most of them would rather resign their post than dirty their hands with "negro emigration." Roest van Limburg also learned that two of these consuls could not even read Dutch (a consequence, he complained, of the failure of his government to pay for competent help) and that instructions forwarded from The Hague had gone unread.

Although Roest van Limburg's relationship with his government appeared to sour at times because of his cautious opposition to the project, he worked to find a way to satisfy the Dutch government and the Surinamese planter class. He suggested waiting for improved circumstances, paying the consuls, and either employing special recruiting agents from the Netherlands or letting the Surinamese administrators handle the hard work themselves. It's unclear how seriously he intended his proposals; he must have known that any mention of financial contribution on behalf of the Dutch government would discourage the project, since the Dutch treasury was already stretched thin.

However, it seemed that no matter what Roest van Limburg wrote to discourage the colonization project, his superiors in The Hague continued to promote it. They took every development in the conflict—a battlefield victory, news of refugees fleeing to General Ulysses S. Grant's camps—as an opportunity to again engage the American government on the matter. Part of the trouble was a revolving door that landed four separate men in charge of the Dutch Ministry of Foreign Affairs between 1862 and 1865, four men who seldom questioned the desirability of colonization in Suriname and who pressed Roest van Limburg to continue despite his objections against the project.

As 1865 arrived and the Americans had yet to ratify the treaty, the Dutch sought other ways to recruit black laborers. The government transitioned from organizing a large-scale

An enslaved mother and her child. Library of Congress Prints and Photographs Division, LC-USZ62-15385.

colonization to promoting a voluntary emigration. In this context the distinction between colonization and emigration was not always clear, although the former generally meant heavier government involvement in the process. Instead of dreaming of receiving a few thousand freed blacks as laborers, the Dutch minister of colonies and the Surinamese planters now hoped for a few hundred, any in fact, who might limit the costs of importing workers from Asia.

Although the Senate never ratified the treaty, the executive branch, even after Andrew Johnson took over from the slain President Lincoln, hardly presented any clear obstacles to colonization. In a letter from November 13, 1865, Roest van Limburg referenced a discussion with interim secretary of state William Hunter, who "let it slip that nothing hinders the intended colonization." Perhaps Hunter and others in the cabinet had realized that no treaty was necessary if the only requirement for emigration was that it be of a voluntary nature.

Freed from the regulations of a potential treaty on the matter, the Dutch provided a Boston merchant with a letter of recognition, allowing him to recruit and transport freed slaves from anywhere in the United States. By 1866 agents working on behalf of the Netherlands were actively recruiting African Americans for resettlement in Suriname.

Whether any freed slaves left for Suriname is another question that has not yet been answered. In the United States interest in colonization died out because few freedmen were willing to go. Though they faced a perilous future at home, nothing offered by the Dutch or others could alleviate concerns that they would not be treated any better abroad.

The Civil War and Hawaii

JEFFREY ALLEN SMITH

Almost five thousand miles and half an ocean away from the killing fields of Gettysburg, Chickamauga, and Spotsylvania, Hawaii and Hawaiians might be assumed absent from the Civil War. Yet regardless of proud protestations of neutrality by the Hawaiian monarchy—the islands were not American territory at the time—many of the islands' residents participated in the conflict, on both sides. And for good reason: though they lived on one of the most geographically isolated island chains in the world, Hawaiians kept abreast of international events, knowing that the outcome of the war could greatly affect Hawaii as well.

The presidential election of Abraham Lincoln received a positive response in Hawaii, where the Hawaiian-language newspaper *Ka Hoku Loa* wrote that America was "blessed" to have him at such a problematic time. Nevertheless the Lincoln administration was worried about Hawaiian neutrality and what it saw to be growing British influence in the islands. Understandably preoccupied with more pressing domestic matters, Lincoln and Secretary of State William H. Seward did what they could. Seward replaced the boorish and tactless American commissioner to Hawaii, Thomas Dyer, with the more capable

King Kamehameha V. Courtesy of Hawaii State Archives.

James McBride and promoted McBride to minister, making him the highest-ranking foreign official in the kingdom.

Later, after the passing of King Kamehameha IV Alexander Liholiho in 1863, Lincoln sent a personal four-page letter to the new monarch, Kamehameha V Lot Kapuāiwa, professing sorrow while congratulating the king and extending offers of support from "Your Majesty's Good Friend."

However, the Hawaiian monarchy had its own reasons to improve relations with the United States, as it wanted a new trade treaty. To that end Kamehameha V sent an emissary, Chief Justice E. H. Allen, to Washington in 1864. In June Allen met with Lincoln, Seward, and other politicians to discuss the prospects for a new treaty. He returned to Hawaii frustrated yet optimistic, without a treaty in hand but reporting that Lincoln and Seward were receptive to the idea. The only problem, Seward told Allen, was that the "civil war renders such negotiation inconvenient and inexpedient." Still, the secretary of state promised, "at no very distant period . . . the subject will be resumed with pleasure." Private correspondence revealed that Seward planned to request a "port, sufficient for a wharf and buildings for a naval depot" in what appeared to be a forebear of Pearl Harbor.

Similar geopolitical wrangling played out in the newspapers. Mid-nineteenth-century newspapers were unabashedly slanted, and the Hawaiian press was no different. Many papers were published in Hawaiian, English, or a combination of the two. The Hawaiian-language press was to varying degrees antimonarchy and quasi-independent, but above all it was pro-Union. The *Polynesian* was one of the biggest and the self-proclaimed "official organ of the Hawaiian government." It promoted a curious combination of abolitionism and states' rights advocacy that liked to reprint articles from England in favor of neutrality. Engaging in a bit of yellow journalism, the *Polynesian* used the Civil War as a proxy fight against the *Pacific Commercial Advertiser*, its main rival and the voice of American business interests in Hawaii. For example, in January 1863 he *Polynesian* claimed that the *Pacific Commercial Advertiser* had "never approved" of Lincoln's removal of General George B. McClellan, unlike the *Polynesian*, and now Lincoln and the *Polynesian* had been vindicated by Union advances on the battlefield.

Hawaiians themselves decidedly favored the North. Union victories were celebrated, and a Honolulu bookstore sold red, white, and blue envelopes imprinted with "Union must be preserved" alongside copies of *Uncle Tom's Cabin*. Neighbors of a Southern-born woman living in Honolulu ripped up a Confederate flag she had hung from her veranda. In fact support for Lincoln in Hawaii was greater than in the United States; he did better in 1860 and 1864 mock elections with American expats in Hawaii than among the Northern voting public. American residents on Hawaii island threw a grand Fourth of July celebration in 1861, complete with bands, the firing of guns, and toasts to Lincoln and the Union.

Perhaps too caught up in the revelry, a Hilo merchant named Thomas Spencer organized about forty Hawaiians into a volunteer auxiliary corps that pledged its support should Lincoln call upon them. The group was later dubbed "Spencer's Invincibles" and drilled in military tactics. The *Pacific Commercial Advertiser* reported, "All the company now wants is a chance of a shot at Jeff Davis' bloodhounds" and that the men hoped that Hawaii's proclamation of neutrality "will not spoil the fun." The Hawaiian government did in fact disband the group, but the monarchy could not stop others from joining the fray.

More than a hundred people from Hawaii fought on both sides of the Civil War. Arguably the most famous was the Union general Samuel C. Armstrong. Born on Maui to missionary parents who ran a school for Hawaiian children, after the war Armstrong used that educational experience as the inspiration for his founding and running of the Hampton Institute, which trained African Americans as teachers and engineers. It was at the Hampton Institute that Booker T. Washington received his education, and he used his alma mater as a model for his Tuskegee Institute.

However, unlike the white Armstrong, native Hawaiians who fought for the Union risked segregation because of their skin color. One volunteer, Prince Romerson, served in the 5th Massachusetts Volunteer Cavalry, an all-black regiment, and mustered out as a sergeant. Exceptions did occur, though; Henry Hoolulu Pitman, son of the Hawaiian chief Kinoole O Liliha, was a private in the 22nd Massachusetts Volunteer Infantry, a white regiment, who was captured and died in Richmond's Libby Prison.

A few Hawaiians found themselves fighting for the South. Probably more for employment than the Southern cause, about ten Hawaiian seamen joined the crew of the *Shenandoah*, a Confederate raider that wrought havoc throughout the Pacific.

Interestingly the saga of the *Shenandoah* played an important part in the larger story of the later overthrow of the Hawaiian monarchy. Indiscriminate in sinking both American and Hawaiian whaling vessels, the *Shenandoah* did not directly cause the demise of the whaling industry in the Pacific, but it did hasten it. With whaling ships becoming scarcer and voyages to find whales longer and more cost-prohibitive, commercial agricultural plantations came into their own in Hawaii. After dabbling in cotton, rice, and other products, planters found sugar to be the cash crop of choice. Commercially active in Hawaii since the 1830s, the Hawaiian sugar industry saw one of its greatest expansions during the Civil War era. As a result of the Union boycott of Southern sugar, Hawaiian sugar exports to the United States rose 175 percent a year from 1860 to 1866, while prices jumped over 500 percent.

However, the rise in sugar profits sowed the seeds for the overthrow of the Hawaiian monarchy. Eerily prophetic, the *Pacific Commercial Advertiser* reported that the Lahina Sugar Company paid more in taxes on sugar than the Hawaiian king's salary, which caused the paper to speculate, "We don't advise the Lahina Sugar Company to purchase his sovereignty—that would be treason or treachery, we don't know exactly which." Either way, the sugar industry in Hawaii gradually gained political and economic power in the kingdom, eventually instituting a form of contract labor that verged on slavery.

The consolidation of wealth and power generated on these plantations proved fertile ground for white businessmen and their ilk, some of whom were Civil War veterans, who favored American annexation of the islands and ultimately overthrew the kingdom of Hawaii in a coup d'état on January 17, 1893. The war that strengthened the United States as a country laid the foundation for the destruction of the kingdom of Hawaii and inextricably bound the two for centuries to come.

The Russians Are Coming!

RICK BEARD

The eponymous heroine of Donizetti's opera *Lucrezia Borgia* had just died, and the final notes of music had barely faded into the November night when hundreds of workers began to transform New York City's Academy of Music. Less than twenty-four hours later the 4,000-seat entertainment emporium—an opera house, theater, and meeting and exposition hall, all under one roof—was to host the social event of the 1863 season. The city's elite had quickly snapped up two thousand tickets for the Soirée Russe, a grand ball for the officers of the Russian fleet at anchor in New York.

A rapturous description of the preparations in the *New York Times* on November 5, the morning of the ball, promised that the visiting Russian naval officers would enjoy "their first opportunity of seeing society in New-York in all its full regalia, style and splendor." Guests would begin arriving at the 14th Street entrance to the Academy at 9 p.m., from where they would be conducted into the ballroom for dancing scheduled to begin at 10:30. As the *Times* reported, "There will be two splendid Bands," one "for the Promenade and operatic music," the other "for the dancing." Despite a newly constructed dance floor more than 850 square yards in size, one reporter in attendance later noted, "We will call it a dance out of respect to conventional and popular prejudice. In truth it was a very wonderful and indescribable phantasmagoria of humanity" that "moved a little this way, a little that, but not a dance."

The organizers spared no expense. Over 1,200 gas burners illuminated the building's interior. Dressing rooms for women featured maids to attend to "the multitude of tears, and rips, and damages which dresses are liable to." Hairdressers for both men and women were in attendance, as was "a corps" of bootblacks. The stage on which Ms. Borgia had expired just hours earlier was now enclosed "in a white ornamented tent, thirty feet high" that framed a trompe l'oeil scene of a "terrace, garden, and lake by moonlight." Paintings, engravings, photographs, and sculpture borrowed or executed especially for the occasion depicted everyone from Peter the Great and George Washington to Tsar Alexander II, President Abraham Lincoln, and Union military worthies like Farragut, McClellan, Halleck, Hooker, Frémont, Grant, and Meade.

Irving Hall, a building adjacent to and connected with the Academy by a covered walkway, was the setting for a supper catered by Delmonico, the city's premier restaurant. Beginning at 11 p.m. guests could partake from a menu that, according to an account of the "principal edibles" in *Harper's Weekly*, included 12,000 oysters, 12 "monster" salmon of 30 pounds each, 1,200 game birds, 250 turkeys, 400 chickens, a half ton of tenderloin, 100 pastry "pyramids," 1,000 loaves of bread, and 3,500 bottles of wine. Each heavily laden table was, in the words of a reporter for the *New York Herald*, "triumphant proof of the ability of our great caterer, and excelled all previous displays of the kind."

This evening of lavish entertainment was the culminating moment in a series of events—a visit by Mary Lincoln to the Russian frigate *Osliaba* in New York Harbor on September 16; a Fifth Avenue parade on October 1; and two banquets at Astor House—to celebrate the unexpected arrival of six Russian warships just weeks earlier. The first to arrive in New York Harbor, the *Osliaba*, had been on patrol in the Mediterranean. On September 24 the *Alexander Nevsky, Peresviet, Variag, Vitiaz,* and *Almaz* (with composer Nikolai Rimsky-Korsakov aboard) all arrived from the Kronstadt Naval Base near St. Petersburg. Their presence in American waters was testimony both to the amicability that had characterized Russian-American relations for decades and the growing threat posed by Russia's neighbors.

Formal diplomatic relations between the two nations had begun during the Madison administration, with John Quincy Adams's appointment as American ambassador to St. Petersburg. In 1832 Russia became the first nation to enjoy "most favored nation" trading status with the United States, which also extended its support to the tsarist government during the Crimean War of the mid-1850s. In turn the Russians consistently encouraged the growth of the United States, in large measure as a counterweight to the major European powers.

Shortly after the outbreak of the Civil War the Russian foreign minister, Aleksandr Gorchakov, remarked, "Russia and America have a special regard for each other . . . because they have no points of conflict." The issue of slavery was of no consequence to the Russians, and their economy had no pressing need for cotton and so suffered little collateral damage from the war.

By late October 1862, however, the Russian minister was worried. The Union had "few friends among the powers. England rejoices over what is happening to you" and France "is not your friend," he wrote in a letter to Bayard Taylor, secretary to the American legation in St. Petersburg. Russia, which desires "above all things the maintenance of the American Union as one indivisible nation," will "refuse any invitation" to intervene. "But we entreat you to settle the difficulty. I cannot express to you how profound an anxiety we feel—how serious are our fears."

Russian concerns that European powers might intervene to broker a peace between the North and the South were well founded. The French emperor Napoleon III, eager to reassert France's role on the world stage, spawned a series of plans intended to unite his nation with Britain and Russia in a triumvirate that could force negotiations to halt the American war. But the French efforts repeatedly miscarried because of the Russian distrust of Britain, a remnant of the Crimean War, and Union resistance to any effort to extend recognition to the Confederacy. Lincoln summed up the latter situation when reacting to a French proposal to promote a six-month armistice and lift the blockade. Louis Napoleon's efforts were the result, the president observed, of "a mistaken desire to counsel in a case where all foreign counsel excites distrust."

The political situation in Europe grew more complicated after a spontaneous protest in Warsaw against the conscription policies of the Imperial Russian Army in January 1863 led to a broader insurrection in Poland. Britain and France quickly voiced support for the Polish revolutionaries, while Prussia agreed to help the Russians repel any effort by the French to intervene.

As hostilities grew more likely, Nikolai Krabbe, the Russian naval minister, took steps to guarantee that his ships would not find themselves trapped in port, as had been the case during the Crimean War. On July 14, 1863, he ordered Rear Admiral Stepan Lisovsky, commander of Russia's Atlantic fleet, to leave the Gulf of Finland and "proceed directly to New York." Once there he was "to keep all the ships in that port" unless such an arrangement was "inconvenient for the American government." In that case he was to "dispose of the vessels among the various Atlantic ports of the United States."

Simultaneously Rear Admiral Andrei Popov received orders to lead Russia's Pacific squadron to San Francisco. By the end of October 1863 the *Bogatir, Kalevala, Rinda, Abrek,* and *Gaidamak* were safely anchored in San Francisco Bay. The new arrivals immediately endeared themselves to San Franciscans when they helped put out a major fire in the center of the city. Like his counterpart in New York, Popov was to "be strictly neutral" unless Confederate raiders threatened the civilian population.

The great Russian ball at the Academy of Music, November 5, 1863. Library of Congress Prints and Photographs Division, LC-DIG-ppmsca-18445.

A Northern public eager for good news after the Union's devastating defeat at the Battle of Chickamauga in late September was quick to assume that the Russians had arrived to support the federal cause, an assumption that shaped the prevailing historical interpretation for the next fifty years. Even Secretary of the Navy Gideon Welles, who knew otherwise, was hard-pressed to restrain his enthusiasm. "The presence in our waters of a squadron belonging to His Imperial Majesty's navy," he wrote the Russian ambassador Baron Edouard de Stoeckl, was a "source of pleasure and happiness." He opened the facilities of the Brooklyn Navy Yard to the visitors and later concluded a diary entry with "God bless the Russians."

Years later Henry Clews, a banker involved in marketing Union war bonds, accurately characterized the squadron's visit as a "'splendid bluff' at a very critical period in our history." William Seward, he went on, was "astute enough to see that this visit of the Russian squadron might seem to be what it was not." Their coming "might have a good moral and political effect in depressing the South and encouraging the North, and causing any foreign powers that might have been considering . . . recognizing the Southern Confederacy to postpone action."

Newspapers both here and abroad echoed this view. In the *Moscow Gazette*, M. N. Katov editorialized, "We don't wish to interfere in American affairs; we went there merely for our own convenience." Closer to home, *Leslie's Illustrated Journal* hoped that the Russian ships might "fit out in our ports privateers, as the rebels have done in the ports of England," and that "burning French or perhaps English vessels may throw some light on questions of international law which are now somewhat obscure."

The *Richmond Examiner* unsurprisingly adopted a more jaundiced view of Russian intentions: "The Czar emancipates the serfs . . . and puts forth the whole strength of his empire to enslave the Poles. Lincoln proclaims the freedom of the African, and strives at the same time to subjugate freeborn Americans."

During the winter of 1864 the threat of war in Europe evaporated, and on April 26, 1864, orders arrived directing the Atlantic and Pacific fleets to return to Russia. In retrospect one historian has written that a pro-Union stance for the Russians was smart policy: if the North won, it would be grateful, while if the South won, it would be so elated that it would soon forget its grievances. The *New York Herald* wondered what had been gained by the fleet's presence: "Russia sends her navy here to keep it safe" but "we doubt if she would send it . . . to aid us in fighting England." Her navy, in fact, was "not worth the sending." The author rather accurately, if somewhat insultingly, observed, "One of our Ironsides could blow it out of [the] water . . . in a couple of hours."

While the lavish social events and celebrations may well have provided a needed civic tonic for a city that had recently survived one of the nation's worst riots, they were not without their critics. The day after the grand ball, the *New York World* characterized the event as "one of those thoughtless and shallow demonstrations which have grown with us into a habit." Another newspaper wrote, "Such extravagant festivities were out of place when the Boys in Blue were dying in the trenches." The millions spent "should instead have been given to the Sanitary Commission."

Fighting off the Coast of France

Jamie Malanowski

Sunday, June 19, 1864, the CSS *Alabama*, a swift commerce raider carrying eight guns, steamed out of Cherbourg Harbor, prepared to battle the USS *Kearsarge*, a sloop of war of similar size and firepower.

Built in secret in a British shipyard in Birkenhead, the subject of a determined if unsuccessful Union intelligence effort to prevent its launch, the rebel raider had become at once the most celebrated and most reviled ship in the small Confederate Navy. In the two years since it had been launched the *Alabama* had sailed the north and south Atlantic, the Gulf of Mexico, the Indian Ocean, and the south Pacific. Along the way she captured sixty-four American merchant ships worth $5.1 million, inspiring Confederate sympathizers and vexing unionists. All that, however, was accomplished without ever mooring in a Southern port. Now the wear and tear of two years of prolonged duty and postponed upkeep had taken its toll, and upon returning to European waters from the Pacific in the spring of 1864, she was, in the assessment of her executive officer, John Kell, "loose at every joint, her seams were open, and the copper on her bottom was in rolls." It was not a moment the raider would have chosen for a fight.

Indeed the *Alabama*'s captain, Raphael Semmes, had brought the ship to Cherbourg on June 11 intending to place it in dry dock for a thorough renovation. His choice of port was reasonable: although the *Alabama*'s closest friends in government and commerce had always been British, the Confederacy's battlefield setbacks in 1863 and 1864 had caused Whitehall's feelings about the Confederacy's prospects to harden. Over the past few months Semmes felt that officials in ports in distant British possessions were enforcing the rules governing the treatment of visiting warships far more scrupulously than before. For this reason he decided to head for France, where the officially neutral policy of the government of Emperor Napoleon III was still decidedly gray.

But once Semmes entered Cherbourg Harbor, he found himself face to face with a technicality: all the berths in the Cherbourg dry dock were reserved for the French Navy, a system that was not in effect in Le Havre or any of the other ports. Releasing a berth for the *Alabama* would have required the personal permission of the emperor. He almost certainly would have acquiesced, but he was away on a family vacation in Biarritz. He was due back in a few days, but the *Kearsarge* arrived first and challenged the *Alabama* to leave the harbor and give battle in international waters.

The *Kearsarge* was one of twenty-five Union ships that had been assigned to track down and destroy the *Alabama* and the other seven Confederate raiders that were making war on America's commercial shipping. These raiders had been launched in hopes of weakening the North's blockade of the South's 3,500-mile coast, a slow strangulation that had ruined the South's ability to wage war. If the raiders did enough damage, the thinking went, the U.S. Navy would have to pull ships off the blockade to protect the commercial vessels. In the end the U.S. Navy assigned a rather paltry twenty-five ships to pursue eight vessels across four oceans, leaving the outraged protests of Northern shippers and their legal and political representatives in lonely opposition.

Lonely, but not without effect; when they condemned the stiff and proper Semmes as a pirate, he bristled, even though a decade earlier he had taken the same position, saying that commerce raiders "are little better than licensed pirates; and it behooves all civilized nations . . . to suppress the practice altogether." Now he argued that he was behaving within generally approved codes of behavior; after every capture he punctiliously conducted proceedings in his cabin to make sure that the *Alabama* was entitled under the rules of war to seize the ship and/or its cargo.

In Cherbourg, Semmes decided to accept the *Kearsarge*'s challenge, his ship's tattered condition notwithstanding. He assumed that additional Union vessels would soon arrive and would overwhelm him if he wasn't in dry dock. If he could defeat the *Kearsarge*, however, then he felt that he stood a good chance of escaping to Le Havre, getting into dry dock, and foiling Yankee capture. Semmes liked his chances; the two ships were about the same size and had similar arms, the *Alabama* having an additional gun but the *Kearsarge* superior pieces. The two captains had almost identical credentials; not only were Semmes and the *Kearsarge*'s John Winslow close in age and experience, but they had berthed together aboard the *Cumberland* after the Mexican War. To Semmes it must have shaped up as an eminently fair fight.

But Winslow possessed an advantage of which Semmes may have had no inkling. Following the example of Admiral Farragut in New Orleans, Winslow bought about $75 worth of surplus anchor chain and hung about 120 fathoms' worth of the heavy metal over the hull of his ship, taking particular care to cover the engine room and the magazines. In effect Winslow retrofitted his sloop of war into an ironclad. He then put planking over the chain and painted it black, so that the ship appeared no different from before.

Sometime after 9 o'clock on Sunday morning, after the crew had enjoyed a hot breakfast, the *Alabama* headed out of Cherbourg Harbor. On land an excited, nearly festive atmosphere prevailed: there had been no combat in Western Europe for a half-century, and sightseers lined the shores and followed the rebel raider in small boats, hoping for a view of the coming spectacle. A French frigate, the *Courone*, accompanied the *Alabama*, making sure that no fighting took place within French territorial waters. An English yacht, the *Deerhound*, tagged along; its owner, a wealthy businessman named Lancaster, thought seeing the battle would be just the cherry to top the family vacation.

Just before 11 a.m., with the ships about a mile apart and seven miles offshore, Semmes opened fire. For fifteen minutes the two ships swapped fire without effecting much damage, until a shot from the *Alabama* exploded on the *Kearsarge*'s quarter deck, wounding three members of a gun crew. Moments later what may have been the turning point of the battle occurred: a shot from the *Alabama* struck the *Kearsarge* right near the steering mechanism but failed to explode. Had it gone off, it might well have disabled the Yankee's rudder, leaving the ship dead in the water. Throughout the battle spectators noticed that the *Alabama*'s cannon fire sounded low and dull, and its explosions emitted

The Combat between the Alabama *and the* Kearsarge, *off Cherbourg, on the 19th of June, 1864.* Library of Congress Prints and Photographs Division, LC-USZ62-5862.

a heavy, smoky vapor, whereas the *Kearsarge*'s fire sounded sharp and the vapor was light. Evidently over two years at sea many of the *Alabama*'s projectiles had turned into duds.

Just after the *Alabama*'s misfire, a shot from the *Kearsarge* hit the *Alabama*'s steering equipment; this shell exploded. The raider nonetheless kept fighting, its crew maneuvering by hands in circles to bring broadsides to bear on the *Kearsarge*. Thanks to damp powder and Winslow's DIY armoring project, the firing had little effect. On the other side, however, the *Kearsarge*'s gun devastated the *Alabama*, which had begun to sink. Semmes ran up a white flag, but Winslow kept firing; he later explained that he couldn't tell if the Confederate colors had been lowered, or if they had been shot away, which had happened earlier in the battle. Finally a white flag was stretched across the *Alabama*'s stern, and the fight was over.

Nine members of the *Alabama*'s crew had been killed during the battle, and twenty-one wounded. Another dozen were missing and presumed dead. Most men were rescued: seventy by the *Kearsarge*, twelve by French boatmen, and forty-one by the *Deerhound*, which took them to England. Among this group was a wounded Semmes, who received a hero's welcome. Casualties on the *Kearsarge* were light: three men were wounded, one of whom later died. After the war Semmes maintained that he had not known that the *Kearsarge* had been covered with chains before going into battle, even though his second in command said that he had known, and a French official said that he told Semmes so. And although Semmes deceptively disguised his ship while stalking victims by flying the flag of a European nation, he resented Winslow's use of anchor mail as sneaky and unfair.

America's claim of damages resulting from the actions of the *Alabama*, illegally built in Britain and often supported by sympathetic British officials, soured relations between the countries for several years. But national goals evolved, and by 1872 pragmatists in both Washington and Whitehall determined that a settlement was in the interests of both countries. In the end Britain agreed to pay $15.5 million in damages, a cheap enough price to make Britain's embarrassing involvement disappear.

The most enduring consequence of the duel between the *Kearsarge* and the *Alabama* might be a piece of fine art. A month after the battle a nearly four-foot-square oil painting by thirty-three-year-old Edouard Manet appeared in the front window of La Bibliothèque Impériale in Paris. For years it was believed that Manet, whose early successes, *Olympia* and *Le Déjeuner Sur l'Herbe*, had appeared just the previous year, had been in one of the small boats that followed the *Alabama* out of the harbor, but there seems to be no evidence supporting that surmise. Instead it seems far more likely that Manet, who at one point studied to become a naval officer, was among the thousands of Europeans who were caught up in the excitement of the event and was one of a number of artists who were to create an image of the battle. His painting *The Battle of the "Kearsarge" and the "Alabama"* is a striking work. Dominated by his depiction of swirling smoke and the roiling sea, it seems to convey the terror and turbulence of the moment far more effectively than the realistic works that were also rushed to meet the appetite of an eager public. The painting is now in the collection of the Philadelphia Museum of Art.

9. Abraham Lincoln and the Federal Government

Introduction

Louis P. Masur

In 1854 Abraham Lincoln observed, "The legitimate object of government is to do for the people what needs to be done, but which they can not, by individual effort, do at all, or do so well, for themselves." As examples he cited maintaining bridges and roads, sustaining common schools, aiding the helpless, and defending against war. All of this was in keeping with his Whig political beliefs; Lincoln, like his idol, Henry Clay, advocated using government to promote internal improvements, banking, and tariffs. By contrast the Democrats adhered to the ideal as expressed by Thomas Jefferson: "That government is best which governs least." The Civil War would upend the balance between these two philosophies.

Whatever the differences between the political parties, on the eve of the Civil War Americans had only limited contact with the federal government, which operated just fifteen agencies and bureaus. Most citizens dealt with postal workers, and some with a customs agent or public lands clerk. Americans did not pay a personal income tax. The federal bureaucracy numbered fewer than thirty thousand employees, with under a thousand working in Washington. The army contained just sixteen thousand officers and soldiers.

The Civil War transformed the role of the federal government in the life of the nation. By invoking the war power Lincoln expanded executive authority, and by signing congressional legislation he substantially enlarged the number and scope of governmental functions. The war required, and to Lincoln legitimized, actions that would have been unthinkable during peacetime. In 1864 he explained, "I felt that measures, otherwise unconstitutional, might become lawful, by becoming indispensible to the preservation of the constitution, through preservation of the nation."

With Congress not in session when the war began, Lincoln unilaterally took such extraordinary steps as calling for forty-two thousand three-year volunteers, enlarging the army and navy, providing Treasury funds to a New York committee to promote military measures (despite a constitutional enjoinder against doing so), and declaring a blockade of Southern ports. When Congress assembled on July 4, 1861, he asked it for 400,000 men and $400 million—an unbelievable sum.

Although Lincoln expressed regret in his July 4 message that he had to employ the war power to save the government, as the conflict progressed he expanded his use of that power. Freeing the slaves in those areas in rebellion as of January 1, 1863—the date of the Emancipation Proclamation—was the most striking exercise of his authority as commander in chief, which he justified under the Constitution on the grounds of military necessity. (He also called it "an act of justice.") In keeping with this constitutional rationale, Lincoln rejected Treasury Secretary Salmon P. Chase's plea that the Proclamation be extended to areas of the Confederacy under Union control. To do that, Lincoln asked, "would I not thus be in the boundless field of absolutism?"

Regardless of the details, Northern Democrats thought freeing the slaves made Lincoln a dictator. They also denounced him as a despot for using executive power to suspend habeas corpus and suppress opposition newspapers. Lincoln transferred responsibility for security to the War Department, and during the rebellion at least fifteen thousand citizens were arrested for suspected disloyalty. Lincoln stoutly defended the measures. "Must I shoot a simple-minded soldier boy who deserts, while I must not touch the hair of the wily agitator who induces him to desert?" he asked.

For the most part the president and a Republican-controlled Congress worked in harmony. Starting in 1861 Congress passed a torrent of legislation that would expand the reach of the federal government and transform the nation: the Revenue Act (a 3 percent tax on annual incomes over $800), the Legal Tender Act (authorized issue of $150 million in Treasury notes), the creation of a Department of Agriculture, the Homestead Act, the Pacific Railroad Act, the Morrill Land Grant Act, and the National Banking Acts. In 1863 Congress passed the Conscription Act, providing for the first wartime draft of U.S. citizens. (Ironically the Confederacy, established on states' rights principles and in opposition to strong centralized government, had adopted conscription in April 1862.)

The only substantial difference between the president and Congress came in 1864, over the issue of how best to proceed with reconstruction; many in Congress wanted a more aggressive, more punitive approach than Lincoln was willing to venture. Still, one of the last acts Lincoln signed (in March 1865) created the Bureau of Refugees, Freedmen, and Abandoned Lands, known as the Freedmen's Bureau. The act authorized the bureau for only a year, which reflected misgivings about creating a government agency committed to helping former slaves make the transition to freedom. In 1866 Andrew Johnson would veto the act's renewal on states' rights grounds, but Congress renewed the bureau over his veto for another two years.

Lincoln and the Civil War did not create the leviathan state government that would emerge decades later and come to be feared by many. The huge wartime increases in federal expenditures, the government workforce, and the armed services were all reversed in the postwar years. To be sure, Lincoln had expanded executive power and, along with Congress, welcomed the creation of a national banking and revenue system, development of public lands, and devotion of resources to education and internal improvements. This Civil War was, as Lincoln said, "a peoples contest," and government existed to help the people. But Lincoln was no tyrant. He was a pragmatic politician who utilized war power and executive power to preserve the nation and assure that "government of the people, by the people, for the people shall not perish from the earth." And whatever its size, it was the people to whom Lincoln's federal government still belonged.

The Sound of Lincoln's Silence

HAROLD HOLZER

Less than a month after Abraham Lincoln's election to the presidency the nation's reigning bible of technology, *Scientific American*, shone a startling new light on the incoming chief executive. Lincoln, it revealed, was an inventor. Eleven years earlier he had secured a federal patent (the first and only for a president) for a device to buoy up imperiled ships over dangerously shallow rivers. Amid a growing secession crisis already awash in comparisons to foundering ships of state, the invitation to metaphor must have seemed irresistible.

But the dismal commercial failure of Lincoln's 1849 invention apparently taught the president-elect a valuable lesson: it was not always best to advocate untested ideas. Thus the man who had once proposed an ingenious precursor of the submarine now reined in his creativity, stifling both his voice and his pen. Between his election and his inauguration, Lincoln withdrew into intractable official silence, even as the Union crumbled during a period that Henry Adams memorably dubbed America's "Great Secession Winter."

Supporters called Lincoln's silence "masterful inactivity" because it offended neither abolitionists nor secessionists. But this political hibernation, a void unimaginable in twenty first-century politics and twenty-four-hour news cycles, perplexed and irritated many. One correspondent embedded with the president-elect in Springfield, Illinois, complained, "He laughs and jokes, gulping down the largest doses of adulation that a village crowd can manufacture, and altogether deports himself with the air of one who fails to comprehend the task which abolition fanaticism has thrust upon him." Even generously acknowledging that his "silence is unquestionably creditable to his prudence and his modesty," the pro-Republican *New York Times* lamented that "it has not been without its embarrassments."

Hindsight suggests that Lincoln's refusal to tilt openly toward either coercion or concession still failed to stem the rush of Southern states to quit the Union and was therefore a failure. And it's true that, in one sense, "masterly inactivity" did nothing to discourage secession and war, and perhaps encouraged both, while making Lincoln himself seem unprepared to lead. So why did the great orator and gifted writer go mute at such a critical moment? And how should it affect our evaluation of our sixteenth president?

While many people derided the idea of "masterly inactivity" as a gloss on an inexperienced political mind, Lincoln's approach was very much intentional. For one thing, silence was nothing new for him. He had said nothing for nearly a year, ever since returning from his triumphant Cooper Union address in New York in February. Save for one final attempt to deliver a turgid lecture on "discoveries and inventions" (another invitation to symbolism) he had adopted the ultimate back-porch strategy and retreated in isolation to Springfield.

Nominated by the Republicans in May, he extended his silence into the ensuing six-month general election campaign. Instead he encouraged surrogates, biographers, partisan newspapers, reprints of his old speeches, and picture publishers circulating flattering new portraits to do the electioneering for him. Though one cartoonist depicted him as an organ grinder's monkey with a padlock sealing shut his lips, the strategy paid off yet again with a narrow but indisputable victory in November.

Having won the presidency while withholding new pronouncements, it is hardly surprising that Lincoln resisted requests for policy clarifications after Election Day as well. "I could say nothing which I have not already said, and which is in print and open for inspection for all," he insisted. Conservatives demanding reassurance that he would not interfere with slavery where it existed and progressives eager that he denounce the earliest expressions of Southern secession as treason were equally disappointed. Saying nothing, Lincoln believed, did the least damage to his fragile winning coalition of moderate Westerners and abolitionist easterners—a coalition that yet might be called upon to resist rebellion by force.

Not even South Carolina's secession in mid-December pushed Lincoln back into the public arena. "Party malice," not "public good," he insisted, animated such demands. "They seek a sign, and no sign shall be given them." Ample proof came from his own supporters that silence remained the preferred approach among Republicans. "There are a class of d—d fools or knaves who want him to make a 'union saving speech'—in other words to set down to conciliate the Disunionists and fire-eaters," warned the editor of the pro-Lincoln *Chicago Tribune*. "He must keep his feet out of all such wolf traps." A Republican politician was even blunter: Lincoln, he said, should "not open his mouth, save only to eat."

But there was more to Lincoln's "masterly inactivity" than a reluctance to offend supporters or inflame opponents. Pride was involved too, in a way seldom remembered by history. To "press a repetition" of his long-held views "on those who have refused to listen," Lincoln insisted, "would be wanting of self-respect, and would have an appearance of sycophancy and timidity which would excite the contempt of good men, and encourage bad ones to clamor the more loudly."

He was "not unmindful of the uneasiness which may exist in many parts of the country," he privately conceded. But "nothing is to be gained by fawning around the 'respectable

As president-elect, Abraham Lincoln rarely discussed national affairs with anyone except his private secretaries, John Nicolay, left, and John Hay. Library of Congress Prints and Photographs Division, LC-DIG-ppmsca-19421.

scoundrels' who got it up." As he confided to one visitor, he would rather be "hung by the neck till he was dead on the steps of the Capitol before he would buy or beg a peaceful inauguration."

Besides—and this crucial fact is often forgotten—Lincoln had not yet been formally or finally elected. True, he had won an outright majority of presidential electors in November. But their votes would not be officially counted until February, leaving ample time for mischief.

Indeed an effort soon got under way—in loyal New York, no less—to divert his electors to another candidate in order to block an outright Lincoln victory and throw the decision to the House of Representatives, where, it was presumed, a more experienced and less provocative leader might emerge. Lincoln could ill afford to confront, or even acknowledge, this outrageous threat. (As it turned out, not until General Winfield Scott ordered artillery to Capitol Hill to frighten dissidents would the crucial vote-counting proceed free of sabotage or surprise.)

Meanwhile, as the day of electoral reckoning approached, another effort got under way that similarly threatened to wrest control of the crisis from Lincoln. At Willard's Hotel in Washington veteran politicians from around the country gathered for the National Peace Convention. Its goal was to draft a series of constitutional amendments designed to reverse secession and prevent war—before Lincoln ever took office.

Just as Lincoln feared, the Convention commenced by weighing the extension of slavery all the way to the Pacific (in defiance of the Republican Party platform), a guarantee to preserve it forever where it existed, and a tight restriction on congressional debate about its future. New slave territory meant new proslavery senators—and a permanent congressional majority against free labor.

At this point Lincoln at last broke his long silence, though the results were hardly masterly. Already en route from Illinois to Washington via New York for his swearing-in, he could not help but offer a series of informal, occasionally discordant, and entirely forgettable addresses wherever his train stopped to refuel. Before the largest crowds ever to see a president-elect he showed off his new whiskers, introduced his wife, and urged audiences to wait for his inaugural address to learn his policy. Though neither these chats nor the more extended remarks he offered at various state capitols did much to inspire confidence, they displayed an amiability that at least diverted attention from the crisis—even as Jefferson Davis was making his own way to Montgomery, Alabama, to take office as president of the new Confederacy.

Of much greater consequence, though unknown to the public, Lincoln also commenced issuing instructions to Republican allies on Capitol Hill on precisely how they should vote on whatever compromise bills ultimately reached Congress. These Lincoln marked "private" or "strictly confidential," though he knew his allies would usefully circulate his views anyway. And there was no mistaking his policy now.

"Let there be no compromise on the question of extending slavery," he all but ordered Senator Lyman Trumbull. "Have none if it. Stand firm. The tug has to come, & better now, than any time hereafter." To Congressman Elihu Washburne he was equally explicit: "Hold firm, as with a chain of steel." Masterful inactivity had finally morphed into a form of secret dictatorship: quiet in public, loud and clear behind the scenes. Without his support the Convention's toxic antidotes to the secession crisis died in Congress, just as Lincoln hoped.

By the time he rose on the Capitol portico for his inaugural on March 4, Lincoln had brilliantly employed his secret weapon of masterly inactivity to distance himself from sectional rancor, dispel fears of his alleged radicalism without appearing too conservative, preserve his tenuous political coalition, successfully discourage (at least until then) Upper South secession, buy time for careful cabinet selection, guarantee his once uncertain official election to the presidency, and, most important of all, discourage compromise that would have violated his unyielding opposition to spreading slavery.

Masterly inactivity did not prevent secession or a war over slavery. But that was never Lincoln's point—and any alternative would probably have sped things up. Instead it bought him the time to prepare for the coming conflict, a fact that too few acknowledged at the time or have given him credit for since.

Seward's Folly

RUSSELL McCLINTOCK

By February 1861 the Republican Party was on the verge of taking complete control of the federal government. But internally the party was split in two by the secession crisis and how to respond: the majority believed that concessions to Southern demands would simply produce more threats and demands down the line; the minority believed that such an uncompromising stance risked a suicidal civil war.

The latter group was smaller in number, but it was led by Senator William Henry Seward, one of the party's most adept politicians and the man some still felt deserved

William H. Seward. Library of Congress Prints and Photographs Division, LC-DIG-cwpb-04948.

to be president. Under his leadership the conciliationist wing of the Republican Party punched far above its weight; indeed Seward's efforts at compromise, or at least the appearance of a compromise, managed to convince Southern Unionists, Northern Democrats, Republican hardliners, and the national press that his party was on the verge of announcing a Union-saving compromise, even when nothing of the kind was likely to happen.

The Republicans weren't always dominated by hardliners; compromise was very much in the air during the first weeks of the crisis. But Southern secession and the seizure of federal property had pushed the majority of the party into a hard-line stance, even as the growing risk of war pushed Northern Democrats and border-state politicians of both parties toward compromise.

The result was a tumultuous debate among Republicans. A deeply demoralized minority, with Seward at its head, saw in the hard-liners' attitude the seed of national dissolution. He wasn't wrong; through his close contact with a large network of allies in the border slave states, Seward understood that Unionists there were desperate for a goodwill gesture from the Republicans, something that would take the wind out of secessionist sails and help them preserve their states' loyalty.

But Seward knew that the only point of view that really mattered was Lincoln's; the dramatic impact of Lincoln's carefully placed anticompromise letters a few weeks earlier proved that congressional Republicans would follow his lead. And so he turned his attention to manipulating the president-elect's position. Time was wasting: Virginia was about to elect its state convention delegates. So Seward quietly, desperately began to spread false rumors that a compromise was imminent.

Beginning on January 18, 1861, he arranged a series of private meetings with Stephen Douglas, John J. Crittenden, and a few other conservative senators. He then leaked to Upper South leaders like Representative John Gilmer of North Carolina that they had reached a "definite arrangement on our present national difficulties," though nothing of the kind had occurred, let alone with Lincoln's blessing.

Gilmer took the bait, wiring home to his district, "We will pass in substance Mr. Crittenden's plans. Give no ear to alarms." So did Douglas and Crittenden, who drafted several joint messages to the people of the border slave states expressing hope of an imminent settlement. Douglas assured the Virginia Unionist James Barbour in a public letter, "I can say with confidence that there is hope of adjustment, and the prospect has never before been better." In the Senate he declared cryptically, "I have reasons satisfactory to myself upon which to predicate that firm hope that the Union will be preserved."

Rumors of an agreement soon reached the national press, which helped make them news across the country. Washington correspondents for the major New York papers reported with assurance that congressional Republicans were nearly ready to accept a territorial compromise, possibly even Crittenden's. "The next few days will develop a complete change of policy on the part of the Republican Party," the *Herald*'s Washington reporter affirmed on January 25. By January 28 the story had grown to include Lincoln himself. "It is now certain," reported one paper, "that all the influence of [the] incoming Republican administration will be thrown in favor of a speedy settlement of our national difficulties." One correspondent claimed to have it "on good authority" that Lincoln himself had written "one of his cabinet ministers" in support of the border state plan.

The rumors disturbed hardliners enough that Representative Owen Lovejoy of Illinois was "open in his declaration that the party is sold out." The Wisconsin radical Carl Schurz warned Lincoln, "The moment seems to have arrived which will put manhood to a final test. Next week a desperate effort will be made to crowd the Crittenden—or the border state—resolutions through Congress, and many Republicans have already signified their willingness to yield."

Apparently only Seward knew that the impending compromise was merely smoke, but he could do no more without securing Lincoln's blessing. To manage that he had dispatched a Republican ally, Representative William Kellogg, to Springfield to lobby Lincoln, hoping even to bring him to Washington early. Lincoln's response confirmed Seward's worst fears. According to Kellogg, he declared firmly, "I will suffer death before I will consent or will advise my friends to consent to any concession or compromise which looks like buying the privilege of taking possession of this government to which we have a constitutional right; because, whatever I might think of the merit of the various propositions before Congress, I should regard any concession in the face of menace the destruction of the government itself."

At news of Kellogg's failure Seward realized he would have to deal with Lincoln himself. On January 27, just eight days before the Virginia election, he penned a lengthy letter that at last lay his conciliatory views fully before the president-elect. He opened by describing the "very painful" appeals of Southern Unionists, who warned that without "something of concession or compromise" their states would secede before Lincoln was inaugurated. Yet whether the Upper South seceded or not, Seward pointed out, Lincoln would face "a hostile armed confederacy" in the Deep South; the only question was whether to subdue it through force or conciliation. Although "much the largest portion of the Republican party are reckless now of the crisis before us," he argued, the North would not support a protracted civil war. Therefore "every thought that we think ought to be conciliatory, forbearing and patient, and so open the way for the rising of a Union Party in the seceding states which will bring them back into the Union." After months of intrigue and cloakroom maneuvering, here at last was Seward's position, out in the open and committed to writing: Republicans must make sufficient concessions to keep alive the latent Southern Unionism that he still insisted would rise to the fore.

Sending the letter was a dangerous gamble, because if Lincoln replied directly to Seward with the sentiment he had communicated to Kellogg, the New Yorker would have no choice but to back away from compromise entirely or, by openly defying Lincoln, split his party irreparably.

One year earlier Seward had been one of the most powerful men in the Senate, the presumed presidential nominee of his party, and the odds-on favorite to capture the White

House. Now, in the face of his country's greatest national crisis, he had been reduced to underhanded schemes and back-channel assurances, helplessly awaiting the next move of the western country lawyer who, it was increasingly clear, held all the cards. Yet Seward believed, not unreasonably, that he still had a few tricks to play to save the country from civil war. Whether they would work would be answered over the following weeks.

A Capitol Dilemma

GUY GUGLIOTTA

By the end of February 1862 construction of the enlarged Capitol building in Washington had been suspended for nine and a half months. The federal government had begun the project twelve years earlier, intending to add new House and Senate wings at either end of the original building, topped by a majestic cast-iron dome above the old central section. But now the country was deep in civil war, and the building was left towering but unfinished.

True, much had been completed. Both the Senate and the House had new, elegantly appointed chambers. Floors were tiled in elaborately colored patterns. Many corridors and committee rooms were decorated with frescoes, wall paintings, and ornately patterned motifs, featuring everything from native birds to the signs of the zodiac and trompe l'oeil cameos of famous Americans. Abraham Lincoln had been inaugurated on the East Front Capitol steps below the half-completed dome, an iron shell with a giant wooden derrick sticking out of the top of it, waiting to hoist chunks of metal nearly three hundred feet in the air to be bolted into place.

But on May 15, 1861, Captain Montgomery C. Meigs, the engineer in charge of the project, ordered construction suspended for the duration of the war. For the rest of the year marble porticoes for the new Senate and House sat unfinished, most of the new one-piece marble columns that were to girdle the new construction did not arrive, and terraces and steps still needed to be added in several locations.

There was too much else to do, too many other places to spend money, and too many terrible things to think about. Building the Capitol was a luxury the country could ill afford. Two weeks after Meigs shut down the Capitol construction, Lincoln made him a brigadier general and appointed him chief of the Union Army's quartermaster corps, a job he would hold with great distinction for twenty-one years.

But by February 1862 it was clear Meigs had done the Capitol no favors. For several months the army had used it as a barracks. Soldiers scuffed the carpets, chopped up desks with their knives, lit campfires in the front yard, swung from ropes in the rotunda, and used every byway and storeroom in the building as a privy. The commissary general had put ovens in the basement and was baking bread for the entire Army of the Potomac. Soot from the fires had invaded the stacks in the Library of Congress, with ruinous effect.

Construction of the new Capitol resumed in 1862. The major task as the war dragged on was to finish the cast-iron dome. Courtesy of the Architect of the Capitol.

The army had mercifully departed by the end of the year, but when the second session of the 37th Congress convened December 2, 1861, the picture was truly grim. Loose pieces of cast-iron dome—$205,000 worth—lay on the grounds, stained and rusted. Inside there was considerable water damage and mildew caused by seepage through cracks and crevices around the unfinished porticoes. Plaster was decaying in places and falling off the wall. Many stucco ornaments were already destroyed, and others were heavily damaged. The army had gobbled up most of the workforce. It was a mess.

A plan to resume construction had begun during the summer of 1861. The ringleader was Thomas U. Walter, the illustrious Philadelphia architect who had designed the new wings and the dome. He and Meigs had been close colleagues in the mid-1850s, but the pair had had a colossal and very public falling-out over Meigs's suspicion—justified, it turned out—that Walter was trying to undercut him and take his job, and Walter's fear, also justified, that Meigs was trying to minimize Walter's accomplishments and, where possible, take credit for them. The two men had barely spoken since 1858.

Walter's accomplices were his three most important contractors: John Rice, another Philadelphian whose quarry in Lee, Massachusetts, was supplying the white marble for the façade of the Capitol; a local Washington entrepreneur, Alexander Provest, whose army of craftsmen was sawing, carving, polishing, and setting the stone when it arrived; and Charles Fowler, a Bronx foundryman who was casting the dome.

"We are putting our heads together in reference to future operations," Walter wrote in a letter to his wife, Amanda, in July. "My present impression is that we will put things into a better shape than they have ever been before."

But the climate was not yet ripe. Congress was traumatized and unable to think about anything but the war, and Meigs, organizing the logistical juggernaut that would eventually destroy the Confederacy, could do no wrong. The conspirators' eventual solution, Walter told Rice in a note, was to get the project away from the War Department, which had had control of it for a decade, and transfer it to the Interior Department. Meigs would be bureaucratically eliminated.

It was then that Fowler made the decisive move. When Meigs suspended work on the Capitol there were 1.3 million pounds of dome castings lying on the ground. Fowler could have stopped work, dismantled his workshops, and put the iron in storage. But instead he made a crucial decision to keep going, gambling that he would eventually be paid. Dome construction did not proceed rapidly after Meigs suspended operations, but it did proceed, and it was vital in establishing the earnest intentions of Walter and the contractors.

In mid-August 1861 Fowler made his case for resumption to Vermont's senator Solomon Foot, president pro tempore of the Senate, who endorsed his proposal. Then he went to see Meigs—Walter stayed out of sight—who told them he could not spare any money for the Capitol. So the plotters went over Meigs's head to Secretary of War Simon Cameron, who agreed to recommend that construction be resumed.

But then nothing happened—until Meigs made a crucial mistake in November. In his annual report on the Capitol extension, he spent most of his effort touting his past accomplishments. "The building has been in use for some years, and has realized all that I undertook to accomplish in regard to light, warmth, ventilation and fitness for debate and legislation," he wrote. "The health of the legislative bodies has never been better." The new chambers had conducted more business in a shorter time, he said, and the acoustics were flawless. The "spacious galleries" attracted crowds of people during the prewar hearings, and audiences "were able to hear the words of those who then debated the greatest questions discussed in our Congress since the revolution."

Congress had heard most of this so many times before, and members had long ago made up their minds about it and generally supported Meigs. But then Meigs noted that while troops had used the Capitol as a barracks, "the little injury done by them to the walls has been repaired." This was patently false. Meigs had at once insulted congressional intelligence and made it obvious that he had not visited the Capitol in months. Clearly he had way too much on his plate and needed to be gotten out of the way.

The trap was sprung. On March 5, 1862, Foot introduced a Senate resolution calling for Capitol construction to be transferred to Interior. The debate dusted off many old complaints about the project, several of which had long ago been overtaken by events. What business did the army have building civilian structures? (They had the best, and cheapest, engineers.) Why does the Capitol need such fancy decoration? (It did not, but the decoration had been done.) Was this just another episode in the endless power struggle between Walter and Meigs? (Of course.) And why do the new chambers have no windows? Moving them to the middle of the building, noted the New Hampshire abolitionist Senator John Hale, an outspoken opponent of the new Capitol for more than a decade, was about as useful as putting "a mousetrap in a pot." (The decision to put the chambers in the middle of the building had been made eight years earlier.)

Several things had changed, however. The building had taken a beating from troops and weather and needed to be protected, and quickly. Foot, for one, had nothing against Meigs, but he and the War Department could not give the Capitol the attention it deserved.

Less obvious, but probably also true, Meigs may have had "a laudable ambition to distinguish himself by the completion of all of these works," as Massachusetts Republican Charles R. Train, the chairman of the House Committee on Public Buildings and Grounds, remarked, and "it would be a nice little entertainment for the decline of his life." However, Train asked, "are we to suffer loss" until then because "Meigs would not allow Walter to complete the building?"

Finally, and most important, attitudes toward the Capitol had themselves changed. When the redesign began in 1850 Congress could barely be cajoled into financing it. Many lawmakers—perhaps the majority—were preoccupied with districts or states, regarded Washington as a dreary backwater, and viewed the federal government as a barely necessary evil, to be tolerated but never enhanced. By tripling the size of the Capitol, the United States was putting on airs, like those decadent Europeans.

As the decade wore on, however, the new project had become a rallying point for increasingly fearful Northerners and Southerners who needed something to reaffirm the bonds that still held them together. The new Capitol was about hope for the future during a time of profound distress.

By March 1862 the future had arrived, and it was going to be a prolonged and bloody catastrophe. The Capitol was no longer simply a hope. It was, on the Union side, fulfillment, and by March 1862 Congress saw this clearly. The United States was becoming a nation, embodied in the Capitol. Never again would individual states pretend to dictate the terms of their membership in the Union.

"Sir, we are strong enough yet, thank God, to put down this rebellion and to put up this our Capitol at the same time," Foot said on the Senate floor on March 25. "And when the rebellion shall have been suppressed—as suppressed it soon will be; when this war shall have been terminated . . . and when this union of ours shall have been restored . . . it will furnish a fitting and appropriate occasion to celebrate that welcome event." The joint resolution passed in both houses with fewer than ten votes in opposition. Construction on the Capitol resumed in April.

Andrew Johnson's Difficult Task

AARON ASTOR

In a broadside posted prominently throughout Nashville in March 1862 the newly installed military governor of Tennessee, Andrew Johnson, issued an "appeal to the people of Tennessee." After describing the "lamentable crisis" in which the state's government was "set at defiance, and the Constitution and the Laws contemned, by a rebellious, armed force," Johnson solicited support from all those citizens "desirous or willing to see a restoration of her ancient government, without distinction of party affiliations or past political opinions."

Despite his cooperative tone Johnson quickly discovered that his task of restoring civilian government in Tennessee was far more difficult than he had imagined. He had served as governor in the 1850s and maintained his seat in the U.S. Senate in 1861, even as his state seceded. But none of those experiences quite prepared him for his return as military governor—the first to oversee a rebellious Southern state.

As would be the case later in the war and beyond, Johnson found himself in a struggle for leadership with few political friends on his side. A strict constructionist Jacksonian Democrat, whose staunchest Unionist allies were Southern Whigs, Johnson

Andrew Johnson. Library of Congress Prints and Photographs Division, LC-USZ62-13017.

was appointed to a constitutionally dubious position by a Republican president who did not even appear on Tennessee's presidential ballot in 1860.

That may explain why he took a moderate tack at first. Johnson insisted that the new state government would honor those who supported the Union all through the "dark and weary night of the rebellion." But the "erring and misguided" would also be "welcomed on their return." He offered a "full and complete amnesty" to those who formerly "assumed a private, unofficial hostility to the Government," so long as they now recognized the "just supremacy of the laws."

And yet almost immediately that spring he faced a hostile local population willing to challenge his right to rule—which in turn forced his hand more quickly than he might have expected. At one point he arrested prominent Confederate-supporting clergymen in Nashville, declaring, "I punish these men, not because they are priests, but because they are traitors and enemies of society, law and order." He then required all local officials to take an oath of loyalty to the federal government or face arrest.

When Mayor Richard Cheatham of Nashville was imprisoned for refusing to take the oath, Nashvillians insisted upon their right to elect replacements for imprisoned officers. Johnson acceded, but when a "fierce and intolerable Rebel" was elected to a circuit court judgeship, Johnson asserted that statewide democratic elections would have to wait until the state was free from Confederate military control. He would have to wait two more years for that to happen, and by then he was already on his way to the vice presidency of the United States.

Johnson faced a challenge from supposed allies as well. His military governorship came with the appointment of a brigadier generalship, which ostensibly gave him weight on army matters. But that did little to prevent ongoing disputes with Union officers like General Don Carlos Buell over the protection of Nashville. And his Unionist allies in East Tennessee also proved troubling, especially as most of them remained in exile until September 1863 and many others insisted that East Tennessee be allowed to pursue separate statehood—a proposition that would only weaken Unionist influence in the remaining part of Tennessee.

Later the question of emancipation in Tennessee embroiled him in even more conflict with fellow Unionists. When Johnson came around to support emancipation in 1863, he did so in a clumsy manner; he even called himself "Moses" to a gathering of blacks in Nashville. But this merely opened up new fissures in the state's Unionist coalition, which included some deeply conservative men who insisted that the institution of slavery must remain intact.

Most aggravating for Johnson was the anomalous military position of the state, whose Confederate-leaning middle and western sections lay under federal military control, while the heavily Unionist east continued to suffer Confederate military occupation. Attempts to restore loyal, civilian rule through democratic election would face either military interference in the east or voter rejection in the middle and west.

But Johnson's task was far greater than the establishment of civilian rule in Tennessee. His "appeal to the people of Tennessee" was, in effect, the first great act in the Reconstruction of the South. Long before the surrender of Confederate armies or even the emancipation of the slaves, Johnson set out the basic terms by which the seceded states could return to the federal fold. Though the "appeal" was written and proffered by Johnson, it received the full blessing of and support from President Lincoln and the Union Army.

What this document reveals, more than anything else, is the direct connection between the debate over secession's legitimacy and the course of Reconstruction. During the secession crisis Johnson, then a senator, insisted that secession was "treasonous" and, more important, an act of a "few men" who "conspired" to overthrow the federal government. Throughout the war he maintained that secession was an illegitimate— even criminal—act that was not only politically treacherous but also constitutionally and theoretically impossible. In other words, the "so-called Confederate states" never actually seceded because the power to do so did not exist.

Lincoln agreed with Johnson on this point, and in the early phases of the war it was advanced throughout the federal government as a means of isolating the Confederate leadership and stimulating loyalty of the Southern rank and file toward the Union. In some ways March 1862 was the last moment during which large numbers of Unionists, North and South, accepted that limited understanding of secession.

Nashville, along with the rest of middle and west Tennessee, had fallen to the Union Army after the capture of Fort Donelson in February 1862. With only eight months of allegiance to the Confederacy—and much of its population maintaining loyalty to the Union—Tennessee seemed the perfect state to employ the "individual traitor" descriptor of secession.

But a month later the epic Battle of Shiloh on the state's southern border put an end to the illusion that ordinary white Southerners continued on as secret Unionists waiting for the signal to return to their "ancient government." More radical members of Congress, including Massachusetts senator Charles Sumner, argued that the people of the Southern states had in fact severed ties with the Union. But in doing so the seceded states had effectively committed "state suicide" and could be treated as conquered provinces and territories to be ruled and reconstructed as the victorious federal government saw fit.

Not only did this justify military rule, but it also opened the path to emancipation. Slavery could be eliminated via a wartime measure because the earlier "state rights" to its protection had been rendered obsolete by virtue of secession and war. By the end of 1862 only the most conservative Unionists doubted the constitutionality—not to mention the wisdom—of wartime emancipation.

But if the rest of the Union leadership changed its position, Johnson didn't. His understanding of secession as an illegitimate act of individual treason persisted throughout the war and served as the constitutional foundation for his conservative approach to Reconstruction when he assumed the presidency in 1865. Johnson insisted that Congress had no right to dictate terms to the sovereign states of the South after the war, just as the states of the South had no right to sever their bonds of union with the federal government.

But by then the rest of the North, victorious in war and vindictive toward the South, was firmly against him. Johnson's insistence that the South never actually seceded proved to be a major thorn in the side of Radical Republicans who hoped to remake the South into a wage labor–based, multiracial democracy.

The Do-Everything Congress

MARK GREENBAUM

In 2011 *New York* magazine, in a list of the worst Congresses in history, highlighted "the inarguably awful 37th," which ran between 1861 and 1863: "The very least that can be said for the other congressional classes on this list is that they did not oversee the eruption of a catastrophic civil war." And that's pretty much all the 37th Congress is remembered for—which is a shame, because it was actually one of the most productive and momentous in American history.

Like President Lincoln, Congress took office not knowing if the United States would endure. When it convened, about a third of the seats in both chambers were vacant, as newly declared Confederates had emptied Washington. Fittingly members served under an unfinished Capitol dome—construction on the cast-iron edifice began in 1855 and would not be completed until 1863—at once a symbol of republican government striving to rise up just as fierce fighting mere miles south on the battlefields of Virginia and elsewhere sought to tear it down.

Yet despite the mortal threat that hung over the nation throughout the two-year session, the new Congress was able to pass laws of incredible breadth and significance for both the immediate stability and future growth of the United States. Congress's work in these early years of the Civil War helped lay the track not simply for the Union's victory but for the nation's educational, socioeconomic, and physical expansion. The 37th Congress, in the words of the historian Leonard Curry, set the "blueprint for modern America."

First came the Revenue Acts of 1861 (and later 1862), which created the first federal income tax to help fund the Union war effort. Although the acts would be repealed after the war, their impact on the future economic direction of the nation is clear: with their precedent, income taxes would serve as future keystones of the nation's economy, as would the National Banking Act passed near the conclusion of the session, which established a single national currency.

In 1862 Congress ended slavery in the District of Columbia, a critical forerunner to the Emancipation Proclamation and, eventually, abolition. Soon thereafter it created the Department of Agriculture, a guiding engine for the nation's agricultural expansion during the post–Civil War era, a boom that the same Congress facilitated with the Homestead Act, which enticed over a million Americans westward on the promise of earning 160 acres of land to call their own. Also helping spur that drive was the Pacific Railway Act of 1862, which began the construction of the first transcontinental railroad from Omaha and San Francisco, culminating with the famous linking of the Central and Union Pacific lines at Promontory, Utah, seven years later.

The 37th Congress's contribution to education was also estimable. A week before the brutal Seven Days Battles raged outside of Richmond, it passed the Morrill Land-Grant Colleges Act, which set aside over 15 million acres for the founding of agricultural and mechanics schools. The landmark act led to the founding of Cornell, Berkeley, the University of Wisconsin, and other institutions and established the backbone of the finest public university system in the world.

In one of its final legislative moves in 1863 it passed the False Claims Act to combat abuses by federal contractors. Better known today as "Lincoln's Law," the act remains arguably the most effective antifraud statute ever passed, having recovered over $20 billion from war profiteers.

How did such a visionary slate of legislation come to pass? To be sure, Congress remained focused throughout the session on supporting the war effort, and assorted measures like the Revenue Acts were enacted with that overarching goal in mind.

The quick answer is that Congress was able to move so adroitly because Republicans held the White House and possessed huge majorities in both the House and the Senate. Founded in the mid-1850s, the party had catapulted to immediate success with the

The first known photograph of the House Chamber, taken in 1861. Library of Congress Prints and Photographs Division, LC-DIG-cwpbh-03301.

dissolution of the Whig Party and the collapse of the Know Nothing movement, doing well in the 1856 elections and capturing the House of Representatives just two years later. In 1860 Republicans won nearly three-fifth majorities in each chamber, paving the way for a unified government.

Prior to Republicans' birth and quick rise, Democratic congresses had been stymieing economic growth for years. Looking back in 1863 Maine's Republican senator and future Treasury secretary William Fessenden captured his party's ambitious outlook in the 37th: "I cannot say that the wiser course was not to make the most of our time, for no one knows how soon this country may again fall into a democratic slough."

From the beginning the Republicans had a clear idea about what they wanted. As the historian Eric Foner has observed about the young party, "Their outlook was grounded in . . . its emphasis on social mobility and economic growth, it reflected an adaption of that ethic to the dynamic, expansive, capitalist society of the ante-Bellum North." The party's core principle held that any American could advance himself in society and achieve economic independence and that the future lay with industrial growth and westward expansion, away from the decayed, slaved-based Southern model. The role of government, then, was to make this happen. These were old Whig philosophies Lincoln himself had subscribed to from the very start of his political career in his almost monastic pursuit of internal improvements.

At times the antislavery element of the party platform could overwhelm the economic development element, and the era in Congress is remembered mostly for colorful figures like Thaddeus Stevens, Benjamin Wade, and Charles Sumner, who were dedicated first and foremost to the slave issue. Similarly many Democrats who had switched to the Republican Party in the 1850s, including Salmon Chase, Gideon Welles, and Francis P. Blair, did so over slavery and did not agree with many of their new party's core economic views.

Ultimately, however, Radical Republicans' focus on slavery and former Democrats' misgivings did not derail the enactment of the party's economic agenda. While many early state Republican platforms ignored economic issues to avoid divisions, this had already begun to change near the end of the 1850s, as many converted Jacksonian Democrats began to tone down their antigovernment sentiments in the wake of the Panic of 1857.

Not that infighting was lacking on Capitol Hill. Partisanship during the war was perhaps even more toxic than ever; Republicans created the Committee on the Conduct of the War largely to disgrace Democratic generals in the aftermath of the disastrous Battle of Ball's Bluff (where Republican senator Edward Baker was killed).

But in the end progress would define Congress's work and would build the nation as the old-line Whiggish vision of economic growth and opportunity won out.

It's understandable why the drama of the Civil War should overshadow the grinding legislative activities of Capitol Hill and the 37th Congress. But for anyone who has ever gone to a public university, spent a dollar bill, or ridden a passenger train cross-country, it's a legislative session that deserves to be remembered.

Lincoln's Letter to the Editor

PAUL FINKELMAN

On August 19, 1862, Horace Greeley, the editor of the *New-York Tribune*, published a long open letter to President Lincoln in his newspaper. Titled "The Prayer for Twenty Millions," the letter demanded that Lincoln immediately move to end slavery, not only in the Confederacy but also in the loyal slave states—Delaware, Maryland, Kentucky, and Missouri—as well as in those parts of Tennessee under U.S. control. The letter was noteworthy as a bold, widely read attack on the president by a major figure in his own party. Even more noteworthy, though, was Lincoln's response.

HON. HORACE GREELEY,
Our Next President.

NEW YORK. PUBLISHED BY CURRIER & IVES. 125 NASSAU ST.

Horace Greeley. Library of Congress Prints and Photographs Division, LC-USZC2-2598.

The letter was tough, arrogant, and marginally insulting to the president. Greeley, never known for his tact, said Lincoln was "strangely and disastrously remiss" in not vigorously moving toward emancipation, and he accused him of listening to "certain fossil politicians hailing from the Border Slave States" in his refusal to undermine slavery. But in doing so the president was in fact undermining the war effort; supporters of the Union, Greeley reported, thought it was "preposterous and futile" to fight the rebellion without fighting slavery.

Lincoln responded to Greeley's open letter in a remarkable way: he wrote a letter to the editor, the first and only time a sitting president has done so. Greeley dutifully published it.

The letter is a classic example of Lincoln's political sense and ability to shape events. With brilliant tact he made sure readers knew that much of Greeley's letter was wrong, that he was fully aware of its offensive tone but that he would take the high road on these matters. Greeley was popular with many in the Republican Party, and the *Tribune* was probably the most important Republican paper in the nation. There was no point in feuding with the notoriously acerbic Greeley, even as Lincoln made clear he did not accept Greeley's spin on the development of the war.

Lincoln began by saying that he would not address "any statements, or assumptions of fact, which I may know to be erroneous." He declined to debate "any inferences which I may believe to be falsely drawn" or respond to Greeley's "impatient and dictatorial tone." He did this, he said, out of "deference to an old friend whose heart I have always supposed to be right." He then used his letter to set out his policy on the war and emancipation:

> As to the policy I "seem to be pursuing," as you say, I have not meant to leave any one in doubt. I would save the Union. I would save it the shortest way under the Constitution. The sooner the national authority can be restored the nearer the Union will be "the Union as it was." If there be those who would not save the Union unless they could at the same time save slavery, I do not agree with them. If there be those who would not save the Union unless they could at the same time destroy slavery, I do not agree with them. My paramount object in this struggle is to save the Union, and is not either to save or to destroy slavery. If I could save the Union without freeing any slave I would do it, and if I could save it by freeing all the slaves I would do it; and if I could save it by freeing some and leaving others alone, I would also do that. What I do about slavery and the colored race, I do because I believe it helps to save the Union; and what I forbear, I forbear because I do not believe it would help to save the Union.

Lincoln added, "I have here stated my purpose according to my view of official duty; and I intend no modification of my oft-expressed personal wish that all men every where could be free."

Critics of Lincoln have often said that this letter shows he was not particularly interested in ending slavery and that he did not care about the fate of African Americans. But a careful analysis of the letter, and its timing, suggests otherwise.

By this time a substantial number of slaves had gained their freedom by running to the U.S. Army. Thus Lincoln's claim that he would save the Union "without freeing any slave" was mere rhetoric, designed to placate Northern conservatives and residents of the four loyal slave states. Lincoln had also just signed the Second Confiscation Act, which set out a process—although a fairly cumbersome one—to emancipate slaves of some rebellious masters.

More important, neither Greeley nor anyone else outside the president's cabinet and inner circle knew that more than a month before he wrote this letter Lincoln had drafted the Emancipation Proclamation. He was simply waiting for the right moment—a major U.S. victory in the East—to announce his plan to end slavery in the Confederacy. Thus his claim that he would save the Union without freeing any slaves was shrewdly political. Lincoln was in fact planning to free more than 3 million slaves in the eleven states that had seceded from the Union.

Lincoln was on the mark, however, in noting that he might have to free some of the slaves and leave the others in bondage. The Constitution of 1787 left him no choice: neither Congress nor the president had any power to liberate slaves in the loyal border states. But Lincoln could use his power as commander in chief to strike at slavery in those Southern states that claimed to be out of the Union and were making war on the United States.

Finally, Lincoln made clear to friends and critics alike that he was no friend of slavery by reaffirming his "oft-expressed personal wish that all men every where could be free." The message was unmistakable. Lincoln was personally opposed to slavery and always had been. He was dismantling it as best he could, given the constraints of the Constitution and the necessity of winning the war. In the next month he would elaborate on this position by issuing the preliminary Emancipation Proclamation. But in his letter to Greeley he carefully did not reveal that he in fact intended to turn the war for the Union into a war against slavery.

The letter was, in effect, a presidential address hidden within a response to an attack, one that the president could not have made directly, for political reasons. Lincoln made clear that emancipation would be his policy and not that of the army or Congress, and he made clear to Northern conservatives—the "fossil politicians" Greeley complained about—that emancipation was coming. Northern conservatives were now on notice that slavery might be destroyed to "save the Union."

Emancipation would indeed be a legitimate result of the necessity of saving the Union. That would happen on September 22, 1862 with the release of the preliminary proclamation, exactly one month and one day after his letter to the *Tribune* had helped lay the groundwork for Northern acceptance of emancipation. Despite the rude and obnoxious tone of Greeley's open letter, Lincoln was probably quite happy to have a chance to let the nation know that emancipation was coming—and that it would help save the Union.

The Civil War's War on Fraud

MARK GREENBAUM

Popular memory holds that among the many differences between Billy Yank and Johnny Reb were the clothes on their back. Union soldiers, we are told, had more and better everything, while rebels had to scrounge for uniforms, weapons, and even shoes. But especially in the early years of the Civil War this was more an impression than reality. Union supplies were poor and in short supply, thanks to unimaginable levels of fraud.

Cheaply made shoes plagued the soldiers' feet. Uniforms of lousy fabric would literally fall apart in rain. Standard-issue coats and blankets were too thin to withstand the winter cold. Guns were sometimes unable to fire, and stocks and shells of gunpowder were found filled with sawdust. Newly ordered horses and mules arrived at the front withered, old, sometimes even blind.

A good part of the problem lay in the growing pains of a still-developing war machine for which the lack of Southern cotton made the creation and procurement of quality uniforms and blankets even more difficult for Union soldiers. But the root of the problem was the legion of unscrupulous contractors who knowingly supplied shoddy materials to the Union.

With virtually no checks in place in 1861 to combat fraud, contractors had free rein in their sales to the government, sometimes with the assistance of greedy military men. In response Congress throughout the war worked to counter the ever-evolving economy of fraud that dragged heavily at the war effort—and as a result created an antifraud framework that remains in place today.

Spurred by early war reports and loud calls from Representative Charles Van Wyck of New York, on July 8, 1861, the House approved the creation of the Select Committee on Government Contracts. In his trademark biting hyperbole Van Wyck underlined the necessity of such a body, describing "the mania for stealing . . . almost from the general to the drummer boy." The new committee was tasked with investigating the procurement system and given broad latitude to act.

The small committee of seven members was originally chaired by Van Wyck, but he was replaced by Illinois Republican Elihu Washburne, a close ally of the president and the original political patron of Ulysses S. Grant. The body maintained a significant pace of activity during the 37th Congress, holding field hearings in several cities, receiving testimony from hundreds of witnesses, and ultimately issuing over three thousand pages of findings.

The Committee's three reports identified numerous cases of fraud in the supplying of horses, clothing, ammunition, and other vitals to Union soldiers, and widespread malfeasance out west. The Committee found that both the Department of War under Simon Cameron and the Department of the Navy under Gideon Welles had awarded contracts not to the lowest bidder through proper advertisements but to friends and associates.

The Navy Department was lashed for using private commission agents to procure unseaworthy vessels. One such agent, Alexander Cummings, had secured a ship, the *Cataline*, at an exorbitant price, and another, George Morgan, enriched himself with a high commission for his purchases on behalf of the department. Things were even worse in the War Department. Cameron was assailed for awarding rich contracts to close allies in the railroad industry, much to the delight of his congressional critics.

Perhaps most striking were the findings in the West. In several hearings in St. Louis and Cairo, Illinois, in October 1861 the Committee uncovered rampant fraud by agents working under General John C. Frémont at the center of the Union's Western Department headquarters just three months after the general took the job. Writing the president, Washburne sounded the alarm: "The robberies, the frauds, the peculiarities in the government which have already come to our knowledge are absolutely frightful."

Frémont had done business with a shady California contractor who worked without a contract and received exorbitant compensation. But perhaps even more troubling was the case of Major Justus McKinstry, the Western Department quartermaster. Eventually court-martialed on sixty-three separate counts by evidence exposed by Washburne's Committee, including bribery and outright fraud, McKinstry was cashiered out of the army, one of the biggest rogues in the war. Another purchaser, Simon Stevens, was implicated in the "Hall Carbine" affair, in which the government unknowingly repurchased arms it had already discarded as obsolete.

Coverage of the Committee's activities was insatiably detailed, as the press was fascinated by the reports of stunning thievery. A *New York Times* editorial appraising one of the Committee's reports reflected this colorful interest, calling the findings "a library of corrupt readings" whose "painful and dreadful" disclosures will "produce a feeling of public indignation which would justify the most summary measures against the knaves whose villainy is here dragged into daylight."

Despite its success and the public interest stoked by media coverage of its hearings, the Committee's activities were highly controversial in Congress from the start. The House had fought over Van Wyck's request for expanding his jurisdiction and having the ability to hold field hearings, as many critics asserted turf concerns that the new body would impinge on the oversight of existing standing committees.

Soon after it began its hearings, the Committee came under attack from Radical Republicans. Many were agitated that the Committee's findings were not more sharply critical of enemies in Lincoln's cabinet, including Welles and Cameron (who would be pushed out in January 1862, in part because of the Committee's revelations), and were disappointed that, unlike the Committee on the Conduct of the War, which was dominated by fire-breathers, the Government Contracts Committee was filled with moderates.

The Radicals were also initially infuriated when the Committee described in harsh detail the crimes occurring in the Western Theater under Frémont's leadership, as many of them had lionized the man known as "the Pathfinder" for his 1861 proclamation

Quartermaster's Office, Washington, D.C. Library of Congress Prints and Photographs Division, LC-B817-7918 [P&P] LOT 4161-D.

emancipating captured slaves in his department (which Lincoln quickly had rescinded so as not to upset the then-wavering border states).

Other critics sought to protect allies implicated by the Committee's findings. Simon Stevens, a protégé of the Radical leader Thaddeus Stevens, raged that the Committee had "no honest purpose to know the truth" except to go "scandal-hunting." Similarly an exposed thief, Captain E. M. Davis, whose fraud in procuring military supplies was breathtakingly diverse, was the brother of Republican Representative William M. Davis of Pennsylvania, who savaged the Committee.

Despite these political criticisms, fraud was a difficult issue to politicize completely. The findings offered by the Committee and the positive, heavy media coverage of its hearings—not to mention the scores of letters sent home by soldiers complaining of their poor supplies—shielded the Committee, such that a motion offered by Stevens to curtail its work was soundly defeated. And while earlier moves to pass broadly encompassing antifraud legislation did fail, Congress would finally act on the body's work.

On March 2, 1863, its final day, the 37th Congress approved the False Claims Act to combat the problem of war profiteering. The bill banned the making of false claims to the government, including forgery, embezzlement, and conspiracy to defraud the government in contracts. Punishment was harsh: wrongdoers faced prison time and up to $5,000 in penalties and could also be hit with a fine double the amount they had stolen plus $2,000 for each claim—an enormous sum in 1863.

Equally important were the unique enforcement mechanisms of the bill. In 1863 there was no Department of Justice or federal prosecutorial apparatus to deal with criminal networks. Therefore the legislation included a whistleblower, or *qui tam*, provision to encourage citizens to come forward with knowledge of ongoing fraud; if their claims proved correct, they would receive a share of the recovered money. The principal sponsor of the bill in the Senate, Michigan's Jacob Howard, acknowledged this: "In short, I have based the . . . sections upon the old-fashioned idea of hold[ing] out a temptation" and "setting a rogue to catch a rogue . . . a reward for the informer who comes into court and betrays his co-conspirator . . . widely used to combat instance of fraud by companies supplying the Union Army." *Qui tam* derives from a Latin phrase that means "he who prosecutes for himself as well as the king"; it allowed private citizens (called "relators" in the law), to come forward and file civil suits against fraud merchants. The mechanism was used as far back as fourteenth-century England and was common in colonial America. *Qui tam* provisions were also in several of the first bills passed by Congress as a means of encouraging people to help root out fraud too intricate and pervasive for the young government alone to adequately uncover.

Though often overlooked in general accounts of the wartime Congress's achievements, the False Claims Act remains a significant legacy of the era. After being defanged during World War II, bipartisan amendments passed by Congress in 1986 reinvigorated the bill, and the law has since saved the government over $20 billion in recovered monies, and exponentially more in deterrence. It continues to serve as a robust bulwark against fraud.

Counting the Costs of the Civil War

JEFFREY ALLEN SMITH AND B. CHRISTOPHER FRUEH

While the desire to document military exploits and wars is as old as writing itself, the recording of military medical data is a relatively modern phenomenon. Although some initial attempts to chronicle the health of troops occurred in the first half of the nineteenth century, the first large-scale wartime medical and behavioral health surveillance effort was conducted during the American Civil War.

This is partly a reflection on the dismal state of the medical profession before the mid-nineteenth century. By the Civil War era medical practice had improved markedly over the previous century, but it had yet to shake free of all the fetters of its lingering superstitions and misconceptions. For example, with the germ theory of disease still a generation away, it was commonly held that a variety of fevers and diseases, like cholera, were caused by miasma, the foul-smelling "bad" air that emanated from swamps and decomposing matter. On the other hand, medical sophistry notwithstanding, bloodletting had fallen out of fashion and belief in the prophylactic powers of cleanliness and proper hygiene were more widespread, thanks in part to the hard work of Florence Nightingale during the Crimean War in bringing sanitation to British war hospitals. One ward's mortality rate fell over 30 percent because of her efforts.

Thus, with medical advancements showing tangible results in lowering mortality rates and sickness, placing greater effort and funding into a larger systematic wartime recording of military medical data seemed sensible and feasible.

The U.S. Army Medical Department entered the Civil War understaffed and underfunded. This was partially the fault of Surgeon General Thomas Lawson, an ossified War of 1812 sawbones, who infamously considered updated medical textbooks a superfluous use of funds. After Lawson died a month into the war, President Lincoln replaced him with Clement Finley, who soon ran afoul of Secretary of War Edwin Stanton in a fiery disagreement.

The choice of Finley's replacement, William Alexander Hammond, was a stroke of good fortune for the department. Hammond, who had military experience and previously was the chair of anatomy and physiology at the University of Maryland Medical School, set about updating and modernizing the Medical Department. He is credited with increasing standards for army surgeons, reorganizing the ambulance service, founding the Army Medical Museum, expanding support to field and general hospitals, and helping to establish the Army Nurse Corps.

Hammond also recognized that the medical record-keeping system for sick and wounded soldiers was "insufficient and defective," and in June 1862, barely a month into his tenure, his office announced a plan to compile the *Medical and Surgical History of the War of the Rebellion*.

Still, it was not until November 4, 1863, that the War Department issued General Order No. 355, directing "Medical Directors of Armies in the field [to] forward, direct to the Surgeon General at Washington, duplicates of their reports . . . after every engagement." A week later the Surgeon General's Office requested "all obtainable statistics and data in connection with past and future operations" and drew "particular attention" to a list of medical topics of elevated importance, the first on the list being "morale and sanitary condition of the troops."

By January 1864 the scope and focus of the data collected expanded from the battlefield to include general hospitals. "Medical officers in charge of wards" were issued a "Register of Sick and Wounded" and a "Register of Surgical Operations," in which they kept "minutely and in detail, the particulars of all operations performed, or treated in [the] hospital." These two registers later served as the foundation for the organizational structure of *Medical and Surgical History of the War of the Rebellion*. A month later the military began explicitly requesting medical reports for "sick and wounded rebel prisoners of war" and "white and colored troops." With the inclusion of these medical reports, and a slight modification of a few others, the Surgeon General's Office had in place a comprehensive system for tracking the medical condition of Civil War combatants by the spring of 1864.

William Alexander Hammond. Library of Congress Prints and Photographs Division, LC-DIG-cwpb-05202.

Yet another year would pass before the office started to focus on medical reporting efficiency as well as effectiveness, but Hammond would not be around to see it. In his zeal to modernize Hammond fell victim to the "Calomel Rebellion." After he banned the medicinal use of mercurial poisons like calomel, army physicians—who stood by these drugs as lifesavers—successfully ousted him from his post.

With Hammond gone, Secretary of War Stanton chose Joseph K. Barnes to serve as the fourth surgeon general in four years. Barnes studied medicine at Harvard University and the University of Pennsylvania before joining the military as an assistant surgeon in 1840. Unlike his relationship with the previous surgeon generals, Stanton got along well with Barnes, and it showed in the War Department's increased support of the Medical Department's activities.

One of these endeavors was the organization of medical records. Bureaucratic delay, ineffectiveness, and struggles to conceptualize and implement a final medical recording system notwithstanding, the unprecedented size and scope of the military medical data collected is truly impressive. Still the struggle to organize the mountains of reports, analyze the data, and effectively share the data with the world would last longer than the war itself.

In June 1868, as the nation began to come to terms with the significance of the war, Congress commissioned Secretary of War Stanton to prepare for publication "five thousand copies of the First Part of the Medical and Surgical history of the Rebellion, [as] complied by the Surgeon General."

A decade later the resulting tome, *The Medical and Surgical History of the War of Rebellion, 1861–65*, appeared, consisting of six volumes and totaling approximately three thousand pages. Based exclusively on military and government medical records, it included statistical data on white and black Union troops broken down into a variety of subcategories. More than a hundred separate tables organized by region and army group tracked 150 "diseases," including "serpent bite," gunshot wounds, dysentery, diabetes, "dropsy from heart disease," and even alcoholism and suicide. In addition many of the "diseases" listed in the tables were in subsequent volumes given general descriptions, selective case studies, accounts of treatments, and sometimes even illustrative photographs or color plates to further aid in contextualizing their effects on the health of the Civil War soldier.

Newspapers, photographs, diaries, and soldiers' letters all had the ability to create a visceral and real connection to the horrors and heroism of the Civil War. However, these sources can also prove selective and occasionally obscure the larger war. The *Medical and Surgical History* provides something else: an extremely detailed examination of the medical condition and toll taken on soldiers during the Civil War. Here, almost for the time, there is no euphemism, no soft focus, no attempt to diminish that cold, dispassionate arithmetic reality of the terrible cost borne by Civil War soldiers, both during the war and for decades after.

Rewriting the Gettysburg Address

MARTIN P. JOHNSON

Abraham Lincoln did not give the Gettysburg Address on November 19, 1863—at least, not the one engraved on the Lincoln Memorial, the one memorized by millions the world over. Lincoln actually wrote the words recognized today as the Gettysburg Address months after the cemetery dedication, during a full and complete revision of his speech that he finished in February 1864.

Lincoln's revisions added about 14 percent more words to his original delivery text, the so-called Nicolay Draft, and several key passages. But no addition was more important than the words "under God": Lincoln had spoken those words, and others that were not in the delivery manuscript, in the inspiration of the moment, when he stood on the speaker's platform and dedicated the nation to "a new birth of freedom."

Influential observers, from Henry Wadsworth Longfellow to the editors of *Harper's Weekly*, had immediately recognized the beauty and power of Lincoln's speech as it was reported in the press. Soon it was being recited at funerals and quoted in political speeches, and the next year it began to appear in schoolbooks and handbooks of rhetoric. Even the featured speaker at the ceremony, Edward Everett, whose underappreciated speech was

The crowd gathered to hear President Lincoln deliver the Gettysburg Address. Library of Congress Prints and Photographs Division, LC-DIG-ds-03106.

overshadowed by the president's short address, later praised Lincoln's words. Lincoln told his old friend James Speed "that he had never received a compliment he prized more highly."

Yet the attention given his speech created a problem for Lincoln. In late January 1864 Everett asked Lincoln for "the manuscript of your dedicatory remarks" so that it could be sold at a charity fair. Sending the delivery text would, however, publicize a text that differed markedly from the newspaper reports. According to Lincoln's secretary John Nicolay, who was directly involved, "Lincoln saw" that the newspaper accounts of his spoken words were "imperfect," but also that, when compared with those reports and with his own recollection of what he had said, the delivery manuscript "seemed incomplete."

Lincoln's difficulty is our fortune, however, because rather than choose one text or the other, Lincoln created a new, revised version to send to Everett. The great care Lincoln took in creating the revised, "Everett" version reveals that he recognized that this speech, these words, had undeniable power and meaning at that crucial moment in the Civil War.

Lincoln's first step in creating this new version was to write out a copy, not of his delivery manuscript but of one of the published accounts of the words he had reportedly spoken. This was a sign that, for Lincoln, the additions and changes that he made while speaking at the ceremony were vital elements of his evolving thought, building and enlarging upon the foundation provided by the delivery text. The published version of his words that Lincoln chose as the foundation text of his revision was close at hand: it was the version in the "authorized" report on the Gettysburg ceremony published by Everett, which was essentially a reprinting of the version originally published in the *New-York Tribune* the day after the dedication. Everett had sent the "authorized" edition to Lincoln within a day or two of his request for "the manuscript" of Lincoln's remarks, and Lincoln mentioned having it in his cover letter for the revised manuscript that he sent to Everett dated February 4, 1864.

Lincoln's handwritten copy includes a few changes and is known as the "Hay Draft" in honor of Lincoln's secretary John Hay. For over a century the Hay text puzzled and confused those seeking to understand how Lincoln wrote the Gettysburg Address, and over the years it has been held up as the first draft, the delivery text, and even a souvenir copy made for Hay. But it seems certain now that Lincoln wrote and edited the Hay when he first set about reconciling the delivery manuscript and the reports of his spoken words.

In the second stage of revision, working from the basis of the edited Hay copy, Lincoln wrote a new, clean manuscript to send to Everett that included additional, mainly stylistic changes. Expressing Lincoln's choice of his spoken words as the foundation for his revisions, the final Everett revised manuscript incorporated his spoken "under God" in the passage of his delivery text that had originally read "that the nation, shall have a new birth of freedom."

Lincoln's revised manuscript also retained other spoken innovations, like twice repeating, with slight variation, the phrase that in the delivery text read "It is rather for us, the living." This allowed Lincoln to retain in the revised Everett text a wholly new phrase he had added while speaking—"be dedicated here to the unfinished work that they have thus far so nobly carried on"—in addition to the single phrase of his manuscript delivery text, "be dedicated to the great task remaining before us." Five times Lincoln's delivery manuscript used variations of the word *dedicated*, and Lincoln made sure that his revised version incorporated his sixth, spoken use of the word, affirming and reaffirming his own commitment, and ours, to "the great task" and "the unfinished work" of preserving and extending the promise of a nation born in the struggle for freedom and equality.

But Lincoln's revised Everett manuscript also reverted to the wording of his original delivery manuscript at some points where it differed from the published accounts of what he had reportedly said. Most important, the revised version included the words "and that government of the people, by the people, for the people" that are found in the delivery text, even though all the reports of his spoken words included "and for the people."

Similarly reports of his spoken words agree that Lincoln twice repeated the words "we are met," but in the revised manuscript he returned to the wording of the original Nicolay delivery text, which has instead "we are met" and "we have come." Lincoln's choices here and in other examples underscore the extent to which, throughout both the composition and the revision of his speech, he sought to combine both sound and sense, poetry and policy, in words he knew were widely considered meaningful and beautiful.

The extent of the changes to the original delivery manuscript, even months after the event, reveals that Lincoln himself was striving toward a clearer understanding of his vision of the Civil War, and of the American experiment that he had expressed on that brilliant November day. Lincoln did give a speech at the Gettysburg cemetery on November 19, 1863, but it was his revisions after returning to Washington, and our own national revision and renewal of the ideals he proclaimed, that continue to give us our Gettysburg Address.

The Rise and Fall (and Rise) of Salmon P. Chase

RICK BEARD

On July 4, 1864, four days after President Abraham Lincoln had surprised him by accepting his resignation, Treasury Secretary Salmon P. Chase confided to his diary, "I am too earnest, too antislavery . . . [and] too radical."

Chase surely possessed each of these attributes—in excess—but they had little to do with his unexpected exit from Lincoln's "team of rivals." Rather it was much more personal. Chase's oft-repeated threat to quit had tested the forbearance of a beleaguered president once too often. Out of patience, Lincoln ended Chase's tenure with the observation, "You and I have reached a point of mutual embarrassment in our official relation which it seems cannot be overcome, or longer sustained."

It had been an unlikely partnership from the start. In 1860 Chase's presidential ambitions were second to none. A staunch antislavery man, he had held a Senate seat and the Ohio governor's chair and in one contemporary's words "looked as you would wish a statesman to look." A widower three times over, the aloof, pious Chase had few friends, lived a life governed by unshakable routine, eagerly sought moral perfection, and had no apparent sense of humor. One contemporary said he knew "little of human nature" and was "profoundly ignorant of men." Salmon Chase, in short, was Abraham Lincoln's polar opposite.

The last of Lincoln's three rivals for the presidency to be offered a cabinet post— William H. Seward was named secretary of state and Edward Bates attorney general— Chase was initially inclined to decline the offer because Lincoln had failed "to tender me the Treasury Department with the same considerate respect which was manifested toward Mr. Seward and Mr. Bates." He finally accepted in March 1861.

Chase proved a remarkably able and innovative manager of the Union's finances. He won congressional approval for a national banking system to provide a stable national currency and create a ready market for government bonds. Sale of the bonds enabled the federal government to pay the staggering costs of over $3 billion (over $5 trillion today) for four years of fighting. Working with Jay Cooke & Company, Chase managed the sale of $500 million in government bonds. He also introduced the greenback demand note, the first federal currency.

Salmon P. Chase. Library of Congress Prints and Photographs Division, LC-DIG-cwpb-05620.

Chase's failings lay in his aspirations, not his performance. Convinced he was the ablest man in the cabinet, he also believed he was Lincoln's superior as both an administrator and a statesman. His dream of occupying the White House never deserted him, and he sought to further his ambitions in ways small and large. Responsible for the design of paper currency, for example, he had no compunction about placing his own face on the $1 bill. After all, he told one confidant, he had placed Lincoln's on the $10!

But Chase's mischief could be more serious. In the last months of 1862 he played the major role in precipitating crises that twice threatened the fragile stability of Lincoln's cabinet. This much lauded "team of rivals" was in reality riven by clashes driven more by personality than ideology. As the historian David Donald has observed, Chase and Navy Secretary Gideon Welles both distrusted Seward, who they believed failed to grasp the dangers the war posed. Edwin M. Stanton, the secretary of war, was irascible and secretive and worked well only with Chase, with whom he enjoyed a twenty-year friendship. Welles—"Father Neptune" to his colleagues as well as the president—was a sometimes comical figure, while Caleb Smith, the interior secretary, seemed to all a figure of no account. Postmaster General Montgomery Blair bore particular animus toward Chase and Stanton and seemed primarily self-interested. Only Bates enjoyed cordial relationships with all of his colleagues.

The stunning defeat of General John Pope's Army of Virginia at the Second Battle of Bull Run in late August 1862 precipitated the first of these crises. In league with Stanton, Chase tried to force Lincoln to cashier General George B. McClellan over his apparent refusal to reinforce Pope's army. In an extraordinary "remonstrance" to the president, they warned of "the destruction of our armies" should "George B. McClellan be continued in command." Chase, Stanton, Smith, and Bates endorsed the document, while Welles and Blair expressed their support but chose not to sign it. Seward was out of town.

At a fractious cabinet meeting on September 2, the president overrode their objections. While not unsympathetic to his cabinet secretaries' concerns, Lincoln argued that only McClellan could "reorganize the army and bring it out of chaos."

Despite the Union's success at Antietam a few weeks later, Lincoln did remove McClellan from command of the Army of the Potomac in November, only to see his replacement, Ambrose Burnside, preside over a Union debacle at Fredericksburg. News of this latest defeat provoked a mutiny among Senate Republicans, who were convinced (due in no small part to Chase's machinations) that Lincoln's management of the cabinet and embrace of Seward's conservative ideas were hobbling the Union war effort.

On December 16 and 17 thirty-one Republican senators caucused to express their frustrations and anger with the Lincoln administration, directing most of their venom at Seward. A concerned Lincoln met with a delegation of nine Republican senators for several hours on the nights of December 18 and 19 both to listen and to defend his administration. With his cabinet members (except Seward, who had submitted his resignation) in attendance at the second meeting, Lincoln contended that while the cabinet did not meet regularly, it was informed of most major issues and generally acquiesced to the decisions that were made.

Lincoln then put his Treasury secretary, whom he knew to be at the bottom "of all the mischief," on the spot. Would he support the president? Chase somewhat reluctantly said yes but sought to save face with the senators present by noting that the cabinet was not asked to discuss many important issues. The other cabinet members had little to say, and the meeting ended inconclusively, well after midnight.

The following morning Lincoln summoned Chase again, along with Welles and Stanton, because, he said, this "matter is giving me great trouble." Chase responded that he had decided to resign. Seizing the letter from his hand, the president exclaimed, "This cuts the Gordian knot. . . . I can dispose of this subject now without difficulty. I see my way clear." His same-day refusal to accept the resignations of Chase and Seward defused the crisis by signaling his willingness to listen to both moderate and radical Republicans.

The cabinet crisis greatly diminished the Treasury secretary's standing: Stanton confessed that he "was ashamed of Chase," while Senator William P. Fessenden of Maine (who would succeed Chase in the cabinet) fulminated at the secretary's deliberate sacrifice of "his friends to the fear of offending his & their enemies."

But Chase's loss of face after the 1862 cabinet crisis did little to blunt his presidential aspirations. He continued to fill the fifteen thousand patronage jobs at his disposal with loyalists and maintained a regular correspondence with supporters throughout the North. Well aware of these activities, Lincoln had "determined to shut his eyes to all these performances . . . [because] Chase made a good secretary." The president also recognized that he had his Treasury secretary under control, for Chase could neither be overly critical within the cabinet nor resign and appear unpatriotic.

But Chase continued to maneuver, and the battle looming over Reconstruction policy in late 1863 and early 1864 bolstered his support among radicals unhappy with the administration. It looked increasingly like Chase might make a run for the White House.

Early in 1864 the campaign committee for Chase, headed by Senator Samuel C. Pomeroy of Kansas, issued two pamphlets critical of Lincoln. Too critical, in fact. Even Lincoln's staunchest opponents found the publications too much, and the so-called *Pomeroy Circular* in particular—which asserted that Lincoln's candidacy was doomed—proved so embarrassing to Chase that he aggressively distanced himself from the piece.

But it wasn't enough; the pamphlet, in one contemporary's words, "had utterly annihilated the pretensions and prospects of Mr. Chase." Within weeks his opponents coalesced in support of Lincoln in the fall election, and Chase announced that he would not be a candidate.

In the wake of these events Chase once again tendered his resignation in a long letter filled with self-justifications. By now Lincoln's fabled patience was threadbare. His first response to Chase's letter, a terse promise to "answer a little more fully when I can find the leisure to do so," was followed six days later by a muted vote of confidence: "I do not perceive occasion for a change."

But the occasion for a change would soon arrive, prompted by the politics of patronage. In late June 1864 Chase sought to replace a well-respected assistant treasurer in New York with a clearly unqualified candidate of suspect political loyalty. Lincoln, fearing an "open revolt" among Republicans, urged Chase to select from among three alternative candidates. Chase rejected them and instead persuaded the incumbent to withdraw his resignation. When Chase sought a meeting with Lincoln he was rebuffed "because the difficulty does not, in the main part, lie within the range of a conversation between you and me."

On June 29 Chase once again offered his resignation, and this time Lincoln accepted. "I thought I could not stand it any longer," the president confided to his secretary John Hay. Official Washington was aghast at the news. "In Congress and on the street there is a general feeling of depression and gloom," noted Hay. When the entire Senate Finance Committee descended on the White House to protest, Lincoln stood firm, reading to them each of Chase's previous letters of resignation, as well as his own responses, and noting that the tension between the two men had become such that they "disliked to meet each other." When Governor John Brough of Ohio offered to mediate the dispute, Lincoln replied, "This is the third time he has thrown this at me, and I do not think I am called on to continue to beg him to take it back. . . . I reckon you had better let it alone this time."

Chase's downfall proved short-lived. In December Lincoln appointed him to the Supreme Court to succeed Chief Justice Roger Taney, who had died two months earlier. In a letter to his fiancée Lincoln's other secretary, John Nicolay, wrote, "No other man than Lincoln would have had ... the degree of magnanimity to thus forgive and exalt a rival who had so deeply and unjustifiably intrigued against him. It is only another ... illustration of the greatness of the President, in this age of little men."

10. The Consequences of the Civil War

Introduction

HEATHER COX RICHARDSON

After General Robert E. Lee surrendered his Army of Northern Virginia at Appomattox Court House on April 9, 1865, his soldiers began the long trip home. In 1861 these battered men had taken up arms to protect slavery and the way of life it supported. They had an idealized vision of patriarchs caring for the women, children, and "servants" who depended on them. This vision justified an economic and political system that stratified wealth at the very top of society and put those wealthy men in charge of government, which they designed to protect their interests. They had marched to war to defend this system, past stately plantation homes, thriving urban towns, and valuable fields where slaves planted the cotton that drove the nation's economy.

Four years later they limped home to a different scene. The South was ruined, its elegant plantations shattered, its cities burned. Its draft animals were dead, its fields gone to weeds. Slavery was destroyed beyond recall, taking with it a social order based on white men leading those beneath them. White women and children, widows and orphans, were now starving refugees, and former slaves had escaped, fleeing to the Union, where they worked or fought for the U.S. government. In 1865 Confederate soldiers trudged through a land of bitter partisans who loathed both the federal government that had crushed their rebellion and the former slaves who had sided with that government and now enjoyed its protection.

General Ulysses S. Grant's men loved the same government that white Southerners hated. They rode trains home to a region whose leaders had been afraid in 1861 that the conflict would destroy the government but who had figured out over the course of the past four years how to build a modern nation. In the 1850s Northerners had organized a new political party to stand against slave owners' determination to spread slavery to the new western territories. These Republicans insisted that the government must make it possible for all men to rise to prosperity rather than simply protecting the interests of the very wealthy. When the Republicans elected Abraham Lincoln president, Southern Democrats felt so threatened they abandoned the Union even before Lincoln took office. In doing so they left the fledgling Republican Party in control of the government.

Supplying an army and navy that eventually included more than 2 million men required Congress to put Republican theories into practice. Congress had to create national taxes—including an income tax—to pay for the war. Then they nurtured national industries and gave poor young men land and education to enable them to pay those taxes. Finally, to guarantee that all Americans shared equality of opportunity, the Republicans abolished slavery. By 1865 Northerners of all racial and ethnic backgrounds and many Southern African Americans had died for the government; those who remained supported its $6 billion debt. Washington had repaid those sacrifices by creating a new government that was, as Lincoln said, "of the people, by the people, and for the people." In the decades after the war's end Americans gave it their fervent loyalty.

There was another region vital to the reconstruction of the country. While the North and the South contended on the battlefields, the war was actually fought over the West. Long before the war began Americans asked whether Southerners would extend slavery into that new region or Northerners would preserve it for freedom. Both governments tried to dominate the West during the war, but the U.S. government quickly pushed the Confederates back. Eager to settle the West and to develop the mines there, the wartime Congress brought western states and territories into the Union at breakneck speed. Between 1861 and 1865 Congress added the territories of Colorado, Dakota, Idaho, Arizona, and Montana to the Union and made Nevada first a territory and then a state. The lands Congress organized made the map of the United States look much like it does today, but the reality was that the government did not control those lands. The American Indians who owned them did. When the Civil War ended, the government turned its attention to the Plains, where army troops fought Apache, Comanche, Cheyenne, and Lakota.

The challenge presented by the war's end was simply this: somehow these three distinct regions—the shattered South, the thriving North, and the raw West—would have to be reconstructed into a new nation, overseen by a newly reconstructed government. Would that government continue to develop along the lines Republicans had laid out, expanding economic opportunity for all? Or would it revert to a system like the one before the war, where the government focused on protecting property?

What the new postwar government would look like depended on who would have a say in it. The white men who had fought to defend the Union would be welcome to determine its future, of course, but who else would? White Southerners had traditionally dominated the federal government; did their rebellion against it require excluding them from power? What about former slaves, who had been shut out of a say in American society but who had fought and died for the government their former masters had tried to destroy? What about women, who had labored for the Union and given their sons and their money to it? What about immigrants, who were arriving to work the fields, the factories, the mines, and the railroads? What about the Indians at war with the United States but who were, after all, Americans long before anyone else had been?

The question of who would have a say in American society was not academic in the postwar years. The new national taxes meant that, for the first time, the right to vote conferred the ability to determine how other people's money was spent. Reconstructing and developing the nation would take government officials and government programs, paid for with tax dollars. Were Northerners willing to put their money behind the idea of universal freedom? If so, what would that mean? Deploying troops to protect ex-slaves and, later, Chinese workers from their angry white neighbors? Providing national public schools? Regulating the growing industries in which immigrants risked life and limb for a pittance? Cleaning up the air and water the factories polluted? Protecting a man's right to keep all that he earned? Permitting women to own property, to divorce, and to share custody of their children?

Bitter fights over the meaning of freedom, race, property, and gender came down to the central question of Reconstruction: What is the proper role of the government in American society, and who should determine that role? Born in the Civil War and contested during Reconstruction, that question is still with us today.

Remembering the Gettysburg Address

JOSHUA ZEITZ

John Hay woke with a severe hangover on the morning of November 19, 1863. As one of Abraham Lincoln's closest White House aides, Hay had spent the previous evening drinking copiously with the disparate crew of journalists and politicians who converged on the small town of Gettysburg, Pennsylvania, for the dedication of a new national cemetery later that day. A bystander remembered seeing the presidential party arrive after a long train ride from Washington, "a straggled, hungry set. Lincoln, with that weary smile . . . Seward, with an essentially bad hat; John Hay, in attendance upon the president, and much to be troubled by the correspondents, handsome as a peach, the countenance of extreme youth."

For Lincoln the dedication of the national battlefield cemetery was politically loaded: it offered an important opportunity to convene with Northern governors and newspaper correspondents who would prove critical to his renomination fight the following summer. While his White House aides plied their trade, mixing politics and drink, the president attended a dinner at the home of a local attorney, David Wills, then retired to a guest bedroom to complete his speech.

"I got a beast and rode out with the President's suite to the Cemetery in the procession," Hay noted in his diary the next day. Edward Everett, the former governor of Massachusetts and a noted orator, spoke first, and for over two hours. Then Lincoln rose to give a few remarks. "Mr. Everett spoke as he always does perfectly—and the President in a firm free way, with more grace than is his wont said his half dozen lines of consecration and the music wailed and we went home through crowded and cheering streets. And all the particulars are in the daily papers."

And that was that. At the time, Lincoln's address at Gettysburg was regarded as an important political moment, but little more. A search of fifteen major American newspapers from 1864 through 1889 yields just a handful of mentions of the Gettysburg Address. When Hay and his colleague John Nicolay published their monumental, ten-volume biography of Lincoln in 1890, they devoted eight pages to Everett's keynote address and only two pages to Lincoln's.

In contrast, between 1890 and 1915 the Gettysburg Address merits at least 579 mentions in the same group of papers, and both Hay and Nicolay did an about-face on the speech. After Hay's death Lincoln's son Robert spent almost ten years searching for the original manuscript; it appeared as a facsimile in the Nicolay-Hay volumes but had mysteriously disappeared after Robert reclaimed his father's papers from the Hay family. Eventually Alice Hay Wadsworth, Hay's daughter, found the document among her possessions in 1916 and donated it to the Library of Congress. It seems that her father had pinched the copy from the larger collection. He couldn't stand to part with it.

Ironically the speech became famous just as America forgot what it meant. Readings of the Gettysburg Address became an obligatory part of Memorial Day celebrations at public schools, municipal ceremonies, and regimental reunions. But of the hundreds of newspaper articles noting its public recitation, very few stopped to dwell on the text's original meaning.

As memories of the war faded in the 1880s and 1890s, and as Jim Crow stamped out the brief moment of racial liberalism that the Civil War helped catalyze, Americans adopted a new ritual of Blue and Gray reunions, in which aging veterans relived their battlefield achievements. In 1887 Boston's Granddaughters of the American Revolution post honored Richmond's Robert E. Lee Camp of Confederate Veterans, while the 7th Connecticut Regiment held a reunion honoring a Confederate officer whom they had captured during the war. Two years later the Society of the Army of the Cumberland held a Blue-Gray reunion that drew twenty-five thousand people near the Chickamauga Battlefield.

Such events became commonplace, as many Northerners—their moral memories faded and their racial prejudices hardened—slipped into ideological amnesia. The Civil War was no longer remarkable for what it accomplished but for what soldiers did on the battlefield. Even Oliver Wendell Holmes Jr., who had enlisted as a committed abolitionist and who nearly died in combat, came to believe that "the faith is true and adorable which

Representative Joe Cannon reading the Gettysburg Address on the floor of the House of Representatives on Lincoln's birthday, February 12, 1920. Library of Congress Prints and Photographs Division, LC-DIG-ds-00664.

leads a soldier to throw away his life in obedience to a blindly accepted duty, in a cause which he little understands."

In fact soldiers' letters and diaries written during the war suggest that they did indeed understand what they were fighting for. Moreover, at the time of its delivery the Gettysburg Address—in which Lincoln signaled a new moral turn in the war—was widely understood. In its immediate aftermath an Ohio Democrat denounced the speech as a "mawkish harangue about this 'war for freedom' of the negro." The *Chicago Times*, a fierce enemy of the administration, complained, "Lincoln did most foully traduce the motives of the men who were slain at Gettysburg." They had not perished to give the nation a "new birth of freedom." Instead "they gave their lives to maintain the old government, and the old constitution and Union."

By the 1890s, however, when the Gettysburg Address finally entered America's secular gospel, most people had conveniently forgotten what Lincoln actually attempted to convey in his brief remarks. Even in Montgomery, Alabama, where Jefferson Davis took the oath of office as Confederate president, the local paper thought it unremarkable when "Decoration Day was observed in this city, the 'Cradle of the Confederacy,' with imposing ceremonies, many ex-confederates being in attendance. Lincoln's Gettysburg Address was read at the graveyard and several patriotic speeches were made."

In 1898, as North and South emphasized intersectional unity during the Spanish-American War, it was commonplace for Union and Confederate veterans to link arms during public recitations of the speech, which now represented a vague tribute to battlefield bravery rather than a commitment to Lincoln's "new birth of freedom." In Lincoln's home state the *Chicago Tribune* reported that "veterans of the Confederate Army shared in" Memorial Day exercises that included readings of the address. "Many speakers pointed to the common spirit of patriotism in the North and South today as evidence that the antipathies of a generation ago have been forgotten." In Pacific Grove, California, former enemies marched together to the soldier's cemetery, where they listened to a reading of the address and watched children "strew flowers on the graves of the Nation's heroes slumbering in the shade of Fort Halleck's pines."

Later that year the *Atlanta Constitution* favorably compared the Gettysburg Address to remarks by President William McKinley, a Union veteran, who declared that in the aftermath of the Spanish-American War "sectional lines no longer mar the map of the United States." According to the paper, "Great as have been the achievements of President McKinley's administration in war, the country will turn to his truly patriotic address at Atlanta . . . as ranking with that of Abraham Lincoln at Gettysburg."

Given the popular transformation of the Gettysburg Address into a generic expression of battlefield commemoration, it is little wonder that in 1909, in honor of the centennial of Lincoln's birth, Confederate and Union veterans gathered at Atlanta's Trinity Church, where a retired brigadier general recited the speech.

To be sure, not everyone stripped the document of its broader implications. In New York proponents of women's suffrage opened a meeting with recitation of the speech, followed by a lecture titled "The Next Steps in Political Reform." For many African American audiences the Gettysburg Address would remain, as it had always been, a proclamation wedding the Civil War to the emancipationist project. In his final years John Nicolay insisted that the Gettysburg Address was an expansive document. Lincoln, he explained, gave expression to his long-held belief that " 'he who would be no slave must consent to have no slave.' This rule, translated to our day, plainly is that he who would suffer no wrong from society must do no wrong to society."

It would take several decades before the modern civil rights revolution compelled most white Americans to reacquaint themselves with the ideological aspects of the Civil War. In so doing they would rediscover a speech that was first forgotten, then remembered, and finally, a century after its delivery, understood.

The Birth of Thanksgiving

PAUL QUIGLEY

Though we most often associate Thanksgiving with Pilgrims and New England Indians, the holiday, at least as an official national event, began 150 years ago, at the height of the Civil War.

On October 3, 1863, President Lincoln issued a proclamation setting aside a day to express appreciation for the "blessings of fruitful fields and healthful skies." Even amid war's many horrors, Americans had much to be thankful for. And Lincoln insisted that the rightful object of their gratitude was "the Most High God, who, while dealing with us in anger for our sins, hath nevertheless remembered mercy." Divine mercies required public acknowledgment. And so Lincoln invited all Americans to "observe the last Thursday of November next as a day of thanksgiving and prayer to our beneficent Father, who dwelleth in the heavens."

Of course Lincoln did not create Thanksgiving from nothing; there were historical antecedents. The "original" Thanksgiving feast did happen in 1621. But it was not until the nineteenth century that it became enshrined as the progenitor of the modern event. In the meantime early Americans celebrated Thanksgiving not as a fixed annual event but as a series of ad hoc holidays called in response to specific events. These were religious occasions, intended to invoke God's help to cope with hardships or to offer God thanks for positive developments.

The custom gradually solidified, and by the 1840s and 1850s Thanksgiving was celebrated each November by a majority of states and many localities across the country. But the practice was uneven—a patchwork of local celebrations rather than a national holiday.

Sarah Josepha Hale, a New Hampshire–born writer and editor, was determined to change that. Hale had long recognized the nationalistic promise of Thanksgiving. In her 1827 novel, *Northwood*, she wrote, "We have too few holidays. Thanksgiving like the Fourth of July should be a national festival observed by all the people . . . as an exponent of our republican institutions." Beginning in earnest in the 1840s she campaigned doggedly to nationalize the holiday, publishing editorials in her journal, *Godey's Lady's Book*, and sending countless letters to political and cultural leaders.

As the North-South conflict deepened, Hale's appreciation of Thanksgiving's potential to bind the nation together grew. She explained in an 1859 editorial, "Everything that contributes to bind us in one vast empire together, to quicken the sympathy that makes us feel from the icy North to the sunny South that we are one family, each a member of a great and free Nation, not merely the unit of a remote locality, is worthy of being cherished." Casting nationalism in terms of family, sympathy, and affection placed it firmly within the idealized women's sphere of nineteenth-century culture. Hale herself couched her mission in gendered terms: "God has given to man authority, to woman influence; she inspires and persuades."

Inspire and persuade she certainly did. In a September 1863 letter to Lincoln, the "editress of the 'Gody's Book'" reaffirmed her long-standing quest "to have the day of our annual Thanksgiving made a National and fixed Union Festival."

Hale's insistence on a single day of nationwide celebration foreshadowed the anthropologist Benedict Anderson's work on "simultaneity" in the "imagined communities" of modern nations. Although nations are too large for every member to meet physically, a powerful sense of shared identity comes from the knowledge that one's compatriots are undergoing similar experiences—whether reading a daily newspaper or celebrating an annual holiday—at the same moment in time. Without using Anderson's terminology, Hale doubtless understood the power of simultaneity in forging national community.

So did Abraham Lincoln. Few American leaders have grasped as well as he the capacity of symbols and ideas to bring a nation together. It is not surprising that the same president who spoke so eloquently of "the mystic chords of memory"—the same president who delivered the Gettysburg Address shortly before Thanksgiving Day 1863—was the one responsible for instituting the new national holiday.

November 26, 1863, was not the only wartime Thanksgiving. Lincoln designated four Thanksgiving days, not all of them in November. For example, a Union Thanksgiving was held on August 6, 1863, to celebrate Gettysburg and Vicksburg. Nor did observances stop at the Confederate border. Jefferson Davis proclaimed two Thanksgivings, one after each battle of Manassas.

Thanksgiving Day in a Union camp. Library of Congress Prints and Photographs Division, LC-DIG-ppmsca-21210.

Both presidents also called for fast days, a sort of gloomier version of Thanksgiving. Here Davis won out, proclaiming ten fast days throughout the war, compared with Lincoln's three. Fast days and Thanksgivings were emphatically religious occasions; whether the news was good or bad, Civil War Americans' first thought was to invoke divine aid and strengthen the link between God and his chosen people. Both Confederate and American nationalisms were deeply embedded in religious beliefs, and although Thanksgiving was already associated with a family feast at home, it was even more closely associated with a visit to church.

Even after 1863 Thanksgiving was still in flux. Nobody knew whether it would become a lasting national tradition. In October 1864 Hale wrote to Secretary of State William H. Seward, asking him to encourage Lincoln to repeat his proclamation of 1863. It was not yet clear that he would. And in April 1865, in the last week of his life, Lincoln received several letters and telegrams urging him to name a day of "national thanksgiving" to commemorate Union victory. Thanksgiving was not yet exclusively tied to the last Thursday in November. Lincoln could not have known that all future presidents would follow his lead, could not have known that Thanksgiving would become fixed as a single day in the nation's calendar rather than an irregular response to specific events.

Thanksgiving exemplifies what the historians Eric Hobsbawm and Terence Ranger call "the invention of tradition." From its roots in harvest celebrations and New England's religious observances, it rose to prominence amid the impossible suffering of the Civil War, when Americans needed more than ever to publicly reaffirm their collective relationship with God.

Like all invented traditions, Thanksgiving has continued to adapt to changing circumstances. Ad hoc celebrations turned into the fixed, nationwide event required by a modern nation-state. The focus on the church gave way to a focus on the home. Football became a vital element. The turkey consolidated its place at the center of the Thanksgiving table, thanks to the late nineteenth-century marketing efforts of the poultry industry.

Thanksgiving has evolved gradually and unevenly. It is a tradition invented by many hands. But surely the most consequential act of invention came in the fall of 1863, when the American nation itself seemed to be falling apart and the persistence of a New England "editress" met its perfect partner in the presidential architect of a new American nationalism.

My Civil War

TERRY L. JONES

As a teenager growing up in the piney woods of Winn Parish, Louisiana, I frequently looked out our front window to see an old man in well-worn overalls gingerly climb over the fence and walk up the hill toward the house.

Uncle Alce, short for Alson, lived next door, and he would come over to drink coffee and catch up on local news when my father was home from his pipeline construction job. Uncle Alce's father, Elisha, was my great-great-grandfather and is one of six generations of Joneses buried in the local cemetery. Elisha and his extended family were poor dirt farmers in 1861, and they chose to sit out the Civil War after Winn Parish voted against secession. Not until the Yankees captured New Orleans and a conscription law was passed in 1862 did Elisha join several hundred other parish men in enlisting in the 28th Louisiana Volunteers. Military records show that he deserted the following summer while the regiment was serving in southern Louisiana. When asked about it, Uncle Alce quickly answered, "Pa wasn't a deserter. He came home to get in the corn crop and then went back."

Nevertheless Elisha's military career ended less than a year later. On April 8, 1864, he and the other Winn Parish boys in General Alfred Mouton's division made a dramatic bayonet charge at the Battle of Mansfield, Louisiana. "Pa and one of his neighbors were running side by side when a bullet went through Pa's right hand, breaking all the bones but his little finger," Uncle Alce recalled. "The bullet then hit his neighbor in the leg. They were both crippled by one shot and cussed that Yankee for the rest of their lives." When family members learned of Elisha's wounding, they drove a wagon seventy miles to Mansfield to bring him home. His hand drew up into a useless claw, and he was later awarded an $8-a-month state pension.

Elisha Jones, the author's great-great-grandfather. Courtesy of Terry L. Jones.

Like those of many Southerners, my family tree has deep Civil War roots. Elisha's brother also enlisted in the 28th Louisiana; he was captured on Bayou Teche. Two of my maternal great-great-grandfathers also served: John W. Jones, of the 5th Mississippi, was wounded at Chickamauga, and Thomas Walden, of the 46th Mississippi, was captured at Vicksburg. After Grandpa Walden was paroled, he had to walk home to Newton County, and his ill-fitting shoes caused his feet to break out in diabetic sores that never healed. My grandmother lived with Grandpa Walden about fifty years after the war, and she vividly recalled the price he paid for wearing the gray. "I remember he had to get up every morning and change the dressings on his feet," she told me. "His feet never healed, and there were just open sores on them all the time."

Although the guns have been silent for nearly 150 years, I still regularly see reminders of the Civil War and Reconstruction. The small rural community where I grew up is known as Hoghair. (Uncle Alce said it was originally called Possum Neck, but that's another story.) A few miles from my boyhood home is Yankee Springs Baptist Church, which got its name during Reconstruction when former rebels robbed and murdered a Northern payroll officer there. From Yankee Springs one can cut through the woods to a salt flat that still bears the scars of brine wells dug by slaves to gather salt for the Confederate Army. Within site of the farm pond in which I was baptized stands an old oak tree where two carpetbaggers were reportedly hanged. (It was rumored the landowner once plowed up their skulls.)

When sitting on the front porch of the home place on a quiet evening, I imagine hearing the tramp of marching troops in the distance. Our mailbox sits on the very road Grandpa Elisha came down in February 1864 to join General Richard Taylor's small army to stop Nathaniel P. Banks's Union juggernaut coming up Red River. Interestingly one of the soldiers recalled in his memoirs the very day they passed our home place:

> The 28th Louisiana Regiment had been raised in this portion of the state, and as we pursued our journey, their wives, sisters, and sweethearts came on horse back and in wagons to see them, often following for two or three days. The number of women became so great as to cause one of Capt. Patin's Irishmen to exclaim in the fullness of his heart that "Be Jabbers, and the 28th must all have three or four wives a pice." An old lady on horseback, who perhaps had several sons in the command, accompanied us for several days, generally riding in the advance. Upon reaching the top of a high hill, presenting a good view of the line of advancing troops for a long distance in the rear, she halted her horse and, gazing back upon the road filled with men as far as she could see, remarked, "Well, well, there's a heap of sons, and it took a heap of mothers to raise all them sons."

I have often wondered what it would have been like to have joined the nameless woman and watched my great-great-grandfather march by on his way to Mansfield's killing ground.

Even after I began teaching in the 1970s I regularly encountered people who remembered Civil War veterans. I once took a high school class to Vicksburg, Mississippi, and hired an elderly lady as a tour guide. As a young girl in 1917 she witnessed the famous "walking stick war" that occurred when several thousand veterans held a reunion there. "My father and I went to town in the wagon," she told my mesmerized students, "and as we approached the campground we could hear a low rumble, like thunder. We rounded the bend and there were all these old gray-bearded men rolling on the ground. Some didn't even have an arm or leg, but they were hitting, kicking, and biting each other. They got to talking about the battle and somebody must have said something somebody didn't like and they lit into each other again. It was the strangest thing I had ever seen, but Daddy just whipped the horses and we drove on through."

A few years later an acquaintance allowed me to use the diary of Corporal Joseph W. Ely of Michigan for my master's thesis. When I learned that Ely's granddaughter, Leona Farnsworth, still lived in Michigan, my wife, Carol, and I visited her and arranged to return the diary to the family. Ms. Farnsworth showed us some of Ely's letters and photographs and shared her memories of living with the old veteran when she was a young girl. While looking at one photograph, she pointed out he was missing the tip of his ring finger and said he lost it during a battle outside Atlanta. "He said he didn't even know he was wounded until the fighting was over and he noticed his hand felt warm. When he looked down, my grandfather saw the fingertip was just hanging by a piece of skin, so he took out his pocketknife, cut it off, and wrapped the stub with his handkerchief."

Ms. Farnsworth also showed us a letter in which Ely mentioned that his fiancée, Maggie, had married another man while he was fighting in the Atlanta Campaign. "When he returned home, my grandfather went over to Maggie's house and stood in her yard and sang 'When This Cruel War Is Over' as loud as he could. She busted out crying, but he just mounted his horse and rode back home."

Before visiting Ms. Farnsworth I, a son of the Deep South, had never much considered how Northerners felt about the Civil War. But the trip to Michigan demonstrated to me that it was as important a part of their family heritage as it was of mine. In his 1861 inaugural address Abraham Lincoln reminded the nation that all Americans were bound together by the "mystic cords of memory." Those words still ring true today, particularly in regard to the Civil War. That conflict and the Reconstruction period that followed settled the critical issues of secession, slavery, and citizenship, but they also left deep wounds that are still red and angry and painful to the touch. One reason the Civil War resonates so strongly with us today is because it is a recent event in our collective memory. The last Union veteran died in 1956 and the last Confederate in 1959. Incredibly the last Union widow died in 2003 and the last Confederate widow in 2004.

The war may have ended 150 years ago, but many Americans today are only one generation removed from Appomattox, and family history is judged in terms of generations, not years.

During their lifetime most of my fellow baby boomers will personally know relatives whose lives, collectively, will span four centuries: as youngsters we frequently visited with elderly relatives who were born in the nineteenth century and who intimately knew Civil

War veterans; by the time we pass on, we will have known relatives who will live into the twenty-second century. A family's collective memory is strong, and in that memory the guns have not been long silent. The ashes of Civil War campfires are still warm, and Rebel Yells and Yankee huzzahs still echo in the hills.

Teddy Roosevelt's Confederate Uncles

EDWARD P. KOHN

On June 19, 1864, the Confederacy lost one of its most effective weapons of the Civil War: in the Battle of Cherbourg off the coast of France, the Union warship *Kearsarge* sunk the notorious Confederate commerce raider the *Alabama*. In its two-year career the *Alabama* had claimed sixty-five ships, totaling $6 million, a huge hit to the Union war effort. The *Alabama* continued to wreak posthumous havoc after the war; since it had been built in England, in the late 1860s the United States pressed a claim for damages, even threatening to invade Canada as compensation.

But for all that, the most enduring effect of the *Alabama* may have been its influence on a young Theodore Roosevelt.

The New York Roosevelts were sober Yankee bankers and businessmen. Roosevelt's father, Theodore Sr., was a partner in the family business, Roosevelt and Son, a member of the Union League Club, and a leading philanthropist.

But Young Roosevelt's mother, Martha "Mittie" Bulloch, was a classic Southern belle who raised her children on stories of the Old South and the era of slavery, grand plantations, and chivalrous duels. Quite in contrast to the dour Roosevelts, the Bullochs included soldiers and adventurers. "From hearing of the feats performed by my Southern forefathers and kinfolk," Roosevelt wrote in his memoirs many years later, "I felt a great admiration for men who were fearless and who could hold their own in the world, and I had great desire to be like them."

Such feats of heroism included duty toward the Confederacy during the Civil War. Unlike the Roosevelt men, none of whom served in the war, virtually every male relative or acquaintance on the Bulloch side joined the Confederacy. The two leading heroes of Mittie's stories were her brother Irvine Bulloch and her half-brother James Dunwody Bulloch.

Both men served on the water. When war broke out, nineteen-year-old Irvine left the University of Pennsylvania to join the Confederate Navy. James initially became a Confederate captain and blockade-runner but was later tasked with the secret mission of having ships built for the navy in England.

Their exploits made a great impact on Roosevelt. Even during the war letters and news of Roosevelt's two uncles reached the Roosevelt home on East 20th Street in New York City and were shared with the children. In early 1862 the elder Roosevelt

Bulloch Hall, outside Atlanta, where Theodore Roosevelt's mother and uncles were raised. Library of Congress Prints and Photographs Division, LC-DIG-csas-00562.

learned that Irvine had run the Union blockade to deliver fourteen thousand Enfield rifles to Savannah, Georgia. In February 1863 young Irvine wrote movingly, "The life [at sea] is as hard as it is exciting, as painful to be away from home and family as it is pleasant to think I am doing my all for my oppressed country."

The lifetime effect of such words during wartime on a four-year-old boy, already outfitted in his own Zouave uniform—"Is me a soldier?" he asked—is incalculable. In 1905 President Roosevelt visited Roswell, Georgia, the site of Mittie Bulloch's childhood home, Bulloch Hall. In a speech Roosevelt underscored his Southern ancestry. "Men and women," the president asked the crowd, "don't you think I have the ancestral right to claim a proud kinship with those who showed their devotion to duty as they saw the duty, whether they wore the gray or whether they wore the blue?"

Central to the uncles' nautical heroism was the *Alabama*. James had commissioned the construction of the cruiser by the British shipbuilders, Laird Brothers, near Liverpool, testing the limits of British neutrality during the war. Everyone involved in its construction assumed the ship was being built for the Confederacy. Its sides were even pierced for cannon ports. America's minister to London, Charles Francis Adams Sr., collected documents and affidavits testifying to the ship's true nature and presented them to the queen's advocate. The documents lay untouched on the official's desk for five crucial days as the man suffered a complete mental breakdown. Meanwhile Irvine planned the *Alabama*'s escape. On July 29, 1862, the ship took to the seas ostensibly for a trial run, complete with a party of well-wishers on board. Once at sea the sightseers were sent back to shore by tug, while the *Alabama* continued on to the Azores to be outfitted for war. For the next two years the Confederate cruiser wrought havoc on Union shipping.

In the Azores the *Alabama* took on cannon, equipment, and a crew that included Midshipman Irvine Bulloch. Irvine was the cruiser's youngest officer and was said to have fired its last shot before being sunk during the Battle of Cherbourg. After the sinking a notice in the *New York Times* on August 8, 1864, reported the survival of Midshipman Bulloch, presumably for the benefit of his New York relatives.

Roosevelt's contact with his uncles was not limited to letters and stories. In his memoirs he recounted that shortly after the war both uncles had traveled incognito from Britain to New York City to visit their sister and her family—although only Irvine may have actually made the trip. As Irvine and James had been denied amnesty offered to Confederate soldiers, they settled in Liverpool to work in the cotton trade. During the Roosevelt family's European grand tour of 1869, they were reunited with the uncles in Liverpool, and Roosevelt saw the uncles again during his honeymoon in 1881.

Roosevelt recounted these visits in two separate diaries, kept as a boy and as a young man, and also in his 1913 autobiography. "Have enjoyed the time so much," he wrote in his diary on September 14, 1881. "Spent most of the day with the dear old sea captain, Uncle Jimmie Bulloch." By this time Roosevelt was working on a book about the naval history of the War of 1812, and he sought the advice of Captain Bulloch, who familiarized his nephew with naval warfare in the time of sailing ships. Roosevelt published his book the following year, acknowledging his uncle, "without whose advice and sympathy this work would probably never have been written."

His Confederate uncles reinforced an important aspect of Roosevelt's personality that has been mostly forgotten: the twenty-sixth president loved the water. Thanks to his uncles, Roosevelt's mother during his boyhood had spun tales of, as he later recounted, "ships, ships, ships and the fighting of ships, until they sank into the depths of my soul." Indeed, from a young age Roosevelt conducted a love affair with all things nautical. Summers were spent rowing and sailing on Long Island Sound. His most common practice was to row around Center Island, which jutted into Oyster Bay Harbor and was attached to the mainland by a narrow, low-lying isthmus. Low tide would force Roosevelt to portage his boat from the Sound back into the harbor. Diary entries note which sails he used, and he peppered his language with nautical terms ("running sea," "shipped water").

Throughout his life Roosevelt wrote and spoke extensively about the need for a strong American Navy—"Our Peacemaker," as he once put it.

While Roosevelt's actions with the Rough Riders cavalry regiment during the war with Spain have received most attention, arguably his most important role in the conflict came before Congress's declaration of war in April 1898. Until then he had served as assistant secretary of the navy. With Secretary John D. Long of Massachusetts usually away, Roosevelt had significant latitude in the conduct of the office on the eve of war. He helped build up the navy into a modern fighting force that could challenge the Spanish Empire at sea. Indeed the whole point of Roosevelt's famous charge during the Battle of San Juan was that the navy had the Spanish fleet bottled up in Santiago Harbor: the Rough Riders' taking the heights above the city made the Spanish ships' position untenable, and this loss of naval power brought an end to Spanish rule in the Western Hemisphere.

More well-known is the fact that, while assistant secretary during the war with Spain, Roosevelt sent orders to Commodore George Dewey and the Pacific Squadron to resupply at Hong Kong and move on Spain's major holding in the East, the Philippines. Dewey's complete victory at Manila was one shared by Roosevelt; no wonder his family and close friends advocated that Roosevelt stay in that office rather than resign for a cavalry commission. As the navy would play such a vital role in victory, Roosevelt's tenure as assistant secretary of the navy was sure to be rewarded.

Roosevelt received that reward anyway, first becoming governor of New York, and then vice president and president. While president he continued to advocate for a larger and more modern navy. In 1907 he dispatched a battle fleet to circumnavigate the globe to demonstrate America's growing military power, especially after acquiring overseas possessions in the war that he helped win. One of Roosevelt's final official acts as president was to welcome home the "Great White Fleet"—so-called because the hulls of the ships were painted peacetime white rather than wartime gray—when it arrived at Hampton Roads, Virginia, in February 1909.

Early on the morning of June 18, 1910, America welcomed home former president Roosevelt as he returned from a yearlong African safari and trip through Europe. His reception was a decidedly naval affair. As his own ship, the *Kaiserin Auguste Victoria*, steamed toward Manhattan, she was escorted by the new battleship *South Carolina* and five torpedo destroyers, the construction of all the ships having been authorized during his presidency. Roosevelt stood mesmerized as the massive battleship passed to starboard. Along the decks her crew dressed her sides, while the marine band in their scarlet uniforms could easily be spied on the quarterdeck. Just as eight bells struck on all the ships, the band began playing "The Star-Spangled Banner," the large national ensigns were hoisted at the stern, and along the entire length of all the ships red, white, and blue bunting was unrolled. For Roosevelt it was an impressive introduction to the *South Carolina*, the first American dreadnought he had ever seen and an early example of the massive ships that would play such a key role in projecting American power during the twentieth century.

Roosevelt made his final home at Sagamore Hill on Oyster Bay, spending entire days rowing with his wife, Edith, on the Long Island Sound. When he died at home on January 6, 1919, he was buried at a nearby Oyster Bay cemetery, remaining near the water he loved so much.

Despite his later reputation as a western figure—cowboy, rancher, hunter—Roosevelt's lifelong love of all things nautical confirmed his eastern, urban origins as the only American president born in New York City. And he had his Bulloch uncles to thank for this. One of the many ironies of Theodore Roosevelt is that this quintessential American president who spoke of "True Americanism" was so heavily influenced by two infamous members of the Confederacy.

The Civil War's Environmental Impact

Ted Widmer

The Civil War was the most lethal conflict in American history, by a wide margin. But the conventional metric we use to measure a war's impact—the number of human lives it took—does not fully convey the damage it caused. This was an environmental catastrophe of the first magnitude, with effects that endured long after the guns were silenced. It could be argued that they have never ended.

All wars are environmental catastrophes. Armies destroy farms and livestock; they go through forests like termites; they foul waters; they spread disease; they bombard the countryside with heavy armaments and leave unexploded shells; they deploy chemical poisons that linger far longer than the fighting itself; they leave detritus and garbage behind. Rusted-out chemical weapons from the 1980s harmed American soldiers in Iraq—chemical weapons designed in the United States and never properly disposed of. World War II's poisons have been leaching into the earth's waters and atmosphere for more than half a century. In Flanders farmers still dig up unexploded shells from World War I.

Now a rising school of historians has begun to go back further in time to chronicle the environmental impact of the Civil War. It is a devastating catalog. The war may have begun haltingly, but it soon became total, and in certain instances a war on civilians and the countryside as well as on the opposing forces. General William T. Sherman famously explained that he wanted the people of the South to feel "the hard hand of war," and so he cut a wide swath on his march to the sea in November and December 1864. "We devoured the land," he wrote in a letter to his wife.

General Philip H. Sheridan pursued a similar scorched-earth campaign in the Shenandoah Valley in September and October 1864, burning farms and factories and anything else that might be useful to the Confederates. General Ulysses S. Grant told him to "eat out Virginia clear and clear as far as they go, so that crows flying over it for the balance of the season will have to carry their provender with them."

But the war's damage was far more pervasive than that. In every theater Northern and Southern armies lived off the land, helping themselves to any form of food they could find, animal and vegetable. These armies were huge, mobile communities, bigger than any city in the South save New Orleans. They cut down enormous numbers of trees for the wood they needed to warm themselves, to cook, and to build railroad bridges and other military structures. Captain Theodore Dodge of New York wrote from Virginia, "It is wonderful how the whole country round here is literally stripped of its timber. Woods which, when we came here, were so thick that we could not get through them any way are now entirely cleared."

Northern trees were also cut in prodigious numbers to help furnish railroad ties, corduroy roads, ship masts, and naval stores like turpentine, resin, pitch, and tar. The historian Megan Kate Nelson estimates that 2 million trees were killed during the war. The Union and Confederate armies annually consumed 400,000 acres of forest for firewood alone. With no difficulty any researcher can find photographs from 1864 and 1865 that show barren fields and a landscape shorn of vegetation.

When the armies discharged their weapons it was even worse. In the aftermath of a great battle observers were dumbstruck at the damage caused to farms and forests. A New York surgeon, Daniel M. Holt, was at the Battle of Spotsylvania Court House in 1864 and wrote, "Trees are perfectly riddled with bullets." Perhaps no battle changed the landscape more than the Battle of the Crater, in which an enormous, explosives-packed mine was detonated underneath Confederate lines, leaving 278 dead and a depression that is still visible.

Still the weapons used were less terrible than the weapons contemplated. Chemical weapons were a topic of considerable interest, North and South. A Richmond newspaper reported breathlessly on June 4, 1861, "It is well known that there are some chemicals so poisonous that an atmosphere impregnated with them, makes it impossible [for men] to remain where they are by filling large shells of extraordinary capacity with poisonous gases and throwing them very rapidly." In May 1862 Lincoln received a letter from a New York schoolteacher, John W. Doughty, urging that he fill heavy shells with a choking gas of liquid chlorine to poison the enemy in their trenches. The letter was routed to the War Department and never acted upon, but in 1915 the Germans pursued a similar strategy at Ypres, to devastating effect.

But the land fought back in its way. Insects thrived in the camps, in part because the armies destroyed the forest habitats of the birds, bats, and other predators that would have kept pest populations down. Mosquitoes carried out their own form of aerial attack on unsuspecting men from both sides. More than 1.3 million U.S. soldiers were affected by mosquito-borne illnesses like malaria and yellow fever. An Ohio private, Isaac Jackson, wrote, "The skeeters here are—well, there is no use talking. . . . I never seen the like." Flies, ticks, maggots, and chiggers added to the misery.

The army camps were almost designed to attract them. Fetid latrines and impure water bred disease and did more to weaken the ranks than actual warfare. Some

1.6 million Union troops suffered from diarrhea and dysentery; Southern numbers were surely proportional. Rats were abundant on both sides, carrying germs and eating their way through any food they could find.

Probably the worst places of all were the prisoner camps. A Massachusetts private, Amos Stearns, wrote a two-line poem from his confinement in South Carolina: "A Confederate prison is the place / Where hunting for lice is no disgrace." Some Alabama prisoners in a New York prison made a stew of the prison's rat population. ("They taste very much like a young squirrel," wrote Lieutenant Edmund D. Patterson.)

Smart soldiers adapted to the land, using local plants as medicines and food and taking shelter behind canebrakes and other natural formations. In this the Southerners surely had an advantage. A Georgia private, William R. Stillwell, wrote his wife facetiously of Northern efforts to starve the South: "You might as well try to starve a black hog in the piney woods." But the better Northern soldiers adapted too, finding fruits, nuts, and berries as needed. A Vermont corporal, Rufus Kinsley, making his way through Louisiana, wrote, "Not much to eat but alligators and blackberries: plenty of them." Shooting at birds was another easy way to get food; a Confederate sergeant stationed in Louisiana, Edwin H. Fay, credited local African Americans with great skill at duck hunting, writing his wife, "Negroes bring them in by horseback loads."

Nevertheless the Northern effort to reduce the food available to Southern armies did take a toll. In the spring of 1863 Robert E. Lee wrote, "The question of food for this army gives me more trouble than anything else combined." His invasion of Pennsylvania was driven in part by a need to find new ways to feed his troops, and his troops helped themselves to food just as liberally as Sherman's did in Georgia, appropriating around 100,000 animals from Pennsylvania farms.

While the old economy was adapting to the extraordinary demands of the war, a new economy was springing up alongside it, in response to unceasing demands for energy, for heat, power, cooking, and a thousand other short-term needs. As the world's whale population began to decline in the 1850s, a new oily substance was becoming essential. Petroleum was first discovered in large quantities in northwestern Pennsylvania in 1859, on the eve of the war. As the Union mobilized for the war effort, it provided enormous stimulus to the new commodity, whose uses were not fully understood yet but included lighting and lubrication. Coal production also rose quickly during the war. The sudden surge in fossil fuels altered the American economy permanently.

Every mineral that had an industrial use was extracted and put to use in significantly larger numbers than before the war. A comparison of the 1860 and 1870 censuses reveals a dramatic surge in all of the extractive industries and every sector of the American economy, with one notable exception: Southern agriculture, which would need another decade to return to prewar levels. These developments were interpreted as evidence of the Yankee genius for industry, and little thought was given to aftereffects. The overwhelming need to win the war was paramount, outweighing any moral calculus about the price to be borne by future generations. Still that price was beginning to be calculated; the first scientific attempt to explain heat-trapping gases in the earth's atmosphere and the greenhouse effect was made in 1859 by an Irish scientist, John Tyndall.

Other effects took more time to be noticed. It is doubtful that any species loss was sustained during the war, despite the death of large numbers of animals that wandered into harm's way. It has been speculated that more than a million horses and mules were casualties of the war. But the most notable extinction of the late nineteenth and early twentieth century—that of the passenger pigeon—began to occur as huge numbers of veterans were returning home, at the same time the arms industry was reaching staggering levels of production and designing new weapons that nearly removed the difficulty of reloading. The Winchester Model 66 repeating rifle debuted the year after the war ended, firing thirty times a minute. More than 170,000 would be sold between 1866 and 1898. Colt's revolvers sold in even higher numbers; roughly 200,000 of the Model 1860 Army Revolver were made between 1860 and 1873. Gun clubs sprang up nearly overnight; sharpshooters became popular heroes; and the National Rifle Association was founded by two veterans in 1871.

History does not prove that this was the reason for the demise of the passenger pigeon, a species that once astonished observers with flocks so large they darkened the sky. But a culture of game-shooting spread quickly in the years immediately after the war, accelerated not only by widespread gun ownership but by a supply-and-demand infrastructure developed during the war, along the rails. When Manhattan diners wanted to eat pigeon, there were always hunters in the upper Midwest willing to shoot at boundless birds—until suddenly the birds were gone. They declined from billions to dozens between the 1870s and the 1890s. One hunt alone, in 1871, killed 1.5 million birds. Another, three years

Soldiers escaping a forest fire during the Battle of the Wilderness, 1864. Library of Congress Prints and Photographs Division, LC-DIG-ppmsca-21457.

later, killed 25,000 pigeons a day for five to six weeks. The last known passenger pigeon, Martha, died on September 1, 1914.

That was only one way Americans ultimately came to face the hard fact of nature's limits. It was a fact that defied most of their cultural assumptions about the limitless quality of the land available to them, but it was a fact all the same. Some began to grasp it even while the war was being fought. If the fighting left many scars upon the land, it also planted the seeds for a new movement to preserve what was left. As the forests vanished, a few visionaries began to speak up on their behalf and argue for a new kind of stewardship. Though it was simplistic at first (the world *ecology* would not be invented until 1866), it is possible to see a new vocabulary emerging and a conservation movement that would grow out of these first, halting steps. Henry David Thoreau would not survive the war—he died in 1862—but he borrowed from some of its imagery to bewail a "war on the wilderness" that he saw all around him. His final manuscripts suggest that he was working on a book about the power of seeds to bring rebirth—not a great distance from what Abraham Lincoln would say in the Gettysburg Address.

Another advocate came from deep within Lincoln's State Department: his minister to Italy, George Perkins Marsh, a polymath who spent the Civil War years working on his masterpiece, *Man and Nature*, which came out in 1864. With passion and painstaking evidence it condemned the unthinking, unseeing way most Americans experienced their environment, dismissing nature as little more than a resource to be used and discarded. Marsh was especially eloquent on forests, which he had studied closely as a boy growing up in Vermont and then as a businessman in lumber. With scientific precision he affirmed all of their life-giving properties, from soil improvement to species diversification, flood prevention, climate moderation, and disease control. But he was a philosopher too, and like Thoreau he worried about a consumerist mentality that seemed to be conducting its own form of war against nature. In a section titled "The Destructiveness of Man" he wrote, "Man has too long forgotten that the earth was given to him for usufruct alone, not for consumption, still less for profligate waste."

Slowly the government began to respond to these voices. After some agitation by the landscape architect Frederick Law Olmsted, then living in California, a bill to set aside the land for Yosemite National Park was signed by Abraham Lincoln on June 30, 1864. The land was given to California on the condition that it "shall be held for public use, resort, and recreation" and shall, like the rights enshrined by the Declaration, be "inalienable for all time." In 1872 even more land would be set aside for Yellowstone.

Southerners too expressed reverence for nature. On August 4, 1861, General Lee wrote his wife from what is now West Virginia, "I enjoyed the mountains, as I rode along. The views are magnificent—the valleys so beautiful, the scenery so peaceful. What a glorious world Almighty God has given us. How thankless and ungrateful we are, and how we labour to mar his gifts."

But neither he nor his fellow Southerners were able to resist a second invasion of the South that followed the war: the rush by Northern interests to buy huge quantities of forested land in order to fill the marketplace for lumber in the decades of rebuilding and westward migration that ensued, including the fences that were needed to mark off new land, the railroads that were needed to get people there, and the telegraph lines that were needed to stay in communication with them. Railroad tracks nearly tripled between 1864 and 1875, to 90,000 miles in 1875 from 32,000 miles in 1864. Between 1859 and 1879 the consumption of wood in the United States roughly doubled, to 6.84 billion cubic feet a year from 3.76 billion. Roughly 300,000 acres of forests a year needed to be cut down to satisfy this demand.

The historian Michael Williams has called what followed "the assault on Southern forests." As the industry exhausted the forests of the upper Midwest (having earlier exhausted New England and New York), it turned to the South, and over the next generation reduced its woodlands by about 40 percent, from 300 million to 178 million acres, of which only 39 million acres were virgin forest. By about 1920 the South had been sufficiently exploited that the industry largely moved on, leaving a defoliated landscape behind, and often found loopholes to avoid paying taxes on the land it still owned. In 1923 an industry expert, R. D. Forbes, wrote, "Their villages are Nameless Towns, their monuments huge piles of saw dust, their epitaph: The mill cut out."

Paradoxically there are few places in the United States today where it is easier to savor nature than a Civil War battlefield. Thanks to generations of activism in the North and South, an extensive network of fields and cemeteries has been protected by state and federal legislation and is generally safe from development. These beautiful oases of tranquility have become precisely the opposite of what they were during the heat of battle. (Indeed they have become so peaceful that Gettysburg officials have too many white-tailed deer, requiring what is euphemistically known as "deer management," as shots again ring out on the old battlefield.) They promote a reverence for the land as well as our history, and in their way they have become sacred shrines to conservation.

Perhaps we can do more to teach the war in the same way that we walk the battlefields, conscious of the environment, using all of our senses to hear the sounds, see the sights, and feel the great relevance of nature to the Civil War. Perhaps we can do even better than that, and summon a new resolve before the environmental challenges that lie ahead. As Lincoln noted, government of the people did not perish from the earth. Let's hope that the earth does not perish from the people.

How the Civil War Created College Football

AMANDA BRICKELL BELLOWS

At a ceremony in Cambridge, Massachusetts, on June 10, 1890, the philanthropist Henry Lee Higginson declared, "I ask to make [Soldiers Field] a memorial to some dear friends who gave their lives ... to their country and to their fellow men in the hour of great need—the War of the Rebellion." The thirty-one acres of marshlands and pasture that Higginson donated to Harvard College, his alma mater, would serve as the site of the country's oldest concrete football arena, Harvard Stadium, built over a decade later in 1903. As he memorialized the Civil War dead, the Union veteran addressed a group of four hundred male students and alumni, most of whom were too young to have experienced and learned from the horrors of battle during the nation's bloodiest war. Like Higginson, however, many late nineteenth-century Americans saw a deep connection between the battlefield and the athletic field, believing that collegiate athletics, including football, could teach the next generation their "own duties as men and citizens of the Republic" and train them to manage "the burden of carrying on this country in the best way."

Prior to football's postwar rise in popularity, antebellum Americans enjoyed sporting events like boxing, harness racing, and early forms of baseball. According to the historians Elliott J. Gorn and Warren Goldstein, however, the Civil War "engendered an ethos of sacrifice, of dedication to the heroic cause" in male soldiers who played a variety of organized sports on teams within military units. After the war's end universities took on the role of creating student athletes through organized sports initiatives that inculcated in young men the Victorian virtues of masculinity and sportsmanship. Educational institutions began to emphasize the importance of athletics; in 1872 the *New York World* remarked, "There can scarcely be any question . . . that the increasing impulse towards athletics in all our colleges is in itself a good thing."

The Rutgers University football team, 1891. Library of Congress Prints and Photographs Division, LC-DIG-ds-03688.

Football was one of the most popular of these new collegiate activities, and it developed rapidly. The first intercollegiate American football game occurred on November 6, 1869, when students from Princeton and Rutgers faced off in an informal match. Rutgers confronted Columbia in 1870, and Harvard and Yale first battled in 1875. University football teams continued to multiply in number after Princeton, Yale, Columbia, and Harvard established the Intercollegiate Football Association in 1876.

A hybrid of early American folk football and British rugby, postbellum American football was a violent sport that, according to the historian Allen Guttmann, appealed to young men hoping to "demonstrate the manly courage that their fathers and older brothers had recently proved on the bloody battlefields of the Civil War." Bravery was a prerequisite for players in an era preceding the widespread use of helmets. In 1905 alone 18 players were killed and 159 sustained severe wounds, statistics that motivated several universities to shut down the sport on their campuses. Yet despite its rough nature, football continued to flourish at many leading institutions.

In the late nineteenth and early twentieth century Americans imbued football games with military significance. In 1908 the *New-York Tribune* reported, "Football as played in America to-day between schools or colleges is not a mere game [but] an intercollegiate contest [that] assumes in the minds of players, coaches, students, graduates, and the affiliated public the importance of war."

Many viewed football as a way of training the next generation of men for military service. *Harper's Weekly* stated in 1898 that "the value of football as a means of keeping alive a martial spirit in time of peace has been abundantly dwelt upon" and that "veteran football-players would be expected to excel ... if war came." Describing Princeton's triumphant football team in 1897, the sportswriter Caspar Whitney declared, "Had those same men been drilled in the science of war instead of in the science of football, the same

Civil War veterans and reenacters gathered in Florida for a sham battle, 1895. Courtesy of Florida State Archives.

persistency of purpose and unity of endeavor would have attained the same conquest over their opponents."

For many football was itself training for war. Football manuals of the late nineteenth and early twentieth century describe the sport as a military endeavor. In his 1895 *Book of College Sports*, Yale's coach Walter Camp encouraged players to exhibit the bravery of a soldier entering a difficult battle; a player should "face it like a man . . . on the side of the men who want no chance of retreat or escape, only a fair contest and certain victory or defeat at the end of it." In 1921, in his manual *American Football: How to Play It*, Charles Daly, the coach of the U.S. Military Academy, called football "a war game" and described troops marching to battle, teams combating an enemy squad, scouts reconnoitering, and linemen charging. Striving to show the "remarkable similarity [that] exists between war and football," Daly even advocated the application of military exercises to players, arguing, "No soldier ever benefited more by intensive and carefully planned drill than does the football player."

Football's traditions further reveal its martial sensibilities; for example, as the political scientist Michael Mandelbaum notes, athletes stream onto the field in brightly colored uniforms, marching bands perform rousing tunes, and students collectively sing to encourage their champions. Intriguingly, early fight songs reveal that memories of the Civil War persisted during the postwar era. Just six years after the war ended, Rutgers students chanted their "Foot-Ball Song": "We'll quickly bury all the slain / And to-morrow the living are ready again, / To follow that bully foot-ball."

Reflecting on the nation's wartime wounds, educators sought to equip young men for military action by teaching them about masculinity and courage through collegiate football. Americans' desire to remember or learn from the conflict shaped the sport's militaristic rules, lexicon, rituals, and popular perceptions. As a result football's Civil War lineage is still perceptible today.

How Lincoln Became Our Favorite President

JOSHUA ZEITZ

Today Americans almost universally regard Abraham Lincoln as our greatest president. And yet he was not always the revered figure that he has become.

Writing many decades after Lincoln's assassination, John Hay, who served as one of Lincoln's secretaries, observed that if the president had "died in the days of doubt and gloom which preceded his re-election," rather than in the final weeks of the Civil War, he would almost certainly have been remembered differently, despite his great acts and deeds. Indeed just months before his death many leading members of his own political party agreed with Governor John Andrew of Massachusetts, who found Lincoln "essentially lacking in the quality of leadership."

John Hay, circa 1897. Library of Congress Prints and Photographs Division, LC-USZ62-48334.

Though his assassination on Good Friday essentially apotheosized the martyred president, as emotions receded the initial wave of commemorations was far from adulatory.

The first person to memorialize Lincoln officially was the celebrated historian George Bancroft. A Democrat who had served in James Polk's cabinet, Bancroft was an odd choice for the job. In his official eulogy before Congress, delivered in February 1866, he delivered a cool if polite rebuke of Lincoln's administrative skills and fitness for high office. The speech was well received in literary and political circles, though Lincoln loyalists like Hay fumed that it "was a disgraceful exhibition of ignorance and prejudice."

To Hay, Lincoln was "the greatest character since Christ." But to others, like the diplomat Charles Francis Adams, he was a kindhearted, well-meaning politician, ill suited to the challenges of the wartime presidency. "I must affirm without hesitation," Adams said in his eulogy for William Henry Seward, "that in the history of our government, down to this hour, no experiment so rash has ever been made as that of elevating to the head of affairs a man with so little previous preparation for the task as Mr. Lincoln." By good grace and fortune Lincoln had been wise enough to make Seward the "master mind" of the administration.

Adams was not alone in this opinion. In his popular account of the war years, *The American Conflict*, Horace Greeley remembered Lincoln as a hapless leader who squandered countless opportunities to end the war early, either on the battlefield or through negotiation.

Aiding this pejorative rendering of Lincoln was a strain of popular history that sought to humanize the slain president, often in the extreme. The most important figure in this movement was William Herndon, Lincoln's former law partner, who complained that Lincoln "was not God—was man. He was not perfect—had some defects & a few positive faults: [but] he was a good man—an honest man." Herndon scoured the Indiana and Illinois countryside for people whom Lincoln had known in his youth to interview, and then took to the lecture circuit in an attempt to remind his countrymen that the sixteenth president had been flesh and blood and hardly without flaws.

From Herndon's lectures and, later, from a popular biography penned by the politicians Ward Hill Lamon and Chauncey Black, based on Herndon's notes, Americans learned (incorrectly) that Lincoln's mother was a "bastard" and that she, like her own mother, had cuckolded her husband. The president's father was not, they said, Thomas Lincoln but one Abraham Enlow. How else to explain the achievements of one born so low? Herndon also insisted that his former partner was an atheist or deist and not a "technical Christian," provoking a violent debate about Lincoln's religious beliefs. Herndon portrayed him as an able country lawyer with relentless ambition for political office, not the disinterested statesman of Lincoln Memorial fame.

"Mr. Wm. H. Herndon is making an ass of himself," Robert Todd Lincoln wrote in a blind rage, but since he "speaks with a certain amount of authority from having known my father for so long," his story, "even if it were . . . all true," would do great injury to his family's reputation.

It ultimately fell to the president's former secretaries, John Hay and John Nicolay, to salvage the Lincoln legacy. Working closely with Robert, who gave them exclusive access to the president's papers (the collection remained sealed to other researchers until 1947), the secretaries spent over twenty years researching and writing a monumental, ten-volume life of Lincoln. Their work, which was serialized between 1886 and 1890 in the *Century* magazine, replaced the popular imagery of an ill-schooled, rough-hewn western lawyer with the Lincoln we know today: the wise and knowing leader, the master of a fractious cabinet, the emancipator of slaves, the kind father figure to a nation.

Most important, Hay and Nicolay swam against the tide of intersectional harmony and historical amnesia to place slavery, not states' rights, at the center of the Civil War and to declare emancipation, not Unionism, Lincoln's signature accomplishment.

Though Hay and Nicolay's biography became the standard-bearer for over half a century, many artists and writers still chose to emphasize the martyred president's human qualities, albeit more respectfully than did Herndon, Lamon, and Black. In 1917 the city of Cincinnati unveiled a new statue of Lincoln by George Grey Barnard. Barnard's work portrayed the president as a clean-shaven western lawyer with plain clothes and a chiseled, rugged face. The sculptor intended to show "the mighty man who grew from our soil and the hardships of the earth. . . . He must have stood as the republic should stand, strong, simple, carrying its weight unconsciously without pride in rank and culture."

Robert was incensed. He viewed the statue as "monstrous," a "grotesque . . . likeness of President Lincoln . . . defamatory as an effigy." Genuinely taken aback by the family's response, Barnard explained, "Your father belongs to future ages, and all sculptors of this generation and those to come, must have as their birthright, as children of Democracy and Art, full liberty to express their interpretation of the life of Lincoln." But Robert was unmoved. His opposition was so compelling that the British government scuttled plans to erect a copy of the statue in Parliament Square.

By contrast the official keepers of the presidential flame were immensely happy with early plans for the Lincoln Memorial, with a sculpture by the renowned Daniel Chester French. Its placement on the Potomac Flats, at the western end of the Mall, pleased Hay, who believed that Lincoln's "monument should stand alone, remote from the common habitations of man, apart from the business and turmoil of the city; isolated, distinguished, and serene."

In contrast to Barnard's rendering, French, in his own words, set out to create a statue that would "convey the mental and physical strength of the great President and his confidence in his ability to carry the thing through to a successful finish." Robert gave the final product his official endorsement when, in 1922, he attended the memorial's dedication.

Though the Lincoln Memorial quickly became an immensely popular tourist attraction and national icon, it was not until 1939 that the modern civil rights movement staked a claim on its symbolism. That year the Daughters of the American Revolution denied Howard University permission to use Constitution Hall for a concert by the renowned black opera soloist, Marian Anderson. Walter White, the head of the NAACP, asked the National Park Service for permission to stage the event in Lafayette Park, across from the White House. Upon learning that the park was off limits, White proclaimed, "Oh, my God, if we could have her sing at the feet of Lincoln!" He took the request to Interior Secretary Harold Ickes, who took it to Franklin Roosevelt. "Tell Oscar he has my permission to have Marian sing from the top of the Washington Monument if he wants it," the president replied, referring to Assistant Interior Secretary Oscar Chapman.

But it was the Lincoln Memorial, not the Washington Monument, that was of the moment. There scores of Supreme Court justices, cabinet members, and congressmen—as well as the first lady Eleanor Roosevelt, who resigned her DAR membership in protest—joined seventy-five thousand attendees, most of them black, to hear Anderson sing. Ickes introduced her, calling the concert a "glorious tribute" to Lincoln's memory "by a daughter of the race from which he struck the chains of slavery." Pointing to both the Washington Monument and the Lincoln Memorial, he lamented that "in our time too many people pay mere lip service to these twin planets in our democratic heaven."

The political and emotional power of Anderson's concert influenced the decision by organizers of the proposed Negro March on Washington in 1941 to end their protest at the Lincoln Memorial, where "Marian Anderson sang at the feet of the great emancipator."

The contrast between Lincoln, the "freer of the slaves," and the current plight of African Americans had by then become painfully obvious. The Negro March on Washington never occurred. In return for Franklin Roosevelt's promise to create a wartime equal employment commission, its organizers called off the march.

How Kentucky Became a Confederate State

CHRISTOPHER PHILLIPS

In the late winter of 1865 Abraham Lincoln was completing a reconciliation-themed second inaugural address, pledging the nation to embrace the end of slavery "that this mighty scourge of war may speedily pass away."

His thoughts were not solely on the last days of the war deep in the Confederacy. Closer to home a war of another kind seemed ongoing. On February 20 the president wrote to Missouri's new governor, Thomas C. Fletcher, troubled by persistent violence and distrust among civilians there. "Waiving all else, pledge each to cease harassing others, and to make common cause against whomever persists in making, aiding or encouraging further disturbance," the president implored. "At such meetings old friendships will cross the memory, and honor and Christian charity will contrive to help." Less than two months later Lincoln was dead at the hands of a Marylander, John Wilkes Booth. Had he lived he would have learned, painfully, that amity would be difficult to find in slaveholding border states, especially over the end of the peculiar institution there.

Lincoln's letter to the new Missouri governor was not sent randomly. His was one of two states, along with Maryland, both controlled legislatively by Radicals, to have emancipated slaves by the time of his second inauguration—Maryland by constitutional convention and plebiscite, Missouri by Fletcher's executive proclamation. Violence erupted, particularly in Missouri. Less than a month before Lincoln's death, one militia commander there explained the late-war violence. "Slavery dies hard," he wrote. "I hear its expiring agonies and witness its contortions in death in every quarter of my district."

Slavery died even harder in the other two border states, Kentucky and Delaware, especially politically. Although polar opposites in terms of slave ownership (Kentucky the largest, Delaware by far the smallest), self-styled Conservative Democrats held political power in both states and rejected the Thirteenth Amendment. (Kentucky would not ratify it until 1976, second to last, ahead of Mississippi.) In the summer of 1865 the Kentuckian Lizzie Hardin returned home after a two-year exile in Georgia to portents of a lingering war. "Slavery in such a condition that neither masters nor Negroes know whether it exists or not, lawlessness of every shade," she wrote, "and in the midst of it all, between Southerners and the Union people a hatred, bitter, unrelenting, and that promises to be eternal."

Postwar violence in the border states was widespread. For Lincoln's murder outraged Unionists "ought to [argue] that Rebels should have but a short rope," wrote one. He would "turn mercy into vengeance." In Wilmington, Delaware, Unionist mobs

A copy of Missouri governor Thomas C. Fletcher's emancipation proclamation, issued January 11, 1865. Library of Congress Prints and Photographs Division, LC-DIG-pga-01806.

tormented known dissenters, demanding they display patriotic emblems or face reprisal. In Louisville, Kentucky, where troops returned from the South to be mustered out, street violence between soldiers and civilians was a daily occurrence.

Now waves of racial violence, characterized by the historian T. J. Stiles as the "war after the war," tore through the border states in this rehearsal for Southern-style Redemption. Newly paroled former Confederates who did come home joined ranks with current and former guerrillas and even anti-emancipation Unionists as "Negro Regulators" or "Ku Klux." In gangs that often numbered in the hundreds they used terror to maintain the political and racial status quo, as well as to undermine or impose new political mandates. In Missouri they threatened entire towns with mass slaughter if all black residents did not leave the state. The counties of southern and western Kentucky, where Klan activity was heaviest in the state, lost on average 17 percent of their black populations. In rural Maryland freed people's churches, which often served as schools, were particular targets of mobs that included doctors, lawyers, and even magistrates. One federal officer claimed, "The civil authorities of the lower part of Delaware and the Eastern Shore accord [freed people] no rights; their churches are burned, their schools broken up, and their persons and property abused by vicious white men."

Especially in the former slaveholding centers of these border states, but also in their white belts, such as on Maryland's Eastern Shore, a three-way struggle soon raged between the occupying federal forces—by the summer of 1865, mostly black—who tried to protect freed people's rights of black citizenship; black residents, who now sought to exert those rights; and embittered white residents (some of them former Unionists and even federal soldiers), who violently denied them rights.

In places like Paducah, Kentucky, the local presence of troops largely suppressed mob attacks on freed people. Many white residents thus begged to have federal troops removed, especially because most were black; Maryland soon sent them to Texas. In areas with few or no garrison troops state authorities maintained restrictive "Black Codes" against freed people, including imposing forced labor.

Violence, especially by former guerrillas and returning Confederates, was widespread enough for the Kentucky legislature to keep its militia mobilized and in service until 1866. In Missouri Governor Fletcher called out the militia to aid county sheriffs in "break[ing] up lawless bands" and authorized another militia enrollment of more than 117,000 men. Unionists in many communities called for protection, and civil authorities and garrisons arrested large numbers of miscreants. Others took up arms themselves as paramilitary "Union regulators." For years many communities witnessed virtual reenactments of the war, with former rebels—"Southern men," as they referred to themselves—exchanging shots with former and federal soldiers in pitched battles, complete with military formations.

Opposition to Radical Republican politics of black freedom went far to change the loyalty of many former Unionists in these border states. White solidarity, as the historian Aaron Astor has claimed, "overwhelm[ed] any residual bitterness over competing loyalties or wartime atrocities." In southern Maryland, where one Unionist claimed many whites "do not hesitate to say that we robbed them of their property," another remarked in the summer of 1865, "The treatment of loyal men in this section has been similar to that received by the freedmen."

As early as 1866 the newly formed *Weekly Caucasian* of Lexington, Missouri, blared to disfranchised white voters that they should resist the state's Radical constitution by fraudulently taking the ironclad oath and registering to vote. Two years later similar white supremacist tropes blared from the first issue of St. Joseph's *Missouri Vindicator*: "We are Caucasian in blood, in birth, and in prejudice."

Inverting Carl von Clausewitz's famous dictum, white border state residents employed postwar politics to achieve thwarted war goals. Ratification of the Thirteenth Amendment and the establishment of the Freedmen's Bureau in Maryland, Kentucky, and portions of Missouri spurred obstructionist political responses in these states. In December 1865 Kentucky's legislature repealed its four-year-old Expatriation Law, reenfranchising former Confederates, and by 1866 insurgent Confederates there swept into office at all levels, replacing the Conservative coalition leadership and reconstituting the Democratic Party as a virtual rebel entity. Many former emancipationists quickly switched to the Democrats or stood with them against the later Reconstruction measures. By 1871 the first of six consecutive Confederate sympathizers, secessionists, or ex-Confederate officers held the governorship.

The Kentucky pattern was replicated in Delaware and Maryland after Radicals were trounced in the latter state's 1866 state legislative elections. Only in Missouri did they maintain legislative power. Consequently, of the border states only Missouri ratified the Fourteenth and Fifteenth Amendments, guaranteeing civil and voting rights to African Americans. But the state would hold out only briefly before a political conversion to a Confederate state nearly as complete as Kentucky's. In 1875 a state constitutional convention met in Jefferson City and overturned the postwar "Drake" constitution (named for the Radical leader Charles D. Drake) to reenfranchise former Confederates. In 1875 the legislature elected Francis M. Cockrell, a former Confederate general, to the U.S. Senate, joined four years later by George G. Vest, who had represented the state in both houses of the Confederate Congress. (Both would serve at least a quarter-century.) In 1884 John Sappington Marmaduke, a former Confederate general, was elected governor.

For many whites in these border states the politics of war memory accomplished a commemorative bridge between their contested Confederate tradition and slaveholding pasts to achieve cultural affinity with the South. With help from Southern contributors, white Kentuckians constructed perhaps the apotheosis of their new Southern memory: the 1924 dedication of the Jefferson Davis birthplace memorial near Fairview in Todd County, among the state's largest antebellum slaveholding counties. The obelisk stands 351 feet tall, some two-thirds the height of the Washington Monument, dedicated to a president to whom the state only collaterally swore allegiance, and within two years the legislature adopted the sentimental antebellum "plantation" song "My Old Kentucky Home" as its state song.

Just over a dozen years later Maryland did the same with the defiant Confederate anthem "Maryland, My Maryland," adapted to pro-Confederate resident James Ryder Randall's dissent poem warning against overweening governmental power. Indeed, after shooting Lincoln, Booth had offered the horrified audience at Ford's Theater a pithy variant of a line from it, referencing Virginia's motto: "*Sic* semper tyrannis!"

These articulations of shared experience between the antebellum and the wartime Souths, and their collective acts of defiance to federal authority during and after the war, allowed white residents a potent reinterpretation of the war by way of a partisan, Southernized collective memory of it. The reimagining of these states transformed them into their more modern incarnation—the Border South—accomplishing, ironically, what the anything but dead Confederacy could not for itself.

Was Abolitionism a Failure?

JON GRINSPAN

On Jan. 31, 1865, Congress passed the Thirteenth Amendment, banning slavery in America. It was an achievement that abolitionists had spent decades fighting for — and one for which their movement has been lauded ever since.

Destruction by Fire of Pennsylvania Hall,

The New Building of the *Abolition Society*, on the night of the 17th May,

Published by J. T. Bowen, 94 Walnut Street, and Sold by George and Cately, 95 Chesnut Street.

Entered according to the Act of Congress, in the year 1838, by J. T. Bowen, in the Clerk's Office of the District Court of the Eastern District of Pennsylvania.

A fire engulfs an abolitionist hall in Philadelphia as anti-abolition activists look on, 1838. Library of Congress Prints and Photographs Division. LC-DIG-pga-04482, Library of Congress, Washington, D.C.

But before abolitionism succeeded, it failed. As a pre-Civil War movement, it was a flop. Antislavery congressmen were able to push through their amendment because of the absence of the pro-slavery South, and the complicated politics of the Civil War. Abolitionism's surprise victory has misled generations about how change gets made.

Today, diverse movements cast themselves as modern versions of the struggle against slavery. The former Republican senator Jim DeMint, now the president of the Heritage Foundation, claimed that small-government "constitutional conservatism" has inherited the cause; the liberal TV host Chris Hayes, writing in *The Nation*, said battling climate change was the "new abolitionism." That term has become shorthand for "fighting the good fight." But the long struggle against slavery shows how jerky, contingent, and downright lucky winning that good fight was.

It's hard to accept just how unpopular abolitionism was before the Civil War. The abolitionist Liberty Party never won a majority in a single county, anywhere in America, in any presidential race. Ralph Nader got closer to the presidency. In 1860 the premier antislavery newspaper, *The Liberator*, had a circulation of under three thousand, in a nation of 31 million.

Even among Northerners who wanted to stop the spread of slavery, the idea of banning it altogether seemed fanatical. On the eve of the Civil War, America's greatest sage, Ralph Waldo Emerson, predicted that slavery might end one day, but "we shall not live to see it."

In a deeply racist society, where most white Americans, South and North, valued sectional unity above equal rights, "abolitionist" was usually a dirty word. One man who campaigned for Abraham Lincoln in 1860 complained: "I have been denounced as impudent, foppish, immature, and worse than all, an Abolitionist."

While we remember the war as a struggle for freedom, at its outset neither Lincoln nor the Republican Party planned to ban slavery. To calm talk of secession, Congress passed a never-ratified, now-forgotten Thirteenth Amendment promising that no amendment could ever end slavery. Lincoln backed it. Going into the conflict, Congress offered to abolish abolitionism, not slavery.

Abolitionism gained strength thanks to the uncompromising stance of radical "fire eating" Southerners. By ostracizing Northern allies, seceding and then starting a war, Southern radicals gave abolitionism gift after gift after gift. When South Carolina militiamen fired on Fort Sumter, Frederick Douglass exalted: "Thank God!—The slaveholders themselves have saved our cause from ruin!"

The war's length and brutality gave further fuel to the abolitionist fire. The historian Gary W. Gallagher has argued that the successful generalship of Robert E. Lee ultimately helped emancipation, pushing bloodied and vengeful Northerners to free slaves. Moderates like Lincoln became convinced that "we must free the slaves or be ourselves subdued."

Still, the war, not the strength of abolitionism, made the difference. When he finally issued the Emancipation Proclamation, Lincoln operated under the president's war powers. And when thousands of slaves freed themselves and fought the Confederacy, they mostly did so as the Union army entered their regions. Antislavery blacks fought bravely and lobbied cannily, helped by the radicalism of their former masters.

By January 1865 the tide had turned. Congress moved to ban slavery everywhere (not just in the Confederacy, but in loyal slave states like Maryland and Kentucky). A body that had tried to make slavery un-abolishable a few years before voted to free 4 million men and women. It could never have passed the amendment if all those Southern congressmen had stayed in Washington to vote against it. Every politician who stormed off to join the Confederacy cast an inadvertent ballot for abolition.

Here's where the confusion emerges. After the war many Americans interpreted slaveholder mistakes as abolitionist victories. Abolition looked like a road map for reform. Many claimed to have been on its side before the war. Publishers printed a torrent of memoirs by supposed abolitionists; everyone who ever cast a ballot for the Liberty Party seemed to write a book about it.

The generation of Americans raised after the Civil War modeled diverse movements on abolitionism, from supporters of labor, women's rights, and socialism to opponents of popular democracy and mass immigration. The Boston poet James Russell Lowell even compared a movement to suppress poor voters to abolitionists, writing: "They emancipated the negro; we mean to emancipate the respectable white man."

Today we point to abolition as proof that we can improve society by eliminating one glaring evil. This is what unites "new abolitionists" across the political spectrum, whether they're working to end the death penalty or ban abortion. We like the idea of sweeping change, of an idealistic movement triumphing over something so clearly wrong.

The problem is, that's not really how slavery ended. Those upright, moral, prewar abolitionists did not succeed. Neither did the stiff-necked Southern radicals who ended up destroying the institution they went to war to maintain. It was the flexibility of the Northern moderates, those flip-floppers who voted against abolition before they voted for it, who really ended 250 years of slavery.

Abolitionists make better heroes, though, principled and courageous and seemingly in step with twenty-first-century values. But people from the past who espoused beliefs we hold today were usually rejected at the time. We can only wonder which of today's unpopular causes will, in 150 years, be considered the abolitionism of 2015.

How the Civil War Changed the World

DON DOYLE

Even while the Civil War raged, slaves in Cuba could be heard singing, "Avanza, Lincoln, avanza! Tu eres nuestra esperanza!" (Onward, Lincoln, Onward! You are our hope!), as if they knew, even before the soldiers fighting the war far to the north and long before most politicians understood, that the war in America would change their lives and the world.

The secession crisis of 1860–61 threatened to be a major setback to the world antislavery movement, and it imperiled the whole experiment in democracy. If slavery was allowed to exist, and if the world's leading democracy could fall apart over the issue, what hope did freedom have? European powers wasted no time in taking advantage of the debacle. France and Britain immediately sent fleets of warships with the official purpose of observing the imminent war in America. In Paris a *New York Times* correspondent with the byline "Malakoff" thought that the French and British observers "may be intended as a sort of escort of honor for the funeral of the Great Republic."

Spain, its fleets already in position in Havana, struck first that March, landing in the Dominican Republic and proclaiming that its former colony had returned to Spanish rule. Seeing no sign of resistance from the Lincoln administration, France, Spain, and Britain met in London in October 1861 to plan an allied invasion of Mexico for the end of the year. Spain and Britain later withdrew, but Emperor Napoleon III of France saw the conquest of Mexico as the key to his Grand Design to regenerate the "Latin race" and thwart the insidious influence of the Anglo-Saxon in both hemispheres. With the collaboration of Mexican conservatives, the French forced Benito Juárez, the republican leader, to flee the capital and eventually installed the Austrian archduke Maximilian as emperor of Mexico.

European conservatives welcomed the dismemberment of the "once United States" and the bursting of the "republican bubble" that, beginning with the French Revolution, had inspired revolution and unrest in Europe. Republicanism had been in retreat in Europe since the failed revolutions of 1848, and some predicted that all the wayward American republics would eventually find their way back to some form of monarchy or seek protection under European imperial rule. When Lincoln, in the darkest days of the war, referred to America as the "last best hope of earth," he was hardly boasting.

Four years later, against all expectations, the world beheld a victorious Union with a powerful navy and 1 million men at arms. Republicans enjoyed a thrill of vindication. "The newspapers and the men that opposed the cause of the great Republic," the Italian hero Giuseppe Garibaldi wrote to the American minister in Italy, "are those like the ass of the fable that dared kick the lion believing him fallen; but today as they see it rise in all its majesty, they change their language."

European powers, seeing the American lion rise, almost immediately began a dramatic retreat from the Western Hemisphere. Spain, exhausted by four years of fierce jungle fighting with Dominican guerrillas, withdrew from Santo Domingo in June 1865, setting its barracks ablaze while Dominican collaborators scrambled to get aboard ships departing for Havana.

In Paris Napoleon III faced growing opposition at home and the rise of Otto von Bismarck's powerful united German state across the Rhine. In early 1866 he announced that the French civilizing mission in Mexico had come to an end. Mexico's republican forces, aided by arms and volunteers from the United States, won stunning victories

Giuseppe Garibaldi. Library of Congress Prints and Photographs Division, LC-DIG-ppmsca-08351.

against Maximilian's diminished army as the French troops withdrew. In May 1867 the emperor of Mexico took his last stand in Querétero, the final battle of the dual civil wars fought in North America. After being captured Maximilian, standing bravely before a Mexican firing squad, spoke a fitting epitaph to the European monarchical experiment in Latin America: "Mexicans! Men of my class and race are created by God to be the happiness of nations or their martyrs." The shots from Querétero provoked indignant cries for retaliation among European royals, but nothing came of them.

The British Empire also withdrew from North America. In 1867 it set up the Dominion of Canada, a confederation of British colonial possessions that remained part of the empire but would operate as a self-governing nation. That same year the Russian Empire, which had stood by the Union during the war, decided to peacefully cede its claims in North America and sold Alaska to the United States. Except for a few vestiges, the European imperial project that began in 1492 had vanished from the American hemisphere.

One of those vestiges, Cuba, remained the jewel in the crown of the crumbling Spanish Empire. Fear of slave rebellions had kept Cubans loyal to Spain, but republicans, fed up with Spanish rule, rose in rebellion 1868 and promised freedom to slaves who joined them in arms. The Ten Years' War failed to emancipate Cuba, but it dealt a fatal blow to slavery on the island. In 1870 the Spanish government answered with a "free womb law," granting freedom to children of slave mothers, and offered freedom to slaves who took their side against the republicans.

Brazil, the last bastion of American slavery, watched nervously. In 1864 Emperor Dom Pedro II wrote that the Union's successes "force us to think about the future of slavery in Brazil." In 1871 Brazil followed Spain with its own free womb law. As one Brazilian senator explained it, "There was no need for a war against us to push us toward emancipation; the world laughing at us was enough; becoming the scorn of all nations . . . was enough." Cuba finally freed all its slaves in 1886, and Brazil followed two years later. A deeply entrenched and hugely profitable system of labor that had been integral to the economy, law, and society of American nations for nearly four centuries was at an end.

The Union's victory also shook the thrones of Europe. John Lothrop Motley, the American minister to Austria during the war, told the New-York Historical Society in 1868 that something like an "electric chain" had united America and Europe. "The American Civil War, at least in Western Europe, became as much an affair of passionate party feeling as if it were raging on that side the Atlantic," he said, and the "effect of the triumph of freedom in this country on the cause of progress in Europe is plain."

It was poetic justice that Motley's electric chain helped transmit stunning shocks to the very European empires that had menaced the Union during the war. In Britain radicals immediately interpreted the Union triumph as the robust vindication of their republican ideals. They organized the Reform League to push for "universal suffrage" on the American model and staged enormous rallies across Britain. Hundreds of thousands of working- and middle-class men and women, many waving red flags and donning the red liberty caps of the French Revolution, provoked fear of revolt; they toppled barricades and swarmed into London's Hyde Park. Faced with extensive civil disobedience, Parliament quickly passed the 1867 Reform Act and put Britain on the road to democracy.

Coinciding with Cuba's republican revolution in 1868, Spain's liberal Progresista Party, fed up with the imperialist party's disastrous forays in Latin America, began what would be known as the Glorious Revolution. They forced Queen Isabella II from her throne and for the first time, the *New York Times* reported, stood before the world as "a State without a King and a Government existing by popular will."

France's Second Empire was next to fall. Napoleon III's Mexican venture and his unpopular commitment to defend Pope Pius IX and Rome against Garibaldi and the Italian Risorgimento undermined support at home. The republican opposition was emboldened by the Union victory, and news of Lincoln's death inspired them to defy government censorship with open demonstrations of solidarity. When the government tried to quash a public subscription to buy a medal for Mrs. Lincoln, it became a cause célèbre. Forty thousand French citizens defiantly contributed their two sous. In 1870, after Napoleon III recklessly provoked war with Prussia and was ignominiously captured in battle, Parisian republicans abruptly deposed him and proclaimed the Third Republic. France, the cradle of European republicanism, resumed its volatile experiment with government by the people.

At the end of America's war Charles de Montalembert, a French liberal, announced that "grave teachings will result for us" from the victory of the North in America, "for, in spite of ourselves, we belong to a society irrevocably democratic." America's arduous trial of democracy, instead of returning a verdict of failure, had proven the remarkable resilience of popular government. "Under a strain such as no aristocracy, no monarchy, no empire could have supported," one English radical noted, "Republican institutions have stood firm."

The trial of democracy was not over; it would face far graver challenges in the twentieth century. But during this perilous moment in America's youth the Civil War demonstrated to friends and adversaries throughout the world that the "last best hope of earth" shall not perish.

AFTERWORD

Ted Widmer

Disunion ended with a flurry of final pieces in May 2015, including a final meditation I wrote, wondering when the war had ended. The series had already opened up so many questions about the Civil War, but here was a new one that had become quite urgent that spring. How could we plan a final piece, timed around the 150th anniversary, if we could not agree on when the war had ended?

Some, of course, would simply say *never*.

In a 1949 address at Harvard, Ralph Ellison said, "It is still in the balance, and only our enchantment by the spell of the possible, our endless optimism, has led us to assume that it ever really ended."

For William Faulkner, in this famous passage from *Intruder in the Dust*, the war can never end, for it exists outside of time itself, like a favorite film, eternally downloaded and ready for screening:

> For every Southern boy fourteen years old, not once but whenever he wants it, there is the instant when it's still not yet two o'clock on that July afternoon in 1863, the brigades are in position behind the rail fence, the guns are laid and ready in the woods and the furled flags are already loosened to break out and Pickett himself with his long oiled ringlets and his hat in one hand probably and his sword in the other looking up the hill waiting for Longstreet to give the word and it's all in the balance, it hasn't happened yet, it hasn't even begun yet, it not only hasn't begun yet but there is still time for it not to begin against that position and those circumstances.

Still there was an ending of sorts, in 1865. Sometimes it came cleanly, as with General Robert E. Lee's surrender at Appomattox Court House, Virginia, on April 9. At other times the war just seemed to give out, as soldiers melted away from their regiments and began to find their way home. Other generals in more distant theaters fought on gamely, before giving in to the inevitable. Joseph Johnston surrendered the Army of Tennessee near Durham, North Carolina, on April 26. Richard Taylor, the son of Zachary, surrendered twelve thousand more in Citronelle, Alabama, on May 4. The Trans-Mississippi Department surrendered on May 26. On June 23 Stand Watie, a Cherokee chief and a Confederate brigadier general, signed a cease-fire agreement at Doaksville in what is now Oklahoma.

The last Confederates were the farthest away. Throughout the spring, the CSS *Shenandoah* was raiding ships in the Bering Sea, trying to find a part of the world that was not dominated by the United States (as Alaska would be, two years later). She sailed around Cape Horn, all the way to England, where her officers surrendered on November 6 in Liverpool Town Hall. In 1964 the Beatles would receive the key to the city in the same building, having invaded the United States far more successfully than Robert E. Lee.

Then there was Abraham Lincoln's assassination on April 15. This sickening act of violence, when added to all the others, brought a definitive feeling that an era had ended, as surely as Lincoln's election in November 1860 had precipitated it. The funeral train that carried Lincoln's remains home to Springfield, Illinois, drew millions of Americans, and while the tragedy felt senseless, it also offered the nation a chance to mourn something much larger than the death of a single individual. To the end Lincoln served a higher cause.

After he was laid to rest on May 4, the armies united for an epic display of glory, worthy of Rome. Over two days, on May 23 and 24, more than 150,000 soldiers marched down Pennsylvania Avenue before a reviewing stand where President Andrew Johnson and General Ulysses S. Grant stood. That was a political as well as a military statement, for this vast army did not exactly disappear. The Grand Army of the Republic, founded in 1866, would become a potent lobbying force for veterans. Its immense gatherings helped to choose Lincoln's successors for decades.

More than a year later, on August 20, 1866, President Johnson proclaimed that final pockets of resistance in Texas were "at an end." We could call this too the close of the war.

But much remained "in the balance," as Ellison said, uncomfortable, unfinished. Certainly the presence of so many veterans was a new fact for Americans and kept the war alive, simmering, for decades. More than a few required help to cope with their trauma, and the federal government, which had grown so much during the war, grew again to address their needs. It paid out pensions, built hospitals and cemeteries, maintained service records, and assumed more responsibility for the mental and physical health of those who had given so much. That was an important precedent for the New Deal and the Great Society. As of 2014, the *Wall Street Journal* reported, an elderly North Carolina woman, Irene Triplett, collects $73.13 a month for her father's pension. He served in both the Confederate and the Union armies; his tombstone avoids that complexity by saying simply, "He was a Civil War soldier."

Reintegrating these former soldiers took decades. What we now regard as the best Civil War fiction, such as the work of Stephen Crane and Ambrose Bierce, did not even appear until the 1890s, as if the war's memory was at first too potent. A new product, Coca-Cola, was introduced in 1885 by a former Confederate officer, John Pemberton, who had been slashed by a saber in the final fighting of the war, after Appomattox, then wrestled with an addiction to morphine to dull the pain. A pharmacist, Pemberton experimented with a mysterious formula that derived from the coca leaf and the kola nut to ease his suffering. The early marketing for the elixir suggested that it could reduce the symptoms that veterans suffered from, including neurasthenia, headaches, and impotence.

Many veterans retained their sidearms, including Confederate officers, and weapons were easily available, thanks to an arms industry that had done great service to the Union cause. They could hardly be expected to go out of business voluntarily. With new products like Winchester's Model 1866 rifle, sophisticated distribution networks, and a public eager to buy, the industry entered a highly profitable phase. Winchester's repeating rifles needed hardly any time for reloading and sold briskly in Europe, where American arms often tipped the balance in local conflicts.

The Winchester was easily transported to the American West, where new military campaigns were undertaken against Native Americans, and few could be blamed for wondering if the Civil War had in fact ended. Many of the same actors were present, and it could be argued that this was simply another phase of the crisis of Union, this time reconciling East and West rather than North and South.

This tragic epilogue does not fit cleanly into the familiar narrative of the Civil War as a war of liberation. Peoples who had lived on ancestral lands for thousands of years were no match for a grimly experienced army, eager to occupy new lands, in part to reward the soldiers who had done the fighting. Natives called the repeating rifles "spirit guns" and had no answer for them. They fought courageously, but in the end had no choice but to accept relocation, often to reservations hundreds of miles away.

The relocation of the Navajo between 1864 and 1868, still remembered as "the Long Walk," was a particularly inhumane chapter. Estimates vary, but a population of twenty-five thousand was eventually reduced, due to disease, malnutrition, and exhaustion, to as few as two thousand people. Adolf Hitler would cite these removals as a precedent for the Nazi concentration camps.

In other ways the war endured. The shift westward created a huge market for building products, furnishings, and all of the technologies that had advanced so quickly during the fighting. One skill that amazed observers was the speed with which Americans could build railroads and the bridges that they needed to cross. During General William T. Sherman's Atlanta Campaign his engineers built a bridge over Georgia's Etowah River 75 feet high, 625 feet long, in six days. Between 1865 and 1873 more than thirty-five thousand miles of tracks were laid, greater than the country's entire rail network in 1860.

This activity was very good for business. Huge profits were made as those who had become wealthy supplying the war effort adapted to the needs of a civilian population eager to start anew. Indeed it is difficult to tell from the 1870 census that any war at all had taken place. The 1860 census had valued the total wealth of the United States, in real and personal estate, at $16 billion; ten years later it was nearly twice that, $30 billion. So many immigrants came between 1860 and 1870 that the population grew 22.6 percent, to 38.5 million, despite the massive numbers of war dead. Deep within the census are statistics revealing a country hard at work, rebuilding itself, with significant new outlays for iron and steel. There was also an uptick in the manufacture of artificial limbs and in "marble and stone work, monuments and tombstones."

To careful observers in 1865 it was palpable that something important had happened during the war. To organize victory a grand consolidation had taken place, in which leading concerns had improved their organization, crushed their smaller rivals, and strengthened distribution networks. The railroad was a key part of this consolidation; so was the telegraph, often built along the tracks. Military goods needed to move quickly around the country to supply armies, and all of those skills were instantly transferable to private enterprise. American Express, an express freight delivery service founded in Buffalo, moved its goods slightly faster than the competition. In 1875 an article in *Harper's* explained, "The source of [its] present vast wealth was the immense business during the war of the rebellion."

Information was vital to make all of these systems work. During the war the Military Telegraph Corps built eight to twelve miles of telegraph line a day, and the military alone sent 6.5 million messages during the war. By the end of 1866 more than eighty thousand miles of line existed, and these were rapidly extended into the West and South, reknitting some of the strands of Union. But a different kind of Union—Western Union—was emerging as a force, to the dismay of many. It would enjoy a long monopoly on the information economy, facilitated by a new force in Washington: the corporate lobbyist.

Entirely new sectors of the economy had sprung up as well. In 1859, on the eve of the conflict, oil was discovered in northwestern Pennsylvania, and throughout the war its value became clear to a war economy that urgently needed to lubricate the machinery of production. By the time the war was over oil had established itself as a major new fact of life in America, well before the invention of the automobile. John D. Rockefeller bought a refinery in Cleveland in 1863, a major step on the way to the creation of Standard Oil. As soon as the war ended, the search for oil in new locations began; the first well in Texas was dug in 1866, in Nacogdoches County.

Many veterans, having paid so dearly for freedom, were troubled to come back from the war only to find a new economy dominated by industrial barons, quite a few of whom had paid substitutes to do their army service. These included Rockefeller, J. P. Morgan, James Mellon, Jay Gould, and Philip Armour of the immense meatpacking business that grew out of supplying pork to the Union Army. Lincoln's words about freedom continued to move people, but his emphasis on equality seemed to fade as the power of money rose to new heights. It was not only that a small elite had become extremely wealthy; money itself seemed to move in new ways, fast and loose. The stock ticker was invented in 1866.

In other words, it was unclear to many Americans what, exactly, they had won. A great evil had been defeated and the Union forcibly defined and defended. But so rapid were the changes unleashed by the war that soldiers blinked their eyes in amazement when they returned home. Like Ulysses, the Greek hero their commander was named after, they often did not recognize the country they came back to.

Perhaps the most complicated legacy of the war was its claim to have liberated millions of African Americans from slavery. This was not the official purpose of the war when it began in 1861, but it became so, especially after the scale of the war required a cause worthy of so great a sacrifice. One of the achievements of the *Disunion* series was to follow Lincoln's steps on the circuitous path toward emancipation. But one of its necessary omissions will be that we cannot follow the story of race relations deeper into the 1860s and 1870s, when it achieved important progress and devastating setbacks a century before the modern civil rights movement.

So when did slavery actually end? Was it with the ratification of the Thirteenth Amendment on December 6, 1865? Or the day Mississippi ratified the Thirteenth Amendment, in 1995? Or the day that ratification was certified, in 2013? Or the recognition of full citizenship, including voting rights, for African Americans? Though landmark legislation did as much in the 1960s, there are those who would argue that we are still waiting for that Day of Jubilee. Powerful recent works argue that slavery's demise simply led to new forms of servitude, invisibility, and degradation. To read the stories of racial turmoil in recent years—all communities that remained in the Union—is to realize how distant the victory of the Civil War feels to large numbers of African Americans.

Of course that does not minimize the importance of the Confederacy's defeat. It ended forever a way of life and politics that had dominated the United States from the beginning. It accelerated the demise of slavery where it still existed, in Cuba and Brazil, and encouraged liberals around the world. In the fall of 1865 Victor Hugo wrote in a notebook, "America has become the guide among the nations." In France Napoleon III was destabilized by Lincoln's victory and pulled back from his adventure in Mexico, where his puppet was shot by a firing squad in 1867. Three years later, he was removed after his defeat in the Franco-Prussian War, and the transfer of Alsace and Lorraine left a bitterness that would fuel the World Wars of the twentieth century.

The world wars of the twentieth century made the Civil War look puny in comparison. But its example lived on. In July 1938 thousands of veterans returned to Gettysburg to celebrate the seventy-fifth anniversary of that battle, a reunion captured in newsreel footage. Franklin D. Roosevelt gave a spirited speech, remembering 1863 in a way that seemed to speak to the threat Hitler posed to democracy that summer as he edged toward Czechoslovakia: the Civil War soldier, he said, "understood that battle there must be; that when a challenge to constituted government is thrown down, the people must in self-defense take it up; that the fight must be fought through to a decision so clear that it is accepted as being beyond recall."

Without the Civil War, and its tempering of the national character, would the United States have been able to mount a great global campaign against fascism? Surely it would have been feebler without the manufacture of war materiél across all the regions or the rhetoric of freedom FDR used to inspire the world. Nearly all of the national triumphs of the past century, from the civil rights movement to the exploration of space and the birth of the digital age, stemmed from the contributions of Southerners, Northerners, and Westerners working together. We have had failures too—we see them on a daily basis. But the refusal to fall apart in 1861 made a difference.

The war will remain "in the balance," as Ellison put it, as long as there are historians willing to write about it and readers willing to read them. *Disunion* proved there were quite a few in each category. It could not provide all of the answers, but it tried to ask the right questions.

ACKNOWLEDGMENTS

The *Disunion* project had many parents: Jamie Malanowski, who brought the kernel of the idea to the *New York Times* Opinion section in mid-2010; David Shipley, the section editor who took a risk on an audacious five-year project; Trish Hall, who took over from David early in *Disunion*'s career; and Andy Rosenthal, the *Times* editorial page editor and not so secret Civil War buff, who gave the project a green light and his unwavering support. But *Disunion* would never have happened without the contributions of scores of writers—the professors, graduate students, novelists, artists, journalists, and lawyers who were, collectively, the series authors.

Though it is the writers' names that appear on the articles, and our names on the cover of the book, much of the hard work in producing the series was performed by our web team, Taylor Adams, Whitney Dangerfield, Kari Haskell, and Snigdha Koirala; our copyeditors, John Guida, Kristie McClain, and Roberta Zeff; and our indefatigable accounts payable team, Lauren Ricci, Natalie Shutler, and Inell Willis.

Finally our thanks to Alex Ward, who helped take this project from a vague idea to a concrete plan, and to the entire team at Oxford University Press, who took that plan and turned it into the book you now hold in your hands.

CONTRIBUTORS

Adam Arenson is an associate professor of history at Manhattan College. He is the author of *The Great Heart of the Republic: St. Louis and the Cultural Civil War* and coeditor of *Civil War Wests: Testing the Limits of the United States*.

Aaron Astor is an associate professor of history at Maryville College. He is the author of *Rebels on the Border: Civil War, Emancipation and the Reconstruction of Kentucky and Missouri* and *The Civil War along Tennessee's Cumberland Plateau*.

Jean H. Baker is a professor of history at Goucher College and the author of several books on Civil War history, including *James Buchanan* and *Mary Todd Lincoln: A Biography*. She is writing a biography of the architect Benjamin Henry Latrobe.

Thom Bassett lives in Birmingham, Alabama. He is at work on a novel.

Rick Beard is an author and consultant who writes frequently on the Civil War, particularly on the role of enslaved and freed African Americans, as well as topics related to history museums in the United States. His work appears regularly in *Civil War Times, Civil War Quarterly*, and *History News* and has appeared in several collections of essays.

Amanda Brickell Bellows is a Bernard and Irene Schwartz postdoctoral fellow at the New-York Historical Society.

David Blight is a professor of history and the director of the Gilder Lehrman Center for the Study of Slavery and Abolition at Yale. He is the author of *American Oracle: The Civil War in the Civil Rights Era* and is writing a biography of Frederick Douglass.

Glenn David Brasher is a history instructor at the University of Alabama and the winner of the 2013 Wiley-Silver Award from the Center for Civil War Research.

Jennifer R. Bridge is a curator at the Naper Settlement, outside Chicago.

Carol Bundy is the author of *The Nature of Sacrifice: A Biography of Charles Russell Lowell Jr. 1835–1864.*

Ken Burns has been making documentary films for almost forty years. Since the Academy Award–nominated *Brooklyn Bridge* in 1981, he has gone on to direct and produce some of the most acclaimed historical documentaries ever made, including *The Civil War, Baseball, Jazz, The War, The National Parks: America's Best Idea, The Roosevelts: An Intimate History,* and *Jackie Robinson.*

Michael David Cohen is a research associate professor of history and the editor of the James K. Polk Project at the University of Tennessee, Knoxville. He is the author of *Reconstructing the Campus: Higher Education and the American Civil War* and an editor of volumes 12 and 13 of *Correspondence of James K. Polk.*

Boyd Cothran is an assistant professor of history at York University in Toronto and the author of *Remembering the Modoc War: Redemptive Violence and the Making of American Innocence,* which received the 2015 Robert M. Utley Prize for best book in military history from the Western Historical Association.

Peter Cozzens is a retired Foreign Service officer and the author or editor of seventeen books on the Civil War and the American West, including *The Earth Is Weeping: The Epic Story of the Indian Wars for the American West.*

Michael J. Douma is the director of the Georgetown Institute for the Study of Markets and Ethics at Georgetown University.

Gregory P. Downs is an associate professor at the University of California, Davis, and is the author of *After Appomattox: Military Occupation and the Ends of War, Declarations of Dependence: The Long Reconstruction of Popular Politics in the South,* and the short story collection *Spit Baths.*

James Downs is an assistant professor of history at Connecticut College, the author of *Sick from Freedom: African-American Illness and Suffering during the Civil War and Reconstruction,* and the coeditor, with David Blight, of the forthcoming *Beyond Freedom: Disrupting the History of Emancipation.*

Don H. Doyle is the McCausland Professor of History at the University of South Carolina and the author of *The Cause of All Nations: An International History of the American Civil War.*

Sue Eisenfeld is the author of *Shenandoah: A Story of Conservation and Betrayal.* She teaches in the Johns Hopkins University M.A. in Writing and M.A. in Science Writing programs.

David Eltis is an emeritus professor of history and the co-principal investigator for slavevoyages.org at Emory University. He is the author of *The Rise of African Slavery*

westward expansion and, 141, 143–44, 157–59
See also emancipation; Emancipation Proclamation
Smith, Andrew J., 182–83
Smith, Edmund Kirby, 218–20, 218*f*
South Carolina
    burning of Columbia, 135–39, 136*f*
    Confederate battle flag in, 2
    emancipation in, 58–65, 58*f*, 62–65, 63*f*
    Fort Sumter, 16, 18, 19, 20, 23, 205
    Fort Wagner, 118–22, 119*f*
    martial law in, 229–30
    nullification, 201
    prisoner camp in, 328
    secession, 7, 10–16, 170–74, 173*f*, 277
    slavery in, 29, 35, 44*f*, 49–52
South Carolina (ship), 325
South. *See* Confederacy/South
Spain, 245, 254, 325, 344, 346, 347
Spalding, George, 194–95
Stanton, Edwin, 37, 85, 179, 187–88
Stanton, Elizabeth Cady, 68
Star of the West (ship), 16
states' rights, 11, 35, 49, 157–59, 170–74, 173*f*
Stevens, Thaddeus, 189, 298
Stone, Charles P., attack on Washington and, 20,
    21, 22
Stowe, Harriet Beecher, 69
sugar industry, 49–51, 55, 56, 236, 266
Sumner, Charles, 70, 71
Sumner, Edwin V., 114*f*
Supreme Court, 47
Suriname, 260

Taney, Roger B., 190, 191*f*, 203, 309
taxes, 311
Taylor, Zachary, 47, 100
Tennessee, 8, 16, 23, 28, 29, 35, 182, 205, 219,
    220, 287–90
Terry's Texas Rangers, 157
Texas
    cotton in, 146–47
    federal troops in, 340
    Houston, Sam, 26, 144–48, 145*f*, 156
    joining Confederacy, 155–57, 155*f*
    military action in, 99–100
    oil in, 352
    Pickens and, 16
    Rangers, 132
    resistance in, 350
    secession and, 25–28, 27*f*
    slavery in, 14
    Washington, D.C. attack and, 22
Texas v. White, 201
Thirteenth Amendment
    abolition morality and the, 198
    Civil War roots of the, 199–203, 200*f*
    Kentucky and the, 338, 340
    Mississippi and the, 353
    Missouri and the, 340
    non-U.S. slavery and the, 39

passage of the, 341, 343
private matters and the, 97
Virginia manumission laws and the, 25
Thomas, George, 127
Thoreau, Henry David, 330
Tubman, Harriet, 69
Twain, Mark, 165–67, 166*f*
Twenty-second Amendment, 208
Twiggs, David, 155–56, 155*f*, 157
Tyler, John, 47

Uncle Tom's Cabin (Stowe), 69
Underground Railroad, 69–70
Union Army
    aftermath of war and the, 310–11
    Capitol and the, 283
    the draft and the, 86–90, 87*f*
    emancipation and the, 33–35, 55–58
    fraud and the, 296–99, 298*f*
    freed slaves in the, 43, 179, 221
    illness/food shortages in the, 327–28
    immigrants in the, 67
    prostitution and the, 193–95, 195*f*
    rape and the, 180–83, 181*f*
    slave liberation by the, 37
    Thanksgiving and the, 317, 317*f*
    women in the, 92–95, 93*f*
    See also battlefield; Grant, Ulysses S.; *Specific battles &
        units*; veterans
Unionists
    Appomattox terms and, 234
    Johnson and, 287–90
    in North Carolina, 30–31
    slavery compromise and, 282
    Southern, 23–25, 24*f*, 35, 71, 205
    in Texas, 25–28, 27*f*, 148, 156
    in Union Army, 100
Union/North
    abolition failure and the, 341–44, 342*f*
    Black baseball, 95–98, 96*f*
    contraband policy of the, 34
    the draft in the, 86–90, 87*f*
    emancipation and the, 34–35
    environmental impact of war in the, 326–31
    family heritage, 321–22
    fighting off the Coast of France, 270–73, 272*f*
    food production in the, 219
    fugitive slave laws and the, 171–74, 173*f*
    goal of the, 253
    Hawaii and the, 265
    home front, 66–69
    Jews and the, 227
    Lee's surrender and the, 232–35
    proslavery presidents, 200
    public opinion in the, 241–42
    railways in the, 20
    secession and the, 12
    Thanksgiving and the, 316–18
    transportation and communication links to the, 20
    See also Lincoln, Abraham; *Specific states*; West

Vallandigham, Clement, 183–86
Van Buren, Martin, 47
Venezuela, 236
Vermont, 171
veterans
    Appomattox, 233
    arms industry and, 329, 351
    black, 203
    comedy and, 73, 74
    disabled/ill, 92, 351
    family heritage, 318–22, 319f
    Gettysburg Address and, 315
    Grand Army of the Republic and, 350
    in Hawaii, 266
    last veteran to serve, 109
    Lee's army, 232
    memoirs of, 3
    post-war economy and, 352
    Reconstruction and, 225
    reunions, 313, 315, 321–22, 353
    survivor benefits, 350
    women, 92, 95
Veterans of the Second Corps, 115
Virginia
    attack on Washington and, 20
    capital of Confederacy, 16
    cartoon regarding, 72f
    environmental impact of war in, 327
    nullification, 201
    passports in, 231
    Peninsula Campaign, 212–13, 219
    secession, 15, 16, 28, 31, 205
    Seward and, 281
    slavery density in, 23–25, 24f, 35–37, 36f
    slavery in, 29, 42, 46–47, 46f, 47, 53f
    the Union and, 15

Walter, Thomas U., 284–86
war crimes, 135–39, 136f, 183
war law, 174–80, 176f
War of the Triple Alliance, 237–38
Warren, Robert Penn, xiv
Washburn, Elihu, 296
Washington Artillery, 104
Washington, Booker T., 42, 52, 265

Washington, D.C., 10–23, 19f, 46–48, 46f, 283–86, 284f, 290
Washington, George, 47, 106, 211
Webb, William, 42, 43–46
Webster, Daniel, 211
Welles, Gideon, 25, 73, 196, 269, 292, 296, 297, 306
West
    expansion in the, 43, 141, 143–44, 153–54, 157–59, 158f, 168–69, 311
    slavery expansion in the, 42, 151–54, 152f
    Winchester rifles and the, 351
    See also Native Americans; Specific states
Western Reserve of Ohio, 161
West Virginia, 164, 188
Whig Party, 15, 45, 50, 187–88, 274, 287–88, 292
Winchester rifles, 329, 351
Wisconsin, 90, 201, 327
women
    aftermath of war and, 312
    Butler and, 78–80, 78f
    Chicago Sanitary Fair, 90–92, 90f
    Civil rights legislation and, 3
    as domestic servants, 55–56
    equality of, 71
    Garibaldi and, 252
    North vs. South, 66–69
    origins of Civil War and, 69–72
    prostitution and, 193–96, 195f
    rape and, 180–83, 181f
    scrapbooking, 80–83, 81f
    slave mother and child, 262f
    as soldiers, 92–95, 93f
world and Civil War
    Bismarck, 253–56
    consequences of the War, 344–47
    emancipation in the U.S., 35, 38–41, 38f
    foreign policy correspondence, 256–60, 258f
    Garibaldi, 249–53, 251f
    Hawaii, 263–66, 264f
    overview, 240–42

Yellowstone National Park, 330
Yosemite National Park, 330

Zouaves, 102–3, 104